Regulation in Asia

Unlike much analysis about regulation in Asia which focuses on globalization and the transplant effect, leaving domestic influence over commercial regulation under-researched and under-theorized, this book focuses on how local actors influence regulatory change. It explores the complex economic and regulatory factors that generate social demand for state regulation and shows how local networks, courts, democratic processes, and civil society have a huge influence on regulatory systems. It examines the particular circumstances in a wide range of Asian countries, provides transnational comparisons and comparisons with Western countries, and assesses how far local regulatory regimes increase economic value and convey competitive advantages.

John Gillespie is Director of the Asia Pacific Business Regulation Group, Monash University, Australia.

Randall Peerenboom is Director of the Oxford Foundation for Law, Justice and Society's Rule of Law in China Programme, Associate Fellow in the Oxford University Centre for Socio-Legal Studies and Professor of Law at La Trobe University, Australia.

Routledge law in Asia
Series editor: Randall Peerenboom

Regulation in Asia

Pushing back on globalization

Edited by
John Gillespie and Randall Peerenboom

Routledge
Taylor & Francis Group

LONDON AND NEW YORK

First published 2009
by Routledge
2 Park Square, Milton Park, Abingdon, Oxon OX14 4RN

Simultaneously published in the USA and Canada
by Routledge
270 Madison Ave, New York, NY 10016

Routledge is an of the Taylor & Francis Group, an informa business

Typeset in Times New Roman by
Value Chain International Ltd
Printed and bound in Great Britain by
CPI Antony Rowe, Chippenham, Wiltshire

British Library Cataloguing in Publication Data
A catalogue record for this book is available from the British Library

Library of Congress Cataloging in Publication Data
Regulation in Asia: pushing back on globalization / edited by
John Gillespie and Randall Peerenboom.
    p. cm. – (Routledge law in Asia; 5)
    Includes bibliographical references and index.
    1. Trade regulation–East Asia. 2. Trade regulation–Southeast Asia.
I. Gillespie, John (John Stanley) II. Peerenboom, R. P. (Randall P.), 1958–
    KNC764.R44 2009
    343.5′087–dc22

                                                    2008040859

ISBN13: 978-0-415-48986-7 (hbk)
ISBN13: 978-0-415-49003-0 (pbk)
ISBN13: 978-0-203-09160-9 (ebk)

Contents

Tables

Contributors

Christoph Antons is Professor of Comparative Law and Director of the Centre for Comparative Law and Development Studies in Asia and the Pacific, University of Wollongong, Australia. He is a QEII Fellow of the Australian Research Council (ARC), Chief Investigator in the ARC Centre of Excellence for Creative Industries and Innovation, and Adjunct Research Fellow at the Max Planck Institute for Intellectual Property, Competition and Tax Law in Munich, Germany. He recently co-edited *Intellectual Property Harmonisation within ASEAN and APEC* (2004, with Michael Blakeney and Christopher Heath) and *Globalisation and Resistance: Law Reform in Asia since the Crisis* (2007, with Volkmar Gessner).

Aishah Bidin is Professor of Corporate and Insolvency Law and former Deputy Dean (2001–6) at the Faculty of Law, Malaysian National University (University Kebangsaan Malaysia (UKM)). Her areas of specialization include company and corporate finance law, securities regulation, bankruptcy, and insolvency law. She has completed numerous research projects about corporate financing, governance of insolvency, and *Syariah* corporate tax, and is a member of the Steering Committee of the Malaysian Corporate Law Reform Committee (CLRC). She is the co author (with Ian Ramsey, Pamela Hanrahan, and Geof Stapledon) of *Commercial Applications of Company Law in Malaysia* (2008, 3rd edn).

Simon Butt is a Lecturer in the Faculty of Law and a member of the Centre for Asian and Pacific Law at the University of Sydney, Australia. Prior to joining the Faculty, Simon worked as a consultant on the Indonesian legal system to the Australian government, the private sector, and international organizations, including the United Nations Development Programme (UNDP) and the International Commission of Jurists (ICJ). He has published extensively on Indonesian legal development issues, and his PhD dissertation is titled "Judicial review in Indonesia: between civil law and accountability? A study of constitutional court decisions 2003–2005".

Michael W. Dowdle is Visiting Professor of Law in the Law Faculty of the National University Singapore and Chaired Professor of Globalization and Governance at the Institut d'études Politiques de Paris (Sciences Po). Prior to that, he was a Fellow at the Regulatory Institutions Network (Regnet) of the Australian National University. His research interests include regulatory and globalization theory and law reform in China, and he is the editor of *Public Accountability : Designs, Dilemmas and Experiences* (2006).

John Gillespie is Professor of Law and Director of the Asia Pacific Business Regulation Group, Department of Business Law and Taxation, Monash University, Australia. He specializes in East Asian legal systems, especially Vietnam, and legal transplantation and regulatory theory. He has consulted widely with international donor agencies on law and development projects in East Asia. His most recent book is *Transplanting Commercial Law Reform* (2006).

Terence C. Halliday is Co-Director, Center on Law and Globalization, American Bar Foundation and University of Illinois College of Law; Senior Research Fellow, American Bar Foundation; and Adjunct Professor, Department of Sociology, Northwestern University, USA. He has recently completed a book entitled *Law's Global Markets*, which includes case studies of insolvency reform in China, Indonesia, and Korea.

Jakkrit Kuanpoth is a Senior Lecturer, Faculty of Law, University of Wollongong, Australia. Before coming to Wollongong, he taught at the School of Law, Sukhothai Thammathirat Open University, Thailand. He holds LLB (Hons) (Ramkhamhaeng University); Barrister-at-Law (of Thai Bar); LLM in International Economic Law (University of Warwick); PhD (University of Aberdeen).

Bui Bich Thi Lien is the Deputy Director of the Judicial Development and Grassroots Engagement Project (JUDGE)—a bilateral aid project supporting judicial reform in Vietnam. Before joining JUDGE, Lien worked in various areas of Vietnam's legal system, including legal education (Hanoi Law University), private practice (international and national law firms), and legal development (the Asia Foundation).

Tim Lindsey is Professor of Law, ARC Federation Fellow, and Director, Centre for Asian Law, and Director of the Centre for Islamic Law and Society at the University of Melbourne, Australia. He has worked extensively on law and development projects in Indonesia, and his publications include *Chinese Indonesians* (2005, with Helen Pausacker), *Law Reform in Developing and Transitional States* (2007), and *Indonesia Law and Society* (2008).

Soogeun Oh is Professor of Law at the Law School, Ewha Woman's University, Seoul, South Korea. His research interests include commercial law, insolvency law, and law and development in East Asia. He was the chair of the Drafting Committee for the Korean Insolvency Law and is the Chief Editor of the *Ewha Law Journal*.

Randall Peerenboom is Professor of Law at La Trobe University, Australia; Director of the Oxford Foundation for Law, Justice and Society's Rule of Law in China Programme; Associate Fellow at Oxford University Centre for Socio-Legal Studies. A Professor of Law at UCLA Law School from 1998 to 2007, he specializes in Chinese and comparative law, Asian legal systems, human rights, legal theory, and law and development. His most recent books are *China's Long March Toward Rule of Law* (2002) and *China Modernizes: Threat to the West or Model for the Rest?* (2007).

Brendan Sweeney is an Associate Professor in the Asia Pacific Business Regulation Group, Department of Business Law and Taxation, Monash University, Australia. His research interests include commercial law, trades practices, marketing law, and international trade. His most recent publication is *Globalisation of Competition Law* (2009).

Veronica L. Taylor is the Dan Fenno Henderson Professor of Law and Director of the Asian Law Center at the University of Washington, USA. Her work focuses on law and society in Asia, Japanese commercial law, applied regulatory theory, and law and development. With Professors Tom Ginsburg (Illinois) and John Ohnesorge (Wisconsin), Professor Taylor established the *Rule of Law, State-Building and Transition Collaborative Research Network* in the Law and Society Association, and is active in shaping new intellectual approaches to law and development initiatives. She has consulted widely with international donor agencies on law and development projects in Asia. Her recent writing on regulation in Asia includes "Dollars to Donuts: Japanese Courts and Corporate Accountability", in Pip Nicholson and Andrew Harding, eds, *New Courts in Asia,* Routledge (in press) and "The Legal and Regulatory Environment for Business in Post-Reform Indonesia", in Pitman Potter, ed., *Business Law in Asia*, Lexis/Nexis Canada/Butterworths (in press).

Dali L. Yang is Director of and Professor at the East Asian Institute, National University of Singapore, and former Chairman of the Political Science Department, University of Chicago, USA. His research interests include political institutions and political economy, with special reference to China. His most recent publications include *Discontented Miracle: Growth, Conflict, and Institutional Adaptations in China* (2007).

Preface

Regulation in Asia: Pushing back on globalization is part of a larger project consisting of a series of volumes that compare the legal systems in several Asian countries, European Union countries, and the US across a wide range of issues.

Specifically, the project seeks to examine legal system development and rule of law in Asia, using Western legal systems as comparison points. Given the great diversity among legal systems, the purpose is to understand how rule of law is conceived and implemented, and the role of law and the legal system with respect to economic growth, political reform and democratization, the protection of human rights, geopolitical stability, and the engagement of Asian countries with other countries in the international arena.

The project will also address the Euro-American centricism of comparative law by replacing outdated stereotypes with empirically grounded, in-depth, and up-to-date analyses of Asian legal systems across a wide range of issues and areas of law.

In terms of methodology, each volume involves specialists in the relevant area of law from different Asian countries or jurisdictions along with specialists from Western countries. Each volume examines specific areas of law or topics in law to determine: (i) whether there are differences/similarities between the countries with respect to legal rules; (ii) outcomes in particular cases (or the way events are handled if they are not subject to formal legal resolution); and (iii) the justifications/explanations for such outcomes (legal reasons, cultural/philosophical explanations, or economic/political/institutional explanations).

In this volume, an impressive group of international experts in law, regulatory theory, and related fields address regulation in Asia, and the ways in which local actors have adopted, adapted, and resisted global regulatory systems and practices. Like its predecessors, this volume demonstrates the complex interplay between international practices and trends and local factors, and the wide variation within Asian legal systems.

Acknowledgements

The chapters in this book are based on edited papers delivered by the authors at a conference entitled "Pushing against globalisation: A local perspective on regulation in Asia" that was run by the Asia-Pacific Business Regulation Group, Monash University in Melbourne during November 2007. The conference was supported by a grant from the Australian Research Council: Asia-Pacific Futures Research Network and funding from the Department of Business Law and Taxation, Monash University. John Gillespie and Randall Peerenboom co-organized the conference and wish to thank Leanne Hunt and staff at the Department of Businesses Law and Taxation for their invaluable assistance.

1 Pushing back on globalization

An introduction to regulation in Asia

John Gillespie and Randall Peerenboom

Much of the discussion about legal globalization focuses on the transnational regulatory arena. It ponders the interaction between international law and nation-states, legal harmonization within regional trading communities such as the European Community, and the regulatory power of international organizations such as the World Trade Organization (WTO). It also discusses regulatory competition among the great trading powers. But it seldom considers regional responses to global regulation. What little is written in this area primarily focuses on Western countries, leaving legal globalization in Asia comparatively under-researched and under-theorized.

This volume aims to redress this gap in the literature by broadening our understanding about how state and non-state actors in Asia influence legal globalization. The chapters shed light on the way in which state and non-state actors adopt, adapt, and resist global commercial law scripts, as well as the complex economic and regulatory factors that generate social demand for global laws and principles while at the same time often resulting in their transformation within the local context. Contributors demonstrate how Asian countries are beginning to create their own modes of regulation that are influential in the region and increasingly have an impact on global regulatory systems, even though, overall, Asia remains an importer of legal knowledge.

Despite being home to a third of the world's population and its fastest growing economies, Asian countries remain secondary players in the international debates that shape global regulation. Although some Asian countries, especially China and Japan, are beginning to assume a more prominent role in international forums such as the WTO, they remain under-represented in the committees that formulate and refine global laws. Overwhelmingly, most global regulation circulating in Asia is Western (especially American) in origin.[1] This is unfortunate as many Asian countries have been remarkably successful in recent decades in achieving sustained growth, reducing poverty, and establishing effective institutions capable of providing good governance.

Nevertheless, there are signs of change. Japan is now a major supporter of legal reforms from The Philippines to central Asia. It also exerts a strong influence over law reforms sponsored by the Asian Development Bank (ADB). More recently, the so-called "Beijing Consensus," which promotes economic development without democratization, is gaining prestige within Asia and beyond.[2]

Chapters in this volume consider the role that courts, democratic processes, civil society, and local networks play in giving local actors—including business associations and business people (whether local or foreigners investing in the country), social and political groups, and international agencies operating in-country—opportunities to localize and influence global regulation. The chapters combine "micro" or interpretive methods that generate finely grained analysis with "macro" or structural approaches that give a broader picture of state and non-state regulation. By contrasting experiences in East Asia with Western countries, this volume investigates to what extent demand for regulation is path dependent and how much is a function of economic and institutional development.

More specifically, the chapters in this volume address a number of issues, including:

- Who are the most influential global and local players, and how do they interact?
- How does demand for regulation and access to regulators combine to shape the substance and style of state regulation?
- What drives regulatory change? When is there local resistance and adaptation, and when is there not?
- Does locally responsive regulation generate economic value and competitive advantages?

Before summarizing our results, we provide a brief overview of the evolving regulatory theory field, noting parallels with the evolving law and development field. Many of the authors have either explicitly or implicitly used regulatory theory to conceptualize the interaction between global regulation and domestic regulatory systems. It is therefore useful to outline the main ideas they employ and consider how regulatory theory advances our understanding about domestic engagement with legal globalization and the efforts to export particular regulatory forms and paradigms of development.

Globalization and domestic regulation

Authors locate the interaction between global and domestic forces in a regulatory domain. This is a notional space where state and non-state actors variously compete and collaborate with each other to steer the domestic adoption and implementation of global regulation.[3] As Veronica L. Taylor observes in her chapter, "the regulatory space metaphor is illuminating because it suggests a suspended sphere with multiple planes, rather than the vertical channel of state–citizen command and control regulation, or a purely horizontal axis of private player interactions."

A brief account of regulatory development explains how changes in the regulatory space influence how global regulation is localized. For much of the twentieth century, commercial regulation was regarded by Western and Asian governments, both empirically and normatively, as a state function.[4] A narrow range of state bodies were responsible for commercial regulation; they included legislatures, the executive and, to a lesser extent (especially in Asia), the courts. The dominant feature of state-centered regulation was that it was a form of command-and-control or top-down regulation, built on Weberian institutions of the modern state and guided by principles of rational and efficient governance, and in Northeast Asia by the twin goals of rapid economic growth combined with social stability.

Regulatory approaches are not static, however, and have always waxed and waned in line with changing endogenous political contingencies and global influences.[5] From the 1950s to the 1980s, developmental states in Asia used regulation to increase national competitiveness.[6] Take Japan, for example. A form of collaborative capitalism developed during the high-growth period (1960–90) that commanded considerable prestige within and beyond Asia. Although its precise workings remain a matter of controversy, in essence the system consisted of an elite bureaucracy staffed by the best managerial talent working closely with big business to develop regulatory policy.[7] The state, represented by the Ministry of International Trade and Industry (MITI), used negotiated policies to guide industries in their investment decisions and marketing practices through formal and informal directives known as administrative guidance. Precisely how administrative guidance shaped business outcomes is debated. What is clear is that state officials negotiated with non-state actors to shape official policy regarding the adaptation of global regulation.

Meanwhile, a different regulatory history developed in the US. Cass Sunstein has described the explosion of legislation that followed the "rights revolution" of the 1960s and 1970s.[8] In addition to enhanced protection of civil and political rights, the rights revolution increased the role of the state as the provider of social welfare. This period, reflecting the transition in Euro-America from classical Millian liberalism to Rawlsian social welfare liberalism, corresponds to the "First Moment" of law and development described by Trubek and Santos, where the state was seen as playing a prominent role in managing the economy, achieving social goals, and modernizing traditional societies.[9]

This idealistic period was followed by the rise of neoliberal economic thinking in the late 1970s, corresponding to the "Second Moment" in law and development. Neoliberalism advocated a smaller state, emphasizing deregulation, privatization, and decentralization to combat the perceived "inefficiencies" caused by state interference in market regulation in the economic sphere and limitations on welfare in the social sphere, with an emphasis on trickle-down economics as the way to address poverty and the needs of the most vulnerable members of society.

Although the neoliberal deregulatory movement reached its zenith in the Anglo-American world, it made modest inroads elsewhere. What neoliberalism meant in practice varied from place to place. For example, in the Anglo-American world, it sought to roll back the welfare state. But more generally it aimed to reduce state control over particular industries in an attempt to make them more responsive to market forces.

By the 1990s, the work of New Institutional Economists such as Douglass North began to challenge the notion that left alone markets always yield optimal results.[10] In a landmark report in 1993 entitled *The East Asian Economic Miracle*, the World Bank moderated its deregulatory mantra and conceded that states play a vital role in regulating markets.[11] The economic success of Japan and the newly industrialized Northeast Asian states, combined with the failures of developing countries that adopted neoliberal policies and complied with the International Monetary Fund (IMF)'s structural adjustment policies, provided the impetus to bring the state back into the regulatory arena.[12]

During the 1990s and especially following the Asian financial crisis in 1997, administrative guidance lost prestige in Japan and South Korea.[13] Japan and South Korea responded to their economic problems by re-regulating. They not only enacted a raft of new commercial laws, but also sought to judicialize administrative processes by shifting discretionary power from bureaucrats to judges and citizens, a process that was occurring globally and in other East Asian states as well.[14]

This period of re-regulation in Northeast Asia coincided with, and was influenced by, what has been termed the rise of the "regulatory state" in the West.[15] States that had moved to privatize companies, reduce red tape, and use market-like incentives were not really deregulating, but rather finding new ways to regulate the economy. Neoliberal deregulation moved in tandem with regulatory reforms that have spread new institutions, technologies, and regulatory instruments around the globe. For example, the World Bank advocates neoliberal reforms, but also promotes re-regulation throughout Asia as a method of stabilizing private markets through a range of measures bundled together as "good governance."[16]

In contrast with previous regulatory periods, the regulatory state challenges the convention that norms must be imposed by the public sphere on the private sphere. It developed new forms of "responsive" regulation that involve privatization, market competition and increased state reliance on self-regulating organizations and regimes.[17] In short, it re-engineers the way in which state and non-state actors think about who is permitted within the regulatory space and who is excluded from exercising regulatory power.

In a related development, empirical work by John Braithwaite and Toni Makkai, among others, has challenged the assumptions regarding the relationship between compliance and the certainty or severity of sanctioning.[18] They favor a flexible approach that combines different strategies that rely on persuasion and more cooperative regulation. Thus, the flexible regulator's toolbox includes a wide range of tools, both formal and informal, legal and non-legal. In addition to the previously mentioned privatization, deregulation, centralization, and decentralization, there are corporatist and negotiated rulemaking approaches that involve key stakeholders in the lawmaking and implementation processes; self-regulation and other informal (non-state or quasi-non-state) approaches, including restorative justice programs; public disclosure and sunshine laws that emphasize transparency and openness; increased participation and supervision by consultative committees, non-governmental organizations (NGOs), and the media; and the list goes on.

If the regulatory state contrasts old-style governance – reliance on command-and-control legislation – with "new governance" based on a flexible array of regulatory techniques, the "post-regulatory state" suggests a pluralistic understanding of governance and corresponds to the "Third Moment" in law and development.[19]

It unshackles regulation from state-based processes and opens the regulatory space to complex forms of private or non-state mechanisms. Much of the literature concerning the post-regulatory state seeks to correct the impression conveyed by some writers about the regulatory state that the state is central to regulatory governance and that state law is the central instrument of regulatory governance.[20]

The notion of a post-regulatory state is used in this volume both as a diagnostic device to understand how globalization affects state and non-state regulators and as an empirical tool to explain the changes in the regulatory space within East Asian states. Implicit in these usages is the notion of the state withdrawing from some regulatory functions and supporting non-state actors to engage with global laws and principles. States are described as performing a "steering" function, leaving the "rowing" function to others. In practice, this means that states not only provide policy guidelines and criteria to assess regulatory objectives, they also design regulatory structures and processes that stimulate and respond to non-state regulation. In post-regulatory states, one task of state regulators is to regulate self-regulation by non-state actors.

Authors in this volume explore how states in Asia have responded to the bundle of ideas associated with the post-regulatory state to evaluate the state's willingness to give non-state actors a regulatory role. This shift in thinking is important because it gives non-state actors more opportunities to go it alone, or come together with the state to shape global regulation.

The chapters show that the role reserved for non-state regulation depends on which regulatory modes dominate the regulatory space. Two distinct regulatory regimes inform decentered regulation and the higher importance attached to non-state regulation. The first is the neoliberal project of removing (or at least reducing) the regulatory burden imposed by the state on industry. Neoliberalism hypothesizes that human wellbeing will be advanced by the practices associated with free markets. It is the role of the state to "create and preserve an institutional framework appropriate to such practices."[21] Technocratic regulators are supposed to shape entrepreneurial preferences by designing regulation that mimics market outcomes, which in practice means correcting market failures.[22] The state does not need to concern itself overly with broader notions of public interest because decentralized decision-making based on private preferences generates outcomes that are beneficial to everyone. States should only intervene in self-regulation to preserve market competition and "fair practice." As Julia Black puts it, "in the standard treatments of 'regulation' the 'why regulate?' question is nearly always answered in terms of the correction of market failures, with the occasional nod to distributional or other ancillary aims."[23]

Although neoliberalism argues for deregulation, in practice it seems to expand and extend regulation. As David Levi-Faur and Jacint Jordana observe, "for every regulation that in the past quarter of a century has been removed from the books, many new ones have been added."[24] Not only has neoliberalism failed to open much regulatory space for non-state actors, it discourages participation in the formulation of regulatory policy. It proposes a set of interventions that impose technical limitations on the functioning of markets, an instrumental approach to regulation that does not invite non-state actors to engage with the state in any way other than on narrow economic grounds.

This narrow focus on market failure is strongest in the Anglo-American world. Elsewhere, more faith is placed in the capacity of state regulators to promote the public interest.[25] In Japan, for example, policymakers think about regulation in social rather than purely economic terms. Regulators combine the neoliberal economic objective of deregulating the developmental state with public interest regulation that stresses redistributive policies and greater state openness, accountability, and public participation in lawmaking. They treat regulation as a process that balances competing values about the sort of society people wish to live in. Regulation plays a role in creating an ethical framework from which to develop not just the economy but also social unity or solidarity.[26] Rather than treating regulation exclusively as a constraint on markets, it becomes the social underpinning of mutual trust and social cohesion necessary for functioning markets.

Case studies considered in this volume show that the mix of neoliberal and public interest regulation affects the role played by state and non-state actors in influencing global regulation. For example, the strong emphasis on public interest regulation in Northeast Asia has translated into a pluralistic understanding of public participation in global regulation. As shown here and elsewhere, this gives non-state actors many opportunities, such as democratic representation, notice and comment procedures, and litigation, to influence the way in which the state deals with global regulation. In these countries, the regulatory space has broadened to include commercial lawyers as transactional intermediaries, foreign investors, courts, and social organizations.

Socialist transforming states are also concerned with public interest regulation, although they place more stress on redistributive policies than on open governance. Nevertheless, during the last two decades, non-state actors have gained more say over state policy formation and can use constitutional and informal mechanisms to convey their views about global regulation. At the same time, an opening of the regulatory space has provided opportunities for transnational entities such as multinational companies, international lawyers, and other professionals to bring global regulation into the domestic space. Much of this private regulation, such as supply chain agreements and International Organization for Standardization (ISO) protocols, bypasses states and directly engages non-state actors.

Who are the global players?

Most discussion about legal globalization starts with international regulatory bodies (such as the WTO, Asia-Pacific Economic Cooperation (APEC), and the Association of Southeast Asian Nations (ASEAN)) and international donor agencies (such as the IMF, World Bank, and ADB).[27] These bodies project local regulations and practices primarily (although not exclusively) developed in Western countries onto the international stage. Which local rules dominate global legal scripts generally depends on power struggles played out in international forums.[28] Most, but certainly not all, global regulations are constructed in transnational settings that bring together interests representing international bodies, dominant nation-states, and industry/professional bodies. The ideas and the documents that express them are then disseminated by international agencies to nation-states and other elites around the world. In developing Asia, conditions attached to loans for structural development under the World Bank's Comprehensive Poverty and Growth Strategy and international market access treaties (especially the WTO and bilateral trade agreements) constitute an important source of global regulation.[29] From this global perspective, nation-states are *the* local arena in which the adaptation, transposition, and resistance to global scripts take place.

Different international agencies often promote slightly different iterations of global regulation. Soogeun Oh and Terence C. Halliday (in this volume), for example, argue that the IMF and ADB championed different approaches to insolvency law in Asia. The recently passed People's Republic of China (PRC) Anti-Monopoly Law, which involved repeated lobbying by both US and EU government and non-government commercial actors, combines aspects of both US and EU anti-competition law.

Further adding to the regulatory mix, bilateral donors (e.g., Sweden and Denmark) and international NGOs (e.g., Oxfam and Friedrich Ebert Stifung) promote civil rights, environmental sustainability, and democratic and social pluralism. Non-state transnational organizations are also an important source of global regulation. International contracts and ISO protocols transfer regulatory ideas into Asia. For example, the Forest Stewardship Council has created a global regulatory system that promotes the sustainable exploitation of timber in many Asian countries.[30] In another example, the ISO has promulgated standards covering corporate governance that have been adopted by tens of thousands of companies in Asia.

What differentiates global from local regulation?

Boaventura de Sousa Santos famously observed that the global and local are interdependent.[31] The global does not exist outside of, and is mutually constituted by, the way local communities regulate themselves. Michael W. Dowdle (in this volume) develops the related point that local actors often deploy one set of global ideas and tactics to resist another set of global ideas. This notion is clearly illustrated in Christoph Antons' discussion of the debates regarding traditional knowledge and in Jakkrit Kuanpoth's description of the political battles over agriculture and the use of natural resources in Thailand, where all protagonists selectively use aspects of globalization and globalized legal regimes to advance their positions.

In fact, throughout Asia, most domestic regulatory systems are constructed from different knowledge systems— such as neo-Confucian, Islamic, colonial, socialist, and contemporary East Asian and Western—with the new overlying and intermingling with the old. As Maurice Halbwachs put it, the past we know is constantly being constructed and reconstructed from contemporary epistemological settings.[32] For Halbwachs, "invented traditions"[33] and "imaged communities"[34] derived from global knowledge are as valid to domestic actors as traditions with an "objective" historical provenance. In studying the complex interaction between Dutch, Islamic, and Amboneses traditional law, Franz and Keebet von Benda-Beckmann found that, "in the perception of local actors what was once transnationalized or globalized colonial law had become 'local' history."[35] What is considered local and authentic depends upon the views of particular observers. This suggests that the perception of difference is a significant factor shaping domestic rejection, transposition, or acceptance of global regulation.

While noting the interdependency between global and local regulators, several contributors emphasize that, without the support of domestic regulators, global legal rules and practices would lack effective implementation and legitimacy.[36] As Oh and Halliday point out, resistance and adaptation to globalization is most prevalent in the implementation phase. But as this is also the most difficult process to observe and measure, there is a tendency to equate the adoption of legislation that mirrors and incorporates global scripts with global convergence and harmonization.

The vigorous interaction between global and local is amply demonstrated by the case studies in this volume. But that does not mean that there is no meaningful difference between the global and the local, or that there is nothing to push back against.

What are domestic actors pushing against?

A recurrent theme in this volume is that domestic actors (both state and non-state) throughout Asia are rejecting, amending, or transmogrifying—pushing back on—global regulation. But what are they pushing against?

At the most general level, some countries have resisted the trend toward liberal democracy and a liberal interpretation of human rights, most notably Vietnam and China. However, as the brouhaha over Asian values showed, there is a broader based resistance to secular liberal norms promoted by Western countries. Most Asian countries continue to be less liberal than Western countries at similar levels of development, as indicated by both general multicountry empirical studies and comparative studies that look at particular issues.[37]

Northeast Asian states have also rejected aspects of the dominant development models promoted by Western states and the major international donor agencies such as the IMF and the World Bank. In particular, they have rejected certain aspects of the Washington Consensus. While they generally accepted the basic macroeconomic principles for their domestic economy, they have rejected or modified the neoliberal emphasis on a small state, deregulation, and privatization. They also rejected or modified the prescribed relationship between the domestic and international economies by advocating that the domestic economy be only gradually exposed to foreign competition.[38]

While China and Vietnam are following a modified version of the developmental state model that proved so successful for other East Asian countries in the past, Japan and South Korea are now moving away from that model. This suggests that the model may be useful for developing countries in their rapid-growth, catch-up phase, but an obstacle to sustained growth once a country reaches a higher level of wealth.

There are of course many variations within Asia. Some countries followed the policy advice of the Washington Consensus more closely. However, the Asian financial crisis, which affected most severely some of the developing Asian countries that had opened their markets, particularly their financial markets, to foreign competition, has led to a nationalistic backlash against globalization, skepticism of the motives and wisdom of international financial institutions, and a rising protectionism.

The rising nationalism and protectionism in Asia is also a response to rising protectionism globally as well as the inability of developed and developing countries to reach agreement on key issues in the Doha round of the WTO negotiations. Realizing that developed countries pursue trade policies that benefit themselves, Asian countries are pushing back.

Thus, Jakkrit Kuanpoth shows how Thai farmers joined with NGOs to resist imported neoliberal deregulatory policies that threatened to undermine deeply entrenched agricultural and social regulatory practices. Their political leaders adopted the reforms, with minimal democratic consultation, to comply with IMF funding conditionalities imposed after the Asian financial crisis in 1997. Similarly, Antons shows how Southeast Asians have pushed against limitations of the existing intellectual property rights (IPR) regime to seek protection for traditional knowledge related to biodiversity, agriculture, medicine, and the cultural and artistic expressions used to transmit knowledge.

In China, the pushback takes the form of new market access restrictions, the championing of domestic companies in key sectors, and increased reliance on anti-dumping and merger and acquisitions (M&A) rules to limit "exploitative" or "unfair" foreign competition. In South Korea, the pushback comes in the form of widespread demonstrations against the pro-US, pro-free market Lee administration and its beef importation policies. In Indonesia, the pushback is reflected in a controversial decision by the constitutional court in a case that highlighted the conflict between global economic principles, in particular neoliberal principles, which emphasize efficiency and aggregate growth through privatization, and constitutional principles that seek to protect domestic industries and groups, with the court deciding in favor of the latter.

This type of interest-based resistance is nothing new. Brendan Sweeney notes that the first competition law in Australia in 1906 was not primarily designed to foster a competitive environment, but rather to restrict foreign competition, particularly cheap imports from US firms. The battle was between the proponents of protectionism and supporters of free trade, and in particular between labor, which sought to protect jobs and a "fair and reasonable wage," and the farming industry, which wanted to import cheaper equipment.

In other cases, domestic actors push back on regulatory practices that are inconsistent with existing regulatory systems or with traditions and norms. For instance, John Gillespie and Bui Bich Thi Lien describe how small-scale traders in Vietnam form relational connections with state officials to flexibly apply global rules to suit local regulatory patterns. It does not seem to matter to the traders that domestic regulatory settings are partially constructed from imported ideas and practices. Aishah Bidin offers another example of local resistance to neoliberalism and global practices when they conflict with local norms and traditions, noting how

Malaysian business leaders have invoked Islamic law/*Syariah* to naturalize the domestic penetration of global corporate law principles.

Which local actors exert most influence on the penetration of global regulatory norms and practices and how?

The chapters discuss a wide range of local actors, from socially vulnerable farmers and villagers to economically, socially, and politically powerful state-owned enterprises (SOEs), multinational corporations (MNCs), bureaucrats, legislators, technocrats, lawyers, academics, and other professionals. The regulatory space is clearly now more crowded than in the past, whether in authoritarian states such as China or Vietnam or in post-developmental states such as Japan or South Korea, where the influence of the technocratic elite has waned in the wake of the Asian financial crisis and economic stagnation. Nevertheless, the polycentric nature of the new regulatory state does not mean that state and non-state actors are on equal footing, or that small businesses, NGOs, and civil society exert as much influence as big businesses.

States that are economically or geopolitically important are better able to resist globalization than states that are not. China has been able to resist foreign pressure and refuse conditions on aid, whereas Thailand, for example, has been less successful at resisting US pressure to sign a bilateral agreement that many Thais find objectionable. States' leverage has also waxed and waned in relation to geopolitical developments such as the end of the Cold War, the rise of China, and the war on terrorism. For better or worse, non-democracies have been better able to resist global trends, with widely divergent results in Vietnam and China compared with North Korea and Myanmar.

State actors also continue to play a greater role in non-democracies, although the policymaking process is now more contested, at least in Vietnam and China. Even in democracies, the relationship between state actors and non-state actors varies. In Singapore, the policymaking process continues to be driven by a technocratic elite, notwithstanding increased public participation and a more active civil society.

Among non-state actors, not surprisingly, the most powerful groups generally have the biggest impact on national rules. Thus, big businesses, whether large domestic companies or MNCs, are often able to influence whether laws reflecting global scripts are adopted and to ensure that particular provisions are drafted in ways that suit their interests. Kennedy and others have found that the influence of lobbyists and business associations is closely related to their percentage of gross domestic product (GDP).[39] As Gillespie notes, small and medium-sized enterprises (SMEs) have been ineffective in voicing their concerns in the national lawmaking process. Oh and Halliday suggest that the influence of big business is particularly pronounced in technical areas such as insolvency law. Nevertheless, sometimes the underdogs can win, as Kuanpoth shows in his chapter on the efforts of Thai human rights organizations and NGOs to protect natural resources and traditional knowledge.

Moreover, while large corporations have an advantage when it comes to influencing national level policies, smaller economic actors often have an advantage when it comes to resisting implementation. MNCs are generally held to higher standards and compelled by the authorities or their own internal corporate policies to comply with national laws. Smaller actors often fly under the radar, as it were. The costs of compelling compliance outweigh the benefits and, in any event, compliance may not be economically or technically feasible for many small operators. Thus, small operators may in effect opt out of the formal state regulatory system and establish their own informal regulatory systems.

Chapter synopses

Chapters 2 and 3 provide theoretical perspectives in which to locate later case and country studies. In Chapter 2, John Gillespie develops a framework for classifying the concrete processes that underlie the phenomena of legal globalization. The framework departs from most of the globalization literature by directing attention away from nation-states and refocusing on the myriad ways in which non-state actors influence global legal scripts and practices. The framework is based on three core regulatory regimes: constitutional regulation, self-regulation by non-state actors, and deliberative regulation. The first regulatory regime is based on constitutional mechanisms that give the state coercive powers to regulate global scripts through legislation, administrative regulation, and court decisions. The second regulatory regime is based on non-state or hybrid public–private mechanisms that use self-regulation to localize global scripts. The third regulatory regime is based on public discourse that both forms communicative bridges among the regulatory regimes and regulates global scripts. Various examples from Asia are provided to illustrate the modes of regulation and how they interact.

The chapter concludes that global scripts are more likely to gain acceptance when they are epistemologically compatible with local assumptions and attitudes toward regulation. Globalization is best understood as fitting new ideas into local contexts. Successful transfers occur when global scripts are repacked into domestic idioms and practices—new wine in old bottles. Global scripts also gain acceptance where they provide solutions to problems that domestic precepts and practices have failed to deliver.

In Chapter 3, Michael W. Dowdle examines what "globalization" and "pushback" look like as system phenomena. He draws a distinction between norm setting and enforcement or implementation, and argues that transnational actors have a comparative advantage in the former, whereas local actors have a comparative advantage in the latter. He then shows that opposition to globalization can occur with respect to norms at either the rule-setting stage or the implementation stage. In many instances, local actors may use other global norms, for example environmental norms promoting sustainable growth, to oppose global business norms, including neoliberal principles that emphasize efficiency and aggregate growth. However, he claims that local pushback against globalization is actually integral to and definitive of globalization as, like the globalization it opposes, it too ends up using globalized norms, and hence promotes the comparative advantages that are driving globalization per se.

The remaining chapters focus on particular issues and countries. In Chapter 4, Christoph Antons examines the conflicting discourses regarding traditional knowledge and biopiracy in Asia, including knowledge related to biodiversity, agriculture, and medicine, and traditional cultural and artistic expressions used to transmit this knowledge. The chapter gives examples of the debate at the national level, but it also shows competing visions of the various United Nations organizations involved in the discussion and illustrates how global standards and new development paradigms have been implemented at the national and grassroots level. Antons shows that the dichotomies of North versus South and industrialized versus developing fail to capture the full complexity of the debates or reflect accurately the various interests involved. At times, some developing countries are pitted against other developing countries, while in other cases the interests of some majority groups conflict with the interests of minority groups, or the central state conflicts with local communities, within a given developing country. Even within local communities, some people may favor development of land and exploitation of resources while others favor their protection. What is abundantly clear is that local actors will use global scripts, including intellectual property rules, to pursue their agendas in whatever forums seem most promising, whether norm-setting transnational forums such as Doha or local courts.

In Chapter 5, Brendan Sweeney examines the forces that have affected the enactment and implementation of competition rules in Australia and Japan. The chapter begins with a brief discussion on the globalization of competition rules and then proceeds to investigate three major episodes in the 100-year history of Australian competition law. In each case, the implementation of the law was shaped by domestic economic and political forces. In the first round, labor won out over the farm industry, obtaining restrictions on the import of farm equipment. By the time the high court held the competition law to be invalid, domestic industries had already found other ways to protect themselves, relying on tariffs and quotas. The second round, centered on the 1965 Restrictive Trade Practices Act, pitted small family retailers against large retailers, and domestic big business against foreign investors. The resulting law was incoherent, reflecting the political compromise needed to gain support from groups with competing interests and goals. In contrast, the 1974 Trade Practices Act, introduced by the Labor Party, favored small businesses, individual consumers, and workers rather than big business. Over time, with a change in the political fortunes of the parties and changes in the global economic environment, small businesses and workers lost their protection, first at the hands of the legislature and then in the courts. However, in 2007, small businesses were able to take advantage of a tightly contested national election to push through an amendment that brought some relief. The battle will now shift to the administrative agency in charge of prosecuting violations of the Trade Practices Act and the courts and judges who interpret the Act.

The story in Japan is rather different because Japan did not choose to introduce a competition law; rather, one was imposed by the US following World War Two. Initially, the competition law did not suit the Japanese economy or Japanese regulatory culture. Yet over time it has become a good fit for the economy, although the regulatory culture has changed only slowly, if at all, making the competition law difficult to enforce.

In Chapter 6, Randall Peerenboom first discusses how China, like other Asian countries, resisted aspects of the Washington Consensus. He then examines various policy areas where there has recently been resistance to economic globalization or signs of retrenchment, including WTO compliance, enforcement of IP rights, M&A regulations, anti-monopoly law, securities litigation, anti-dumping cases, property law, and bankruptcy and labor law. In analyzing the reasons for the pushback, he notes that it is to a large extent the response to protectionist measures implemented globally. Nevertheless, he argues that, despite rising protectionism in China, the general trend is still toward greater openness and a more competitive economy. He also demonstrates that in China, as elsewhere, the policymaking arena is crowded with numerous actors—international and domestic, state and non-state—who adopt a variety of strategies and form shifting alliances to pursue their own interests depending on the issue at stake.

In Chapter 7, Dali L. Yang argues that China's less than successful attempt to model the State Food and Drug Administration (SFDA) after the US Food and Drug Administration (FDA) demonstrates the challenges of regulatory globalization. The SFDA was created with noble goals in mind: to rationalize and improve administration in an area plagued by overlapping responsibilities and turf struggles among administrative agencies. Major reform initiatives included the establishment of national drug standards, an overhaul of the approval and registration system, and the promotion of best practices for manufacturing, research, and sales. These reforms all failed to one degree or another for various reasons: lack of resources, including adequate professional staff able to complete in a timely way the demanding task of testing and certifying the safety of new and existing drugs, which led to the delegation of authority to lower level government agencies; the need to produce cheap and affordable drugs; corruption and rent-seeking; lack of respect for intellectual property and the confidentiality of trade secrets; the need for local government officials to ensure high growth rates, which prevented them from shutting down companies that violated laws but played an important role in the local economy; and the limited effectiveness of party and government discipline and oversight mechanisms.

The crisis in the SFDA led to the execution of the head of the agency and the arrest of many other senior officials, as well as to a shake-up of the industry and wide-ranging institutional reforms that affected all agencies and industries. The SFDA's budget was increased, high-risk areas were identified for enhanced supervision, inspectors are rotated and carry out random checks, and there have been calls for greater monitoring by NGOs, civil society, and the media.

Nevertheless, problems remain in the food and drug industries and elsewhere. As Yang notes, the crisis in the SFDA is attributable in part to the personal shortcomings of those in charge. However, it was also the result of systemic factors that affect other industries. Most fundamentally, the SFDA saga once again demonstrates that what might work in a rich, developed country, such as the US, where the food and drug industries are (now) relatively stable, will not necessarily work in a lower-middle income developing country such as China, where the food and drug industries are characterized by many small players and rapid change, and where the government lacks the resources and staff to meet the technical challenge of adequately testing new drugs and food products. Successful reforms must take into consideration local circumstances, including resource constraints and limitations in technical capacity. Designing cost-effective solutions that work in a particular context requires significant local knowledge, and thus de-emphasizes the role of foreign experts who rely on "international best practices" that are often idealized abstractions of existing practices and institutions from developed countries.

In Chapter 8, John Gillespie and Bui Bich Thi Lien examine the ways in which businesses influence commercial regulation in Vietnam. They find a bifurcated system in which an elite group of state-owned enterprises and foreign investors exert influence over the enactment and implementation of commercial legislation, resulting in a legislative framework that increasingly reflects international treaty provisions. However, this internationalized economic framework is largely irrelevant to the vast majority of economic actors in Vietnam, including small and medium-sized businesses and farmers. For a variety of reasons, most domestic businesses are unable to effectively communicate their preferences to central-level lawmakers. Instead, they influence commercial regulation at the local level through relational connections with officials or establish self-regulatory mechanisms that often draw on local norms to govern their business activities.

Vietnam appears to be undergoing several types of regulatory transformation simultaneously. The state is cautiously experimenting with new governance techniques to implement global scripts. At the same time, while most small and medium-scale businesses self-regulate with little reference to the state, they are also increasingly prepared to adopt transnational standards and processes (e.g., ISO 901:200) that provide regulatory solutions that are not found in domestic practices.

In Chapter 9, Jakkrit Kuanpoth notes that, while Thailand has joined the WTO and rushed to open its markets to foreign investment, the Asian financial crisis and the conditionalities imposed on Thailand in exchange for foreign assistance have led to criticisms of the way national development decisions are made, and to warnings about the direct and indirect effects of globalization, including growing income inequality and environmental damage. He then analyzes forms of local resistance against the globalization of business power, focusing on the movements of non-state groups in the areas of agriculture, natural resources, and protection of traditional knowledge. Civil society is not monolithic, of course. Different groups have different agendas, and they invoke or oppose global scripts as suits their purposes. Although NGOs and other non-state actors have influenced policies in some areas, they have failed to have an impact in other areas. All the same, Kuanpoth sees local grassroots movements as a powerful force in determining economic, environmental, and cultural policy, and ultimately in shaping a particular type of society for Thais within an increasingly globalized world.

In Chapter 10, Veronica L. Taylor summarizes the discourses, processes, and outcomes of regulatory reform in Japan during the period 1989–2007. A key theme is the re-regulation of Japan, in which government and industry began to deploy formal law, legal institutions, and lawyers as mechanisms for implementing dereg-ulatory policy and economic restructuring, while at the same time informal forms of regulation such as industry practices and codes of conduct and ethics emerged or were reshaped. This new post-regulatory state involves the delegation and contract-ing out by the state of some traditional functions and services to private actors or quasi-state actors; a proliferation of new actors in the regulatory space, including consumer advocates, non-governmental organizations, lawyers, prudential regula-tors, shareholder activists, and electronic commerce networks (some of whom are foreign actors); and the elevation of formal law and legal institutions as legiti-mized regulatory tools available to both the state and its citizens. She concludes by warning against the assumption that formal law and lawyers will become the main actors in the new post-regulatory state. Rather, as elsewhere, the state is drawing on diverse modes in response to changes in the relationship between the domes-tic and international economy and to the emergence of new regulatory theories, institutions, and practices being promoted domestically and globally.

In Chapter 11, Soogeun Oh and Terence C. Halliday discuss the transforma-tion of Korean insolvency laws over the last several decades. They argue that the comprehensive and far-reaching revisions of insolvency laws in 2005 brought to culmination both a domestic impetus for change that had gathered pace during the 1990s and urgent international pressures for reform in the wake of the Asian financial crisis. More specifically, they found that insolvency reforms involved four distinct patterns. Some reforms were developed domestically. Others reflected global pressures but were accepted locally. Still others were based on global norms that were initially rejected but eventually accepted, while some global norms were explicitly and consistently rejected.

As is generally true in the insolvency area, the main protagonists have been the National Assembly, market actors brokered by the Ministry of Finance and Economy, including banks and representatives of big business, the Korean Supreme Court and local district courts, and insolvency specialists including lawyers, econ-omists, and legal academics. Not surprisingly, given collection action problems and the technical nature of these commercial law reforms, trade creditors, small businesses, NGOs, and individual citizens played, at most, minor roles.

In Chapter 12, Simon Butt and Tim Lindsey use a series of recent cases decided by the Constitutional Court in Indonesia to examine the conflict between global economic principles and the constitutional provision to protect and nur-ture domestic industries. The cases also shed light on how institutional conflicts have undermined attempts to import neoliberal deregulatory policies, but have strengthened the role of the court in constitutionalizing political and economic disputes. Nevertheless, the judicialization of controversial economic disputes has put the Constitutional Court on a collision course with the Supreme Court and the legislative and executive branches, and raised concerns about the technical competence of the courts to decide such issues.

In the final chapter, Aishah Bidin examines efforts to reform corporate governance in Malaysia in accordance with global standards. She argues that the direct importa-tion of foreign models is not wholly appropriate for many of Malaysia's corporate governance problems. Corporate governance in Malaysia has reflected local concerns and circumstances, including cultural values and the desire to preserve the rights of Malays, the relatively weak state of legal institutions and limitations on access to the courts, and state ownership of or influence on businesses.

Conclusion

We end with some preliminary thoughts on two sets of questions, both of which require that the research begun in this volume be further developed and extended. First, what drives regulatory change? When do you get resistance, and when do you not?[40] And second, have the developments in regulation within Asia, including locally responsive regulation, generated economic value and competitive advantages?

One of the key factors in driving both regulatory change and resistance to global scripts is the increased interaction with the global economy. Asian countries have entered into the WTO, signed bilateral agreements, and sought foreign direct investment (FDI). All have required regulatory changes. Conversely, the rise of global protectionism, the Asian financial crisis, and the rising inequality and environmental damage that have followed in the wake of increased trade and penetration of domestic economies have produced a backlash.

Changes in the domestic economy have also resulted in regulatory change. In Japan, "the lost decade" of economic stagnation has driven wide-ranging reforms in all sectors. In China, rapid growth has led to more demand for modernist regulatory techniques—a strengthening of the legislature, administrative agencies, and the judiciary. There are even signs that China may be beginning to take IPR seriously as domestic companies increasingly have their own intellectual property to protect. Chinese trade officials are also now more assertive in preaching to other developing countries the need for good governance as they increasingly invest in and export to these countries. Nevertheless, as a lower-middle income country, China lacks the resources and its institutions are still too weak to meet the rising expectations of its citizens. As a result, the government has turned, albeit in limited and cautious ways, to new governance techniques, including the contracting out of state functions to private actors, a greater monitoring role for civil society, and public–private hybrids. In low-income Vietnam, higher levels of wealth and a more diversified economy are also giving rise to more demand for regulatory systems and rules found in advanced economies. At the same time, however, much of the economy operates on the basis of self-regulatory and traditional, informal systems.

Political factors also affect regulatory patterns and choices. The nature of the regime is perhaps less significant than one might expect. Both democracies and non-democracies employ a mix of regulatory forms and techniques. Democracies can rely heavily on top-down, command-and-control techniques; authoritarian regimes can contract out state functions to private actors, establish public–private hybrids, and permit self-regulation. Similarly, both democracies and non-democracies have adopted various development strategies from neoliberalism to chastened neoliberalism[41] to the (new) developmental state[42] to Venezuela's leftist neo-nationalism. Some strategies are more receptive to international trade rules than others.

More important than the nature of the regime is a shift toward pluralism and state toleration of non-state actors participating in governance. It is the opportunity to engage in public discourse more than participation in an essentially discourseless electoral system that appears to give non-state actors a public voice to oppose or adapt global scripts.

There is a considerable range in East Asia in the nature and robustness of civil society and opportunities for public participation. In general, civil society plays a more active role in policymaking in democratic Asian states. But even in authoritarian China and Vietnam, civil society is growing where there is greater tolerance of social organizations in the commercial area, such as business associations. Less growth is found in politically sensitive areas such as religion. However, the impact of business associations and civil society on policymaking in commercial law is often limited.

Perhaps the most salient political factor is simply the importance of everyday politics. The everyday politics of interest group competition is clearly evident in all countries, whether agricultural policy in Thailand, competition law in Australia, insolvency law in Japan and Korea, corporate law in Malaysia, anti-dumping claims in China, or competition between the Constitutional Court and other state organs in Indonesia.

In contrast, whether the constitutional structure of the state is federalist or unitary, or whether the legal system is common law or civil law, does not appear to be particularly important. To be sure, some reforms are easier to assimilate when they are consistent with the existing regulatory framework and institutional culture. However, most legal systems are now mixed to one degree or another.

More important is the size of the country. The bigger the country, the more difficult it is for state law to penetrate everywhere, particularly when there are wide regional differences. In China, for example, some of the large eastern cities such as Beijing and Shanghai are as rich and developed as in upper-middle income countries, while other areas in the center and west are as poor as low-income Bangladesh. Not surprisingly, the demand for state law (whether or not based on global scripts) and the appropriateness of particularly regulatory mechanisms also vary.[43]

Cultural factors were also evident in some cases: in the appeal to the notion of fair play in Vietnam, in the modification of corporate governance in Malaysia in light of Islamic *Syariah* principles, in the emphasis on traditional knowledge and forms of life in Thailand and Indonesia, in the balancing of efficiency and short-term profits with public interests and social goals in Japan, and in Korean sensitivity to their national image, as evident in the desire to be seen as a modern, developed country, whose laws reflect the latest international standards.

Cognitive factors have also shaped regulatory choices in Asia. Later developing Asian states have taken note of the developmental state model of earlier success stories in Japan, Taiwan, Korea, Hong Kong, and Singapore. Korean insolvency law was heavily influenced by interaction among members of a relatively small transnational epistemic community of insolvency specialists. In Australia, the Australian Competition and Consumer Commission (ACCC), the administrative agency in charge of prosecuting violations of competition laws, is one of the founding members of the International Competition Network (ICN), consisting of national competition authorities. The ACCC has been actively involved in the production of, and is influenced by, international best practices and guiding principles that seek to address global competition concerns through policy coordination. In Vietnam, local epistemic communities influenced the self-regulatory networks that arose in different industries and gilds.

These epistemic communities are fluid and dynamic. Today's prevailing wisdom is likely to be replaced by a new set of ideas that become intellectually fashionable tomorrow. Thus, Sweeney shows how, in early competition law cases, the Australian court, Privy Council, and House of Lords favored laissez faire principles in vogue at the turn of the century, similar to the US Supreme Court during the Lochner era. In other periods, competition law reflected other principles and concerns, including the need to protect the consumer and SMEs.

Similarly, Korean judges were initially reluctant to take on the role of economic policymaking in competition cases. Their views changed over time, in part because the Asian Financial Crisis and poor economic performance during the 1990s called into question the special expertise of government officials, but also in part because judges were influenced by the global trend to judicialize disputes. This in turn led to a more general change in the role of courts. As Oh and Halliday note, once courts entered the fray, they were subject to public scrutiny and criticism. In the process, they began to see themselves as significant players in national politics, and thus they began to take "an institutional interest in the national matrix of power."

The chapters in this volume have documented changing trends and patterns of regulation, both globally and within countries in the Asian region. But are the new forms of regulation superior? Do they add value?

There is no simple, or single, answer to whether locally responsive regulation generates economic value and competitive advantages. In part, this is because it is not one question. There are many different forms of regulation. Some may be more useful than others. But evaluative standards will also vary. Different actors will assess the costs and benefits, advantages and disadvantages of different modes of regulation and particular reforms or rules according to their interests. In many cases, empirical data are also lacking or contested. In addition, assessment often turns on contested normative judgments.

At the most general level, there has been much debate about the East Asian developmental state and the East Asian (or Chinese) model of development.[44] Even if one accepts that this model of development has proven economically successful, one may still object to its normative costs in terms of restrictions on civil and political rights and the postponement of democratization.

Moreover, what works in one context or at one level of development may not work later on. Low-income countries have different regulatory needs and capabilities from middle-income countries, which in turn have different needs and capabilities from high-income countries.

Most fundamentally, although there are trends in regulation, there is no perfect regulatory system. For example, debates continue about the relative advantages and disadvantages of top-down (command-and-control) approaches versus bottom-up or post-Fordist approaches in general, and in developing countries where institutions are weak and resources lacking in particular.[45] Similarly, various studies have traced a cycle of centralization, decentralization, and recentralization in Asia and globally.[46] Intersecting with this line of research in an interesting if complicated way is the work of Håkan Hyden, who points out that China is undergoing three significant transformations at the same time.[47] Parts of the economy are still based on a gild society, other parts are at different stages in the transition to an industrial society, and there is now beginning to emerge a post-industrial information society. Hyden notes that each of these economic modes has its own form of regulation, which follows a general cycle in the shape of an S-curve, emerging, maturing, and then decaying and giving way to another form. The different phases lead to different types of regulation, which may explain to some extent the regulatory cycles noted by others. The gild sector in China is increasingly more open and less dependent on internal rules binding on its members. Parts of the industrial sector, already heavily regulated, have undergone deregulation, and in some cases re-regulation. Meanwhile, the emerging information society is now giving rise to a host of new laws and regulations as the government grapples with the Internet, the role of foreign investment in key information sectors such as telecommunications, the media, and banking and finance, and the need to set technical standards that will determine the development path of key industries and China's competitiveness in the global economy.

While there are vast literatures on the various "new governance" approaches, there is as yet no overall agreement about what constitutes optimal regulation. Perhaps there never will be, given the diversity in levels of development, institutional culture, social and cultural practices, and a host of other contingent factors that differentiate countries. Indeed, the quest for a unified theory or optimal approach to regulation may be at odds with the emerging view that what is needed is a pragmatic, flexible, balanced approach that takes into consideration these differentiating contingent factors.[48] Unfortunately, the general advice to policymakers to adopt a pragmatic, flexible, balanced approach does not provide much guidance. Even in the absence of a general theory of regulatory design, however, there are many specific issues that can be clarified through research and experimentation. This volume begins that task.

Notes

1 See Terence Halliday and Bruce Carruthers, 'Foiling the Financial Hegemons', in Christoph Antons and Volkmar Gessner, eds, *Globalisation and Resistance: Law Reform in Asia since the Crisis*, Oxford: Hart Publishing, 2007, pp. 255–301. Curtis Milhaupt and Geoffrey Miller, 'Cooperation, Conflict, and Convergence in Japanese Finance: Evidence from the "Jusen" Problem' *Law and Policy in International Business* 29 (1), 1997, p. 1.

2 See Randall Peerenboom, *China Modernizes: Threat to the West or Model for the Rest?*, London and New York: Cambridge University Press, 2007 [hereafter, Peerenboom, *China Modernizes*].

3 The concept of the regulatory space emerged in the regulatory literature in the 1980s but it has been popularized by Colin Scott. See Colin Scott, 'Analysing Regulatory Space: Fragmented Resources and Institutional Design', *Public Law* 2001, pp. 283–305.

4 See Leigh Hancher, Michael Moran, eds, *Capitalism, Culture and Regulation*, Oxford: Clarendon, 1989; Kanishka Jayasuriya, 'Introduction: A Framework for the Analysis of Legal Institutions in East Asia', in Kanishka Jayasuriya, ed., *Law, Capitalism and Power in Asia: The Rule of Law and Legal Institutions*, London: Routledge, pp. 3–19.

5 Yves Dezalay and Bryant G. Garth, *The Internationalization of Palace Wars: Lawyers, Economists, and the Contest to Transform Latin American States*, Chicago: University of Chicago Press, 2002.

6 See Robert Wade, *Governing the Market: Economic Theory and the Role of Government in East Asian Industrialization*, Princeton, NJ: Princeton University Press, 1990.

7 Frank Upham, 'Privatized Regulation: Japanese Regulatory Style in Comparative and International Perspective', *Fordham International Law Journal* 20, 1997, p. 396.

8 See Cass Sunstein, *After the Rights Revolution*, Cambridge, MA: Harvard University Press, 1990.

9 See David Trubek and Alvaro Santos, 'Introduction: The Third Moment in Law and Development Theory and the Emergence of a New Critical Practice', in *The New Law and Economic Development. A Critical Appraisal*, David Trubek and Álvaro Santos, eds, Cambridge: Cambridge University Press, 2006, pp. 103–31.

10 See Douglass North, *Institutions, Institutional Change and Economic Performance*, Cambridge: Cambridge University Press, 1990.

11 World Bank, *The East Asian Economic Miracle*, New York: Oxford University Press, 1993, pp. 553–62.

12 Peter Evans et al., eds, *Bringing the State Back In*, Cambridge: Cambridge University Press, 1985; Joseph E. Stiglitz, *Globalization and Its Discontents*, New York: Norton, 2003.

13 See Tom Ginsberg, 'The Regulation of Regulation: Judicialization, Convergence, and Divergence in Administrative Law', in Eddy Wymersch, Hideki Kanda, Harald Baum, and Klaus Hopt, eds, *Corporate Governance in Context: Corporations, States and Markets in Europe, Japan and the U.S.*, New York: Oxford University Press, 2006, pp. 321–38; Halliday and Carruthers, 2007, *supra*.

14 See John Ohnesorge, 'Politics, Ideology and Legal System Reform in Northeast Asia', in Christoph Antons and Volkmar Gessner, eds, *Globalisation and Resistance: Law Reform in Asia since the Crisis*, Oxford: Hart Publishing, 2007, pp. 110–12; Martin Shapiro and Alec Stone Sweet, *On Law, Politics, and Judicialization*, New York: Oxford, 2002; Tom Ginsburg and Robert Kagan, eds, *Institutions and Public Law: Comparative Approaches*, New York: Peter Lang, 2005; Tom Ginsburg and Albert Chen, eds, *Administrative Law and the Judicialization of Governance in Asia*, London: Routledge, 2008.

15 See John Braithwaite, '*The New Regulatory State and the Transformation of Criminology*', *British Journal of Criminology* 40 (2), 2000, pp. 222–38.

16 See Kanishka Jayasuriya, ed., *Asian Regional Governance: Crisis and Change*, New York: RoutledgeCurzon, 2004.

17 See Anil Hira, 'Governance Crisis in Asia: Developing a Responsive Regulation', in M. Ramesh and Michael Howlett, eds, *Deregulation and its Discontents*, Cheltenham, UK: Edward Elgar, pp. 13–25.

18 John Braithwaite and Toni Makkai, 'Testing an Expected Utility Model of Corporate Deterrence', *Law & Society Review* 25 (1), 1991, p. 7.

19 See Colin Scott, 'Regulating in the Age of Governance: The Rise of the Post-Regulatory State', in J. Jordana and D. Levi-Faur, eds, *The Politics of Regulation in the Age of Governance*, Cheltenham: Edward Elgar, 2004, pp. 145–74; Julia Black, 'Decentring Regulation: The Role of Regulation and Self-Regulation in a "Post-Regulatory" World', *Current Legal Problems*, 54, 2001, pp. 103–46. For a discussion of the "Third Moment," see Trubek and Santos, *supra*, and below. Given the multiple, often inconsistent, and competing visions of development in the present era, this new phase is better described as the Third Moments in law and development.

20 Both David Levi-Faur and John Braithwaite use the term "regulatory capitalism" to decenter regulation by emphasizing the growth of non-state regulation. See John Braithwaite, 'Neo-Liberalism or Regulatory Capitalism?', Regnet Occasional Paper No. 5, Canberra: Australian National University, 2005; David Levi-Faur, 'The Global Diffusion of Regulatory Capitalism', *Annals of the American Academy of Political and Social Science* 598, 2005, pp. 12–32.

21 David Harvey, *A Brief History of Neo-Liberalism*, Oxford: Oxford University Press, 2005, p. 2.

22 See Tony Prosser, 'Regulation and Social Solidarity', *Journal of Law and Society* 33 (3), 2006, pp. 376–78.

23 Julia Black, 'Critical Reflections on Regulation', LSE Centre for the Analysis of Risk and Regulation Discussion Paper 4, 2002, p. 21.

24 David Levi-Faur and Jacint Jordana, 'The Making of a New Regulatory Order', *Annals of the American Academy of Political and Social Science* 598, 2005, p. 6.

25 See Tony Prosser, *supra*, pp. 364–87.

26 See Gillespie and Kuanpoth's chapters. See also Peerenboom, *China Modernizes*.

27 See John Braithwaite and Peter Drahos, *Global Business Regulation*, Cambridge: Cambridge University Press, 2000; David Held and M. Koenig-Archibugi, eds, *Global Governance and Public Accountability*, Oxford: Blackwell Publishing; Dimity Kingsford Smith, 'Networks, Norms and the Nation State: Thoughts on Pluralism and Globalized Securities Regulation', in Catherine Dauvergne, ed., *Jurisprudence for an Interconnected Globe*, Aldershot: Ashgate, pp. 1–34.

28 Santos, *supra*; Dezalay and Garth, *supra*.

29 See Erik Jensen, 'The Rule of Law and Judicial Reform: The Political Economy of Diverse Institutional Patterns and Reformers' Responses', in Erik Jensen and Thomas Heller, eds, *Beyond Common Knowledge*, Stanford: Stanford University Press, 2003, pp. 330–35.

30 Benjamin Cashmore, 'Legitimacy and the Privatization of Environmental Governance: How Non-state Market-driven (NSMD) Governance Systems Gain Rule-making Authority', *Governance*, 15, 2002, pp. 502–29.

31 See Boaventura de Sousa Santos, *Towards a New Common Sense: Law, Science, and Politics in the Paradigmatic Transition*, New York: Routledge, 1995.

32 Maurice Halbwachs, *On Collective Memory*, transl. Lewis Coser, Chicago: University of Chicago Press, 1992. As Karl Popper observed, "there can be no history of the past as it actually did happen; there can only be historical interpretations and none of them final … the so called sources of history only record such facts as appeared sufficiently interesting to record, so the sources will often contain only such facts as fit with preconceived theory." See Karl Popper, *The Open Society and Its Enemies*, London: Routledge, 1993, pp. 265.

33 Upham argues that the social elites constructed the social perception that Japanese have a low legal consciousness. See Frank Upham, 'Weak Legal Consciousness and Invented Tradition', in S. Vlastos, ed., *Mirror of Modernity: Invested Traditions in Modern Japan*, Berkeley: University of California Press, 1998, pp. 48–68.

34 See Benedict Anderson, *Imagined Communities: Reflections on the Origin and Spread of Nationalism*, 2nd edn, London: Verso, 1991.

35 Franz von Benda-Beckmann and Keebet von Benda-Beckmann, 'Transnationalisation, Globalisation and Pluralism: a Legal Anthropological Perspective', in Christoph Antons and Volkmar Gessner, eds, *Globalisation and Resistance: Law Reform in Asia since the Crisis*, Oxford: Hart Publishing, 2007, pp. 64–65.

36 See David Schneiderman, 'Transnational Legality and the Immobilization of Local Agency', *Annual Review of Law and Social Science*, 2, 2006, pp. 387–482.

37 Randall Peerenboom et al., eds, *Human Rights in Asia: A Comparative Legal Study of Twelve Asian Jurisdictions, France and the U.S.*, London: Routledge, 2006.

38 See Peerenboom, *China Modernizes*; see also Butt and Lindsey's chapter in this volume.

39 Scott Kennedy, *The Business of Lobbying in China*, Cambridge: Harvard University Press, 2005.

40 In an early attempt to predict the success or failure of legal transplants, Kahn-Freund emphasized political factors including interest group politics over social, economic, and cultural factors. Daniels and Trebilcock group obstacles to the rule of law into three general categories: resource and institutional capacity shortcomings, social–cultural–historical problems and political–economy barriers. They argue that political–economy obstacles, including opposition by key interest groups, have been the biggest barriers in Latin America and Central and Eastern Europe. Kahn, Licht et al., Friedman, and Perez-Perdomon all focus on cultural factors. Friedman calls for more attention to *legal* culture. Cooter highlights the importance of law complying with efficient social norms. Mattei emphasizes the economic efficiency of the laws themselves. Kanda and Milhaupt emphasize the motivation for adopting the reform (e.g., colonial imposition or desire for enhanced economic efficiency, prestige or professionalism) and how well the transplant fits with the existing legal infrastructure and the broader political economy. See also Gillespie, Chapter 2 in this volume. Otto Kahn-Freund, 'On Uses and Misuses of Comparative Law', *Modern Law Review* 37, 1974, p. 1; Ronald J. Daniels and Michael J. Trebilcock, 'The Political Economy of Rule of Law Reform in Developing Countries,' 26 *Michigan Journal of International Law* 99, 2004; Paul W. Kahn, *The Cultural Study of Law: Reconstructing Legal Scholarship*, Chicago: The University of Chicago Press, 1999; Lawrence M. Friedman and Rogelio Perez-Perdomon, eds, *Legal Culture in the Age of Globalization – Latin America and Latin Europe*, Stanford: Stanford University Press, 2003; Lawrence M. Friedman, 'On Legal Development,' *Rutgers Law Review* 24 (11), 1969; Robert Cooter, 'The Rule of State Law and the Rule-of-Law State: Economic Analysis of the Legal Foundations of Development', *Annual World Bank Conference on Development Economics*, 1996; Ugo Mattei, 'Efficiency in Legal Transplants: An Essay on Comparative Law and Economics', *International Review of Law and Economics* 4, 1994, pp. 3–19; Hideki Kanda and Curtis J. Milhaupt, 'Re-examining Legal Transplants: The Director's Fiduciary Duty in Japanese Corporate Law', March 24, 2003, Columbia Law and Economics Working Paper No. 219. Available from http://ssrn.com/abstract=391821.

41 David Kennedy, 'Political Choices and Development Common Sense', in David Trubek and Álvaro Santos, eds, *The New Law and Economic Development. A Critical Appraisal*, Cambridge: Cambridge University Press, 2006, pp. 103–31. Chastened neoliberalism involves awareness of the limits of markets and the need for the state to correct market failures, greater emphasis on institutions, a greater role for constitutionalism and the courts (judicialization), and more emphasis on human rights, albeit primarily civil and political rights rather than a more progressive agenda that focuses on the broader changes required to generate a more equitable society.

42 See David Trubek, 'Law and Development in a Time of Multiple Visions: The Challenge of Law in the New Developmental State', paper presented at the International Conference on Chinese Experience of Law and Development, 10–11 May, 2008, Beijing, China. The new developmental state looks strikingly similar to the East Asian developmental state, particularly as modified to fit the WTO era. See the description of the East Asian Model in Peerenboom, *China Modernizes*. Common features include a significant role for the state in regulating the economy and protecting domestic industries against foreign competition while nevertheless gradually exposing the domestic economy to global competition; an emphasis on exports and relative openness to imports; promotion of productive foreign investment and restrictions on exploitative foreign investment; primary reliance on the private sector rather than direct state ownership yet with a controlled process of privatization and continued state ownership in key sectors; support for globally competitive national champions; attention to poverty reduction, income inequality, and other social goals; and significant investment in human capital, including education and health, and in institutions, including legal and administrative

institutions. One notable feature of the new developmental state is the greater role for private actors and for public–private hybrids that characterize new governance and the post-regulatory state. As these chapters demonstrate, there has always been a role for public–private hybrids and self-regulation in Asian developmental states, although that role has increased and changed in many countries in recent years. Another difference is that most Western proponents of the new developmental paradigm assume a liberal democratic state, whereas in Asia democracy has been postponed until a relatively high level of economic (and institutional) development was obtained, and states have been less liberal, restricting civil and political rights during the high-growth period in the name of economic growth and sociopolitical stability. Nevertheless, it is surprising that scholars groping toward a new development paradigm to capture the Third Moment have not drawn more explicitly on the experiences of Asian countries, given the many similarities between the demonstrably effective East Asian model and the new developmental paradigm. One reason for this is that the role of law in Asian development is often misunderstood and understated because of a narrow emphasis on the role of courts in resolving disputes, particularly in Japan. This misses the broader role of law and regulation in Asian development. Moreover, although the role of courts in Asia has expanded recently in keeping with a global trend toward judicialization, the jury is still out on whether courts in developing countries have the competence and authority to provide effective remedies in cases involving land takings, welfare claims, and labor rights. These cases are at bottom economic in nature, and difficult to resolve in any developing country where resources are limited and institutions weak. As a result, there has also been a pushback on judicialization in some Asian developing states, including China. See Randall Peerenboom, 'More Law, Less Courts: Legalized Governance, Judicialization and Dejudicialization in China', in Tom Ginsburg and Albert Chen, eds, *Judicialization of Administrative Law in Asia*, London: RoutledgeCurzon, 2008 (forthcoming).

43 Randall Peerenboom and He Xin, 'Dispute Resolution in China: Patterns, Causes and Prognosis', in Randall Peerenboom, ed., *Dispute Resolution in China*, Oxford: Oxford Foundation for Law, Justice and Society, 2008.

44 See, generally, Peerenboom, 2007, *supra*.

45 World Bank, *Greening Industry, New Roles for Communities, Markets and Governments*, Oxford: Oxford University Press, 2000. The World Bank advocates a flexible approach that relies on local communities and non-state informal mechanisms.

46 See, for example, Dali Yang, *Remaking the Chinese Leviathan: Market Transition and the Politics of Governance in China*, Stanford: Stanford University Press, 2004; Andrew Mertha, *The Politics of Piracy: Intellectual Property in Contemporary China*, Ithaca: Cornell University Press, 2005. Yang and others have documented the recentralization of regulation through vertical or semi-vertical integration of the administrative hierarchy in a number of areas, including tax collection, environmental protection, food and drug administration, workplace safety, and information collection, with the State Statistical Bureau conducting more of its own surveys rather than relying on reporting from local governments. Michael Howlett and M. Ramesh, 'Preface: The Evolution of De/Reregulation', in M. Ramesh and Michael Howlett, eds, *Deregulation and its Discontents: Rewriting the Rules in Asia*, Cheltenham, UK, and Northampton, MA: Edward Elgar, 2006, pp. 1–10.

47 See Håkan Hyden, 'Putting Implementation into Context: Implementation of Law in China', in Marina Svennson and Mattias Burel, eds, *Making Law Work*, 2009 (forthcoming).

48 See generally the chapters by Michael Dowdle, Jerry Mashaw, Michele Ford, and Colin Scott, all of which challenge, to one degree or another, the notion that a system of governance and accountability can be created by design, in *Public Accountability: Designs, Dilemmas and Experiences*, Michael W. Dowdle, ed., Cambridge: Cambridge University Press, 2006.

2 The role of state, non-state, and hybrid actors in localizing global scripts in East Asia

John Gillespie

Introduction

After the East Asian economic crisis in 1997 exposed shortcomings in state-managed commercial regulation, many countries in the region accelerated the harmonization of their domestic legal systems with global regulatory regimes (e.g., World Trade Organization (WTO) and bilateral trade agreements). Research considered in this volume suggests that global scripts,[1] such as treaties, laws, legal principles, and practices, not only interact with state-based institutions, but also with a multitude of non-state actors, including businesses, professional bodies, non-governmental organizations (NGOs), social activists, and citizens. New modes of global governance have also extended their reach into Asia, such as supply chain agreements and private standard-setting organizations (i.e., International Standards Organization (ISO)). What this suggests is that the key dynamic is not between global scripts and the state, but rather between global scripts and the multiple actors (state and non-state) that form domestic regulatory systems.

This polycentric understanding of regulation calls for a decentered understanding of globalization where states are only one of many regulators competing to control the domestic adaptation and implementation of global scripts. State-centered explanations for globalization fail to adequately explain how non-state and state/non-state hybrid actors influence nation-states to select and adapt global scripts and have themselves become players in adapting and localizing global forces.

Definitions of globalization abound. William Twining writes of "those processes which tend to create and consolidate a world economy, a single ecological system, and a complex network of communications that covers the whole globe, even if it does not penetrate every part of it."[2] If Twining emphasizes the intensification of worldwide social relationships, others draw our attention to the diversity of global regulatory techniques ordering the interaction between the local and the global.[3]

This chapter will argue that, in polycentric regulatory systems, the diffusion of global knowledge is not simply unidirectional, from the global to the nation-states, or from states to society. As Anne-Marie Slaughter reminds us, nation-states are not monolithic but rather resemble disaggregated entities in their dealings with global scripts.[4] Both transnational and local non-state actors influence the transmission and adaptation of global scripts.[5] For example, global scripts bypass the state and engage with non-state actors in areas where the state claims jurisdiction and in areas where it does not.[6] At the same time, the diffusion of legal ideas takes place through transnational advocacy networks, foreign education, lawyers, foreign investment, and technology transfers.[7] Taken together, there are myriad institutions, norms, and processes through which state and non-state actors influence global scripts.

The first section of this chapter briefly reviews analytical approaches to legal globalization that posit a role for non-state actors. It finds existing theories either preoccupied with the "fit" or congruence between global scripts and recipients, or overly actor centered. They do not account for the dynamic interaction and intersubjectivity that generates preference convergence and shared regulatory approaches to global scripts.

The second section develops a framework for mapping the regulatory regimes that govern the domestic adaptation and implementation of global scripts in East Asia. The first regulatory regime is based on constitutional mechanisms that give the state coercive powers to regulate global scripts through legislation, administrative regulation, and court decisions. The second regulatory regime is based on non-state or hybrid state/non-state mechanisms that use self-regulation to localize global scripts. The third regulatory regime is based on public discourse that both forms communicative bridges among the regulatory modes and regulates global scripts.

The conclusion suggests how the interconnectivity among the regulatory regimes shapes particular regulatory approaches to global scripts. It ends by suggesting that further research is needed to understand why state and non-state actors come together to regulate global scripts in particular ways. This work needs to predict how domestic actors are likely to respond to global treaties such as the WTO and ultimately provide more accurate ways of forecasting whether domestic actors are likely to play by global regulatory rules.

Analytical approaches to legal globalization

Most studies about legal globalization emphasize the authority, capacity, and resources of nation-states to engage global forces. Some commentators have triumphantly declared the death of the Westphalian state to make way for a "new world order" composed of international organizations.[8] Others worry that transnational law and international governance institutions have constrained the sovereignty of nation-states and their capacity to protect their citizens from global forces.[9] Still others see global forces and nation-states in dialogue, creating regionally appropriate regulatory networks.[10] In each case, nation-states are the primary focus of attention—an approach that underestimates the state/non-state dynamic that underlies global regulation.

A few scholars have moved beyond Westphalian imagery to assess the interaction between state and non-state actors in adapting global scripts. It is argued, however, that they do not adequately explain how and why state and non-state actors come together to regulate global scripts. Neither do they fully acknowledge that non-state actors have themselves become players in localizing global scripts—a shortcoming this chapter will address.

Alan Watson takes an economic view of this interaction by proposing that fixed preferences about global scripts compete in a "marketplace" of ideas.[11] In his estimation, global scripts generally prevail over local opposition, because they are promoted and resourced by legal elites.

Pierre Legrand and others sensitive to local contexts and epistemologies take exception to Watson's economic explanation.[12] Their main disagreement with Watson concerns the level of interaction between global scripts and domestic social conditions. Watson sees few points of interaction, making legal globalization relatively easy. Legrand, on the other hand, sees so much interaction that legal globalization generates too many variables and too much uncertainty to readily succeed. Both theoretical approaches neglect the complex regulatory interaction among state and non-state actors that localizes global scripts.

Recent sociological studies about globalization partially address this shortcoming by focusing on the intermediaries who bridge global legal knowledge and local understandings. Yves Dezalay and Bryant Garth pioneered an actor-centered approach that examines the personal histories of the main actors dealing with global scripts and the institutions they served.[13] They found that the localization of global scripts depends on who supports this process, where they are located in the structure of government, and whether they enjoy close working relationships with international development agencies promoting legal reform. What matters most are power differentials and the distance between global and local actors.[14]

Anthropological studies also consider the interaction between state and non-state actors. Daniel Lev used ethnographic research to explain the diffusion of colonial legality in Indonesia.[15] This style of research is well illustrated by recent studies about transnational advocacy networks that distribute organizational techniques to reduce violence against women to NGOs throughout East Asia.[16] However, even studies about non-state activists tended to focus on elite-level discourse surrounding central law reform initiatives or "middle-class" concerns about human rights.[17] Few investigations move beyond the central state to examine how global scripts are interpreted at the provincial, district, or village levels. They rarely consider what ordinary people think about global scripts.

Systems theory

Systems theory proposes another conceptual understanding of legal globalization. It posits that society is differentiated into numerous self-referential modes of communication.[18] For example, people within institutions such as companies, political bodies, or universities use communication to create their own kind of reality and meanings. Virtually the whole of society, including legal systems, is fragmented into subsystems that have become so self-referential that they understand their environments from internal frames of reference.[19]

Gunther Teubner[20] uses this theory to argue that recipient legal systems are "cognitively" open to global scripts, yet remain operationally closed. By this, he means that recipient systems absorb global knowledge, but interpret it according to an internal logic. Global scripts thus act like "legal irritants in host-country legal systems. They unleash an evolutionary dynamic in which the external rule's meaning will be reconstructed and the internal context will undergo fundamental change."[21] Systems theory adds to this discussion by suggesting the circumstances in which recipients are likely to understand and learn from global scripts.

Evidence supporting systems theory is found in numerous case examples discussed in this volume. For example, in countries as different as Japan, Vietnam, and Malaysia, lawyers and international donor agencies disseminate global scripts by communicating with each other in a mutually comprehensible legal code or grammar. But global scripts are only likely to move out of legislation into daily life where the domestic subsystems relevant to regulation—the political, legal, social, and economic systems—have "co-evolved" and are well aligned with global scripts. For example, in most Western countries, contract law and market principles of exchange correspond and act on each other. As authors in this volume have observed, the problem for global scripts in much of East Asia is that they do not correspond to underlying regulatory patterns.

Although not free of its own conceptual problems,[22] this novel way of understanding global scripts as communicative events avoids problems associated with other socio-legal approaches to globalization It has the added benefit of decentering analysis and directing attention to the interaction between global scripts and a broad range of domestic regulatory actors.

Shortcomings with the theories reviewed

Despite its variety and richness, the transplant, sociological, and anthropological literature focuses narrowly on specific aspects of legal globalization such as the "fit" between global scripts and legal institutions in recipient countries and power struggles among elite-level lawmakers. They seldom acknowledge the growing number of "local" networks that contest, both normatively and practically, state-centered understandings of global scripts. For example, the self-regulatory business networks discussed by Gillespie and Bui Bich Thi Lien (Chapter 8 in this volume) largely by-pass state-based regulation and interact directly with global scripts.

Attempts to use quantitative analysis to capture general social attitudes to global scripts suffer from their own shortcomings.[23] Although this form of analysis usefully tries to understand what ordinary people think, it has been criticized for reducing complex and contested ideas into unrepresentative generalizations.[24] With the exception of systems theory, existing approaches to legal globalization de-emphasize the regulatory dynamics that research outlined in this volume suggests is a pivotal force in localizing global scripts.

State, non-state, and hybrid actors

The terms "state" and "non-state" are used in this chapter to distinguish those regulators that have a legal mandate to compel compliance and those regulators who do not.[25] This distinction is not intended to suggest that there is a hierarchy of state–non-state regulators or that "state" and "non-state" regulators function separately. On the contrary, much of the following discussion aims to demonstrate that they are interconnected in many ways. Hybrid actors take many forms that can resemble state agencies but pursue private (non-state objectives) or look like non-state agencies but aim to realize state policies. This distinction is useful, however, because it opens the discussion to the possibility that states are not the only site of interaction with global scripts even though many transactional organizations such as the WTO privilege nation-states. State, non-state, and hybrid actors variously collaborate and compete to influence the domestic regulation of global scripts.

To better understand how state, non-state, and hybrid regulators come together to influence the domestic adaptation and implementation of global scripts, an analytical framework must do two things. First, it needs to provide a means of unraveling the complexity of regulatory systems and mapping the diversity of regulatory approaches to global scripts. Second, it needs to suggest how different regulators are likely to learn from each other and form coherent approaches to global scripts.

Mapping the regulatory space

This section aims to develop a framework in which to map the concrete processes—direct and indirect—through which state, non-state, and hybrid actors influence global scripts. The framework will classify the ways in which domestic actors (state and non-state) regulate global scripts in East Asia into discrete regulatory regimes. To capture the broadest range of regulatory interaction with global scripts, it will avoid privileging state institutions as the sole or even primary regulators. Regulatory theory provides a useful framework for analysis because it is not considered an activity exclusively performed by the state—leaving open the possibility of mutually constituted state- and self-regulatory systems.[26]

"Regulatory space" is an analytical construct whose boundaries are defined by the events or conduct being regulated.[27] It assists this project by suggesting a framework in which to place and analyze the myriad ways in which state and non-state actors come together to regulate global scripts. It anticipates research in East Asia that shows laws and formal state authority may not always play a determining role in localizing global scripts, and that state and non-state actors may collaborate or compete with each other in the regulatory space. Furthermore, the notion of a space or arena of regulation invites examination of not only those within the space, but also those excluded from exercising regulatory power.

The regulatory space governing global scripts is divided into three regimes. The first regime is based on constitutional mechanisms that give the state coercive powers through legislation, bureaucratic regulation, and court orders to localize global scripts. The second regime encompasses non-state regulation such as self-regulation by non-state or hybrid state/non-state collaborations. The third regime is composed of state and non-state deliberation that regulates and localizes global scripts.

The first regulatory regime: constitutional regulation

Constitutions control power and allocate it between different state organs, more specifically the legislature, executive, judiciary and, in socialist Asia, the procuracy. Under most constitutions in Asia, regulatory power is primarily vested in the legislature, but it is also delegated or directly ceded to the executive. Although it is sometimes overlooked, courts have a residual power to regulate. Anne-Marie Slaughter makes the important point that, in dealing with global scripts, "all of the different institutions that perform the basic functions of governments—legislation, adjudication, implementation—interact both with each other domestically and also with their foreign and supranational counterparts."[28]

State regulation over the adoption and implementation of global scripts is not a unidirectional phenomenon. Non-state actors can enlist constitutional mechanisms such as representative democracy, "notice and comment provisions," and litigation to influence the ways states deal with global scripts. This section is interested in how state and non-state actors use constitutional processes to regulate global scripts in East Asia.

Statutory regulation

Most global scripts enter domestic regulatory spaces through statutory enactments. Authors in this volume describe how legislatures re-enact global scripts into domestic laws that govern insolvency in Korea, corporations in Vietnam, business cartels in China, and copyright in Indonesia.[29] In each case, the lawmakers were exposed to internal and external views (from the perspective of the state) regarding the appropriate ways to adopt and implement the global scripts. This discussion will focus on the mechanisms that non-state actors use to influence the selection, codification, and interpretation of global scripts by the state.

Representative democracy is the constitutional mechanism with the most potential to give ordinary people a say in shaping the way states regulate global scripts. Citizens express ideals and opinions about globalization through an electoral system that allows representatives to aggregate preferences that are in theory acceptable to most. This is generally a discourseless participation in which regulatory preferences are not verbally articulated.[30] Nevertheless, electoral processes can sensitize lawmakers to public concerns about globalization.

Since the mid-1980s, many states in East Asia have become popularly elected democracies.[31] Yet in each country democratic structures have been superimposed over much older notions of statecraft. Mindful of the problems generated by such reforms, Thomas Carothers claims that electoral democracy does not automatically consolidate the democratic practices and habits that make representative processes an important avenue for citizens' complaints.[32] For this transformation to happen, he argues that the state and citizenry need to reject authoritarian modes of governance, such as clientelism, in favor of some form of democratic governance.[33] As clientelist modes of communication exist in every society, even those claiming to be liberal democracies, it is their relative importance that affects the emergence of democratic processes. What the literature tentatively suggests is that democratic governance needs a citizenry that recognizes representative processes as important (but not exclusive) modes of conveying their views to lawmakers.[34]

Studies show that the consolidation of democratic governance in East Asia lags well behind electoral reforms.[35] For example, *majoritarian* democracy has not necessarily made legislatures more receptive to voters' concerns.[36] Even in Japan, representational democracy mirrors and rarely disrupts deeply entrenched clientelist networks.[37] But studies suggest that there is no democratic threshold and each incremental change affects the ability of citizens to use representative mechanisms to convey their regulatory concerns.[38] Even so, if representative processes are to assume a central organizing role, citizens need to not only embrace democratic governance, but in addition abandon clientelist modes of communication formed under authoritarian rule.

In countries such as China and Vietnam, where democratic processes are poorly developed, citizens must rely on state-sponsored "notice and comment" provisions that require state agencies to consult the public in drafting legislation.[39] In both countries, drafting committees are expected to consult with business associations and the public before finalizing bills.[40] Gillespie and Bui Bich Thi Lien (Chapter 8 in this volume) suggest that the efficacy of these processes is limited by the reluctance of lawmakers to codify viewpoints that contradict political policy.

Bureaucratic regulation

Evidence considered in this volume suggests that bureaucratic power is Asia plays a more important regulatory function than command-and-control legislation. Both state and non-state actors are more likely to respond to personalized discretionary power than abstract legislative norms, standards, and procedures.

If bureaucratic regulation is understood as an interpretative practice, then it is the relative indeterminacy of global scripts that provides scope for their adaptation to local contexts. The first factor to consider is the power invested in bureaucrats to regulate global scripts. Bureaucrats exercise significant powers in countries such as China and Vietnam where the state retains extensive discretionary control over businesses.[41] Neoliberal deregulatory policies pursued throughout East Asia have only marginally diminished bureaucratic power in countries where broad delegations of power are the norm.[42] Compounding the problem, open-ended drafting techniques used by many legislators give bureaucrats a wide latitude to interpret global scripts.

The second factor concerns differences in the way in which central and local bureaucrats interpret global scripts. Research discussed in this volume shows that different narratives about global scripts circulate among central- and local-level bureaucrats. For example, central elites in Malaysia who are engaged in global law reform debates hold very different views about the role of corporations from regional authorities promoting Islamic law/*Syariah*.[43] Similarly, local-level bureaucrats in China, Indonesia, and Vietnam are far removed from global discourse and tend to regard rights-based commercial laws promoted by international trade agreements and international donor agencies as alien and imposed. They interpret the meaning and purpose of law according to conflicting local interests, goals, and norms.[44]

All this suggests that what is often considered a national regulatory system is actually composed of provincial regions with different dialects and languages, ethnicities, and regulatory histories. Global scripts are not shaped by monolithic state regulators, but rather by multiple regulators in a polycentric regulatory space.

Throughout East Asia, citizens can use state-based mechanisms to voice their concerns about the bureaucratic implementation of global scripts.[45] Complaint and denunciation laws give citizens rights to challenge official action that contradicts the meaning given to global scripts by central-level legislators. In practice, however, it is often difficult to discern whether local-level officials have deviated from central interpretations of global scripts or, alternatively, whether bureaucrats are flexibly applying central rules. In developing economies, it sometimes suits all levels of government to allow local officials to arrogate discretion to experimentally adjust rigid central laws to local conditions.

Court actions

Non-state actors can use courts to challenge the adoption and interpretation given to global scripts. This may take the form of constitutional challenges to legislation implementing global scripts or judicial reinterpretation of the meaning attributed to global scripts. Courts may also serve as agents for the expansion and implementation of global scripts.

What role courts perform in resisting and reshaping global scripts depends on their powers and willingness to hear disputes concerning new global ideas and practices. Judicialization—the willingness of states to submit new social and economic spheres to regulation by courts—is taking hold in some East Asian countries.[46] The review of administrative action by courts is arguably better developed in Northeast Asia than elsewhere in the region. For example, the administrative procedure statutes introduced in Japan, South Korea, and Taiwan were intended to legally define the state–society interface and give courts additional powers to constrain bureaucratic action within legal parameters. As Song observed in South Korea, "reforms aimed to increase citizens' participation in, and the transparency and accountability of, the policy-making process."[47]

Simon Butt and Tim Lindsey in this volume marshal evidence for judicialization by examining the emergence of the constitutional court in Indonesia.[48] They describe how NGOs and citizens petitioned the court to strike down legislation that aimed to privatize key industries such as oil and gas exploration, water supply, and electricity generation. The privatization laws were based on global scripts prepared by the World Bank and the International Monetary Fund (IMF) as a condition for bailing Indonesia out of the East Asian financial crisis in 1998. To the surprise of international donor agencies, the court decided that Article 33 of the Constitution 1945 (amended) required the state to retain control over key industrial sections. By finding that the privatization laws offended the constitution, the court extended its powers into a policy arena in which it had not previously participated. It also invoked domestic narratives to push back global scripts that promoted neoliberal privatization.

In another example, for decades foreign investors pressed Japanese, South Korean, and Taiwanese regulators for greater corporate accountability.[49] They wanted procedural rights to force companies to privilege shareholder value over the private interests of managers and controlling shareholders. As domestic companies internationalized they too needed less state protection. Regulators responded to these changes by making derivative actions by shareholders more viable. Courts in Japan now routinely reinterpret the corporations law according to global standards of corporate governance that make managers more accountable to minority investors.

Judicialization is further advanced in China than in Vietnam.[50] In both countries, the judiciary is being asked to play a larger role in resolving commercial disputes. Party leaders stress the need for a more independent, competent, and authoritative judiciary. For the present, however, well-founded concerns about the competence, impartiality, and authority of courts have moderated social demand for litigation.[51] Another problem is the uncertainty surrounding the meaning of laws incorporating global scripts. Without a well-developed interpretative system through which individual court decisions can cohere into a uniform body of statutory interpretation, citizens struggle to use courts to give global scripts coherent and uniform meanings.

Courts are nevertheless slowly gaining power to make decisions over economically important areas. This process is partially facilitated by party reforms that promote judicial resolution of commercial problems.[52] But it is also demand driven, because courts cannot continue to delay and avoid making decisions in complex commercial cases brought by foreign investors and state-owned enterprises (SOEs). Courts will undoubtedly play an increasingly significant role in interpreting and moderating the implementation of global scripts.

To summarize, with the exception of the most advanced democracies in the region, such as Korea and Japan, governments can embrace globalization without fear of electoral backlashes. Nevertheless citizens in countries lacking representational democracy can use constitutional mechanisms such as "notice and comment" processes and court decisions to influence government policy. Even in socialist developing countries, governments seem willing to allow non-state actors to harness judicial power to change the way global forces affect local regulation. In the process, states in the region are beginning to recognize a role for private litigants in shaping regulation.

The second regulatory regime: self-regulation

The second regulatory regime is self-regulation. Although the phenomenon has come under increased control by Asian states, self-regulation remains the principal controlling device for a wide range of activities.

The discussion is divided into three subsections that examine how non-state:

- transnational organizations project global scripts into domestic regulatory systems;
- business consultants supervise and in some cases regulate the way states respond to globalization;
- business networks use self-regulatory regimes to localize global scripts.

Section one: Transnational non-state regulatory regimes

TRANSNATIONAL ORGANIZATIONS

Global regulatory standards are established by transnational non-state organizations such as corporate governance bodies or labor standard monitoring organizations. In exercising regulatory power, these non-state authorities transcend conventional understandings about boundaries separating state and non-state spheres of action.[53] A growing number of these regulatory systems are projecting binding and enforceable rules into domestic regulatory systems in Asia.

The Forest Stewardship Council (FSC) provides a particularly interesting example. It is a transnational environmental organization created in 1993 to promote the sustainable exploitation of timber around the world.[54] Forestry companies in Indonesia and Malaysia joined the FSC to gain certification and preferential market treatment for their products. Although the FSC lacks the coercive powers of state-backed regulatory regimes, it nonetheless has inspection powers and sanctions to enforce compliance with its standards.

Following the FSC's lead, other non-state transnational organizations aim to control different regulatory spaces. The Fair Trade Labelling Organization and Social Accountably International, for example, set and enforce standards governing internationally traded commodities and labor practices in East Asia.[55] What is significant about these organizations is their capacity to manufacture global scripts outside the policymaking sphere of nation-states. They enable associations composed of domestic actors to steer themselves toward collective goals such as environmental and labor protection.

TRANSNATIONAL COMMERCIAL TRANSACTIONS

Transnational commercial transactions have produced another kind of non-state global regulation. The complex multilevel networks in transnational commerce constitute a non-state regulatory sphere that is independent from the hierarchical forms of state law. As Gunther Teubner notes, this is "global law without a state."[56]

Private international law, based largely on the *lex mercatoria*, is a central component of this global governance system.[57] Global scripts emerge out of networks based on private contracting, private lawmaking, and private arbitration.

Transnational networks have their own means of establishing authority and order that is the result of unplanned evolutionary processes rather than state-directed strategies.[58] Non-state actors can enforce agreements through international arbitration centers that function like private courts. The importance of arbitration to international trade is implied by the fact that more than 90 percent of international contracts contain arbitration clauses.[59]

Transnational trade agreements project global scripts into domestic regulatory systems. Take, for example, the transfer of globalized labor standards through transnational supply chain agreements in the clothing, footwear, and textile industries in East Asia. In one representative case, Nike contractually bound a Vietnamese footwear manufacturer (Maxsport) to adopt labor standards that exceeded domestic statutory standards.[60] Maxsport now acts as a node in a global regulatory network. It imports new organizational thinking through supply chain agreements and then disseminates a localized version of this knowledge to subcontractors and suppliers. The new organizational thinking bypasses state institutions and stimulates creative ways for companies to deal with each other.

Standards and rules promulgated by the ISO are playing an analogous role.[61] In order to comply with ISO 9001:200 management standards, family-owned firms need to develop internal bureaucracies that cut across familial and relational hierarchies. Global accounting standards have a similar effect on domestic organizational practices.[62] In each case, the global scripts are interpreted and implemented according to local understandings and habits.

In another example, foreign lawyers use global scripts to spin protective webs around their domestic clients.[63] They exert pressure on state regulators to open domestic legal systems to global scripts and foreign competition.[64] They also use litigation to shape the way in which state and non-state actors interpret and apply global scripts.

Although there are no centralized regulatory organizations controlling the global scripts disseminated by law firms, by setting professional standards international bar associations exert some control over the range of norms and principles promoted by lawyers. International arbitration centers also standardize global scripts. Although the role of lawyers, particularly transnational lawyers, in diffusing global scripts in the Asian region is poorly researched, enough is known to suggest a permanent tension between some global norms and local regulatory spaces. It is also interesting to speculate whether the willingness of domestic legislatures and courts to deal with imported legal concepts affects the domestic influence of transnational lawyers.

Section two: Using global scripts to regulate the state

This section considers evidence that non-state actors use global scripts to monitor and even regulate East Asian states. One way in which this happens is when transnational professional advisors are given powers to oversee state regulatory functions. Among many examples, some East Asian states use logistics and inspection firms such as Société Générale de Surveillance to monitor state compliance with customs rules.[65] The organizational rules promoted by these firms contain global customs and import–export protocols. In another case, state agencies are audited by accounting firms.[66] The powers of oversight invested in these firms aim to ensure that state officials follow global accounting and budget standards.

Transnational management consultancies also play an important role in shaping the norms and procedures followed by East Asian states.[67] They are called in to advise governments about the implementation of regulatory policies and organizational structures. Although some consultants hire local staff and attempt to adapt their message to domestic circumstances, studies suggest that the regulatory template used by these firms is overwhelmingly derived from global (mainly Western) norms and practices.

What these accountability mechanisms have in common is that they act as sites of contestation between different conceptions about the role of the organization and how it can make sense of itself. They provide a conceptual framework that enables state agencies to discuss how pre-existing modes of regulation can be adapted to the new operational environment. Ultimately, they create opportunities for non-state actors to regulate the way states engage global scripts.

Section three: Self-regulatory networks

Throughout East Asia, non-state actors decide for themselves how to respond to global scripts, and their self-regulatory networks constrain the regulatory options available to states. In this section, the discussion explores the role of self-regulation in shaping global scripts.

On one level, self-regulation seems uncomplicated. Self-regulatory rules governing the conduct of individual organizations or networks are self-specified, self-monitored, and self-enforced. In practice, however, state regulators shape many aspects of self-regulation. State involvement ranges from direct legislative intervention to administrative guidance by state officials. Voluntary self-regulation, where there is no role for the state beyond criminal and civil law, generally occurs where the state does not demand or encourage regulation. There are few areas of commerce without state involvement.

Research in Western countries suggests that the scope for self-regulation depends to some extent on the regulatory policies pursued by the state.[68] Once states recognize the limitations of "command-and-control" legislation in regulating commercial behavior, they are more prepared to open the regulatory space to hybrid state/non-state and self-regulatory practices. For example, the shift from "command-and-control" to "new governance" techniques such as "responsive regulation" (discussed in Chapter 1) gives non-state actors opportunities to self-regulate within an overarching policy framework that is constructed from informal agreements and tacit understandings. The discussion next considers instances where state and non-state actors develop regulatory regimes that steer themselves toward collective responses to global scripts.

REFLECTIVE REGULATION

One of the most striking aspects of commercial regulation throughout East Asia is the use of reflective (sometimes termed responsive) regulation. This regulatory technique uses state power not to impose substantive objectives, but rather to sensitize government decision-making to industry structures and needs.[69] Reflective regulation alters the role of government from dictator of rules to facilitator of agreements with stakeholders. The government becomes one of many interest groups and is discouraged from exercising a determining judgment about what the public interest involves and how best to achieve it.

By allowing self-regulation to operate within the overarching regulatory goals imposed by the government, the autonomy and special knowledge of non-state actors are harnessed for public purposes. Studies show that reflective regulation works most effectively where state–societal interaction is mutually beneficial and promotes reciprocal learning.[70] These exchanges give non-state actors opportunities to shape the way in which the state responds to global scripts.

There is abundant evidence that reflective regulation operates in East Asia.[71] The subtle network of long-term ties between ruling political parties, centralized bureaucrats, and managers of large private enterprises that ran Asian developmental states before the East Asian economic crisis in 1997 constituted a type of reflective regulation. Representatives from these groups met in consultative or deliberative councils to formulate policies, rules, and regulations that would eventually govern an economic sector or entire industry.[72]

The regulatory system that developed in Japan during the high-growth period (1960–90) exemplifies this mode of regulation. Commentators differ about which groups played the dominant role, or whether bureaucrats exercised "authority without power" because they lacked a sufficient legal basis to direct corporations and citizens.[73] But they agree that the regulatory policy developed through consultation—"cooperative capitalism"—profoundly influenced state and non-state responses to global scripts both within and outside Japan.[74]

Another form of reflective regulation underlies the everyday exchanges between local-level officials and businesses in China and Vietnam[75] and other developing states such as Indonesia.[76] Local-level officials often negotiate with businesses in a personal and contextual language that focuses on problem-solving rather than legal rules or macroeconomic policy. They risk losing trust unless central laws, which are often based on global scripts, are flexibly applied according to local sentimental and moral precepts such as "good heart," compassion, and "good neighborliness." Through such regulatory exchanges, global scripts are reinterpreted, transposed, or simply ignored.

As Gillespie and Bui Bich Thi Lien show (Chapter 8 in this volume), reflective regulation at the local level can exacerbate regulatory fragmentation and undermine the coherence of central legislation containing global scripts. Efforts in China and Vietnam to bring highly contextual local regulation under central control face considerable hurdles. The state-based mechanisms that manufacture regulatory coherence in Western jurisdictions, such as constitutional and administrative courts, function most effectively in Northeast Asia. And as we shall shortly see, non-state actors are unaccustomed to participating in lawmaking and thinking beyond pragmatic self-interest—"What is good for me?" More work is needed to determine how reflective regulation in East Asia affects the way in which states and non-state actors deal with global scripts.

SELF-REGULATORY BUSINESS NETWORKS

Non-state actors are not merely passive recipients of state regulation, they have agency to develop their own self-regulatory networks. By sharing tacit understandings and codes of practice, non-state actors can develop regulatory strategies that localize global scripts. Self-regulatory networks have the capacity to limit the regulatory options available to states as well as to engage directly with global scripts such as *lex mercatoria* and transnational governance standards.

Self-regulation is not merely a function of underdevelopment; on the contrary, it plays an important role in the most economically and legally developed parts of East Asia. For example, the success of organized crime in some parts of Japan has been attributed to its effective protection of property rights.[77] Ulrike Scheade makes the broader argument that self-regulation in Japan is not "contained by domestic antitrust enforcement or foreign pressure" and performs a central regulatory function.[78]

In less economically developed states, such as Vietnam, self-regulating business networks govern entire industries such as copper wire distribution, sunglass retailing, construction, and furniture manufacturing.[79] Analogous self-regulatory systems exist elsewhere in East Asia. What these diverse types of regulation have in common is their capacity to shape responses to global scripts with little direct reference to state-based institutions such as statutes, administrative directives, and courts. As previously noted, however, self-regulation does not imply a complete severance between state and non-state actors.

In summary, self-regulatory regimes influence global scripts by:

- importing global scripts;
- joining with the state in establishing reflective regulatory regimes;
- negotiating with state officials, especially at the local level, to naturalize the implementation of global scripts.

The next section considers another way in which self-regulation influences global scripts.

REGULATING STATE RESPONSES TO GLOBAL SCRIPTS

Self-regulatory networks shape the way in which entire markets are structured. The argument goes something like this: self-regulatory networks interact with each other to form an interlocking system of financial agreements, corporate governance, industrial relations, and market entry controls that structure the way transactions are formed, financed, and enforced. They create a regulatory environment that influences the demand for legal services, insurance, auditors, quality-standard organizations, and other institutions associated with particular types of market regulation. In order to remain socially relevant, states adjust their regulatory approach to suit the underlying market structure.[80]

Take, for example, self-regulatory networks (*keiretsu*) in Japan. During the high-growth decades, corporations relied on bank finance, undemanding share-holders, and opaque corporate governance to build market share at the expense of short-term profits.[81] When this strategy became unviable during the 1990s and transnational companies moved production offshore, some of the bonds that held the *keiretsu* together began to unravel. This in turn led to less demand for govern-ment protection and more support for law-based transactions backed by a func-tioning legal system. At the same time, demand increased for legal services and derivative processes that gave shareholders more say over the payment of divi-dends.[82] The Japanese experience suggests that states respond not only to global pressures but also to particular market configurations produced by self-regulatory networks.[83]

To recap, self-regulation influences global scripts in two main ways. One, states modify their adaptation and implementation of global scripts to accommodate self-regulatory patterns. Two, states may expand their regulatory reach beyond existing jurisdictional boundaries to control new forms of self-regulation based on global scripts. This response is demonstrated in Vietnam where the state is amend-ing its labor law regime to take into account labor standards imported through supply chain agreements by domestic clothing and footwear manufacturers.

The third regulatory regime: deliberative regulation

Deliberation transmits global scripts into recipient legal systems.[84] By setting the ground rules for discussing global scripts, deliberation constitutes a form of regulation because it shapes the way in which actors think about global scripts. It also performs the dual role of giving state and non-state actors a means of learn-ing from each other and coming together to form coherent responses to global scripts.

Both systems and deliberation theory categorize the types of deliberation that are likely to convey regulatory meaning. As we have seen, systems theory pro-poses a highly fragmented world that is divided into self-referential subgroups that struggle to communicate with each other. Deliberative theory is more opti-mistic about the capacity for public discussion to formulate agreed positions about common social problems. It claims that public values are shaped by morals, ethics, and practices that are synthesized from deliberative exchanges.[85] Recent neo-Habermasian scholarship has loosened the reliance of deliberative theory on Western European democratic models.[86] Theorists in this tradition prefer to build up small pieces of evidence bearing on the regulatory role of deliberation, while avoiding the broader functionalist explanations proposed by Habermas. For exam-ple, they argue that deliberation does not necessarily need a public dimension; it may occur in face-to-face interactions at home or in workplaces and other social meetings. This recalibration anticipates the findings in this volume that delibera-tion not only influences regulation in public forums organized by trade unions, NGOs, business associations, and law reform commissions, but also in private forums based on familial and relational networks.[87]

Although the unstructured open communication presupposed by neo-Habermasians can occur in a wide range of social settings, discussants need a social space or civil society in which to raise new and controversial ideas.[88] Civil society is a highly contested notion, but contemporary debates presuppose formal and informal associations and networks in society that exist outside the state, but are "communicatively interdependent" with state bodies.[89] In practical terms, this means that non-state regulators need space from state bodies to formulate their own views, but at the same time they require a deliberative environment that facilitates learning from, and preference convergence with, the state. Iris Young argues that, once the cultural trappings of particular societies are stripped away, civil society should at minimum allow non-state actors to "self-organize and develop communicative interaction that supports identities, expands participatory possibilities and creates networks of solidarity."[90]

Closely related to the rise of democratic governance in some East Asian countries, non-state actors have gained more deliberative space to communicate their concerns about global scripts to lawmakers.[91] The state–societal boundaries that give state and non-state actors room to maneuver and voice their concerns are constantly changing. The active participation of non-state actors in post-Suharto Indonesia provides a striking example of what can happen when state controls over public deliberation are eased.[92]

Although political discourse in newspapers and Internet sites is broadening in socialist transforming Asia, many commentators[93] believe that civil society concepts do not readily extend to these countries because the party and state exercise extensive powers to co-opt and suppress social organization and public discussions. Not only does the state control discourse in public forums, it also tightly manages the formation of member-directed associations that could mobilize the resources that non-state actors need to lobby for social and legislative reforms.[94] Some Chinese intellectuals have invoked the Habermasian notion of the public sphere to challenge party ideology that the "state is the prime agent of progress."[95] But they have made limited headway in convincing party leaders to loosen their grip on the formation of business associations and public discourse.[96]

In contemporary China and Vietnam, business networks struggle to consistently voice their concerns about global scripts in public channels.[97] In consequence, much discussion is conducted in private, via communication channels that are easily co-opted by state officials into clientelist and essentially corrupt relationships.[98] As the purpose of these secretive exchanges is to secure short-term personal advantage, they produce highly contextual outcomes and rarely propose viable local alternatives to global scripts.

The governments in both China and Vietnam recognize the need to increase public participation to make commercial rules based on global scripts more socially relevant, but are reluctant to give non-state actors a prominent role in shaping public policy. Tight controls over public discourse have less effect on well-resourced and politically connected state- and foreign-owned companies than politically unconnected small-scale producers. As a result, small-scale producers struggle to communicate their concerns to state and non-state regulators about the market competition unleashed by neoliberal deregulation.[99]

Asymmetric deliberation is not just a function of state control and power differentials. What often triumphs in deliberation is the better argument. But the rules and values that determine who is permitted to speak and what form of deliberation is preferred are culturally specific and can operate as forms of power that silence or devalue the views of others.[100] Discursive rules weigh heavily on small-scale producers. As they lack coercive force to ensure compliance with their regulatory preferences, small-scale producers must translate their demands into a language that other regulators (especially the state) recognize.[101]

The rational deliberation favored by elite-level lawmakers throughout East Asia privileges speech that moves from premise to conclusion in an orderly way, and it tends to discount passionate, contextual, and figurative communication.[102] This discursive preference advantages well-resourced businesses, especially foreign investors and domestic elites that communicate their preferences in the legal language understood by lawmakers. As a corollary, it disadvantages small-scale producers who lack the skills to convert highly pragmatic preferences and tacit understandings into a general normative language. To make matters worse, small-scale producers are often more interested in pressing narrow personal interests than expanding the deliberative circle to engage with others in the regulatory space.

This bias toward rational discourse is offset to some extent, however, by the role of the media and populist pressures that arise in reaction to particular events. Thus, in China for example, the brutal death of a college graduate in administrative detention led to a public uproar that eventually resulted in the elimination of that form of detention.[103]

Ordering the regulatory space

To this point, the discussion has proposed a framework to analyze how constitutional, self-regulatory, and deliberative regimes localize global scripts. This next section builds on this "thick description" to propose an explanation for how state and non-state regulators steer themselves toward common responses to global scripts.

As conventionally conceived, globalization is an impersonal process of diffusion and normative alignment.[104] Research in this volume shows, on the contrary, that globalization is not a mindless force, but rather it is constructed from below by actors with varying identities and strategies.[105] But this conceptualization leaves open the question, how do actors come together to regulate global scripts? Some authors in this volume suggest that individuals regulate global scripts by their collective actions,[106] while others argue that what individual actors think about global scripts is shaped by the groups in which they are embedded.[107] The next section suggests a way to transcend this structure-versus-agency dilemma.[108]

Epistemic communities

We have seen that regulation in East Asia is polycentric. It is composed of myriad state, non-state, and hybrid regulatory groups. What makes central-level regulators take a different approach to global scripts from, say, local-level regulators or non-state business networks cannot be entirely explained by either the pragmatic decisions of self-interested individuals or political and economic structures.

The idea that social institutions and regulatory practices are first created in the mind is not new.[109] Sociologists have long recognized that major differences exist in the distribution of knowledge in society brought about by diverse educational, economic, and social backgrounds. Peter Berger and Tomas Luckmann characterize this fragmentation as "socially segregated sub-universes of meaning."[110] Within these subgroups, actors make sense of the world from a shared set of perspectives. As Robertson opined, "being embedded in a background context of beliefs, practices and goals is what makes the perception of anything possible and what gives that perception shape."[111]

Research considered in this volume suggests that local actors interpret global scripts through domestic institutions and epistemological frames of reference.[112] Take, for example, the groups of like-minded people that coalesce around law reform projects in East Asia.[113] Research in East Asia shows that global scripts gain a toehold in the collaborative structures that bind foreign donors/lawyers, consultants, and state officials in law reform projects.[114] These communities inculcate regulatory ideas by bringing foreign advisors into a close working relationship with their local counterparts.

Most local members of donor projects are either Western educated or, through training programs and study tours, are familiar with the legal canon that explains and legitimizes global scripts. Although they are encouraged to follow stylistic and methodological approaches prescribed by foreign donors, the language used by members of law reform projects is heterogeneous. While foreign advisors emphasize the "rule of law," "market deregulation," and other ideals promoted by funding agencies and foreign investors, to avoid offending domestic elites, local members of the community strategically stress national development and international competitiveness. In attempting to fit new ideas into their own context, local members repackage global scripts in domestic idioms and practices—new wine in old bottles.

Over time, members develop shared views about the nature of regulatory problems and the correct regulatory responses. These epistemic clusters should not be thought of as communities in a physical sense, but rather as abstract bonds with the potential to generate cooperation and shared understandings and responses to global scripts.

In another example, business networks are established and maintained by storylines that contain a "creation myth" that explains why there was a need to form the group and how the group continues to benefit members. For example, members of a battery trading network in Northern Vietnam repeat stories that stressed the need for mutual assistance to protect each other against unconscionable competitors. Eventually, particular storylines about the nature of business problems and the correct regulatory solutions gather authority. Storylines not only appeal to pragmatic self-interest by promising to stabilize market competition, they also provide a shared sense of community and identity for the members.

Overlapping values and strategic interests predispose members to develop trust and understanding, as well as the shared perception that they inhabit an island of ethical business practices in a sea of sharp practices and dishonesty. They also draw from the network a source of identity as ethical people, a notion that recalls the neo-Confucian *quan tu* (gentlemen). Over time, the storylines reshape attitudes and norms by convincing members that the network benefited them both pragmatically and ethically. By providing members with shared understandings about their common interests, the networks were used strategically to variously support or oppose particular global scripts.

Epistemic communities advance our study by suggesting reasons for collective action toward global scripts. They also explain why members of epistemologically compatible communities are likely to learn from each other—a prerequisite for the high levels of consensus required to change regulatory behavior.[115] Finally, as systems theory informs us, epistemic communities are not hermetically sealed against outside influence, but rather they interpret exogenous knowledge from internal perspectives.

Interconnectivity within the regulatory space

An important feature of epistemic communities is their interconnectivity—in other words, the way they interact with each other. Research considered in this volume suggests that epistemic communities are suspended in an interlocking web of regulatory influences. Interconnectivity depends on whether epistemic communities converse in a mutually cognizable language that promotes learning and preference convergence.[116] Elite-level lawmakers set the rules of regulatory discourse and in the process fix the limits of the regulatory space by determining who gains entry and on what terms. For example, business associations that represent well-resourced, large-scale companies dominate public discourse about global scripts. They communicate effectively with state regulators, not only because they have access to the resources required to run public relations campaigns, but also because they have the expertise to transpose their personal interests into general normative idioms that appeal to lawmakers. Litigation provides another way for the well-connected to influence global scripts.

What seems to increase the opportunities for small-scale business networks to influence global scripts is a shift toward pluralism and state toleration of non-state actors participating in governance. It is the opportunity to engage in public discourse more than participation in an essentially discourseless electoral system that appears to give non-state actors a public voice to oppose or adapt global scripts.

The regulatory mix may also influence how those excluded from the regulatory space challenge global scripts. In a society where public discourse is constrained, non-state actors may resort to civil disobedience, such as anti-globalization demonstrations or, more typically, silent resistance to global modes of regulation. This may take the form of mass non-compliance or the formation of defensive self-regulatory networks that collude with state officials to subvert the implementation of global scripts. In some cases, the intersubjective processes that bind epistemic communities are simply too robust for legislation to control. Even authoritarian states such as China and Vietnam are unwilling to pay the high political and economic cost of forcing compliance against broadly based opposition.

The detailed case studies in this volume explore at close range how deliberation operates in particular countries. They provide answers to important questions. For example, what social institutions and narratives determine who should participate in the regulatory space? Do asymmetries in public discourse enable particular regulatory groups to dominate discourse about the appropriate regulation of global scripts?

Conclusion

This chapter has attempted to broaden the analytical focus beyond Westphalian imagery to show that states do not monopolize the adaptation of global scripts, although of course the state remains a significant actor in all East Asian countries. We have seen that the regulatory space governing global scripts in East Asia is polycentric. It is composed of numerous state, non-state, and hybrid actors that are both regulators and regulated. Non-state actors influence the way in which nation-states select and adapt global scripts and have themselves become players in adapting and localizing global forces.

Globalization has proved an elusive subject. Not only is it difficult to pin down the main actors, because sometimes global and local scripts merge in the regulatory discourse. Despite the uncertainty, it has been possible to map a diverse range of regulatory modes. Each mode orders the way in which other modes connect state and non-state actors with global scripts. The resulting regulatory mix conceives of state and non-state actors in different ways; and different regulatory mixes allow different groups of actors access to the regulatory space. Much depends on the regulatory style adopted by state regulators and whether they allow non-state actors to participate in governance.

For example, neoliberal deregulation was rolled out in Japan during political reforms in the 1990s that aimed to give citizens more say over state policymaking. From this political perspective, neoliberalism was not just a technique to revitalize the economy, it was also used to enable non-state actors to participate in governance and determine the type of society in which they wanted to live. In contrast, neoliberal deregulation in countries such as China and Vietnam is treated as a technical instrument for engineering economic reform without necessarily giving non-state actors more access to the regulatory space.

A pressing question arising from this chapter is what factors induce domestic regulators to come together to coherently regulate global scripts? This is not merely an academic concern because the factors that determine why actors form regulatory communities have a direct bearing on the pace and depth of globalization. The notion that cohesive regulation seems to need epistemic communities that share similar views about global scripts goes some way to explaining the fragmented responses to global scripts in East Asia. But it does not adequately explain what motivates state and non-state actors to develop coherent regulatory approaches toward global scripts. Further research in this area may more accurately forecast whether domestic actors are likely to play by global regulatory rules.

Notes

1 The term "global scripts" refers to the globalization of norms, standards, principles, and rules that regulate (shape the behavior of) businesses. It encompasses not only written laws and doctrines, but also spoken and subverbal communication.
2 William Twining, 'Globalization and Legal Theory: Some Local Implications', *Current Legal Problems* 49, 1996, p. 2.
3 See Boaventura de Sousa Santos, *Towards a New Common Sense: Law, Science and Politics in the Paradigmatic Transition*, New York: Routledge, 1995, p. 65; John Braithwaite, 'Responsive Regulation and Developing Economies', *World Development*, 34 (5), 2006, pp. 884–98.
4 Anne-Marie Slaughter, *A New World Order*, Newhaven: Princeton University Press, 2005, p. 5.
5 Colin Scott, 'Private Regulation of the Public Sector: A Neglected Facet of Contemporary Governance', *Journal of Law and Society* 29 (1), 2002, pp. 56–76.
6 See Franz von Benda-Beckmann and Keebet von Benda-Beckmann, 'Transnationalisation, Globalisation and Pluralism: a Legal Anthropological Perspective', in Christoph Antons and Volkmar Gessner, eds, *Globalisation and Resistance: Law Reform in Asia since the Crisis*, Oxford: Hart Publishing, 2007, pp. 60–64.
7 Yves Dezalay and Bryant Garth, *Dealing in Virtue: International Commercial Arbitration and the Construction of a Transnational Legal Order*, Chicago: University of Chicago Press, 1996.
8 See David Held, 'Democratic Accountability and Political Effectiveness from a Cosmopolitan Perspective', in Gunnar Folk Schuppert, ed., *Global Governance and the Role of Non-State Actors*, Baden-Baden: Nomos, 2005, pp. 9–30.
9 See Andrew McCrew, 'Global Legal Interaction and Present-Day Patterns of Globalisation', in V. Gessner and A. Budak, eds, *Emerging Global Certainty: Empirical Studies in the Globalisation of Law*, Aldershot: Dartmouth Publishing, 1998, pp. 337–38.
10 See Wolf Heydebrand, 'From Globalisation of Law to Law under Globalisation', in David Nelken and Johannes Feest, eds, *Adapting Legal Cultures*, Oxford: Hart Publishing, 2002, pp. 123–29.
11 See Alan Watson, 'Comparative Law and Legal Change', *Cambridge Law Journal* 37 (2), 1978, pp. 313–36.
12 See Pierre Legrand, 'Comparative Legal Studies and Commitment to Theory', *Modern Law Review* 58, March 1995, pp. 263–70.
13 See Yves Dezalay and Bryant Garth, *Dealing in Virtue: International Commercial Arbitration and the Construction of a Transnational Legal Order*, Chicago: University of Chicago Press, 1996.
14 See Bruce Carruthers and Terrence Halliday, 'Negotiating Globalization: Global Scripts and Intermediation in the Construction of Asian Insolvency Regimes', *Law & Social Inquiry* 31 (3), 2006, pp. 521–84; Halliday and Oh in this volume.
15 See Daniel Lev, 'Judicial Authority and the Quest for an Indonesian Rechsstaat', in Daniel Lev, ed., *Legal Evolution and Political Authority in Indonesia: Selected Essays*, Leiden: Kluwer Law International, 1996, pp. 215–44.

16 See Sally Engle Merry, *Human Rights and Gender Violence: Translating International Law into Local Justice*, Chicago: University of Chicago Press, 2006.

17 See Sally Engle Merry, 'Constructing a Global Law – Violence against Women and the Human Rights System', *Law and Social Inquiry* 28 (4), 2003, pp. 941–77.

18 See Niklas Luhmann, *A Sociological Theory of Law*, London: Routledge, 1985; Niklas Luhmann, 'The Unity of the Legal System', in G. Teubner, ed., *Autopoietic Law: A New Approach to Law and Society*, New York: W. de Gruyter, 1987, pp. 21–35.

19 See Hugh Baxter, 'Autopoiesis and the "Relative Autonomy" of Law', *Cardozo Law Review* 19, 1998, p. 1987.

20 Gunther Teubner, 'Legal Irritants: Good Faith in British Law or How Unifying Law Ends up in New Divergences', *Modern Law Review* 61 (1), 1998, pp. 11–32.

21 Ibid., p. 12.

22 Some theorists applaud the insights generated by systems theory but believe that Luhmann overstates the epistemological divisions within society. They envision a less divided world composed of "semi-autonomous" communicative subsystems that, albeit imperfectly, converse with each other. See M. Van Hoecke, *Law as Communication*, Oxford: Hart Publishing, 2002, pp. 203–7; Julia Black, 'Proceduralizing Regulation: Part I', *Oxford Journal of Legal Studies* 20, 2000, p. 597.

23 Daniel Berkowitz, Katharina Pistor, and Jean-Francois Richard, 'The Transplant Effect', *American Journal of Comparative Law* 51, 2003, p. 163.

24 Inga Markovits, 'Exporting Law Reform &—But Will It Travel?', *Cornell International Law Journal* 37, 2004, p. 95.

25 The distinction between state and non-state regulators is blurred in some East Asian countries where constitutions and social conventions do not clearly delineate or respect state and non-state spheres.

26 According to Julia Black, regulation is a sustained attempt to alter behavior for identified purposes. See Julia Black, 'Regulatory Conversations' *Journal of Law and Society* 29 (1), 2002, pp. 163–96.

27 See Leigh Hancher and Michael Moran, 'Organizing Regulatory Space', in L. Hancher and M. Moran, eds, *Capitalism, Culture and Regulation*, Oxford: Clarendon Press, 1989.

28 Anne-Marie Slaughter, *supra*, 2005, p. 5.

29 See Terence C. Halliday and Soogeun Oh; John Gillespie and Bui Bich Thi Lien; Randall Peerenboom, and Christoph Antons in this volume.

30 See Julia Black 'Proceduralising Regulation &—Part I', *Oxford Journal of Legal Studies* 20, 2000, pp. 606–8.

31 Yu-tzung Chang et al., 'Authoritarian Nostalgia in Asia', *Journal of Democracy* 18 (3), 2007, pp. 66–80.

32 See Thomas Carothers, 'The End of the Transition Paradigm', *Journal of Democracy* 13, 2002, pp. 5–21.

33 He is referring to the paternalistic, informal networks that supported undemocratic developmental states. See, for example, Jean-Francois Arvis and Ronald Berenbeim, *Fighting Corruption in East Asia: Solutions from the Private Sector*, Washington, DC: World Bank, 2003.

34 Even in Japan, the East Asian country with the longest history of democracy, clientelist pathways remain important conduits between state and society. Ethan Scheiner, *Democracy without Competition in Japan: Opposition Failure in a One-Party Dominant State*, Cambridge: Cambridge University Press, 2005, pp. 220–30; Takashi Inoguchi and Matthew Carlson, *Governance and Democracy in Asia: Modernity and Identity in Asia Series*, Melbourne: Trans Pacific Press, 2006. See also Yu-tzung Chang et al., *supra*, 2007, pp. 75–78; Doh Chull Shin and Jason Wells, 'Challenge and Change in East Asia: Is Democracy the Only Game in Town?', *Journal of Democracy* 16 (2), 2005, pp. 92–99.

35 For more information about the East Asia Barometer, see http://www.eastasia barometer.org.

36 Inoguchi and Carlson, *supra*, 2006.
37 As the Liberal Democratic Party is the only effective political party, the electoral competition that might have given citizens democratic leverage is comparatively weak. See Ethan Scheiner, *Democracy without Competition in Japan: Opposition Failure in a One-Party Dominant State*, Cambridge: Cambridge University Press, 2005, pp. 220–30.
38 Michael Dowdle argues that delegates in the People's Congress in China have over time become more responsive to voters' concerns. See Michael Dowdle, 'Of Parliaments, Pragmatism, and the Dynamics of Constitutional Development: The Curious Case of China', *New York University Journal of International Law and Politics* 35, 2002, p. 1.
39 A survey conducted in ten Chinese provinces in 2007 found that fewer than 5 percent of businesses surveyed used formal state mechanisms such as appealing to bureaucrats or courts to complain about state regulation. See Kellee Tsai, 'China's Complicit Capitalist', *Far East Economic Review* 171 (1), 2008, pp. 13–15.
40 Jianfu Chen, 'Role/Rule of Law in China Reconsidered', in Christoph Antons and Volkmar Gessner, eds, *Globalisation and Resistance: Law Reform in Asia since the Crisis*, Oxford: Hart Publishing, 2007, p. 100.
41 For a discussion about the problems in controlling administrative regulations by bureaucrats in China, see Vivienne Bath, 'Reducing the Role of Government—The Chinese Experiment', *Asian Journal of Comparative Law* 3 (1), 2007, pp. 1–24.
42 William Fox, *Understanding Administrative Law*, Albany: Matthew Bender, 1997.
43 See Aishah Bidin, Chapter 13 in this volume.
44 See Bath, *supra*, 2007; John Gillespie, 'Localizing Global Rules: Public Participation in Lawmaking in Vietnam', *Law and Social Inquiry* 33 (3), 2008, pp. 673–707; David Linnan, 'Commercial Law Enforcement in Indonesia: The Manulife Case', in Tim Lindsey, ed., *Indonesia: Law and Society*, Sydney: Federation Press, 2008, pp. 596–619.
45 See Albert Chen and Tom Ginsberg, *Administrative Law and Judicialized Governance in Asia*, London: Routledge, 2008.
46 For a review of administrative courts in East Asia, see Chen and Ginsburg, *supra*, 2008.
47 Hee Joon Song, *Building E-Government through Reform*, Seoul: Ewha Woman's University Press, 2004, p. 9.
48 The Constitutional Court in Thailand has also given citizens opportunities to refine imported social beliefs. See Andrew Harding, 'Buddhism, Human Rights and Constitutional Reform in Thailand', *Asian Journal of Comparative Law* 2 (1), 2007, pp. 1–25.
49 Courts in Malaysia and Singapore have been protecting minority shareholders' interests for decades. See Li-Ann Thio, 'Rule of Law in Singapore', in Randall Peerenboom, ed., *Asian Discourses of Rule of Law: Theories and Implementation of Rule of Law in Twelve Asian Countries, France and the US*, London: Routledge, 1997, pp. 191–201. See also John Ohnesorge, 'Politics, Ideology and Legal System Reform in Northeast Asia', in Christoph Antons and Volkmar Gessner, eds, *Globalisation and Resistance: Law Reform in Asia since the Crisis*, Oxford: Hart Publishing, 2007, pp. 109–10; Johneth Chongseo Park and Doo-Ah Lee, 'The Business Judgment Rule: A Missing Piece in the Developing Puzzle of Korea's Corporate Law Reform', *Journal of Korean Law* 3 (2), 2003.
50 See Randall Peerenboom, *China's Long March to the Rule of Law*, Cambridge: Cambridge University Press, 2002, pp. 319–30; John Gillespie 'Rethinking the Role of Judicial Independence in Socialist Transforming East Asia', *International Comparative Law Quarterly* 56 (4), 2007, pp. 847–66.
51 See Kellee Tsai, *Capitalism without Democracy: Politics of Private Sector Development in China*, Ithaca: Cornell University Press, 2007.
52 See Joseph McLaughlin, Kathleen Scanlon, and Catherine Pan, 'Planning for Commercial Dispute Resolution in Mainland China', *American Review of International Arbitration* 16 (1), 2005, pp. 133–56; Gillespie, *supra*, 2007.

53 See Steven Bernstein and Benjamin Cashmore, 'Can Non-state Global Governance be Legitimate? An Analytical Framework', *Regulation & Governance* 1, 2007, pp. 347–71; Julia Black, 'Constructing and Contesting Legitimacy and Accountability in Polycentric Regulatory Regimes', *Regulation and Governance* 2, 2008, pp. 1–15.

54 Benjamin Cashmore, 'Legitimacy and the Privatization of Environmental Governance: How Non-state Market-driven (NSMD) Governance Systems Gain Rule-making Authority', *Governance* 15, 2002, pp. 502–29.

55 See T. Bartley, 'Certifying Forests and Factories: States, Social Movements, and the Rise of Private Regulation in the Apparel and Forest Products Field', *Politics and Society*, 31, 2003, pp. 433–64.

56 See Gunther Teubner, 'Global Bukowina: Legal Pluralism in the World Society', in G. Teubner, ed., *Global Law without a State*, Aldershot, UK: Ashgate, 1997, pp. 3–38. Also see Filip De Ly, 'Lex Mercatoria (New Law Merchant): Globalisation and International Self-Regulation', in Richard Appelbaum, William Felstiner, and Volkmar Gessner, eds, *Rules and Networks: The Legal Culture of Global Business Transactions*, Oxford: Hart Publishing, 2001, pp. 159–88.

57 See John Braithwaite and Peter Drahos, *Global Business Regulation*, Cambridge: Cambridge University Press, 2000, pp. 39–63; Goldman, 'The Applicable Law: General Principles of Law &—the *Lex Mercatoria*', in J. Lew, ed., *Contemporary Problems in International Arbitration*, London: Centre for Commercial Law Studies, Queen Mary College, University of London, 1986, p. 116.

58 See Sigrid Quack, 'Who Fills the Legal "Black Holes" in Transnational Governance? Lawyers, Law Firms and Professional Associations as Border-crossing Regulatory Actors', in Gunnar Folke Schuppert, ed., *Global Governance and the Role of Non-State Actors*, Baden-Baden: Nomos, 2006, pp. 85–86.

59 Dezalay and Garth, *supra*, 1996, p. 90.

60 See Gillespie and Bui Bich Thi Lien, Chapter 8 in this volume.

61 See Kaewta Rohitratana and Skaun Boon-itt, 'Quality Standard Implementation in the Thai Seafood Processing Industry', *British Food Journal* 103 (9), 2001, pp. 623–31.

62 See Teemu Ruskola, 'Conceptualizing Corporations and Kinship: Comparative Law and Development Theory in a Chinese Perspective', *Stanford Law Review* 52 (6), p. 1599; M. Power, *The Audit Explosion*, Oxford: Oxford University Press, 1995.

63 See Quack, *supra*, 2006, pp. 88–97.

64 See Yves Dezalay and Garth Bryant, *The Internationalization of Palace Wars: Lawyers, Economists and the Contest to Transform Legal Order*, Chicago: The University of Chicago Press, 2002.

65 See Amiruddin Saud, 'Indon Importers Recommend Re-Employing SGS for Pre-Shipment Inspection', *Antara Press*, Jakarta, 26 November, 2002, p. 1.

66 Ramkumar, 'Expanding Collaboration between SAIs and Civil Society', *International Journal of Government Auditing* 34 (2), 2007, p. 2; Kunreuther et al., 'Third Party Inspection as an Alternative to Command and Control Regulation', in Eric Orts, ed., *Environmental Contracts and Regulatory Innovation: Comparative Approaches in Europe and the United States*, London: Kluwer Law International, 2001.

67 The major management consultants active in East Asia are McKinseys, PriceWaterhouseCoopers, and Deloittes. See also Christopher Wright and Seung-Ho Kwon, 'Business Crisis and Management Fashion: Korean Companies, Restructuring and Consulting Advice', *Asia Business Review* 12 (3), 2006.

68 See Colin Scott, 'Private Regulation of the Public Sector: A Neglected Facet of Contemporary Governance', *Journal of Law and Society* 29 (1), 2002, pp. 56–76.

69 See Anil Hira, 'Governance Crisis in Asia: Developing a Responsive Regulation', in Michael Howlett and M. Ramesh, eds, *Deregulation and Its Discontents: Rewriting the Rules in Asia*, Cheltenham, UK: Edward Elgar, 2006, pp. 13–28. See also Ayres and Braithwaite, *Responsive Regulation: Transcending the Deregulation Debate*, New York: Oxford University Press, 1992.

70   See Shawn Rosenberg, ed., *Deliberation, Participation and Democracy: Can People Govern?*, New York: Palgrave Macmillan, 2007.
71   Andrew MacIntyre, *The Power of Institutions: Political Architecture and Governance*, Ithaca: Cornell University Press, 2003.
72   Jose Campos and Hilton Root, *The Key to the East Asian Miracle*, Washington, DC: The Brooking Institution, 1996, pp. 78–99.
73   See John Haley, *The Spirit of Japanese Law*, Athens, GA: University of Georgia Press, 1998.
74   See Ulrike Schaede and William Grimes, *Japan's Managed Globalization: Adapting to the Twenty-First Century*, Armonk, NY: M.E. Sharpe, 2002.
75   See Kellee Tsai, 'Adaptive Informal Institutions and Endogenous and Institutional Change in China', *World Politics* 59 (1), 2007, pp. 116–41. See also John Gillespie, *Transplanting Commercial Law Reform: Developing a 'Rule of Law' in Vietnam*, Aldershot, UK: Ashgate, 2006, pp. 189–93.
76   Von Benda-Beckmann, 'Transnationalisation, Globalisation and Pluralism: a Legal Anthropological Perspective', in Christoph Antons and Volkmar Gessner, eds, *Globalisation and Resistance: Law Reform in Asia since the Crisis*, Oxford: Hart Publishing, 2007.
77   See Curtis Milhaupt and Geoffrey West, 'The Dark Side of Private Ordering: An Institutional and Empirical Analysis of Organized Crime', *University of Chicago Law Review* 67, 2000.
78   See Ulrike Scheade, *Cooperative Capitalism: Self-Regulation, Trade Associations, and the Anti-monopoly Law in Japan*, Oxford: Oxford University Press, 2000; Schaffer, G.C., *Defending Interests: Public–Private Partnerships in WTO Litigation*, Washington, DC: Brookings Institution Press, 2003, p. 1.
79   Gillespie, *supra*, 2006, pp. 275–84.
80   The "varieties of capitalism" approach raises the analogous argument that each type or variety of capitalism has it own distinct interlocking set of economic institutions that produce particular regulatory outcomes. See P. Hall and D. Soskice, *Varieties of Capitalism: The Changes Facing Contemporary Political Economics*, Cambridge: Cambridge University Press, 2000.
81   See Ohnesorge, *supra*, 2007, p. 112.
82   See Kenji Sanekata and Stephen Wilks, 'The Fair Trade Commission and the Enforcement of Competition Policy in Japan', in G. Bruce Doern and Stephen Wilks, eds, *Comparative Competition Policy: National Institutions in a Global Market*, Oxford: Clarendon Press, 1996.
83   Frank K. Upham, 'Privatized Regulation: Japanese Regulatory Style in Comparative and International Perspective', *Fordham International Law Journal* 20, 1996, p. 396. Also see Chapters 5 and 10 by Brendan Sweeney and Veronica Taylor in this volume.
84   For a discussion about deliberative theory, see Jurgen Habermas, *Structural Transformation of the Public Sphere: An Inquiry into a Category of Bourgeois Society*, trans. Thomas Burger, Cambridge: Polity Press, 1992; John Dryzek, *Deliberative Democracy and Beyond: Liberals, Critics and Contestations*, Oxford: Oxford University Press, 2000.
85   Jurgen Habermas, *The Theory of Communicative Action*, Vol. 2. Boston, MA: Beacon Press, 1987, pp. 164–97.
86   See, for example, Michael Neblo, 'Thinking Through Democracy', *Acta Politica* 40, 2005, pp. 169–81; Bernhard Peters, 'Seeing Bifocally: Media, Place Culture', in Akhil Gupta and James Ferguson, eds, *Culture, Power, Place: Explorations in Critical Anthropology*, Durham, NC: Duke University Press, 1996, pp. 104–11; Maarten Hajer, 'A Frame in the Fields: Policy Making and the Reinvention of Politics', in Maarten Hajer and Hendrik Wagenaar, eds, *Deliberative Policy Analysis: Understanding Governance in the Network Society*, Cambridge: Cambridge University Press, 2003, pp. 88–112; Carolyn Hendriks, 'Participatory Storylines and their Influence on Deliberative Forums', *Policy Science* 38, 2005, pp. 1, 5.

87 See Chapter 8 by Gillespie and Bui Bich Thi Lien and Chapter 13 by Aishah Bidin in this volume. Also see Wenfang Tang, *Public Opinion and Political Change in China*, Palo Alto: Stanford University Press, 2005; Scott Kennedy, *The Business of Lobbying in China*, Cambridge, MA: Harvard University Press, 2005, pp. 5–56.
88 Habermas proposed a set of preconditions for effective public deliberation such as "communicative rationality" that reflect communicative structures in Western Europe. This does not automatically disqualify his theories from applying in other cultural settings, but it does suggest caution in applying them too literally. See also Kevin Dowd, 'Participation in Civil Society', in N. Douglas Lewis and David Campbell, eds, *Promoting Participation: Law or Politics?*, London: Cavendish Publishing, 1999, pp. 31–43.
89 Michael Walzer, ed., *Towards a Global Civil Society*, Providence, MA, and Oxford: Burghahn Books, 1995.
90 See Iris Marion Young, *Democracy Inclusion*, Oxford: Oxford University Press, 2000, p. 163.
91 Inoguchi and Carlson, *supra*, 2006.
92 See Chapter 12 by Simon Butt and Tim Lindsey in this volume.
93 Norman Stockman, *Understanding Chinese Society*, Cambridge: Polity Press, 2000, pp. 222–24; Ben Kerkvliet et al., *Getting Organized in Vietnam: Moving in and Around the Socialist State*, Singapore: Institute of Southeast Asian Studies, 2003.
94 See Chapter 8 by John Gillespie and Bui Bich Thi Lien in this volume.
95 Gloria Davis, 'Habermas in China: Theory as Catalyst', *The China Journal* 57, 2007, p. 66.
96 See Kennedy, *supra*, 2005.
97 See Kennedy, *supra*, 2005, pp. 25–56.
98 See Pitman Potter, 'Guanxi and the PRC Legal System: From Contradiction to Complementarity', in Thomas Gold, Doug Guthrie, and David Wank, eds, *Social Connections in China*, New York: Cambridge University Press, 2002. See also Peerenboom, *supra*, 2002, p. 430.
99 See Chapter 6 by Randall Peerenboom and Chapter 8 by John Gillespie and Bui Bich Thi Lien in this volume.
100 See Iris Marion Young, 'Justice and Communicative Democracy', in Roger Gottlieb, ed., *Radical Philosophy: Tradition, Counter Tradition, Politics*, Philadelphia: Temple University Press, 1993.
101 See Bronwyn Morgan, *Social Citizenship in the Shadow of Competition*, Dartmouth: Ashgate, 2003.
102 See Thomas Heberer, 'Discourses, Intellectuals, Collective Behavior and Political Change Theoretical Aspects of Discourse', in Claudia Derichs and Thomas Heberer, eds, *The Power of Ideas: Intellectual Input and Political Change in East and Southeast Asia*, Copenhagen: NIAS Press, 2006, pp. 20–22, 25–31.
103 Keith Hand, 'Citizens Engage the Constitution: The Sun Zhigang Incident and Constitutional Proposals in the People's Republic of China', in Stephanie Balme and Michael Dowdle, eds, *Constitutionalism and Judicial Power in China*, New York: Palgrave, 2008.
104 See, for example, John Meyer, John Boli, and George Thomas, 'World Society and the Nation-State', *American Journal of Sociology* 103 (1), 1997, pp. 144–81.
105 See, for example, Chapter 11 by Soogeun Oh and Terence C. Halliday and Chapter 9 by Jakkrit Kuanpoth in this volume.
106 Hayek and Popper are the founders of methodological individualism, which reduces any collective phenomenon to the intentional actions of human individuals. See, for example, Friedrich Hayek, *Law, Legislation, and Liberty*, Vol. 1, *Rules and Order*, London: Routledge and Kegan Paul, 1973.
107 See, for example, Chapter 3 by Michael W. Dowdle, Chapter 6 by John Gillespie, and Chapter 10 by Veronica Taylor in this volume.

108 For a discussion about this dilemma, see Victor Nee and Richard Swedberg, eds, *On Capitalism*, Palo Alto: Stanford University Press, 2007; Pierre Bourdieu, *The Social Structure of the Economy*, Malden, MA: Polity Press, 2005.

109 See Peter Berger and Thomas Luckman, *The Social Construction of Reality*, Garden City, NJ: Anchor Books, 1967. Also see Gunther Teubner, 'How the Law Thinks: Toward a Constructivist Epistemology of Law', *Law and Society Review* 23 (5), 1988, p. 733.

110 Berger and Luckman, *supra*, 1967, p. 65.

111 Michael Robertson, 'Picking Positivism Apart: Stanley Fish on Epistemology and Law', *Southern California Interdisciplinary Law Journal* 8, 1999, p. 417.

112 See Chapter 3 by Michael W. Dowdle and Chapter 8 by John Gillespie and Bui Bich Thi Lien in this volume. Also see Joachim Savelsberg and Ryan King, 'Institutionalizing Collective Memories of Hate: Law and Law Enforcement in Germany and the United States', *The American Journal of Sociology* 111 (2), 2005, pp. 582–85.

113 See Gillespie, *supra*, 2006, pp. 66–82.

114 See Chapter 11 by Soogeun Oh and Terence C. Halliday and Chapter 8 by John Gillespie and Bui Bich Thi Lien in this volume.

115 See R. McAdams, 'The Origin, Development, and Regulation of Norms', *Michigan Law Review* 96, 1997, pp. 338, 382–86.

116 See John Gillespie, 'Developing a Discursive Analysis of Legal Transfers into Developing East Asia', *New York University Journal of International Law and Politics* 41 (2), 2008, pp. 101–61.

3   Pushing against globalization

Toward an analytic template

Michael W. Dowdle

Introduction

In this chapter, I examine what the concepts of "globalization" and "pushing against" look like as system phenomena. I will argue that what we call globalization can be characterized as a kind of reciprocal regulatory borrowing between transnational and local regulatory actors, and that this borrowing is likely to be subject to a kind of law of comparative regulatory advantage that tracks David Ricardo's similar law. As we shall see, because of this, a significant portion of what we are likely to categorize as local "pushing against" globalization is not really pushing against globalization at all, but is instead actually acting to promote globalization. And in fact, the most effective "pushing against" globalization is likely coming from globalization itself.

"Regulation" and its components

At its heart, globalization describes a regulatory phenomenon. "Regulation," in this sense, involves inducing individuals to engage in large-scale social coordination. (As described further below, in the case of globalization, the induced social coordination transcends national boundaries.) Regulatory coordination is achieved by rationalizing individual behavior into large-scale patterns.[1] Inducing such coordination requires the presence of a number of component institutions that collectively comprise a regulatory regime. Perhaps principal among these components are "norms" and "enforcement institutions."[2] "Norms" refer to the particular conceptual *patterns* of social coordination that identify or define a particular regulatory framework. These norms may be conscious or pre-conscious; they may be written, customary, or tacit; they include patterns that are the product of design as well as patterns that are more spontaneous in origin. These patterns of behavior are also constantly evolving as the regulatory framework itself is continually encountering new kinds of regulatory problems. Many of these patterns will be contested among the subjects of that framework, especially in their application, but also in their abstract substance or even in their status as norms. Nevertheless, without such *a priori*, conceptualized patterns—relatively stable, relatively known and agreed upon, and relatively rational—social coordination, of which regulation is a type, would be impossible.

Another important aspect of a regulatory framework is enforcement. Patterns of social coordination are often vulnerable to breakdown, resulting from individual acts of defection. Within most regulatory frameworks, situations will frequently occur in which, for any particular individual, the immediate gains from not cooperating in some particular instance will outweigh the immediate gains she receives from cooperation. For this reason, a regulatory framework will often, if not invariably, include institutions that incentivize their particular patterns of cooperation (i.e., its particular norms) beyond that produced by individual expectation of immediate gain.

When a particular regulatory entity possesses authority to generate both the norms and the necessary enforcement institutions for a particular regulatory framework, I will refer to that entity as a "regulatory agent." Regulatory agents, in this usage, may be transnational, national, or local; they may be formal or informal. They may even be spontaneous, as according to Hayek's notions of "markets," for example.[3]

Regulatory agents do not operate in isolation, however. Constructing and disseminating new sets of regulatory norms or new enforcement institutions can be costly. For this reason, a particular regulatory regime may sometimes, perhaps often, piggyback on other regulatory regimes, using one or more of those other regimes' components for its own ends.

For convenience, we might call this "regulatory borrowing."[4] For example, in late nineteenth-century United States, large companies developed a standardized set of accounting practices called "cost accounting" in order to help them keep track of their increasingly geographically dispersed economic activities. In this sense, cost accounting can be said to have been originated as a normative component of a particular kind of regulatory agent that would become known collectively as "corporate governance." When the American government, in the form of the newly established Interstate Commerce Commission (ICC), started regulating certain forms of market competition, it found that the information generated by cost accounting could also be used to evaluate the competitiveness of the particular markets. It then began requiring that regulated companies both adopt a standardized form of cost accounting, called a uniform system of accounts, and make these accounts available upon demand to the ICC.[5] This would be an example of regulatory borrowing: the ICC in effect borrowed a set of regulatory norms that corporate governance had developed to regulate the economic activity of its internal actors for its own use in regulating market competition among corporations themselves.

Regulatory regimes can also borrow enforcement components from other regimes. A good example of this kind of regulatory borrowing can be found in a Lawrence Lessig's study of American efforts to outlaw dueling in the late nineteenth century.[6] Dueling had long been illegal in the various states of the US. But the social demands of preserving one's honor caused it to remain a common practice, nevertheless. Early laws that simply criminalized dueling were largely ineffective—particularly in the American south, where refusing a challenge was regarded as dishonorable, even in the face of possible criminal sanction. Eventually, southern states were able to put an end to this practice, not by increasing the criminal penalties associated with the crime, but by passing laws that made one who had been convicted of dueling ineligible for public office. This allowed people to refuse a dueling challenge by claiming a desire to someday enter public service. Entering public service was a highly honorable calling, and the honor that accompanied such service was seen as being stronger than the dishonor of refusing to duel. In this case, the regulatory regime of the criminal law could be said to have borrowed certain regulatory enforcement patterns, those associated with reputation, of gentrified southern society.

Globalization as transnational regulatory borrowing

Regulatory agents can be "local," in the sense of being innately restricted to a particular geography, or they can be what we call transnational, meaning that their geographical reach is not *innately* fixed. With this in mind, I propose the following definition of globalization: globalization describes a phenomenon in which transnational regulatory agents borrow particular regulatory components of local regulatory agents.

I propose such a definition primarily because it allows us to distinguish globalization from simple colonialism. In contrast to globalization, colonialism causes the local regulatory agents to effectively lose *all* regulatory autonomy. This is not to suggest that the regulatory borrowing that accompanies globalization is not at times achieved through particular forms of coercion. But even where it is, the norms of the transnational agent are such that they nevertheless and at the very least allow local regulatory participants a means by which these local participants may formally and autonomously remove themselves from cooperation with that regime if they so choose. Of course, the costs of doing this may be so great as to make this theoretical option virtually suicidal. But the notion of autonomy is concerned with potentiality rather than reasonability. And thus, the fact that no reasonable regime would choose such an option does not extinguish its ultimately autonomous character.

Autonomy, in this regard, is the *transnational* and *regulatory* parallel to the *international* and *public law* concept of sovereignty. Within the context of public international law, a country is regarded as sovereign to the extent that it enjoys ultimate formal capacity to choose and conduct its domestic policies as it sees fit. Of course, this status does not protect a sovereign country from nevertheless sometimes being functionally compelled—perhaps by international agreement, for example, or by threat of economic or political sanction, or simply by concern for self-preservation—to adopt or not adopt particular domestic policies independent of its own desires. But what distinguishes a sovereign country from a colony is precisely the fact that, even under such conditions, the latter always and in every instance retains a formal, *potential* capacity to break its agreement, to endure the sanction, and even to risk its very preservation.

In contrast, colonies generally lack such capacities, at least insofar as their relationship with the colonizing country is concerned. Of course, this does not mean that colonial populations cannot contest that relationship informally—through rebellion, for example, or by lobbying colonial authorities. But invariably, colonial regulatory regimes simply do not articulate any formal set of means (norms) through which the colony could autonomously absolve itself of its colonial relationship.

But why do we need to distinguish between globalization and colonialism? Some have argued that, in fact, the actual impact of globalization on local populations has been no less invidious than that of colonialism. But even if this is the case, there is still a critical difference between the two: simply put, since the end of World War Two, colonialism has been in decline; globalization, in contrast, has been ascendant. And as we shall see in the next section, our particular definition offers an explanation of why this might be the case.

Positing a law of "comparative regulatory advantage"

I posit that the reason why globalization may be succeeding where colonialism failed is because, by preserving the innate autonomy of the local regulatory regimes, globalization is able to take advantage of a particular evolutionary dynamic that was first identified by David Ricardo in his germinal 1817 book, *On the Principles of Political Economy and Taxation.*[7] This was his famous law of comparative advantage, or "Ricardo's law." Basically, I am going to suggest that, because of their innate autonomy, transnational and local regimes can at least sometimes have complementary "comparative advantages" in constructing transnational regulatory systems, and that, when this is the case, these comparative advantages will favor the evolution of a transnational regulatory *system* through a dynamic similar to that which encourages the evolution of trade specialization as per Ricardo's law. A regulatory system, in this usage, designates that the regulatory framework is a collaborative product created by the interaction of multiple regulatory agents, rather than being the autochthonous product of a single, autonomous regulatory agent.

But before I explain what I mean by all this, I first want to make clear what I do *not* mean. I am not suggesting, nor do I believe, that globalized regulatory systems that have been constructed out of complementary comparative advantages are in any way better or more efficient than their possible alternatives. Similarly, when I suggest, for example, that under some conditions a particular kind of regulatory regime, say a transnational regime, has a comparative advantage in the production of norms for a particular regulatory system (as opposed to the production of enforcement), I am not at all implying that the particular norms produced by that regime are at all likely to be socially, economically, or morally better or more efficient than those produced otherwise. I simply mean that the norms produced for the system by that particular regime will be more effective in catalyzing the particular patterns of behavior that define the system's regulatory framework. The comparative advantage of globalized regulatory systems (at least *vis-à-vis* colonialism) lies simply in the fact that they are now better able to perpetuate themselves over time. Whether this is a good thing, whether we should actually want them to perpetuate themselves, is a completely different question—one which, unfortunately, I will not address in this chapter.

Along these lines, we m ight review what Ricardo's law is really about. Ricardo's law addresses itself to a very simplified abstraction of an international trading system: one that involves only two nations, two products, governed by only two complementary coordinating logics, these being free trade and a desire for increasing return on investment. What it shows is that, in such a system, the combination of these two logics will cause the two national economies to evolutionarily gravitate to different forms of production. For example, it will cause a national economy that is the most efficient producer of wine to focus its resources increasingly on producing wine, and other national economies to focus their resources increasingly on producing some other distinctive product, such as cloth. This will be the case even if the wine-producing economy is also the most efficient at producing cloth. It will also be the case even if the economy that ends up producing cloth is actually more efficient at producing wine than it is at producing cloth (but still not as efficient at producing wine as the wine-producing economy). The evolutionary dynamics described by Ricardo's law are also spontaneous—they operate independent of any policy intentionality of the involved economies. They are the product simply of the innate autonomy of the involved national economic actors.

The globalized regulatory arena evinces parallels to the particular logic that drives Ricardo's law. Imagine a globalized regulatory space—a social space in which there is demand for regulation. This demand could be economic, it could be public-minded, or it could involve both. This potential regulation would involve the two components discussed above: norm-setting and enforcement. Let us also assume that the greater the resources devoted to it, the more effective the regulation—effective in the sense of being better able to structure and rationalize the relevant behavior in the relevant social space.

Within this space are two potential regulatory agents. One is a transnational regulatory agent, called "T," the other a local regulatory agent, called "L." Let us assume that, as between these two regulators, T is the more effective norm producer. Again, by effective, I mean not that its norms are likely to be better for society but simply that its norms are better able to shape and continue shaping social activity within the regulated space. This might be because T is more prestigious, or because it is better able to communicate its norms throughout the relevant social space, or simply because it is the preferred choice of the more powerful actors within the regulated population.

Now, in such an environment, if L turned out to be the more effective *enforcer*, and if L and T decided to cooperate in the regulation of that environment, then obviously this would cause T to focus on norm production and L to focus on enforcement—resulting in an archetypical example of globalization as we have defined it. But Ricardo's law argues that complementary specialization will arise even when one party is more cost effective at producing both elements of the system. So let us assume: (1) that T is not only the more effective norm producer, but also the more effective enforcer as well; and (2) that T's resources are more efficient at structuring social space when they are directed to norm production than when they are directed to enforcement. Because T's norms are more effective, they will tend over time to crowd out L's norms. This being the case, L's contribution to regulation will be principally in the area of enforcement. But as L assumes increasing responsibility for enforcement, this allows T to direct its resources increasingly to their most effective use, namely norm production. So T will still end up producing norms and borrowing L's enforcement capacity—as per our definition of globalization.

All this suggests that the evolutionary dynamics of transnational regulatory space at least sometimes conform to those posited by Ricardo's law so long as: (1) regulatory effectiveness (meaning its ability to structure its relevant social environment) is proportionate to resources; (2) the regulators wish to maximize their contribution to the regulatory system; and (3) the regulators have a fixed set of resources. And this, in turn, would explain why globalization is replacing colonialism as the dominant form of transnational regulation. The combining of local and transnational regulatory agents brings more regulatory resources to bear on a particular transnational social space. This results in transnational regulatory systems that are often more effective at shaping and maintaining particular patterns of social behavior. Within this system, different agents will tend to specialize in particular regulatory components as a means of conserving their own resources and maximizing their own input into the system. Again, this is not to claim that globalization results in better or fairer regulatory systems. Simply, all it means is that it results in a more durable regulatory system.

In the above example, I posited that the transnational regulatory agent had a comparative advantage in norm production. I suspect that this is generally the case, particularly with regard to the regulation of transnational economic activity, because transnational regulators tend to enjoy a wider geographical regulatory reach (thus ensuring that their patterns of coordination are able to normatively extend throughout the transnational regulatory environment), greater prestige, and greater support from powerful transnational economic actors that are the principal subjects of the regulation.[8]

But this is not necessarily always the case. There may exist transnational regulatory regimes in which local regulatory agents enjoy a comparative advantage in, and will thus gravitate toward, a specialization in norm production. A possible example of this might be the transnational regulation of development. Here, the dominant model appears increasingly to be one in which the particular normative emphasis of that development is formally set by local developmental agents (contractors), while the principal focus of the transnational agent lies primarily in giving funds to the local development project (giving funds can be broadly seen as a form of enforcement, albeit a form that works through the use of positive incentives—i.e., money—rather than the much more common negative incentives that are paradigmatic of legal enforcement).[9] The reason why local agents might have a comparative advantage in norm production in this particular regulatory arena is because, in contrast to, say, economic globalization, the actors regulated in developmental globalization tend to be local (e.g., local courts, local governments, local society). In such a situation, local agents may enjoy greater prestige, greater access to social norms (which they can borrow from), and thus be better able than transnational agents to construct norms that perpetuate.[10]

"Pushing against" globalization: a preliminary mapping out

Having hypothesized a way of thinking about globalization, and a dynamic that might be underlying it, I now want to examine how we might think about the dynamic of "pushing against" globalization. In order to do this, however, I first want to review and systematize our previous discussions. Our description of globalization posits that globalization operates in two dimensions. On one hand, a globalized regulatory component can issue from a local regulator or a transnational regulator (or perhaps even somewhere in between). This is the first dimension, which we will refer to as "spatial." On the other hand, as we have seen, globalized regulation can involve a number of different regulatory components. This is the second dimension, which we will call the regulatory dimension.

With this in mind, one way in which we might describe a particular, global-ized regulatory system is by mapping which regulatory components emanate from which regulatory spaces. Such a map would allow us to identify the developmental regulatory trajectory of a particular globalized system, as per the developmental patterns established by Ricardo's law. So, let us assume for the moment that trans-national regulation operates in only two discernible kinds of regulatory space, the local and the transnational, and that it involves only two components, norm-setting and enforcement. This would give us a potential developmental template that would look like that produced in Table 3.1. With this matrix, we could describe any transnational regulatory system in terms of two variables: X and X'. We could also define its developmental trajectory in the same way: as a movement towards a space defined by an X and an X' variable. Within this framework, the particu-lar form of regulatory borrowing that we have associated with globalization, and their attendant developmental trajectories, would map out as either (A, A') (i.e., local norm-setting combined with transnational enforcement) or (B, B') (i.e., transnational norm-setting combined with local enforcement).

We might also note that pushing against globalization can itself be seen as a kind of transnational regulation. Most organized opposition to globalization is itself globalized, and so is more properly described as pushing against a particular form of globalization, such as that normally associated with neoliberal economic ordering. And even where the pushing against refers to an effort to resist a (perhaps only a particular aspect of) globalized or transnational social ordering per se, we might still note that an *affirmatively structured* lack of order can itself be regarded as a particular and desirable kind of social ordering.[11] So even there, what the pushing against is really pursuing is an alternative vision of globalization.

Table 3.1 Mapping transnational regulatory space

	Norm-setting	*Enforcement*
Local	A	B'
Transnational	B	A'
(Both)	C	C'

For this reason, the dynamics of pushing against can themselves be mapped using the same mapping template we developed for mapping transnational regulation (see Table 3.1). This template would locate pushing against by identifying where in particular the resistance was located or focused (i.e., on a local or a transnational regulatory space) with regard to each regulatory component that was being resisted.

As a general matter, we would probably expect that a mapping of some particular pushing against dynamic would generally correspond to a mapping of that particular regulatory system against which it is pushing. In the context of neoliberal global trade regulation, for example, opposition to the *normative* aspects of that system naturally tend to focus on transnational regulatory space, such as meetings of the G8 and the International Monetary Fund (IMF). This only makes sense, as normative resistance at a local level would seem not likely to be effective given the comparative advantages that the transnational space is likely to hold in that particular regulatory system. On the other hand, if resistance is more focused on or located within the local part of that space, it would make sense for that resistance to focus more on disruption of particular enforcement patterns, as that is where the coordinate comparative advantage of the local regulatory space lies.

For convenience, we will refer to this type of pushing against, that whose mapping parallels the regulatory mapping of the system it seeks to push against, as "symmetrical." But we might note that resisters may also choose to push against such transnational norms *asymmetrically*, by encouraging local regulators to develop alternative norms despite their lack of comparative advantage in this regulatory component. A good example of this might be the Final Declaration of the Regional Meeting for Asia of the World Conference on Human Rights, more generally known as "the Bangkok Declaration." The Bangkok Declaration sought to contest particular, internationalized human rights norms associated with the International Covenant on Civil and Political Rights by arguing that the transnational level was not the appropriate venue for the setting of human rights norms. Instead, it argued that human rights norms were more effectively and properly to be set at the local (national level).[12] Presuming for the moment that transnational regulatory agents enjoy the same comparative regulatory advantages in norm production in the context of global human rights regulation as they appear to enjoy in the context of global trade regulation, then the pushing against promoted by the Bangkok Declaration would be asymmetric, in the sense that its focus on local production of alternative regulatory norms runs against the comparative advantage dynamics of the larger system.

As we saw above, a symmetrical pushing against would appear to be the natural strategy for those seeking to oppose globalization in some way. Such a strategy is consistent with the comparative competencies of the globalized regulatory environment it is trying to effect. But at the same time, however, it is also consistent with the developmental tendencies of this environment, because our law of comparative regulatory advantage posits that: (1) these complementary comparative competencies are themselves symbiotic with the phenomenon of globalization; and (2) globalization is being driven by the increasing segregation of these competencies. To the extent that some pushing against is pushing debates over norms into one arena (transnational or local) and debates over enforcement into another, and to the extent that this division of labor corresponds to the division that is driving globalization via our regulatory Ricardo's law (i.e., it is symmetrical), then that pushing against is likely to actually be catalyzing, in the long run, the further, overall globalization of the relevant regulatory environment.

An example of this can be found in the argument advanced by many environmentalists that local grassroot regulators in rural locales should be given greater latitude to resist the demands of globalization in the regulation of their physical environments. This is because, it is argued, indigenous populations are much more attuned to their local environmental ecology, and are therefore much more disposed to adopt strategies of sustainable development than transnational economic actors. On its face, this argument thus portrays globalization as a conflict between a globalized regulatory environment that is driven by economic concerns, and local regulatory environments that are more conscious of the value of a distinctly sustainable development. And its proposed solution to this conflict, that is giving greater autonomy for local regulators *vis-à-vis* the transnational, would seem to run counter to the process of globalization.

But in fact, this argument has promoted rather than hindered globalization. For example, localized political factions in rural Indonesia have begun deploying these arguments to enlist international support for their efforts to deny land use rights to immigrant populations, claiming that their efforts to deny such rights reflected and reified these factions' superior understanding of what would be best for the sustainable development of "their" land. Previously, questions of local land use rights had been purely local. In this way, the arguments of environmentalists, while seemingly pushing against globalization in their efforts to promote the capacity of local regulators to resist particular norms of global economic regulation, have in fact catalyzed globalization by introducing into previously localized policy debates over land usage the globalized discourse and politics that surround the globalized normative debate over sustainable development.[13]

Despite pushing for local autonomy *vis-à-vis* globalized regulators, the symmetricality of the environmentalist pushing against ended up injecting global policy debates into local politics. The pushing against represented by this argument was in fact not a case of global versus local. It was a case of global versus global—global environmentalists versus global trade and capital. It sought to use (or borrow) supposedly spontaneous patterns of local regulatory behavior to support a distinctly global environmentalist norm of sustainable development. But in so linking global norm-setting, in the form of debates over sustainable development, to local enforcement capacities, it created a potential commonality of interests between globalized actors engaged in these global policy debates and local political actors engaged in local regulatory politics—so long as these local actors could appeal to and did not challenge the supremacy of the global norms of sustainable development. In this way, the symmetry of this particular form of pushing against allowed global environment politics to colonize local land use politics, and thus promoted rather than impeded overall globalization.

In this sense, a true pushing against would not only have to contest the outcome of globalization, it would have to contest the particular pattern of regulatory comparative advantage that is driving that particular globalization. It would have to be asymmetrical to the divisions of labor that are driving the globalization of that particular regulatory environment. But the asymmetrical nature of such pushing against suggests, paradoxically, that it will be unlikely to be a preferred or effective strategy of local resisters, because it will prevent these resisters from gaining transnational allies that would be necessary to contest the distinctly transnational aspects of globalization. It is probably for these reasons that the most visible of asymmetric domestic resistance to globalization, such as that associated with militant nationalism in North Korea and Myanmar, for example, appear to have had little significant effect on the globalization process.

But this does not mean that asymmetric pushing against is a relative non-factor in the globalization dynamic. It simply suggests that asymmetric pushing against is not likely to be a preferred or common strategy among domestic or transnational actors who are *consciously* pushing against some aspect of globalization. But as we shall see below, asymmetric styles of pushing against can emerge—and can be effective in impeding the globalization of transnational regulatory space—as *unintended* regulatory epiphenomena induced by some other transnational regulatory system.

An example of this kind of "epiphenomenal" asymmetric pushing against can be found in American efforts to structure a transnational, regional, economic regulatory system—Asia-Pacific Economic Cooperation (APEC)—for countries in Asia and the Americas that border the Pacific Ocean.[14] In contrast to most trade globalization, the US's preferred strategy for developing this regulatory ordering was not one of transnational norm generation, but what has been called a hub-and-spoke strategy in which regional ordering, including regional economic ordering, was maintained primarily from a collection of *bilateral* relationships involving the US and other countries in the region. The US sought to use APEC to leverage the locally negotiated content of these bilateral relationships into the status of transnational norms.[15]

But this hub-and-spoke strategy actually appears to have prevented APEC from developing into an effective regulator of transnational trade within the Asia-Pacific region. APEC was intended to be a truly multilateral free-trade regional arrangement like that of the European Union (EU) or North American Free Trade Agreement (NAFTA). But by seeking to derive regulatory norms primarily from bilateral (i.e., local) international agreements, the American hub-and-spoke strategy was asymmetric. In a larger regulatory environment in which the comparative regulatory advantage favored transnational norm formation, this strategy promoted a regulatory framework in which formal norms would issue from what were in fact the least effective norm producers.

These norms therefore had difficulty penetrating the transnational regulatory environment. In particular, they had difficulty competing with often contradictory transnational norms that were emerging from other truly multilateral regulatory spaces operating in the region. One such space was that associated with the Association of Southeast Asian Nations (ASEAN), whose transnational regulatory norms, while sparse when compared with similar multilateral organizations, had the advantage *vis-à-vis* those of APEC of being created transnationally. Because of this, and despite having a significantly narrower geographical coverage (at least formally), ASEAN has eclipsed APEC as the principal regulator of international trade and economic cooperation within the Asian part of the Asia-Pacific region, albeit as a regulator that is still significantly less ambitious in ordering social behavior than other transnational trade regulators.

The irony in all this is that the hub-and-spoke strategy was itself a product of the globalization of a different transnational regulatory environment affecting the Asia-Pacific region, one that had earlier emerged to promote international stability and security. In this particular regulatory environment, the hub-and-spoke strategy was consistent with the comparative advantages that governed that environment. The US military represented a commanding and stabilizing force in that region. For a transnational regulatory system devoted to preserving such stability, the US thus represented the most effective promulgator of norms of stability. The comparative advantage of the transnational agent, in contrast, lies primarily in its ability to coordinate more effective cooperation with American stabilization efforts (a form of enforcement). Transnational trade within this region was intimately linked to its overall security and stability, and thus it made sense to structure the initial regulation of this trade symmetrically with this security arrangement, because this allowed these two, related transnational regulatory systems to better coordinate with each other, by having the same regulatory agent, that of the US, assume responsibility for norm development in both systems.[16]

However, over time, the stability of the region became increasingly embedded in intraregional relationships. It became, in other words, an increasingly spontaneous aspect of the regional structure. For this reason, organized transnational regulation of this stability became less significant to regional ordering.[17] At the same time, the region also found itself increasingly exposed to transnational economic forces emanating from outside its geographical boundaries.[18] This meant that the older regulatory–evolutionary logic of US-led stabilization, in which local norm production was comparatively advantageous, was increasingly being supplanted by another regulatory–evolutionary logic of globalized trade, in which transnational norm production was comparatively advantageous. It was thus the shifting interactions of existing global regulatory systems that caused the US hub-and-spoke strategy, and through it APEC, to become asymmetrical with larger regulatory–evolutionary trends, and in that way ultimately to impede globalized transnational trade regulation within the Asia-Pacific region.

The reason why the asymmetrical pushing against represented by the American hub-and-spoke arrangement was effective in impeding the globalization of Asia-Pacific trade was therefore precisely because that asymmetrical pushing against was at the same time symmetrical with other transnational regulatory systems. Its effectiveness in resisting trade globalization was catalyzed by its effectiveness in promoting the transnational regulation of regional security. In this way, the most effective incidents of pushing against globalization are likely to come from globalization itself.

Conclusion: "so what?"

My point in all this is to show how a systems-like approach to the issue of globalization and pushing against can help us to see and explore more clearly the evolutionary tendencies and obstacles that affect globalization. One might complain, however, that my descriptions of globalization, regulation, globalization, and anti-globalization are really too simplistic: that regulation involves many more components in addition to norm-setting and enforcement, for example; that there is significant local norm-setting in the area of transnational economic regulation; and that some of this does indeed represent truly asymmetric pushing against. One might also object that the boundaries between what I am calling the transnational and the local, or between norm-setting and enforcement, are often not so clear cut.

All this is true. But I don't think it detracts from my principal argument, which is that when and where we can identify reciprocal forms of regulatory borrowing, and when and where we can relate this borrowing to particular configurations of comparative regulatory advantages that seem to be operating within that particular, transnational regulatory space, we can use such information to generate insight into the evolutionary dynamics and trajectories that might be affecting that space. These are likely to be complex spaces, and our mapping will likely involve many more regulatory factors, much more complex patterns of regulatory borrowing and lending of these factors, and systems that are much more intertwined and interpenetrated than this chapter's portrayal. But underneath it all, I propose, we can still find at the root of these global systems patterns of regulatory borrowing (and lending) that are operating against a background dynamic of comparative advantage. By charting these patterns and dynamics, we can create a crucial window into how globalization and pushing against are really interacting with one another.

Notes

1 See generally James C. Scott, *Seeing like a State: How Certain Schemes to Improve the Human Condition Have Failed*, New Haven: Yale University Press, 1998.
2 These are not the only such components, of course. But they are the two components that will concern us in this essay.
3 Friedrich A. Von Hayek, *Individualism and Economic Order*, Chicago: University of Chicago Press, 1996 (originally published 1948).
4 Günther Teubner, 'Legal Irritants: How Unifying Law Ends Up in New Differences', in Peter A. Hall and David Soskice, eds, *Varieties of Capitalism: The Institutional Foundations of Comparative Advantage*, Oxford: Oxford University Press, 2001, pp. 417–41.
5 See Alfred D. Chandler, Jr, *The Visible Hand: The Managerial Revolution in American Business*, Cambridge: Harvard Belknap, 1977, p. 464; A.C. Littleton, *Accounting Evolution to 1900*, New York: Russell and Russell, 1966, p. 366; Mark A. Covaleski, Mark W. Dirsmith, and Sajay Samuel, 'The Use of Accounting Information in Governmental Regulation and Public Administration: The Impact of John R. Commons and Early Institutional Economists', *The Accounting Historian's Journal* 22 (1), 1995, pp. 1–33; Paul J. Miranti, Jr, 'Measurement and Organizational Effectiveness: The ICC and Accounting-Based Regulation, 1887–1940', *Business and Economic History* 19, 1990, pp. 184–85.

6 Lawrence Lessig, 'The Regulation of Social Meaning', *University of Chicago Law Review* 62, 1995, pp. 943–1045.

7 David Ricardo, *On the Principles of Political Economy and Taxation*, R.M. Harwell, ed., London: Penguin Books, 1971 (originally published 1817).

8 See Yves Dezalay and Bryant G. Garth, *The Internationalization of Palace Wars: Lawyers, Economists, and the Contest to Transform Latin American States*, Chicago: University of Chicago Press, 2002.

9 See, for example, Ford Foundation, *Many Roads to Justice*, New York: Ford Foundation, 2000.

10 Cf. Suli Zhu, *Songfa Xiaxiang: Zhongguo Jiceng Sifa Zhidu Yanjiu* [Sending Law to the Countryside: Research on China's Basic-Level Judicial System], Beijing: The Chinese University of Law and Politics Press, 2000.

11 See, for example, Roberto M. Unger, *The Critical Legal Studies Movement*, Cambridge: Harvard University Press, 1986.

12 Christina M. Cerna, 'Universality of Human Rights and Cultural Diversity: Implementation of Human Rights in Different Socio-Cultural Contexts', *Human Rights Quarterly* 16 (4), 1994, pp. 740–52.

13 Gregory Acciaioli, 'From Customary Law to Indigenous Sovereignty: Reconceptualizing the Scope and Significance of Masyarakat Adat in Contemporary Indonesia', in Jamie S. Davidson and David Henley, eds, *The Revival of Tradition in Indonesian Politics: The Deployment of Adat from Colonialism to Indigenism*, Abingdon: Routledge, 2007, pp. 295–318.

14 See Mark Beeson, 'Multilateralism, American Power, and East Asian Regionalism', in City University of Hong Kong Southeast Asia Research Centre (SEARC) Working Paper Series, No. 64, May 2004. Available from http://www.cityu.edu.hk/searc/WP64_04_Beeson.pdf.

15 See also Peter Drahos, 'Intellectual Property and Pharmaceutical Markets: A Nodal Governance Approach', *Temple Law Review* 77 (2), 2004, pp. 401–24.

16 See Josef Joffe, '"Bismarck" or "Britain"? Toward an American Grand Strategy after Bipolarity', *Foreign Affairs* 14 (4), 1995, pp. 19–34. But see Beeson, *op cit.*, p. 10.

17 See Beeson, *supra*.

18 Ibid.

4 Traditional knowledge in Asia
Global agendas and local subjects

Christoph Antons

Introduction: traditional knowledge and local, national, and global agendas

Over almost two decades, but especially since the 1990s, traditional knowledge and its relationship with intellectual property rights has been one of the topics at the forefront of interest for academics, social activists, and non-governmental organizations (NGOs) critical of globalization.[1] It has been a hotly contested issue between developing and industrialized countries, especially in intellectual property debates[2] and debates about sustainable development and the environment,[3] but also in discussions concerning agricultural practices,[4] medicine and public health,[5] and the human rights of indigenous peoples and local minority groups.[6] So what precisely is "traditional knowledge," how did it gain such prominence among social activists and policymakers, and how does it relate to the "global scripts" referred to in the introductory chapter in this volume?[7]

At first glance, the topic of traditional knowledge is somewhat different from the business regulation topics covered in the other chapters in this volume. With traditional knowledge, social actors who seem of only marginal relevance to debates about the globalization of business laws, take center stage. For example, when Carruthers and Halliday[8] speak of the "truly local," they mean "corporations, judges, lawyers, workers, and banks who are spread across the mainly urban centers of the country." However, according to statistics, in countries such as Thailand and India, 80.2 percent and 72.3 percent of the population, respectively, do not live in such urban centers.[9] As large as this rural population may be, it does not normally come much into contact with the norms and regulations of international business and, as a consequence, it is often disregarded in studies about law and globalization. Yet, rural, traditionally living, and indigenous people do matter for national governments and, to a more limited extent, also to international businesses. First, they are voters, and national governments would be foolish to ignore them. The recent events in Thailand provide an excellent example. Former Prime Minister Thaksin was unpopular with the urban elite, but sections of the rural population, especially in the northeast and northwest of the country, have been vehemently supporting him. These votes were crucial in bringing the People Power Party, which has vowed to continue his policies, into power.[10] Second, sustained rural opposition can become problematic for development projects in rural areas that are backed by international businesses. Third, multinational corporations are eager to be seen as good corporate citizens with ethically principled approaches to the conduct of their businesses. Projects extending into rural areas that lead to human rights violations or to abuse and destruction of local resources would tarnish such carefully acquired reputations.

Traditional knowledge is an example of an area of originally local interest that has repercussions at national and international level. Local groups defend it and use it for bargaining at the national and international level, often assisted by NGOs, by stressing ethnic identity or the economic development of regions, provinces, or districts. National governments use it for nation building and the formation of a national identity as well as for national economic development in bargaining with foreign parties. Multinational corporations interested in pharmaceuticals or biotechnology have discovered that local traditional knowledge can provide substantial insights into the medical application of local plants or their suitability for improved food crops. Finally, global institutions such as the World Intellectual Property Organization (WIPO), United Nations Educational, Scientific and Cultural Organization (UNESCO), United Nations Environment Programme (UNEP), United Nations Conference on Trade and Development (UNCTAD), United Nations Development Programme (UNDP), and the UN Human Rights Council are attempting to smooth and to some extent harmonize the many different interests and approaches that have emerged in the debate.

This chapter therefore attempts to heed John Gillespie's call for an account that canvasses the "myriad" local positions.[11] It does not regard all local interests or positions as identical, or regard the "local" as identical to or exclusively represented by central state actors. The chapter will demonstrate how local and national interests interact with international and regional institutions, foreign governments, and multinational corporations and their demands for internationally harmonized regulation. "Local" in this chapter refers, therefore, largely to the subnational level and it is understood as "locality" linking territory with certain population groups rather than as "local business people, networks, etc." The chapter attempts to go beyond the frequently analyzed dichotomies of North versus South and industrialized versus developing countries. All protagonists in the traditional knowledge debate use aspects of globalization and globalized legal regimes, at times to their advantage, while perhaps opposing other aspects at other times. However, the occasionally paradoxical use of homogenizing globalized legal regimes to defend local cultural identity may ultimately lead to the partial destruction and disappearance of precisely those forms of local traditions that their proponents want to uphold.[12]

Traditional knowledge and its beneficiaries: definitions in global scripts and local implementation

In the introduction to a collection of papers from a workshop in 1997 at the University of Kent, anthropologists Ellen, Parkes, and Bicker noted at least nine different terms that had been used for the topic over the years, including indigenous knowledge, indigenous technical knowledge, ethnoecology, local knowledge, folk knowledge, traditional knowledge, traditional environmental or ecological knowledge, people's science, or rural people's knowledge.[13] And these are only the terms limited to what the authors call "local environmental knowledge with practical implications"[14] rather than more wide-ranging definitions based on the holistic worldview of indigenous people. In the view of many indigenous groups, however, it is incorrect to distinguish between technical and practical knowledge and artistic forms and expressions, which are often used to transmit the material over generations.[15] Thus, the knowledge can be expressed and transmitted within a community, for example, in the form of a song, a poem, a mystical story, or in a painting. Often, the knowledge is transmitted only within a restricted circle of initiated community members, and it is often connected to religious rituals, ancestor mythologies, and/or particular stretches of land.[16] Because of the secret and sacred character of this material,[17] indigenous groups have often asserted that it is impossible to separate the technical knowledge from the particular form of its expression. The holistic understanding of the material becomes visible from the definition of "indigenous cultural and intellectual property" used by Australian Aboriginal lawyer Terri Janke to assert rights to the material on behalf of communities in the report "Our Culture, Our Future," which was submitted to the Australian Aboriginal and Torres Straits Islander Commission in 1998. The term "indigenous cultural and intellectual property" includes not only scientific, agricultural, technical, and ecological knowledge, but also literary, performing, and artistic works, movable cultural property, human remains and tissues, immovable cultural property such as sacred sites and burial grounds, and documentation of indigenous heritage in archives, films, photographs, video and audiotape, and other forms of media.[18]

When the World Intellectual Property Organization (WIPO) began working on traditional knowledge issues in the late 1990s, it sent fact-finding missions to many developing countries, especially in Asia and the South Pacific. The result was a report, published in 2001, which used the following working definition of "traditional knowledge": "tradition-based literary, artistic or scientific works; performances; inventions; scientific discoveries; designs; marks, names and symbols; undisclosed information; and all other tradition-based innovations and creations resulting from intellectual activity in the industrial, scientific, literary, or artistic fields."[19] WIPO at this stage seemed heavily influenced by the holistic understanding of the issue, which had been explained to the fact-finding missions in countries such as Australia. WIPO established an Intergovernmental Committee on Intellectual Property and Genetic Resources, Traditional Knowledge, and Folklore to work on the establishment of appropriate forms of protection. Soon, however, it became clear that the holistic forms of traditional knowledge advocated by indigenous groups did not fit the traditional categories of intellectual property rights. More recently, therefore, WIPO has returned to an intellectual property-inspired distinction between copyright-related folklore or traditional cultural expressions and patent or industrial property-related "technical traditional knowledge."[20] Thus, at the current stage, the debate focuses mainly on the following forms of traditional knowledge: folklore or traditional cultural expressions, biodiversity-related traditional knowledge, agricultural traditional knowledge, and medicinal traditional knowledge. WIPO currently recognizes that many rights holders take an "overall holistic approach" to traditional knowledge,[21] but it has nevertheless divided the topic under several headings using the terms traditional cultural expressions/expressions of folklore, traditional knowledge, and genetic resources.

As a starting point, it is important therefore to notice the strong role that Aboriginal advocacy in countries such as Australia, New Zealand, the US, and Canada has played in shaping the terms of the debate.[22] The reasons for this are simple. First, the discussions in the countries just mentioned are lively and go back for several decades. In Australia, for example, a working party to examine the issue of folklore protection was formed as early as 1974. Its report was published by the Department of Home Affairs and Environment in 1981 and recommended the adoption of an Aboriginal Folklore Act and the establishment of a Folklore Commission.[23] Aboriginal communities have taken their cases to the courts both individually and collectively and, perhaps most importantly, all this precedent and government material is not only easily available, but also published in English. Not surprisingly, Australian and Canadian examples in particular are frequently used at an international level as case studies to illustrate the problems in linking intellectual property and traditional knowledge.[24] But can the interpretation of "traditional knowledge" as it has evolved in Aboriginal communities in English-speaking countries be easily transferred into the context of Asia?

Before I answer this question, I would like to outline the international context of the debate, the international agreements and "global scripts"[25] that have been written in this field. An examination of the history of the debate in an international context helps to explain further why, at the end of the twentieth century, some of the most ancient forms of knowledge are suddenly being combined with some of the most advanced forms of intellectual property.

The story of those global scripts really begins with the counterculture popular in industrialized countries in the 1960s. This was the time when Jimi Hendrix, dressed in colorful Indian or African outfits, was playing "Voodoo Child" at Woodstock, and the Beatles and other pop and rock stars were going on pilgrimages to Indian gurus. During the modernization frenzy of the 1950s and early 1960s, non-Western knowledge was still regarded as superstitious and primitive and as something to be replaced by scientific knowledge. In countries such as Australia, such thinking was often supported by a generation of anthropologists, who justified their research and the urgency for funding with the argument that they were documenting vanishing cultures virtually at the last moment.[26] As the 1960s progressed, a counterculture emerged with a curious blend of Marxist believers in the ultimate progress of mankind and New Age skeptics distrustful of notions such as progress or development. It was the latter element rather than the former that influenced the "hippie" movement and suddenly everything "non-Western" was in vogue. Middle-class children in industrialized countries began to dress in Asian or African Batik, read Carlos Castaneda's explorations of drug use among Mexican Indians, and listen to Ravi Shankar's Indian sitar music. This newly found interest in expressions of cultures from developing countries was part of a popular movement and, as such, superficial and romantic rather than analytical and interested in deeper engagement. For some developing countries, there were some positive effects in the form of greater interest in so-called Third World cultures; a few Asian, African, and Latin American artists became internationally famous. However, with the popular attraction of the "exotic" material came the first cases in which Western artists were accused of appropriating cultural material from developing countries. "The Lion Sleeps Tonight" was an early example of an African song that became a hit record in the early 1960s, but for many years was not attributed to its South African composer. A few years later, Simon and Garfunkel had a world hit record with "El Condor Pasa," a song written by a Peruvian composer and based on a traditional Andean folk song. It was perhaps a first sign of the regional significance of such cultural expressions that it was the Bolivian and not the Peruvian government that raised concern about what was from now on regarded as "appropriation" of Latin American folk songs by US American pop musicians.[27] The debate led ultimately to the inclusion of folklore in the WIPO- and UNESCO-sponsored Tunis Model Law for the Protection of Folklore of 1976 and to further WIPO/UNESCO-drafted "Model Provisions for National Laws on the Protection of Expressions of Folklore against Illicit Exploitation and other Prejudicial Actions," published in 1985.[28]

At the same time, improved transport and communication technologies becoming available meant that previously isolated and remote living communities from all over the world came into contact with each other. In 1982, the UN Working Group on Indigenous Populations was formed within the UN Economic and Social Council. An international movement of indigenous people with similar problems slowly became transformed into a movement of marginalized minorities, when minorities from many Asian and African countries became involved. As a consequence, the meaning of the term "indigenous" was stretched to accommodate the new membership to a point where, as the anthropologist Jeffrey Sissons has critically remarked, it became possible "for almost any people with a subsistence based culture to claim membership in international indigenous forums."[29] Coates[30] reports that, after the formation of a Working Group to draft a Universal Declaration on the Rights of Indigenous Peoples, white Afrikaners from post-apartheid South Africa attended the meetings. He believes, nevertheless, that the strong focus on the activities of European colonial powers "ignores equally disruptive and authoritarian invasions of indigenous territories by Asian, African, and other societies and skips over the experience of indigenous societies separate from their contact with and conquest by outsiders."[31] Kingsbury,[32] however, sees in the broadening of the definition "a significant risk for the indigenous peoples' movement that the existing and highly functional international political distinction between 'indigenous peoples' and ethnic and other minorities will erode, galvanizing opposition to claims of 'indigenous peoples'."

Apart from the widening of the concept "indigenous," the 1980s also saw a further broadening of the traditional knowledge debate, where cultural expressions of folklore were now joined by agricultural and biodiversity-related knowledge. The concept of farmers' rights was introduced in Resolution 4/89 of the United Nations Food and Agriculture Organization (FAO) and further defined in FAO Resolution 5/89 as "Rights arising from the past, present, and future contribution of farmers in conserving, improving, and making available Plant Genetic Resources, particularly those in the centers of origin/diversity. These rights are vested in the International Community as trustees for present and future generations of farmers, for the purpose of ensuring full benefits of farmers and supporting the continuation of their contributions ... ."[33] In 1992, the Convention on Biological Diversity (CBD) brought even broader concepts of indigenous and local knowledge and community participation. Parties to the Convention were required to "respect, preserve, and maintain knowledge, innovations, and practices of indigenous and local communities embodying traditional lifestyles relevant for the conservation and sustainable use of biological diversity and promote their wider application with the approval and involvement of the holders of such knowledge, innovations, and practices and encourage the equitable sharing of the benefits arising from the utilization of such knowledge, innovations, and practices."[34] Thus, within a few decades, the understanding of indigenous and local rural communities had been transformed from that of ignorant subsistence farmers whose unscientific practices were harmful to the environment to custodians of the forests and the environment.[35] However, if read carefully, such "eco-indigenism" (as Sissons has termed it) entails not just rights but also the "moral responsibility to care for the threatened environment and to defend it against the destructive forces of western progress and global capitalism."[36]

The CBD also included detailed provisions on access with prior informed consent and equitable sharing of the "results of research and development and the benefits arising from the commercial and other utilization of genetic resources."[37] It foresaw a quid pro quo deal, in which biodiversity-rich countries would provide access to their resources in return for access to technology created on the basis of the resources by technologically advanced users of the system (Article 15(2), (6), and 16). While indigenous and local groups play an important role in the convention as the bearers and presumably ultimate beneficiaries of their traditional knowledge, it is the nation-state as party to the convention that mediates between the local and the global and assumes a paternalistic role in encouraging local communities to play their roles as custodians of the environment and preservers of the ecosystem. Of great concern from the viewpoint of indigenous and local communities is the changing status of plant genetic resources. The CBD has declared that plant genetic resources, which had previously been regarded as the common heritage of mankind, are now within the nation-states' "sovereign right to exploit their own resources pursuant to their own environmental policies" (Article 3). Equally, the CBD made it perfectly clear that "the authority to determine access to genetic resources rests with the national governments and is subject to national legislation" (Article 15(1)).

The latest turn in the setting of global standards and obligations in this field occurs with the adoption in September 2007 of the United Nations Declaration on the Rights of Indigenous Peoples.[38] This non-binding, soft law document repeats in the preamble the current paradigm that respect for indigenous knowledge, cultures, and traditional practices contributes to sustainable and equitable development and proper management of the environment. The Declaration contains various provisions, which aim to safeguard aspects of traditional knowledge. Perhaps the most relevant of these is Article 31(1), which speaks of indigenous peoples' "right to maintain, control, protect, and develop their cultural heritage, traditional knowledge, and traditional cultural expressions, as well as the manifestations of their sciences, technologies, and cultures, including human and genetic resources, seeds, medicines, knowledge of the properties of fauna and flora, oral traditions, literatures, designs, sports and traditional games, and visual and performing arts." They also have the "right to maintain, control, protect, and develop their intellectual property over such cultural heritage, traditional knowledge, and traditional cultural expressions." There is a separate explicit provision safeguarding the right to traditional medicines and health practices, including the conservation of vital medicinal plants, animals, and minerals (Article 24). There is a right "to participate in decision-making" in matters concerning indigenous peoples' rights (Article 18), and states have "to consult and cooperate" with indigenous people to obtain free, prior, and informed consent on any legislative or administrative measures (Article 19).

How did Asian governments and local communities turn the new global paradigms into national legislation and into policies at the grassroots level? One major problem in accepting the international principles has been the reluctance of most Asian governments to accept the concept of "indigenous people."[39] Asian governments are concerned about equities and imbalances that affirmative action in favor of particular ethnic groups may create in their multiethnic states. They also believe that it is in many cases not historically accurate to speak of indigenous people in nation-states where population movements go back for many centuries and where cultures have intermingled. Difficulties can be observed in particular in Indonesia, where the Indonesian word for native (*asli*) was used for many years to distinguish all indigenous Indonesians from what the Dutch sociologist Wertheim termed "trading minorities,"[40] the latter term meant to refer to people with Indonesian citizenship, whose ancestors had migrated during the colonial period from countries such as China and India or from the Arabian Peninsula.[41] Another example is India, which in many international meetings has opposed the undifferentiated application of the "indigenous" concept to post-colonial Asia.[42] During WIPO deliberations, the delegations of these two countries repeatedly raised concern about this terminology. They also pointed out that traditional knowledge in Asia can often reside in society at large and that it would be inappropriate to attribute it exclusively to relatively small minority groups.[43] Indonesia instead professed a preference for the term "society or community bound by customary law," which is the term currently used in the Indonesian constitution to describe local communities (*masyarakat adat*).

It seems indeed that Asian governments are raising an important point here, because the delineation of communities of custodians and beneficiaries in accordance with who came earlier to a country is clearly more difficult in many parts of Asia than in the post-colonial settler societies of North America, Latin America, or Australia. Especially in South China and Indochina, historical upheavals leading to war and replacement have created migration patterns that can make it very difficult to determine which particular ethnic group arrived somewhere before others. As a further difference compared with Aboriginal populations in settler societies, many written sources of traditional knowledge exist in Asia. These written sources were used by entire regions and later by entire nations or even by several nations. Such materials include, for example, the written traditions of Chinese traditional medicine or Indian Ayurvedic medicine, which were spread across the region by traders and religious teachers. Thus, the form, transmission, and spread of this knowledge make it very different from the much more vulnerable unwritten traditions of tribal people, with such traditions coming under the more narrowly defined term "indigenous" and which were transmitted via rituals and forms of art and protected by secrecy. In the Asian understanding, traditional knowledge is often the knowledge of a dominating majority of the population. From majority knowledge, it is only a small step for it to become national knowledge, which is to be exploited and defended by the nation-state and the national government against unauthorized users from the industrialized world, but also against competitors from other developing countries, who claim the same or a similar kind of knowledge, where such knowledge has traveled across borders. In other words, the distinction between "indigenous," "local," and "national" becomes blurred.[44]

Given this history of a widespread reluctance in Asia to accept the notion of "indigenous people," it comes perhaps as a surprise that all East and Southeast Asian countries and all South Asian countries with the exceptions of Bhutan and Bangladesh voted in favor of the recently adopted UN Declaration on the Rights of Indigenous Peoples. However, the declarations made and statements given by various national representatives in explanation of their votes quickly reveal that the old attitudes have not really changed. Bangladesh, for example, criticized the lack of definition of "indigenous people" in its decision to vote against the Declaration.[45] India, on the other hand, voted in favor, but provided its own definition, drawn from earlier conventions: "indigenous rights pertained to peoples in independent countries who were regarded as indigenous on account of their descent from the populations which inhabited the country … at the time of conquest or colonization or the establishment of present State boundaries and who … retained some or all of their socio-economic, cultural, and political institutions." This interpretation makes the entire population of India with roots going back to pre-colonial times indigenous at the time of the departure of the colonial power. "Indigenous" is, therefore, interpreted as "indigenous Indian" as opposed to foreign elements introduced during colonial rule. Equally, the representative of Indonesia said that "given the fact that Indonesia's entire population at the time of colonization remained unchanged, the rights in the Declaration accorded exclusively to indigenous people and did not apply in the context of Indonesia."[46]

The major exception to the general adverse attitude toward the "indigenous people" terminology in Asia is the Philippines. In the Philippines, both Spanish and US American colonial powers had applied concepts that they were familiar with in their dealings with native Americans in Latin America and North America respectively.[47] The Philippines reacted swiftly to the Convention on Biological Diversity and the Global Agenda 21. In 1995, it was one of the first countries to introduce a regulatory framework for the protection of biological and genetic resources taking into account the requirements of prior informed consent from indigenous and local communities. In 1997, it introduced the Indigenous Peoples Rights Act (IPRA), which covered issues such as traditional resource rights and what the Act defined as community intellectual rights, which in turn extended to indigenous knowledge systems and practices.[48] Nevertheless, in voting for the UN Declaration on the Rights of Indigenous Peoples, the representative of the Philippines stressed his understanding that land ownership and natural resources were vested in the state.[49] In the interest of getting as many countries as possible to agree to the Declaration, territorial integrity and political unity are in fact explicitly guaranteed in Article 46(1).[50]

Traditional cultural expressions as "cultural property": global scripts, local communities, and the nation-state in Indonesia

At this stage, it is useful to examine a few case studies of the implementation, or lack of it, of traditional knowledge concepts and the various conflicting interests associated with it. My first example comes from Indonesia and relates to what WIPO refers to as traditional cultural expressions or expressions of folklore. Earlier in this chapter, I discussed how, during the 1970s and 1980s, international institutions such as WIPO and UNESCO drafted model provisions for the protection of folklore after receiving complaints from developing country governments about "cultural appropriation" of folkloristic material by the entertainment industry of industrialized countries such as the US and the UK. The argument from developing countries was basically that they regarded it as inequitable that their citizens were expected to pay copyright royalties for every use of copyrighted material from the industrialized world, while artists and composers from industrialized countries helped themselves freely to material drawn from the rich repertoire of folklore and traditional cultural expressions in so-called Third World countries.[51] While the WIPO/UNESCO model provisions of 1985 foresaw royalty collection by a "competent authority" of the state or by the "community concerned," many developing countries had by that time already adopted the relevant provisions from the Tunis Model Copyright Law for Developing Countries of 1976, which did not provide a similar choice but left the administration of the remuneration exclusively in the hands of a "competent authority" at the national level.[52]

The national-level solution suited many developing countries in their relationship with local communities. The state could exercise the copyright and collect royalties on their behalf. Not only would this satisfy the aim of getting some returns from the rich consumers in the developed world in a practical manner, it would also be in accordance with other pressing needs. First of all, it would stress national culture as opposed to regional and locally dispersed cultural expressions and, thereby, help to consolidate young nation-states. Second, it would actually assist multiethnic, multicultural, young nation-states in forging a national culture by turning originally local cultural expressions into national heritage.

Indonesia adopted this approach when it enacted its first national Copyright Act, which replaced the Dutch colonial law in 1982. Article 10 of the earlier Copyright Act has been transferred with only small amendments[53] into the current Copyright

Act of 2002, and is included in a part bearing the heading "Copyright to works whose authors are not known." It provides in Article 10(1) that the state holds the copyright to pre-historical and archaeological "works" and to other objects of national culture. According to Article 10(2), the state equally holds the copyright to folklore and to "products of popular culture which become common property such as stories, tales, fairy tales, legends, chronicles, songs, handicrafts, choreographies, dances, calligraphies, and other works of art." According to Article 10(3), non-Indonesians have to obtain approval from a "relevant agency" if they want to publish or multiply such "works." Finally, as is often the case in Indonesia,[54] the details for these arrangements were to be worked out in a further Government Regulation on the basis of Article 10(4). Since the introduction of this provision in its original form in 1982, this Government Regulation has never been issued, and the details of the scheme, including the important appointment of the "relevant agency," have not been further elaborated. In practice, therefore, the envisaged protection of national folklore remains so far unimplemented.

Several points can be made about this part of the Indonesian Copyright Act. First, Article 10(1) relates largely to material in the public domain and is not actually a matter for copyright but for heritage conservation. However, in a "catch all" phrase, the provision also declares the Indonesian state as copyright holder in general to "objects of national culture" (*benda budaya nasional*). Article 10(2) provides examples of a whole range of folkloristic expressions, some of which seem less traditional than others and not necessarily of a collective nature (e.g., choreography, calligraphy). The fact that the state is the copyright holder and grants licenses to foreigners means that it is likely that even quite individual expressions of regional identity would be treated as national property. It would, for example, disentitle a regional artist, who changes citizenship, from drawing on regional symbols that express his/her personal identity.[55] The basis of the scheme is, therefore, a concept of national identity. The state has chosen to adopt an international script that puts state agencies in charge and has further strengthened the role of the national government *vis-à-vis* agencies and potential centers of power in the regions.

As the scheme has not really been implemented thus far, there has been relatively little public debate about it. When it was first introduced in draft form by the Suharto government, some regional communities expressed concern about restrictions to their own use of their folklore and cultural expressions.[56] Apparently as a compromise and to clarify that the provision was not meant to disown local communities, the government then restricted its exercise of the copyright to "foreign countries."[57] This has meanwhile been transferred into the new Copyright Act as a licensing requirement for foreigners. However, the current Article 10(2) has also made it unmistakably clear that the state indeed claims the copyright to folkloristic expressions, whereas the previous version merely provided that such material was "taken care of and protected by the state."

While the legal implementation of these schemes is still lacking, over the past few years, various government departments and agencies have started to compile databases of Indonesia's traditional knowledge, where little attention is often paid to the distinction between folklore and cultural expressions and other forms of traditional knowledge, a distinction made by WIPO. Further, claims have appeared in the Indonesian media about foreigners appropriating Indonesian cultural heritage and claiming intellectual property for it abroad. Perhaps not surprisingly in view of the cultural nature of the claims and regional exchange and similarities in culture, such claims have recently been directed against Malaysia. In 2007, Indonesians disputed claims that had appeared on Malaysian Internet sites that *Angklung*, a musical instrument made from bamboo, and *Angklung* music was Malaysian, locating its origins instead in the Indonesian province of West Java.[58] In the same year, the use of the folk song "*Rasa Sayang*" for a tourism campaign by the Malaysian government almost sparked a diplomatic row between the two countries. The Indonesian Tourism and Cultural Minister wanted to investigate whether Indonesia could claim copyright for the song, while a member of the House of Representatives thought that Indonesia should sue over the use of the song in the tourism campaign, while alleging that there were other cases of appropriation of Indonesian cultural heritage, such as *Batik* and the shadow puppet theatre *wayang*.[59] The Malaysian Tourism Minister responded that he regarded the song as the heritage of *Kepulauan Nusantara* (the Malay archipelago), which also included Malaysia, while the Malaysian press pointed out that *Rasa Sayang* was widely sung throughout the archipelago, although the song was believed to have originated in *Maluku* (the Moluccan islands).[60] The dispute shows how difficult such claims to "cultural property" can be in a part of the world where populations have been migrating, trading, and intermingling for centuries.

"Biopiracy," the patenting of traditional knowledge, and claims over genetic resources

In the more technical field of traditional knowledge related to biodiversity and the question of access to genetic resources, the global scripts show very diverse influences. Earlier in this chapter, I explained how much of the international debate about the knowledge of indigenous people was influenced by case studies and debates from Anglo-American settler colonies, because of the widespread use of the English language and the prominence and visibility of indigenous communities from those countries in the international movement of indigenous people. When these discussions were picked up and developed further by United Nations agencies during the 1980s, these agencies were often focusing on quite diverse issues. In the debate on traditional knowledge and access to genetic resources, currently the most important forums are the Intergovernmental Committee on Intellectual Property and Genetic Resources, Traditional Knowledge and Folklore of WIPO, and the Working Group on Article 8(j) of the Convention on Biological Diversity, which is administered by the UN Environmental Programme. Both have produced guidelines and model provisions aimed at, in the case of WIPO, preventing misappropriation of traditional knowledge and, in the case of the CBD, facilitating benefit sharing and ensuring prior informed consent.

The debate in this area draws on relatively new paradigms in development studies and environmental studies, which aim to empower stakeholders and decentralize responsibilities and custodianship for the environment, while at the same time envisaging new forms of property to act as incentives to local people to protect the environment.[61] The use of genetic resources by people from outside the community is no longer regarded as an issue of access to natural resources only, but also as an intellectual property issue. Developing country governments and provincial and local councils have high hopes for some kind of green trade triggered by the interest of multinational biotechnology and pharmaceutical companies in their resources. Intellectual property protection seems more useful here, at least in the short term, because of the potential of strong international protection. As a consequence, the governments of many developing countries have been pushing the issue at the negotiating table of the World Trade Organization (WTO). Echoing the term "piracy" commonly used by the copyright industry for the copying of their products without paying royalties, developing countries, political activists, and NGOs now frequently use the term "biopiracy" to refer to the acquisition of intellectual property rights for plant material obtained from the developing world without free and prior informed consent. The terminology in both cases is emotionally charged. In fact, it is often the case that piracy activities of any kind take place in a legal vacuum and in an environment where legal protection is simply lacking. As for intellectual property, the WTO Trade-related Aspects of Intellectual Property Rights (TRIPS) Agreement to some extent ensures certain protection standards around the globe. For genetic resources and the traditional knowledge that such resources represent, similar global standards are currently under negotiation, especially within the working group on Article 8(j) of the CBD.[62] Many developing countries argue that, in view of the principles enshrined in the CBD, it needs to be harmonized with the extended intellectual property rights granted by the TRIPS Agreement. A particular focus here is on the so-called "biotechnology clause" of Article 27.3(b) of the TRIPS Agreement. The provision allows member states to exclude plants and animals and essentially biological processes for the production of plants and animals from patenting, but requires the availability of patents for micro-organisms and non-biological and microbiological processes. It is important to note in this context, however, that the term "essentially biological processes" has been interpreted as not including biotechnological inventions, which would be patentable on the basis of their "technical intervention."[63] Article 27.3(b) of the TRIPS Agreement further requires that "Members shall provide for the protection of plant varieties either by patents or by an effective *sui generis* system or by any combination thereof."

Perhaps not surprisingly, the call for harmonization of the principles of TRIPS and CBD from developing countries is often taken up by environmental and human rights lawyers, whereas intellectual property lawyers tend to fear for the consistency of the patent system and the value of patents, if they can be challenged for reasons that lie outside the patent system. The current discussion about the introduction of a requirement for compulsory disclosure of the origin of genetic material in patent applications and the obligation for the genetic material to have been obtained with free and prior informed consent demonstrates these different views.[64] Whatever the outcomes of these debates, those companies accused of "biopiracy" exploit a lack of coordination in the international patent system and a time lag in gaining knowledge of what is in the public domain and constitutes, in patent parlance, prior art elsewhere. Discussions are currently under way to remedy these shortcomings of the system.

In the following section, I will present three examples of how these various debates about the globalization of intellectual property rights play out at the national and local level and how various governments in Asia translate these principles into national law. My first example comes again from Indonesia. In line with many other developing countries, Indonesia had to revise its Patents Act after acceding to the TRIPS Agreement and broaden the scope for patents with regard to biotechnological inventions.[65] As for the plant variety protection required by TRIPS, it decided, again in line with many other developing countries, on *sui generis* protection via a Plant Variety Protection Act modeled after the International Convention for the Protection of new Varieties of Plants, which is better known under the French acronym for its administering international organization as UPOV. To safeguard local interests, the Indonesian Act attempts to integrate protection for local and traditional varieties into the legislation. However, the approach chosen is similar to that in the Copyright Act for folkloristic expression. Articles 7(1) and (2) of the Plant Variety Protection Act No. 29 of 2000 make it unmistakably clear that "local varieties owned by communities are controlled by the State," and that such control is exercised by the government. The term used to describe ownership (*milik masyarakat*) is in fact somewhat ambiguous and can refer to "community ownership" or simply "public ownership." However, the explanatory memorandum to Article 7(4) makes it clear that there shall be economic compensation for the communities that own a local variety. Such a regulation of compensation as well as other details regarding the naming of such varieties, their registration and further use will have to await an implementing Government Regulation referred to in Article 7(4). Thus, as in the Copyright Act, the scheme authorizes the government to administer the rights. However, as in the Copyright Act, such administration is not currently taking place because of a lack of implementation provisions.

As mentioned earlier in this chapter, the Philippines is an exceptional case in Asia with its explicit recognition of the rights of indigenous communities in the Indigenous Peoples Rights Act (IPRA) of 1997. While IPRA guarantees so-called "community intellectual rights" for biological material, the relevant provisions have to be read in conjunction with environmental conservation laws and regulations. On the regulation of access, the various laws sometimes overlap, as in areas designated as national parks, which are under national environmental laws, but often also inhabited by indigenous people.[66] Because of its recognition of ancestral domain title, the Philippine version of native title, IPRA has been unsuccessfully challenged in the Supreme Court of the Philippines,[67] and its implementation was delayed for years pending the decision of the court. The legislation continues to clash with other interests in the Philippine economy, most importantly with the powerful mining industry. Because of the overlaps and contradictions between IPRA and the environmental laws and regulations, the powerful National Commission on Indigenous Peoples

(NCIP) and the Department of Environment and Natural Resources harmonized the various laws in a joint memorandum in 2003.[68] This was followed by a joint administrative order of 2005 with new Guidelines for Bioprospecting Activities in the Philippines.[69] The harmonized approach foresees an important role for the NCIP in documenting free and prior informed consent and in negotiating the benefits on behalf of indigenous communities and the use of fees collected within ancestral domains in accordance with the aims of the Indigenous Peoples Rights Act.[70]

In view of US heritage in policies toward indigenous people in the Philippines, it is not surprising that the policies and solutions adopted for traditional knowledge also show similarities to those in Anglo-American settler colonies. They show an attempt at integrating traditional knowledge and related customary laws into the national legal framework and provide scope for negotiations between local communities and national and international parties with commercial interests. The national government stands, as elsewhere, at the intersection of such negotiations, but in the Philippines it attempts to remain largely in the role of arbitrator and mediator.

My final example comes from India. In view of their large rural population, commentators in India have been particularly critical of the aspects of the TRIPS Agreement related to the patenting of forms of life. India also made headlines when, via its Council of Scientific and Industrial Research, it successfully challenged patents granted for *turmeric* and *neem*.[71] Apart from biotechnological inventions, a main area of conflict with industrialized countries concerns patent protection for pharmaceuticals. Exclusion provisions in the Indian Patents Act until recently ensured that methods of agriculture and horticulture and various forms of treatment for animals or human beings did not qualify for patent protection. Patents only for processes but not products were available for food, medicine, and drug-related inventions. The absence of product patent protection in this field allowed India to become a leading manufacturing country for generic medicines and a major supplier for the rest of the developing world. Judicial interpretation of "manner of manufacture" in the Act as exclusively related to processes resulting in non-living, tangible products was an additional obstacle to biotechnological inventions.[72]

As elsewhere, things began to change with India's accession to the WTO TRIPS Agreement. The exclusion provision of the Indian Patents Act was amended providing patent protection from that point for micro-organisms and biotechnological processes that require substantial human intervention.[73] However, the Indian government newly included several provisions meant to safeguard local interests and to prevent patenting of local knowledge. Controversial grounds for opposition to and revocation of patents were added, where "the complete specification does not disclose or wrongly mentions the source of geographical origin of biological material used for the invention" and where "the invention … was anticipated having regard to the knowledge, oral or otherwise, available within any local or indigenous community in India or elsewhere." Excluded from patent protection was "an invention which, in effect, is traditional knowledge or which is an aggregate or duplication of known properties of traditionally known component or components."[74] The further extension of patent protection remained controversial and did not entirely satisfy foreign pharmaceutical manufacturers, who mounted an unsuccessful challenge to the constitutionality and TRIPS compatibility of those aspects of the Indian Patents Act.[75]

Aspects of traditional knowledge protection have also been included in the appropriately worded Protection of Plant Varieties and Farmers' Rights Act (PPVFRA) of 2001 and in the Biological Diversity Act (BDA) of 2002. The PPVFRA foresees registration of traditional varieties under certain conditions and puts a Protection of Plant Varieties and Farmers' Rights Authority in charge of the administration of the legislation and of a National Gene Fund set up to compensate farmers for their contribution to the development of commercially used varieties. The BDA creates similar mechanisms, a National Biodiversity Authority and a National Biodiversity Fund, for biological resources more generally and not confined to farming. It treats the access applications of Indian citizens and corporations more leniently than those of foreigners, and overlaps in its benefit-sharing mechanisms with the PPVFRA. This, and the weak position of communities, has been criticized and prompted a commentator to conclude that the provisions "even seem to encourage commercial exploitation rather than giving impetus to the conservation of biodiversity or to benefit-sharing with the local communities."[76]

The example from India shows that in some countries the courts may play a significant role in modifying the application of international norms in the interest of local parties. Indian social and political activists have also been successful in public interest litigation.[77] The Indian government has further been eager to safeguard local and traditional knowledge against misappropriation by foreigners. Critics have argued, however, that there is much less protection for local communities against misappropriation by Indian parties and that the entire system of traditional knowledge protection is perhaps too state centered and bureaucratic to appeal to people at the grassroots level.[78]

Conclusion

In sum, development and environment protection paradigms, as well as attitudes toward the commercial use of folkloristic expressions, have changed and there are now continuing negotiations between the new local stakeholders, government agencies, NGOs, international agencies, and domestic and foreign industries. In the process, cultural heritage is reinterpreted as national, regional, local, or as fitting the international criteria of international conventions. Competition between biological and cultural resource providers is tough, however, and the financial benefits are at this stage still far from certain. Rather than generally pushing against globalization, it seems that the various parties involved in the debate all make use of aspects of it in one way or another for their respective purposes by using new telecommunication and networking facilities and/or by trying to fit the criteria to benefit under international conventions and agreements. Ronald Niezen, in a chapter entitled "(Anti)Globalization from Below," has pointed to some of the contradictions in the current movements of indigenous people in particular:

… there is a central ambiguity associated with this global strategy of mobilization, an ambiguity that can be more generally seen as a central feature of the current era of globalization: the defense of distinct societies relies on political forces that exert pressures of global conformity … At the very least, legally based defenses of tradition require the formation of a new elite that meets two new criteria for leadership: skilled literacy and sophisticated familiarity with the workings of bureaucracy. In short, there is a trade-off between global strategies of cultural preservation and the strategic necessity of wearing a one-size-fits-all transnational identity.[79]

To some extent, these contradicting pressures also apply to local communities in Asia, whether indigenous or not, who are overall struggling to see their particular interests recognized by nation-states. Of the various modes for local "pushing against globalization" noted by John Gillespie in his chapter, it seems that the harnessing of global governance and the drawing of international attention to local issues are regarded as particularly promising by local communities. In some countries, social activists have also successfully turned to the courts. Self-regulation by non-state actors in the form of customary law is widely recognized throughout the region, but clearly subordinated to the normative frameworks of the national legal system and of the economic development goals of governments. Finally, democratization and decentralization are making inroads into the formerly exclusive domains of bureaucratic government authority, but there is also much frustration with some aspects of the reform processes, as for example with decentralization in Indonesia,[80] which among other concerns has been criticized as business unfriendly.[81]

Yet, for relatively young, post-colonial nation-states, it remains of paramount importance to defend national unity and to accelerate the processes of economic and social development. Thus, the internal struggle between the perceived developmentalist needs of governments and reformist pressures exerted by internal and external forces[82] will continue for the foreseeable future. The outcome of this struggle is by no means certain.

Notes

1 See, for example, Vandana Shiva, 'Food Rights, Free Trade and Fascism', in Matthew J. Gibney, ed., *Globalizing Rights*, Oxford and New York: Oxford University Press, 2003, pp. 87–108; Vandana Shiva, *Earth Democracy: Justice, Sustainability and Peace*, London: Zed Books, 2006; Boaventura de Sousa Santos, ed., *Another Knowledge is Possible: Beyond Northern Epistemologies*, London and New York: Verso, 2007.
2 Carlos M. Correa, *Intellectual Property Rights, the WTO and Developing Countries: The TRIPS Agreement and Policy Options*, London, New York and Penang: Zed Books and Third World Network, 2000.
3 Darrell Addison Posey, 'Ethnobiology and Ethnoecology in the Context of National Laws and International Agreements Affecting Indigenous and Local Knowledge, Traditional Resources and Intellectual Property Rights', in Roy Ellen et al., eds, *Indigenous Environmental Knowledge and its Transformations: Critical Anthropological Perspectives*, London and New York: Routledge, 2003; Tanya Murray Li, 'Locating

80   *Christoph Antons*

Indigenous Environmental Knowledge in Indonesia', in Roy Ellen et al., eds, *Indigenous Environmental Knowledge and its Transformations: Critical Anthropological Perspectives*, London and New York: Routledge, 2003; Burton Ong, ed., *Intellectual Property and Biological Resources*, Singapore: Marshall Cavendish Academic, 2004; Christoph Antons, 'Traditional Knowledge, Biological Resources and Intellectual Property Rights in Asia: The Example of the Philippines', *Forum of International Development Studies* 34, 2007, pp. 1–18.

4 Peter Drahos and Michael Blakeney, eds, *IP in Biodiversity and Agriculture: Regulating the Biosphere*, London: Sweet & Maxwell, 2001; Christoph Antons, 'Sui Generis Protection for Plant Varieties and Traditional Agricultural Knowledge: The Example of India', *European Intellectual Property Review* 29 (12), 2007, pp. 480–85.

5 Victor T. King, *Anthropology and Development in South-East Asia: Theory and Practice*, Oxford and New York: Oxford University Press, 1999, Ch. 9.

6 Christopher R. Duncan, ed., *Civilizing the Margins: Southeast Asian Government Policies for the Development of Minorities*, Ithaca and London: Cornell University Press, 2004.

7 John Gillespie, Chapter 2 in this volume.

8 Bruce G. Carruthers and Terence C. Halliday, 'Law Between the Global and the Local: Negotiating Globalization: Global Scripts and Intermediation in the Construction of Asian Insolvency Regimes', *Law and Social Inquiry* 31, 2006, p. 535.

9 Adam Szirmai, *The Dynamics of Socio-Economic Development: An Introduction*, Cambridge: Cambridge University Press, 2005, p. 397.

10 Pasuk Phongpaichit and Chris Baker, 'Reversing the Tanks in Thailand', *Far Eastern Economic Review* 170 (7), 2007, p. 38.

11 John Gillespie, see note 7 above.

12 Ronald Niezen, *A World Beyond Difference: Cultural Identity in the Age of Globalization*, Malden, MA, Oxford, and Carlton, Vic.: Blackwell Publishing, 2004, p. 74.

13 Roy Ellen et al., 'Introduction', in Roy Ellen et al., eds, *Indigenous Environmental Knowledge and its Transformations: Critical Anthropological Perspectives*, London and New York: Routledge, 2003, p. 2.

14 Ibid., p. 1, note 1.

15 Terri Janke, *Our Culture: Our Future – Report on Australian Indigenous Cultural and Intellectual Property Rights*, Sydney: Michael Frankel & Co.: 1998, pp. 2–3; Christoph Antons, 'Traditional Knowledge, Biological Resources and Intellectual Property Rights in Asia: The Example of the Philippines', *supra*, 2007, pp. 2–3.

16 Howard Morphy, *Aboriginal Art*, London and New York: Phaidon Press, 1998, pp. 103–42; Christoph Antons, 'Folklore Protection in Australia: Who is Expert in Aboriginal Tradition?', in Elke Kurz-Milcke and Gerd Gigerenzer, eds, *Experts in Science and Society*, New York: Kluwer Academic/Plenum Publishers, 2004, pp. 87–88.

17 Jürg Wassmann, 'The Politics of Religious Secrecy', in Alan Rumsey and James F. Weiner, eds, *Emplaced Myth: Space, Narrative, and Knowledge in Aboriginal Australia and Papua New Guinea*, Honolulu: University of Hawai'i Press, 2001; Eric Kline Silverman, 'From Totemic Space to Cyberspace: Transformations in Sepik River and Aboriginal Australian Myth, Knowledge, and Art', in Alan Rumsey and James F. Weiner, eds, *Emplaced Myth: Space, Narrative, and Knowledge in Aboriginal Australia and Papua New Guinea*, Honolulu: University of Hawai'i Press, 2001.

18 Terri Janke, *supra*, 1998, p. 3, note 2.

19 World Intellectual Property Organization, *Intellectual Property Needs and Expectations of Traditional Knowledge Holders – WIPO Report on Fact-finding Missions on Intellectual Property and Traditional Knowledge (1998–1999)*, Geneva: WIPO, 2001, p. 25.

20 Christoph Antons, 'Traditional Knowledge and Intellectual Property Rights in Australia and Southeast Asia', in Christopher Heath and Anselm Kamperman Sanders, eds, *New Frontiers of Intellectual Property Law: IP and Cultural Heritage,*

Geographical Indications, Enforcement, and Overprotection, Oxford and Portland, OR: Hart Publishing, 2005, p. 51.

21 World Intellectual Property Organization, WIPO/GRTKF/IC/12/5(c) of December 6, 2007, Intergovernmental Committee on Intellectual Property and Genetic Resources, Traditional Knowledge and Folklore, Twelfth Session, Geneva, February 25–29, 2008, *Reproduction of Document WIPO/GRTKF/IC/9/5 'The Protection of Traditional Knowledge: Revised Objectives and Principles'*, Geneva: WIPO, 2007, p. 6.

22 Christoph Antons, 'Traditional Knowledge and Intellectual Property Rights in Australia and Southeast Asia', *supra*, note 20, p. 38. See also Ken S. Coates, *A Global History of Indigenous Peoples: Struggle and Survival*, Houndmills, Basingstoke, and New York: Palgrave Macmillan, 2004, p. 9: "Definitions of indigenous in most common usage arise out of the European colonial experience, originated in western industrial nations, and reflect the historical and contemporary realities of these social relationships."

23 Christoph Antons, 'Traditional Knowledge and Intellectual Property Rights in Australia and Southeast Asia', *supra*, note 20, p. 44.

24 See, for example, Michael F. Brown, *Who Owns Native Culture?*, Cambridge, MA, and London: Harvard University Press, 2003; see also Megan M. Carpenter, 'Intellectual Property Law and Indigenous Peoples: Adapting Copyright Law to the Needs of a Global Community', *Yale Human Rights & Development Law Journal* 7, 2004, pp. 51–78, where she speaks of "Australia's groundbreaking body of case law located at the intersections of indigenous interests and intellectual property" where "a growing pattern of creative lawmaking and dicta shows that judges are beginning to recognize the need for such reconfiguration."

25 Bruce G. Carruthers and Terence C. Halliday, *above*, note 8.

26 Russell McGregor, *Imagined Destinies: Aboriginal Australians and the Doomed Race Theory, 1880–1939*, Melbourne: Melbourne University Press, 1997; Barry Hill, *Broken Song: T.G.H. Strehlow and Aboriginal Possession*, Milsons Point, NSW: Vintage Books, 2002; Geoffrey Gray, *A Cautious Silence: The Politics of Australian Anthropology*, Canberra: Aboriginal Studies Press, 2007.

27 Michael Halewood, 'Indigenous and Local Knowledge in International Law: A Preface to Sui Generis Intellectual Property Protection', *McGill Law Journal* 44, 1999, pp. 967–68.

28 Janice G. Weiner, 'Protection of Folklore: A Political and Legal Challenge', *International Review of Intellectual Property and Competition Law* 18 (1), 1987, pp. 76–80 and 86–88.

29 Jeffrey Sissons, *First Peoples: Indigenous Cultures and Their Futures*, London: Reaktion Books, 2005, p. 17.

30 Ken S. Coates, *supra*, note 22, p. 9.

31 Ibid., p. 8.

32 Benedict Kingsbury, 'The Applicability of the International Legal Concept of "Indigenous Peoples" in Asia', in Joanne R. Bauer and Daniel A. Bell, eds, *The East Asian Challenge for Human Rights*, Cambridge: Cambridge University Press, 1999, p. 344.

33 As cited in Carlos M. Correa, *Options for the Implementation of Farmers' Rights at the National Level*, Trade-Related Agenda, Development and Equity (TRADE), Working Papers No. 8, December 2000, p. 4.

34 Article 8(j) of the *Convention on Biological Diversity*.

35 Martin Chanock, 'Customary Law, Sustainable Development and the Failing State', in Peter Ørebech et al., eds, *The Role of Customary Law in Sustainable Development*, Cambridge: Cambridge University Press, 2005, pp. 348–49.

36 Jeffrey Sissons, *supra*, note 29, p. 23.

37 See Article 15(4), (5) and (6) of the CBD.

38 For a complete text of the declaration in the Resolution of the General Assembly 61/295 as well as the various explanations of countries as to their positions, see *General*

Assembly adopts Declaration on Rights of Indigenous Peoples: "Major step forward" towards human rights for all, says President, Media Release, New York: Department of Public Information, News and Media Division, GA/10612, 13 September 2007. Available from http://www.un.org/News/Press/docs/2007/ga10612.doc.htm (accessed 30 October 2007).

39 Benedict Kingsbury, *supra*, note 32.
40 W. F. Wertheim, 'The Trading Minorities in South-East Asia', in Hans-Dieter Evers, ed., *Sociology of South-East Asia: Readings on Social Change and Development*, Kuala Lumpur: Oxford University Press, 1980.
41 Christoph Antons, 'Ethnicity, Law and Development in Southeast Asia', in Frans Hüsken and Dick van der Meij, eds, *Reading Asia: New Research in Asian Studies*, Richmond, Surrey: Curzon, 2001.
42 Benedict Kingsbury, *supra*, note 32, p. 350.
43 Christoph Antons, 'Traditional Knowledge, Biological Resources and Intellectual Property Rights in Asia: The Example of the Philippines', *supra*, note 3, pp. 5–6.
44 Christoph Antons, 'Traditional Knowledge and Intellectual Property Rights in Australia and Southeast Asia', *supra*, note 20, p. 50.
45 General Assembly GA/10612, 13 September 2007, *supra*, note 38, p. 11.
46 Ibid., pp. 12–13.
47 James F. Eder and Thomas M. McKenna, 'Minorities in the Philippines: Ancestral Land in Theory and Practice', in Christopher R. Duncan, ed., *Civilizing the Margins: Southeast Asian Government Policies for the Development of Minorities*, Ithaca and London: Cornell University Press, 2004, pp. 60–61.
48 Christoph Antons, 'Traditional Knowledge, Biological Resources and Intellectual Property Rights in Asia: The Example of the Philippines', *supra*, note 3, pp. 8–10.
49 General Assembly, GA/10612, 13 September 2007, *supra*, note 38, p. 14.
50 Article 46(1) of the *United Nations Declaration on the Rights of Indigenous Peoples*: "Nothing in this Declaration may be interpreted as implying for any State, people, group, or person any right to engage in any activity or to perform any act contrary to the Charter of the United Nations or construed as authorizing or encouraging any action which would dismember or impair, totally or in part, the territorial integrity or political unity of sovereign and independent states."
51 Christoph Antons, *Intellectual Property Law in Indonesia*, London: Kluwer Law International, 2000, p. 87; Janice G. Weiner, *supra*, note 28, p. 67.
52 Janice G. Weiner, *supra*, note 28, pp. 86–87.
53 The word "folklore" has been added to the protected material in Article 10(2), and a licensing requirement for foreigners to use such material, which was implied in the previous version of the law, is now explicitly included in Article 10(3).
54 Christoph Antons, 'Harmonisation and Selective Adaptation as Intellectual Property Policies in Asia', in Christoph Antons, Michael Blakeney, and Christopher Heath, eds, *Intellectual Property Harmonisation within ASEAN and APEC*, The Hague: Kluwer Law International, 2004; Christoph Antons, 'Law Reform in the "Developmental States" of East and Southeast Asia: From the Asian Crisis to September 11, 2001 and Beyond', in Christoph Antons and Volkmar Gessner, eds, *Globalisation and Resistance: Law Reform in Asia since the Crisis*, Oxford and Portland, OR: Hart Publishing: 2007, pp. 90–92.
55 Christoph Antons, 'Law and Development Thinking after the Asian Crisis of 1997', *Forum of International Development Studies* 20 (12), 2001, pp. 205–32; Christoph Antons, 'Law Reform in the "Developmental States" of East and Southeast Asia: From the Asian Crisis to September 11, 2001 and Beyond', *supra*, note 54, p. 92.
56 Ajip Rosidi, *Undang-Undang Hak Cipta 1982 – Pandangan Seorang Awam* [The Copyright Act – A Layperson's Viewpoint], Jakarta: Pernerbit Djambatan, 1984, pp. 79–80.
57 See Article 10(2) b. of the previous Copyright Act of 1982: "The state holds the copyright to the works mentioned in subsection (2) a. with regards to foreign countries."

58 Catharina Ria Budiningsih, 'Menyoal Paten Pengetahuan Tradisional' [Problematize Traditional Knowledge Patents], *Pikiran Rakyat* 30 July 2007.
59 'Malaysia urges Indonesia to drop plans to sue over folk song', *Jakarta Post*, 8 October 2007.
60 'Rasa Sayang belongs to all', *The Star Online*, 3 October 2007; Marc Lourdes, 'Rasa Sayang "ours too … we have the right to sing it"', *nstonline*, 22 November 2007.
61 See, for example, Fred Bosselman, 'Adaptive Resource Management through Customary Law', in Peter Ørebech et al., eds, *The Role of Customary Law in Sustainable Development*, Cambridge: Cambridge University Press, 2005.
62 Brendan Tobin, 'The Role of Customary Law and Practice in the Protection of Traditional Knowledge related to Biological Diversity', in Christoph Antons, ed., *Traditional Knowledge, Traditional Cultural Expressions and Intellectual Property Law in the Asia Pacific Region*, The Hague: Kluwer Law International, 2009, Ch. 6, in print.
63 See, for example, the *Guidelines for Examination of the European Patent Office*, No. X-232.2, as quoted in UNCTAD-ICTSD, *Resource Book on TRIPS and Development*, Cambridge: Cambridge University Press, 2005, p. 393.
64 For views in favor of disclosure requirements, see Martha Chouchena-Rojas et al., eds, *Disclosure Requirements: Ensuring Mutual Supportiveness between the WTO TRIPS Agreement and the CBD*, Gland and Geneva: IUCN, ICTSD, CIEL, IDDRI, QUNO, 2005. For a view opposing such requirements, see Jon Santamauro, 'Reducing the Rhetoric: Reconsidering the Relationship of the TRIPS Agreement, CBD and Proposed New Patent Disclosure Requirements Relating to Genetic Resources and Traditional Knowledge', *European Intellectual Property Review* 29 (3), 1991, pp. 91–99.
65 Article 7.d. of Law No. 14 of 2001 on Patents. An Indonesian language version of this and other Acts mentioned in this chapter can be found in Tim Redaksi Tatanusa, eds, *7 Undang-Undang – Rahasia Dagang, Desain Industri, Desain Tata Letak Sirkuit Terpadu, Paten, Merek, Hak Cipta, Perlindungan Varietas Tanaman* [7 Laws – Trade Secrets, Industrial Designs, Lay-out Designs of Integrated Circuits, Patents, Trade Marks, Copyright, Plant Variety Protection], Jakarta: P.T. Tatanusa: 2005. For an English language version, see Yasmon (Rangkayo Sati), *Indonesian Intellectual Property Directory*, Jakarta: shortCUT Gagas Imaji, 2006.
66 Christoph Antons, 'Traditional Knowledge, Biological Resources and Intellectual Property Rights in Asia: The Example of the Philippines', *supra*, note 3, p. 12.
67 *Isagani Cruz and Cesar Europa v. Sec. of Environment and Natural Resources*, G.R. No. 135385 of 6 December 2000. Available from http://www.supremecourt.gov.ph/jurisprudence/2000/dec2000/135385.htm (accessed 1 December 2008).
68 Joint DENR-NCIP Memorandum Circular No. 2003–1, 'Harmonization of the Implementation of the Indigenous Peoples Rights Act (IPRA) and Environment and Natural Resources (ENR) Laws and policies', 31 October 2003.
69 Joint Administrative Order No. 1 Series of 2005 of the Department of Environment and Natural Resources (DENR), the Department of Agriculture (DA), the Palawan Council for Sustainable Development (PCSD), and the National Commission on Indigenous Peoples (NCIP).
70 Christoph Antons, 'Traditional Knowledge, Biological Resources and Intellectual Property Rights in Asia: The Example of the Philippines', *supra*, note 3, p. 13.
71 S.K. Verma, 'Plant Genetic Resources, Biological Inventions and Intellectual Property Rights: The Case of India', in Burton Ong, ed., *Intellectual Property and Biological Resources*, Singapore: Marshall Cavendish Academic, 2004, p. 129.
72 Christoph Antons, 'Sui Generis Protection for Plant Varieties and Traditional Agricultural Knowledge: The Example of India', *supra*, note 4, pp. 480–81.
73 Shanti Kumar and Neeti Wilson, 'Biotechnology in the Limelight', *Managing Intellectual Property*, Supplement Life Sciences, 2006, p. 46.
74 S.K. Verma, *supra*, note 71, pp. 147–48.

75 Christoph Antons, 'Sui Generis Protection for Plant Varieties and Traditional Agricultural Knowledge: The Example of India', *supra*, note 4, pp. 481–82.
76 Rajesh Sagar, 'Intellectual Property, Benefit-Sharing and Traditional Knowledge: How Effective is the Indian Biological Diversity Act, 2002?', *Journal of World Intellectual Property* 8 (3), 2005, p. 400.
77 Oliver Mendelsohn, 'Law, Terror and the Indian Legal Order', in Christoph Antons and Volkmar Gessner, eds, *Globalisation and Resistance: Law Reform in Asia since the Crisis*, Oxford and Portland, OR: Hart Publishing, 2007, pp. 163–64.
78 See, for example, N.S. Gopalakrishnan, 'Protection of Traditional Knowledge: The Need for a *Sui Generis* Law in India', *Journal of World Intellectual Property* 5 (5), 2002, p. 735.
79 Ronald Niezen, *supra*, note 12.
80 Franz and Keebet von Benda-Beckmann, 'Between Global Forces and Local Politics: Decentralisation and Reorganisation of Village Government in Indonesia', in Christoph Antons and Volkmar Gessner, eds, *Globalisation and Resistance: Law Reform in Asia since the Crisis*, Oxford and Portland, OR: Hart Publishing, 2007.
81 Owen Podger, 'Why Regional Governments are Unfriendly to Business', *Jakarta Post*, 23 June 2006.
82 Christoph Antons, 'Law Reform in the "Developmental States" of East and Southeast Asia: From the Asian Crisis to September 11, 2001 and Beyond', *supra*, note 54.

5 Giving content and effect to competition rules
Contrasting Australia and Japan

Brendan Sweeney

I Introduction

As more and more countries have shifted away from centrally planned economies towards more market-driven models, there has been an explosion in the number of competition law regimes adopted around the world. Most of these regimes trace to a common ancestry, US antitrust rules. Yet they vary significantly in shape and enforcement. This chapter examines the factors that have determined competition policy in Australia and Japan.

Part II of this chapter provides a brief discussion on the globalization of competition rules. Two factors come out of this discussion. First, there are many ways in which countries are introduced to competition rules. Sometimes they are freely selected. Australia is a prime example. Sometimes they are adopted only under external pressure. Japan typifies this situation. Second, competition rules tend to be very flexible. This is due not only to the open-ended nature of the rules themselves, but also to the lack of an uncontested central object. The result is a set of rules, the content and the effect of which are constantly negotiable.

Part III investigates the history of Australian competition law. Australia was one of the first states in the world to enact competition rules. In 1906, it relied heavily on US antitrust law to enact the Australian Industries Preservation Act. The Act, however, failed to gain traction and fell into disuse. It was not until the 1960s that Australia made a second attempt at adopting a competition regime. This time the attempt was a success.

Part IV investigates Japanese competition law. The Japanese story is quite different. Japan is well acquainted with foreign legal borrowings. When the Tokugawa regime was overthrown, the Meiji government looked to Western sources for a legal system to replace its discredited feudal system. The Japanese Civil Code, based initially on the French Napoleonic Code, was later remodeled on the German Code.[1] The Meiji government also borrowed heavily from the German system for its Commercial and Civil Procedure Codes.[2] These borrowings, however, were Japan's choice. The introduction of competition law to Japan was quite different. Japan did not choose competition law. Rather, it was imposed by the US following World War Two. Competition law did not suit the Japanese economy or Japanese regulatory culture and this is reflected in its treatment. The problem for Japan is that, while competition law may now be a good fit for the economy, the regulatory culture has changed only slowly, if at all. This makes it difficult for competition law to have any effect.

II Global competition rules

Although competition rules can take many forms, they usually contain at least three broad substantive provisions:

- a provision dealing with anti-competitive agreements or arrangements (for example, bid-rigging agreements, price agreements, and market-sharing agreements);
- a provision dealing with single firm conduct, often called monopolization conduct (for example, predatory pricing and other forms of conduct designed either to injure existing competitors or to exclude new competitors); and
- a provision dealing with proposed mergers.

These provisions are generally traced in their modern form to the Sherman Act enacted by the US Congress in 1890. Because the Sherman Act provisions directly attacked the trust structures by which large business cartels sought to control many areas of US commerce, the rules came to be known as antitrust laws. An indication of the US influence internationally is the extent to which the expression "antitrust" is used in other jurisdictions.[3] Although there have been changes over the ensuing 100+ years, the basic structure of US antitrust law remains much the same as it was in 1890. What has changed (and changed quite significantly) is how key concepts (such as competition, anti-competitive, and monopolization) are interpreted. Only a brave soul would predict that these changes are now complete.

From 1890 to the end of World War Two, competition rules developed largely as a US domestic project. Few states showed much appetite for copying this initiative. Australia was one nation that had a brief flirtation. In general, during this period, the most significant event internationally was the growing willingness of US courts to apply their antitrust rules extraterritorially.

The situation changed after World War Two. First, the states of Western Europe, desperate for mechanisms that would reduce bellicose tensions on the European continent, sought some unity in economic union. The common market created by the Treaty of Rome in 1957 contained competition rules. These remain very much a key element of the European Union (EU). Any state wishing to join the EU must implement a competition regime consistent with the EU rules. Second, the UK, not a founding member of the European Economic Community (EEC), introduced competition rules during the 1950s. Third, as part of the policy of fragmenting economic power in Japan, the US-led occupation forces required Japan to adopt the Antimonopoly Act.[4] The Antimonopoly Act was based on US antitrust law. Although largely ignored in its early days, the Act has remained on the statute books.

The next growth period for the adoption of competition rules domestically begins in the early 1990s and continues to the present day. In 1980, there were about twenty competition law regimes. These included the US, the countries of Western Europe (which of course had a European system as well), Canada, Australia and New Zealand, Japan, and Korea. By 2000, the number had grown to ninety-eight and continues to grow. In 2007, China enacted competition laws to come into effect in August 2008. India's Monopoly Act was recently repealed and replaced by the Competition Act 2002. In contrast to the Monopoly Act, the Competition Act is designed along the lines of the European competition regime. That is, it now conforms to the model first set up by the US Sherman Act.

The growth of domestic competition regimes is not accidental. Since World War Two, the US has been very keen to promote this growth. For example, the US insisted on competition rules being introduced to Japan. In more recent times, the EU has been the leader in promoting the need for competition rules. Any country wishing to join the EU must adopt European-style competition rules. The EU took the lead in pushing for competition rules to be added to the Doha round of trade talks at the World Trade Organization (WTO). Pressure has also come from international donor organizations. For example, in the wake of the Asian financial crisis, both the International Monetary Fund (IMF) and the World Bank insisted on competition rules as a condition of their support.

There is no multilateral international competition agreement. All attempts to forge such an agreement have failed. The key reason is probably the open-ended nature of competition rules. Competition policy is a broad church capable of accommodating a variety of views on the nature of competition and harmful monopoly. This lack of precision about its core concepts makes it difficult to construct an agreement except in very broad terms. At the end of World War Two, competition rules were part of the Bretton Woods negotiations that ultimately resulted in the General Agreement on Tariffs and Trade (GATT); thus, competition rules were included in the proposed charter for the International Trade Organization (the Havana Charter). The ITO, however, failed to obtain US congressional approval and never came into effect.[5] One of the reasons why the US Congress refused to approve the ITO was concern that US antitrust rules would thereby be diluted. Fifty years later, the US opposed European attempts to add a competition agreement to the WTO agreements on the grounds that the ensuing rules would be too restrictive. Thus, in both cases, the US backed away from multilateral rules because it feared that it would lose control of its domestic antitrust regime. In the first case, it feared a weakening of those rules; in the second, a strengthening. In those fifty years, US antitrust laws had remained almost untouched by the legislature, but the approach to analyzing competition and monopoly had changed radically, first by antitrust administrators and then by the courts.[6]

Therefore, when examining how local forces have adapted competition rules, it is necessary to bear in mind that there is plenty of scope for adaptation. Different groups can champion competition policy, but have entirely different things in mind. The following histories of competition law and policy demonstrate this.

III Australia

A *The first attempt at competition rules in Australia*

1 *What was the legislative intent?*

The first attempt at competition rules in Australia was the Australian Industries Preservation Act 1906 (Cth) (AIPA). The Act was based on the Sherman Act.[7] It had a provision prohibiting certain restraints of trade and a provision prohibiting monopolization. It also copied some of the Sherman Act's notable remedial features, treble damages and criminal liability.[8]

AIPA was not primarily designed to foster a competitive environment, but rather, as its name suggests, to protect local industry from foreign competition, particularly cheap imports from US firms.[9] The years leading up to and immediately following Australian federation saw a battle between the proponents of protectionism and those who supported free trade. Protectionism succeeded because it was supported by the manufacturing class and because it was able to tap into the growing political strength of the labor movement in a very tangible fashion. The architect of this so-called "new protectionism" was Alfred Deakin, Prime Minister on three separate occasions during the first decade of federation. Deakin brought the labor movement and its political wing, the Labor Party, onside by linking tariff and other protectionist policies not just to the protection of jobs but also to the provision of a fair and reasonable basic wage. Firms that paid a fair and reasonable wage were entitled to protection. This counteracted the strong opposition from the farming lobby, which wanted access to the cheapest farm equipment. The move also neutralized those in the labor movement who preferred nationalization as a solution.[10] Although much of the structure of the so-called "new protectionism" was declared constitutionally invalid by the High Court, the underlying drivers, namely protectionism and the fair and reasonable wage, became mainstays of the Australian economic landscape.

AIPA was a piece of protectionist legislation. Viewed from a modern standpoint, it may seem surprising that a protectionist law was based on the US Sherman Act. Although the Sherman Act is not now viewed as a piece of public interest legislation, this was not the case in 1890. The evidence suggests that the primary object of the Sherman Act was to protect small traders against the corporate giants, in particular the trusts that had sprung up during the second half of the nineteenth century in many US industries (for example railways, oil, and tobacco).[11] It was only later, indeed much later, that the broad provisions of the Sherman Act were provided with their current, free market focus.[12]

Thus, both the US Act and the Australian Act were designed to serve a protectionist purpose.[13] They were both designed to curtail the power of big business. The difference is that in Australia big business was equated with imports. The Australian Act was designed essentially to protect emerging, but still vulnerable, local industries.[14]

Although based on the Sherman Act, the Australian Act was drafted in a more precise manner. Both Acts declared agreements in restraint of trade and attempts to monopolize commerce unlawful. However, whereas the US Congress left it to the courts to work out what amounted to an unlawful restraint of trade and unlawful monopolization, the Australian Act specifically provided that they were only unlawful if the parties intended to cause detriment to the public. The "public" was defined to include not only producers and consumers but workers as well. The inclusion of workers in the definition of "public" reflects the political influence of labor in constructing "new protectionism."

2 Why did the Act fail?

(A) JUDICIAL CONSERVATISM

It didn't take long before AIPA was tested in the High Court. In *Huddart Parker & Co. Pty Ltd v. Moorehead* (1909) 8 CLR 330, much of the potential scope of the Act was held invalid on constitutional grounds. The Act relied on an expansive interpretation of what constituted a "trading or financial corporation" (a constitutional corporation). Instead, the High Court interpreted a constitutional corporation narrowly. Because of this, because most states refused to enact complementary legislation,[15] and the citizens of Australia showed a marked reluctance to amend the Constitution, very few cases were ever heard under the Act. The most significant case decided under the AIPA was the Coal Vend case.

Competition rules are often expressed in broad language (and this was certainly true of the AIPA). This means that interpreting the legislative language becomes the key. The interpreter must resolve a tension that exists between two competing versions of what competition law is.[16] On the one hand, the language of competition law can be consistent with notions that protect individual liberty and freedom of contract. On the other hand, the language can be interpreted as a constraint on that liberty for the purpose of achieving other social goals (for example, the protection of particular interests or the protection of public welfare in the case of market failure). Thus, the institution with the power to interpret is very important. In the case of the AIPA, this was the judiciary.

The judiciary has played a vital role in the development of competition rules in Australia, and even more so in the US. In both countries, the judiciary is largely independent of the legislature and the executive. In Australia, High Court judges are appointed by the Commonwealth government. They cannot easily be removed. This gives them considerable independence from other state actors.

The Coal Vend case involved a classic cartel. New South Wales (NSW) coal producers and the coal shipping companies colluded to exclude competition for the trade in coal and to fix the supply of coal for the purpose of ensuring a "reasonable" price.

The main area for coal production in Australia was Newcastle in NSW. By agreement between the coal producers and their employees, wages were pegged at the beginning of each year to the "probable" price of coal. The coal producers, therefore, had incentives to ensure that the price of coal did not fall below this "probable" price. The natural result was that the coal producers entered into price fixing (market sharing) agreements. The association of coal producers thus formed was called a Vend.

When a new coalfield (with new producers) came onstream at Maitland (also in NSW), the Newcastle Vend became very difficult to maintain. Vigorous price competition replaced the fixed price. As the probable price exceeded the actual price, coal producers risked falling into debt and into the hands of the banks. There was also a risk that miners would be laid off. The shipping companies that were dependent on Newcastle coal and acted as buyers as well as shippers of coal were also concerned about falling prices. Indeed, the town and district of New-castle, being dependent on the coal industry, feared a period of extreme economic strain.

Having established themselves in the market, the Maitland producers also had reasons to try and lift the price of coal. Eventually, all parties entered into negotiations to rectify the situation. An agreement to control supply resulted and continued for four years.

The Federal Government alleged that the agreements breached the AIPA. The trial lasted a marathon seventy-three days. (Lengthy and extremely costly trials continue to plague this area of the law, not only in Australia but wherever the court system plays a major part.) The Act prohibited contracts or combinations in trade or commerce that were entered into with the intent of restraining trade or commerce to the detriment of the public. A contract or combination in trade or commerce clearly existed. Therefore, the critical issue was whether the relevant intent existed.

Justice Isaacs rejected the proposition that just because a restraint of trade was lawful at common law it could not be a breach of the Act. Rather, the Act required an analysis of the public interest. Conspiracies to raise prices were often, but not always, to the detriment of the public. Consequently, it was necessary to examine the full circumstances surrounding the Vend's conduct. The way to do this was to compare the public's position with and without the conduct. When analyzed in this way, the Vend's conduct was an unlawful restraint. Justice Isaacs rejected the notion (taken from common law) that the intention of the Vend was to further its own interests, not harm the public. Justice Isaacs essentially put the onus on the Vend to show that the conduct was reasonably necessary to protect the public interest. A modern antitrust judge could have written this analysis of cartels and their consequences.

The Full Court and later the Privy Council rejected this approach. Both looked to the common law for inspiration.[17] Restraints of trade and conspiracies were well known to the common law. In fact, the House of Lords had handed down major judgments in both areas within the previous decade and a half.[18] In both areas, the common law concentrated on the interests of the parties, not the interests of the public, consumers, or workers. Provided conduct between the parties was rea-sonable, it was lawful. This trend was particularly noticeable in the case of con-spiracies to injure a competitor. In *Mogul Steamship*, their Lordships held that a conspiracy to injure a person in his or her trade was only unlawful if the dominant reason for the conspiracy was to harm that person. If the conspirators acted to further their own commercial interests, then there was no unlawful conduct. This approach by the House of Lords was in keeping with the laissez faire commercial spirit of the nineteenth century.

If the conduct of the coal producers was reasonable, there was no unlawful intent as required by the Act. In language reminiscent of the *Mogul Steamship* case, the High Court and the Privy Council held that the Commonwealth had failed to demonstrate that the Vend had a specific intent to injure the public. Relying on the common law tended to privilege the interests of coal producers because the common law tended to protect a business person's right to carry on their trade as they saw fit. As one commentator said:[19]

> The decision demonstrates the unsatisfactory nature of the common law, which in effect means that if the real and primary object of any restrictive agreement is to promote the commercial interests of the parties, the agreement is not illegal if, as an incidental result, it affects the public adversely through a rise in prices.

(B) POLITICAL REASONS FOR FAILURE

In 1910, Parliament amended the AIPA by removing the need to establish a particular intent. Arguably, this should have made the Coal Vend case easier to prove. Yet the government did not bring an action against the Coal Vend, or indeed anyone else, under the amended Act. The reasons for this inactivity were partly political. The protectionism-versus-free trade debate was won by the protectionists. High tariffs and restrictive quotas became the order of the day. Once they were in a position to construct a more adequate system of protection, the liberal protectionists lost enthusiasm for the Act, particularly where it was turned on local producers. The Labor Party also no longer needed the Act to achieve its goals. Consumers, the real victims of cartel conduct, had no voice. Finally, there was no external pressure to maintain an anti-cartel system. It would take another forty years before the US actively promoted antitrust laws abroad and before Australia felt internal pressure to bring its economic systems into line with international ones. Moreover, the developed world was about to slide into the mayhem of World War One.

3 Conclusion

On its face, the AIPA contained quite radical regulatory possibilities (for example, a broadly based public interest test, the provision of treble damages, criminalization of certain conduct). The way was open for the courts to develop a new set of principles for market regulation, principles that were not merely adaptations of the common law.[20] Justice Isaacs pointed the way. However, in the end, the common law tradition was just too strong. Whether the AIPA would have developed in a similar manner to the Sherman Act (and the extent to which US cases may have influenced that development) will not be known. Judicial conservatism combined with constitutional limitations—itself another example of judicial conservatism—practically ensured the Act's death knell. Politically, in any event, the Act had outlived its usefulness. There was no pressure, internal or external, to implement a competition regime.

B The 1960s: competition rules revived

1 Australian business in 1960

Parliamentary interest in competition rules was not revived until the early 1960s. By this time, Australian business had become used to operating in a regulatory environment that permitted anti-competitive activities.[21] Cartels and anti-competitive vertical conduct were rife. Most trade associations were engaged in some form of restrictive conduct: "In 1961 there were over 600 trade associations in Australia, of which an estimated 58–66 percent operated restrictive trade practices."[22] These practices were often described as "orderly marketing." Intra-industry agreements (both horizontal and vertical) had become so much a part of the Australian commercial landscape that they were a part of local culture. There was nothing unethical about entering into price-fixing agreements.[23] Indeed, some retailers were so inured to the notion of a fixed industry-wide price that they were shocked when offered discounts by manufacturers and assumed that a mistake must have been made.[24]

The Australian economic environment itself was conducive to a culture of collusion and protection. As was said:[25]

> The idea that an increase in competition conditions is desirable will come as a novelty to much of Australian industry, which has been developed against a background of Commonwealth tariff protection, highly concentrated patterns of ownership and control, and a tradition of substantial *ad hoc* bounties and subsidies from both Federal and State governments.

Among owners, managers, and workers, there was a distinct preference for "the objectives of stability and order rather than those of change and competition."[26] This spirit also infected consumers. The fact is that no consumer organizations lobbied for restrictive trade practices legislation. One commentator ascribed this to ignorance about the benefits that flow from a competitive economy.[27] What, therefore, caused the revival of competition rules?

2 Factors influencing a revival of competition rules

The impetus for revisiting competition rules came from a variety of economic, legal, and commercial sources. But, underlying these sources and giving them a significance they would not otherwise have had was a political conviction, shaped by the events of World War Two, that, as a nation, Australia could not just return to the social, economic, and political preferences that characterized its pre-war existence. Australia had to change. It had to become more self-sufficient. It could no longer base its future simply on the ties of empire. It had to increase its population; it had to rapidly expand the economy; it had to become a modern industrial state. It is in this context that the revival of competition rules in Australia must be understood. It explains why a nation that embraced all forms of competitive collusion in 1960 would, some forty years later, be outraged by the price-fixing activities of one of its leading citizens.[28]

Significant developments in competition law and policy had occurred overseas. The UK had introduced competition laws progressively through the 1950s. Europe had included competition rules in the 1956 Treaty of Rome which established the European common market. In the US, antitrust law had moved more into the spotlight as the US Supreme Court adopted a more interventionist approach to antitrust law, triggering a vigorous intellectual response by economists. According to the Court, the function of the antitrust laws was to protect competition, and this was to be done by actively protecting competitors.[29] Thus, the Court protected small retailers—for example the "mom and pop" grocery stores—against the aggression of large chain stores. On the other side, economists and lawyers—drawing in the main on welfare and industrial organization economics—were busy rewriting the theory of antitrust in an altogether different manner. According to them, the object of antitrust law was to maximize consumer welfare. Courts should only intervene in the free operation of markets where it could be reliably demonstrated that the market was producing inefficient outcomes. The Chicago School of antitrust (so called because many of its adherents came from Chicago University) set out to demonstrate that many of the activities proscribed by the Supreme Court were in fact efficient (when properly viewed from a Coasian perspective). Thus, the Chicago School criticized the activist approach of the Courts. This preference for non-intervention was reinforced by a profound distrust in the ability of the state to intervene efficiently.

In Australia, economists, aware of the policy changes overseas, began to investigate Australian industry in more detail. Their studies revealed the anti-competitive and inefficient nature of many Australian industries.[30] Lawyers also pointed to the legal developments occurring overseas, particularly in the UK. The UK had always been a powerful source of ideas for Australia. Australia was clearly out of step with other developed nations.

At the same time, the possibilities inherent in US-style antitrust law (as practiced by the US Supreme Court) resonated with at least one special interest group. By the early 1960s, discount retail chains had arrived in Australia. Large grocery retailers threatened to put small grocery stores out of business. The same was occurring in other retail industries such as petrol, alcohol, and clothing. Just as the small retailers had suffered in the US, so did small retailers in Australia. Small business complained about the power of the chains to extract cheaper prices from suppliers than the small firms were able to extract. For small business, this was unfair price discrimination. Small business also complained about the ability of the chains to offer consumers consistently cheaper prices than small business could offer; this was labeled predatory pricing. Small business turned to the government for help. Competition law, which purported to prohibit anti-competitive activities, seemed just the thing. After all, how more anti-competitive can conduct be than driving competitors out of the market? Of course, the object was to convince the government to regulate big business activities that harmed small business; in other respects, business should be left free to operate as it wished. Small business certainly had no intention to open the door to Chicago School antitrust theory.

3 Restrictive Trade Practices Act (1965)

In 1960, the Commonwealth government announced its intention to investigate the need for a monopolies and restrictive trade practices law.[31] In 1963, the Attorney General, Sir Garfield Barwick, who in practice at the Bar generally represented the interests of large business such as the banks, introduced to the Commonwealth Parliament a proposal for competition laws based on the UK's provisions.[32] The proposals called for the prohibition of many restrictive practices including the total prohibition of collusive tendering and bidding, monopolization, and predatory price-cutting. In other respects, the proposals were quite different from the Australian Industries Preservation Act; there was no mention of criminalization or treble damages. Given the prevailing socio-economic circumstances, if competition rules were to be introduced, it was never going to be possible to just revive the 1906 law (no matter how much economists may have regretted it).

Barwick was undoubtedly driven by a conviction that competitive markets were the best means of serving the public interest.[33] He was also fully aware of the difficulties attending the creation of an effective competition system and the need to ensure that it reflected local conditions and satisfied local aspirations. According to Barwick, "The Government has attempted to develop 'an Australian approach' which might be singularly appropriate to the Australian economy in its developing stage."[34] Barwick was an intelligent political operator and almost certainly his "Australian approach" included due recognition of the need for some horse-trading to be done. Perhaps the most noticeable example of the Australianism of the proposals was that in the main they would not apply to rural industries. As a result, the farming and grazing interests supported the proposals.

Once Barwick's proposals were released, business, particularly big business, responded vigorously. Big business had no desire for change. It was comfortable with the government's prevailing non-interventionist approach. The argument put forward is one that resonates just as strongly today among large business organizations—oligopolies and monopolies were necessary if Australian industry was to expand and compete in foreign markets. Consequently, big business vehemently opposed the changes.[35] The Associated Chamber of Manufacturers listed the evils that could be expected from the new proposals. They would:

- slow down foreign investment;
- adversely affect the balance of payments;
- lead to other undesirable consequences.[36]

The lobbying enjoyed some success. When the Restrictive Trade Practices Act 1965 appeared, monopolization and predatory pricing were no longer prohibited outright, although they were examinable at the instance of the Commissioner of Trade Practices (a newly created position). There was no private right of action. The Trade Practices Tribunal had power to declare an examinable practice unlawful if it was not in the public interest. Certain agreements had to be registered but the penalty for failure to do so was a small fine.[37] The register was confidential.

According to one leading commentator, the intense lobbying and politicking produced an Act without a coherent objective.[38]

> The major difficulty [in turning Barwick's proposals into law], clearly enough, has been political, not only in the narrow sense of finding a bill which will prove acceptable to Liberal Party supporters, but also in the sense of devising a policy with goals and methods which reflect the social and political values of a large section of Australian society. And after five years of discussion, including the two and a half years of sharp controversy which followed the unveiling of the Barwick scheme, it has to be recorded that—if the proposed bill is any indication—there is still no formulated objective for legislation in this area.

Two aspects of the Act demonstrate the lack of a coherent object and suggest that the reason for incoherence was the government's need to placate their diverse supporter groups. First, the list of examinable activities is difficult to explain according to any theory of competition policy. Predatory pricing and inducing price discrimination were listed as examinable practices, but mergers and resale price maintenance were not. Preventing predatory pricing and inducing price discrimination were key aspects of the small business lobby. On the other hand, small business favored resale price maintenance because it helped prevent retail discounting. Small business may have had some concerns about unregulated mergers, but their interest in preventing mergers was not nearly so strong as the interest big business had in keeping government regulation out.

Second, the test for determining whether examinable conduct was in the "public interest" was confusing. When determining whether conduct was in the public interest, the Tribunal had to have regard to a number of factors, including inter alia:

(a) The needs and interests of consumers, employees, producers, distributors, importers, exporters, proprietors, and investors;
(b) The needs and interests of small businesses ...

The Act provided no guide as to how the Tribunal was to weigh these factors against each other and against the other listed criteria.[39] This was a matter upon which the government did not wish to be precise. The government's basic problem was that competition law divided its natural constituency: big business (the non-interventionists) versus small business (limited interventionists). It is difficult to satisfy both these camps at the same time. Consequently, it is not surprising that the government found it more politically convenient to leave the difficult balancing of interests to the Tribunal.[40]

4. Conclusion: the revival of competition rules

There were a variety of influences at work in producing the Restrictive Trade Practices Act 1965. The problem for the Conservative government was that it had divided loyalties: small business wanted some protection from big business and big business wanted to retain the status quo. By exempting most rural industry practices, the government ensured that its other main constituency remained neutral. The Restrictive Trade Practices Act 1965 is thus a compromise. It is doubtful whether the Act had much real impact on the operation of big business; the Act was just too weak to achieve that kind of outcome. Indeed, some commentators have suggested that the basic reason for the Act was a desire on the part of the government to stave off more vigorous alternatives.[41] Nevertheless, the Act did break the hold that business had established over competition policy in Australia for over fifty years.

C Trade Practices Act 1974

In 1974, the Labor government introduced the Trade Practices Act (TPA). Its predecessor, the Conservative coalition government, had been examining the possibilities of a stronger Act, but lost power before producing anything concrete.[42] It is very difficult to be definite about these things, but it has to be doubted that, in its twilight years (it had been in power for twenty-three years), the coalition had the political will or support to produce such a comprehensive piece of legislation as the TPA.

The TPA has been substantially added to over the years since 1974, but the structure and many of the substantive provisions still form the core of Australian competition law. As with the Australian Industries Preservation Act 1906 and the Restrictive Trade Practices Act 1965, the TPA was based on overseas competition regimes, principally the Sherman Act.

The Labor government, elected in 1972, favored socialist policies. It owed no debts to big business. Its concerns lay with workers, consumers as voters— consumer organizations did not agitate for the TPA[43]—and small business. The commitment to small business had something of a Jeffersonian quality about it; it was described by one commentator as "a commitment to small business as the seed-bed of innovation and as the bastion of democracy."[44] It demonstrates a political concern with accumulations of economic power. This is very reminiscent of the forces that gave life to the Sherman Act.

The TPA was much more interventionist than the Restrictive Trade Practices Act 1965. To this end, it proscribed certain conduct outright (price fixing, bid-rigging, market sharing, and third line forcing) and other conduct if it had the effect of substantially lessening competition. The Trade Practices Commission was created with oversight responsibility for the Act. The Commission also had a direct regulatory role in that it was given responsibility for authorizing conduct where it considered that the conduct was justified in the public interest. The importance of the TPA and of the Commission to the regulation of the Australian economy really commenced in earnest with the appointment of an activist chairman, Professor Allan Fels, in 1991.

Although recent Labor governments have been more centrist in their political orientation than the Whitlam government, the Labor government remains the innovator in competition legislation. In 1993, the Keating Labor government set up the Hilmer Committee to enquire into all aspects of Australia's competition law and policy. Most of the Committee's extensive recommendations were accepted and implemented by Labor.

The problem confronting the conservative parties is that they are often torn between two political imperatives. This was particularly noticeable in the last years of the Howard government (1996–2007). On the one hand, it had a decided preference for economic liberalism.[45] On the other, it needed to attract the small business vote by tightening the market power laws against big business. Small business had become disillusioned with the market power provisions of the TPA as a result of a series of judgments by the High Court.[46] The High Court interpreted the market power provisions in a way that restricted their use to monopolies or near monopolies. This interpretation, although available as a matter of statutory interpretation, was contrary to the intention of the original framers of the provision.[47] Thus, just as it had in the Coal Vend case ninety years earlier, the High Court played a significant role in determining Australia's competition policy. The Conservative government was caught in a dilemma. Eventually, just a few months before its electoral demise, it capitulated to the small business lobby and introduced amending legislation. The amending legislation, however, is itself indicative of the problem that this issue presents to the conservatives; it was worded in such a way that it is impossible to be certain what it means. It is inevitably headed back to the High Court.

D Summing up—Australia

Except for Barwick's proposal, the major legislative events in Australian competition law have occurred when the Labor Party has been in government. It was a Labor government that repealed the Restrictive Trade Practices Act 1965 and replaced it with the TPA, which remains the legislative core of competition law to this day. It was also the Labor government that commissioned the broadranging Hilmer Inquiry in 1993 and implemented its suggested reforms. In contrast, conservative governments, apart from the introduction of the Restrictive Trade Practices Act in 1965 (which took five years), have been responsible for few changes.

Conservative governments have a difficult political problem with some of the core elements of competition policy. While reluctant to shift away from policies based on economic liberalism (policies that tend to favor large businesses), conservative governments have a political need to placate small businesses. For this reason, small business has been able to influence the manner in which conservative governments have handled the market power provisions of the TPA, sometimes contrary to the government's preferred position.

IV Japan

A Introduction of competition rules to Japan

1 Background

In 1947, the Japanese Diet passed the Antimonopoly Law (AML). The AML was based on US antitrust law. Its introduction had very little to do with internal Japanese forces. No element of Japanese society had hitherto displayed the slightest interest in competition laws. Rather, the enactment of the AML had everything to do with the political economic agenda of the US-led Allied Occupation Forces that ruled Japan in the years immediately following the end of World War Two.[48] The US was determined to dismantle the hierarchical and militaristic structure that, in its opinion, had brought about the War. Japan was to be politically democratized and, as Japan's industrial organization was seen as a key element of the offending structure, it was to be economically democratized as well.[49]

Prior to World War Two, the Japanese economy was dominated by large industrial conglomerates (*zaibatsu*), some of which had their roots in pre-Meiji Restoration Japan. During the War, these conglomerates worked with the military government to realize Japan's hegemonic aspirations. Consequently, a prime aim of the Allied Powers was to break up the *zaibatsu* and to prevent their restoration.[50] All cartels, whether domestic or international, were to be prohibited.[51] The activities of Japan's powerful and influential trade associations were to be severely curtailed.[52] Japanese industry was to be restructured along more competitive lines, similar to the US. The AML was to be Japan's Sherman Act.

2 Enactment of the AML

As originally proposed, Japanese competition law was to be similar to US antitrust law. Like US antitrust law, the AML would target horizontal and vertical restrictive agreements. Responsibility for the AML was to be given to an independent regulator, the Japan Fair Trade Commission (JFTC). The model for the JFTC was the US Federal Trade Commission.[53] An independent regulator was a novel institution in Japan; ultimately, the JFTC was the only independent regulator in Japan to survive the departure of the Supreme Commander of Allied Powers (SCAP). As with US antitrust law, violations of the AML were to attract severe penalties as well as civil liability.

Japanese bureaucrats began the push against US-style antitrust law right from the beginning.[54] While the substantive aspects of the AML remained very much in the mold of US antitrust law,[55] the remedial and procedural provisions proposed by SCAP were changed in important ways. The JFTC's powers were deliberately reduced; the JFTC could issue cease and desist orders, but it had no power to impose civil penalties. A criminal penalty could be imposed by the Tokyo High Court, but the procedure was complex, time-consuming, and relied on cooperation from the Ministry of Justice. Private actions were permitted under the AML, but they could only be implemented after the JFTC had made a final administrative order against the impugned firm. Should industry cooperate with the JFTC or should the JFTC find no need to proceed to an administrative order, there was no possibility of a damages claim under the AML.[56] Unlike the US, there was no provision for treble damages.

These changes were deliberately designed to make the enforcement structure of competition law more amenable to prevailing Japanese regulatory norms.[57] A powerful, independent JFTC could prove difficult for the bureaucracy to control. An attractive scheme for private enforcement might prove impossible to control.[58] Both, therefore, could seriously interfere with industrial policy development and implementation based on centralized coordination and cooperation.

B 1952–72—rejection of competition policy and law

1 Introduction

From the early 1950s (when SCAP vacated Japan) until the 1970s, the AML and the JFTC were almost wholly ineffective. This period has been described by the present Secretary General of the JFTC as the dark ages of competition law in Japan.[59] The majority of cases that came to the attention of the JFTC were dismissed for lack of evidence.[60] Generally, this was simply a pretext; as the 1959 newspaper case demonstrated, the JFTC often had sufficient evidence, but lacked the power (and probably the inclination) to do anything with it.[61] No criminal cases were initiated. Contrary to US intentions, the JFTC was anything but a strong, independent antitrust agency. Private enforcement also failed: there were no actions for damages.

The problem was not just a lack of enforcement. The AML itself came under sustained attack. Significant amendments were made in 1953 and periodically throughout the rest of the 1950s and the 1960s.[62] In 1953, the notion that cartels and market power were bad per se was legislatively discarded. Henceforth, cartels would be subject to a public interest test. Exemptions were introduced for recession and rationalization cartels. The deeply unpopular and ineffective Trade Association Law was also repealed.

The main reason why Japan's competition law was so ineffective was that the major policymakers in the relevant domain—the Liberal Democratic Party, the bureaucrats, and business interests—were united in their opposition to the AML. In fact, given the breadth and intensity of the opposition, the most surprising feature of the first twenty years of the history of competition law in Japan is that it survived at all.

2 Regulatory culture of Japan

From the beginning, the AML had little or no local support. Indeed, it was widely viewed in business circles as a ploy by US industrialists to prevent Japanese firms from becoming competitive.[63] The notion of fostering competition as the dominant driver of economic activity was fundamentally at odds with Japanese administrative practices.[64] Following the Meiji Restoration, the principal economic imperative was to develop the Japanese economy as quickly as possible to catch up with the West. While introducing a market economy, the government maintained a very close relationship with economic institutions. From the private sector side, industry associations and the *zaibatsu* developed as a mechanism to facilitate that relationship.[65] From the beginning, Japanese capitalism was focused on outcomes. Japanese political economy was pragmatic rather than ideological.

When production cartels appeared to be a useful response to the recession that followed the Russo-Japanese War in 1905, the Meiji government supported them.[66] Eventually, the government supported compulsory cartels because they stabilized, organized, and rationalized industry.[67] This prevented over-investment and aided the development cause.

The primary administrative mechanism employed to carry out this policy was administrative guidance (*gyōsei shidō*). Administrative guidance gave the bureaucracy a central role in Japan's quest to modernize. Administrative guidance is an informal process by which the relevant ministry engages with the private sector to achieve certain policy ends. Normally, the ministry does not have any direct legislative powers of enforcement. Thus, the administrative agency uses persuasion, negotiation, and cajolement. It may also threaten.[68] For example, an administrative authority may use its power over subsidies and licenses to create positive and negative incentives.[69]

The bureaucracy's role in the operation of the Japanese economy assumed particular significance from the late 1920s to the end of World War Two. During this period, the Ministry of Trade and Industry (MITI) took a very hands-on approach to tackling the problems of the depression and later the execution of the war.[70] MITI organized and supervised production cartels to allocate resources and control prices.

3 The AML is sidelined

US determination to remake the Japanese economy along more competitive lines was always a political imperative for the US rather than an economic one. Although some economic idealists were involved in shaping the AML, the principal concern of the US was always to emasculate the power of Japan as a military threat.[71] The outbreak of the Korean War in 1950 forced the US to rethink its strategy. What was now required was an economically successful and powerful Japan. As a consequence, the US lost interest in pushing for major systemic changes in Japan.

When the Allied Occupation Forces left in 1952, Japan returned to the political economy that it had known before the war, which had been very successful.[72] Japanese bureaucracy returned to the preferred practice of coordinated planning and guidance. To be effective, administrative guidance requires cooperation between industry and government.[73] Thus, trade associations were reinvigorated. New industrial linkages (*keiretsu*) emerged to replace the *zaibatsu*.

Strategies were developed to carry out the government's policy of giving priority to industry development. These strategies often required market activities to be coordinated and competition to be restrained. This was achieved by encouraging cartels, notably production curtailment cartels (*kankoku sôtan*). The Japanese people accepted this process; it was familiar and it worked—Japan enjoyed phenomenal economic growth during the 1950s and 1960s.

Yet the use of private cartels to organize industrial activity was directly contrary to the spirit and text of the AML. Therefore, MITI and business combined during the early years to sideline the AML. Initially, the preferred option of business was to abolish the AML. MITI, on the other hand, preferred to weaken the law rather than abolish it altogether. It did this by introducing a system of exemptions which MITI controlled. Control of the exemptions increased MITI's power and influence over the private sector while at the same time enfeebling the AML.[74]

Later in the 1950s, MITI saw an advantage in destroying the AML, but this time business opted to oppose MITI's strategy. Business was concerned that MITI should not become too powerful.[75] Both MITI and business favored cartels, but each wanted the upper hand in running them.[76] Small and medium-sized businesses (including the agriculture and fisheries industries) also opposed MITI.[77] Their concern was not to preserve competition per se or to oppose MITI; rather, they believed that the AML might be a useful shield against big business.[78] Not surprisingly, MITI's proposals were lost. Some commentators have claimed that this was a pivotal moment for competition policy in Japan because for the first time a majority had accepted some form of competition law (albeit the weakened 1953 AML).[79]

However, acceptance was at best tepid, and was arrived at more by default than conviction. There was no change to the manner in which the Japanese economy operated. For instance, the JFTC estimated that, by the late 1950s, there was barely an industry without a cartel.[80] In the 1960s, MITI's proposal to exempt investment cartels from the AML was accepted. By the simple practice of declaring all cartels that it favored to be investment cartels, MITI effectively rendered the AML irrelevant to the regulation of cartels.

The JFTC had no power to prevent the emasculation of the AML. It had few supporters, and those it had were no match for the so-called iron triangle of power—the business leaders (*zaikai*), the politicians, and the bureaucrats.[81] The JFTC's inability to oppose even the most egregious cartels (such as the newspaper cartel) meant that it lost the respect of even those who were potentially its supporters. JFTC's weakness was both cultural and structural. As the supposed champion of competition, it was at odds with the dominant practice of cooperation. Even assuming it had the inclination, the JFTC was not structurally ideal for the task; it lacked adequate administrative tools to enforce the AML.

4 Analyzing the forces that sidelined the AML

The AML was ineffective because it failed to win support from any significant sector of the community. Business was hostile from the beginning. Small and medium-sized businesses preferred protection to competition, and were linked in beneficial ways with big business through trade associations and *keiretsu* relationships. Labor supported government and business in return for security of employment and guaranteed promotion through seniority.

The governing Liberal Democratic Party (LDP) built its success on its pro-business policies. In turn, business was the main source of funding for the LDP.[82] Indeed, the peak organization for business (*keidanren*) acted as collector of business donations for the LDP.[83] This was important in a country where the costs of electoral politics were high.[84]

In implementing government policy, the bureaucracy—a powerful institution in the years immediately after the War—favored administrative guidance and industry cooperation. MITI pursued an industry policy that was irreconcilable with the original spirit of the AML. Business worked with the bureaucracy because it required government help (particularly in the early years) and because it was used to the bureaucratic system.[85]

Consumers, although apparently the big losers in a highly protected state, were not a vocal group and, in any event, generally supported government policies out of national loyalty[86] and because of Japan's phenomenal economic growth. For similar reasons, the media also remained quiescent. Even if it were inclined to challenge the prevailing regulatory norms, the JFTC was powerless to do so.

C 1973–89: weak acceptance of the AML

1 Background to the events of the 1970s

The largely uniform hostility to the AML that existed in Japanese society during the 1950s (the early years of growth) had already begun to dissolve during the 1960s. First, rising prices put political pressure on the LDP to do something. Thus, the 1960s witnessed the government for the first time referring economic matters to the JFTC. Second, although restricted mainly to professional circles (economists and lawyers), there was a growing recognition that some consumer protection measures were required.[87] Third, MITI developed a new industrial structure policy to meet the challenges of increasing trade liberalization. Although the policy continued to emphasize central planning, guidance, and a role for cartels, it did not treat competition policy in the dismissive manner of MITI's old policy.[88] Fourth, with greater prosperity, the tensions between big and small business grew. Small and medium-sized businesses perceived that the AML could provide some protection against abuse.[89]

2 JFTC's response to the oil crisis

In 1973, Japan, like the rest of the world, was hit by the oil crisis. Prices skyrocketed and growth stalled. As many businesses felt the cold wind of impending ruin, the Japanese bureaucracy and Japanese business reacted to the crisis by further restraining competition. However, when the oil companies collectively hiked oil prices, Japanese consumers and the Japanese press reacted with widespread hostility for the first time. With public opinion favoring some form of official sanction against the oil companies, the JFTC acted.

The JFTC initiated criminal proceedings against a number of oil companies and their executives for breaches of the AML. This was the first time criminal charges had been brought under the Act. The companies were charged with engaging in unlawful price cartels and unlawful production cartels. In their defense, the companies argued that they were not liable because their compact on prices and output was done under administrative guidance from MITI.[90] Output levels had been set by the companies at the request of MITI and then endorsed by MITI; MITI, however, denied that it had mandated specific prices. The case thus raised a critical question—what was the legal relationship between administrative guidance and legislative provisions?

In 1980, the Tokyo High Court found the oil companies not guilty in respect of fixing production levels. The production restriction cartel was unlawful—despite MITI's involvement, the output levels had been set by the companies and, consequently, this was not a case of administrative guidance,[91] but the element of intent was not established. There was reasonable doubt as to whether the oil companies were aware that, in acting on MITI's request, they were engaging in unlawful conduct.

The High Court, however, did find the companies guilty of engaging in price fixing. On appeal, the Supreme Court indicated by way of dictum that an otherwise unlawful cartel could be justified provided it was done in conformity with administrative guidance, and provided the administrative guidance was not counter to the public interest and was consistent with the overall purpose of the AML.

Thus, the relationship between administrative guidance and the AML remained somewhat opaque. Nevertheless, although its legal scope was still uncertain, it was clear that administrative guidance did not provide a complete shield to violations of the AML. Depending on the circumstances, firms engaging in conduct in breach of the AML could be criminally liable even though they maintained that they were carrying out government policy.[92] In the wake of the oil cartel case, MITI announced that in future it would work more closely with the JFTC. For its part, the JFTC released guidelines concerning the AML and administrative guidance.

3 1977 amendments to the AML

The cartel activity spawned by the oil crisis and the resulting groundswell of support for the AML prompted the JFTC to lobby for reform of the Act. Three years later (1977), significant amendments were made to the administrative provisions of the AML. The JFTC was given the power to impose civil penalties (referred to as a surcharge). Although the amount of the surcharge was inadequate when measured in terms of its deterrent value, the introduction of an administrative fine was an important step. The JFTC's other remedial powers were strengthened; for example, it was given power of divestiture.

The 1977 amendments were a significant event in the history of Japanese competition law and policy. They were enacted in the face of opposition from business, MITI, and large sections of the LDP. How did this happen? The public and press attacks on Japanese business triggered by the price hikes of the early 1970s temporarily silenced business. Public pressure also caused sections of the LDP to push for reform. As the economy stalled, the credibility of the LDP was on the line. At the same time, the Party endured a number of high-profile scandals. This provided a window of opportunity for those pushing for more competition enforcement. This push was significantly aided by the fact that Prime Minister Miki also favored reform.[93] The LDP introduced a reform bill, but internal divisions within the party ensured that it was constantly delayed. It was finally passed when the LDP suffered a rare electoral setback in 1977.[94]

4 Assessing the effect of the oil cartel cases and the 1977 amendments

The 1977 amendments and the decision in the oil cartel case were obviously important, but they did not lead to any long-term increase in formal activity by the JFTC. The reasons for this are illuminating. Although the 1977 amendments were passed by the Diet, business and the ministries, notably MITI, remained opposed. The JFTC was still a minnow in comparison with these two arms of the iron triangle. Therefore, while it could pursue an aggressive role in a popular case such as the oil cartel case, the JFTC could not take this approach on other occasions.[95] For example, when the JFTC tried to bring an action against certain construction companies for bid-rigging, it was forced to retreat in the face of hostility from the construction industry, the Ministry of Construction, and leading LDP politicians (concerned to protect a lucrative source of political funds).[96] To continue functioning, the JFTC had to comply with Japan's dominant regulatory norms, which still favored harmony, guidance, and cooperation.[97] Although independent, the JFTC had connections to the bureaucracy and tended to conform to bureaucratic norms.[98]

As a result, the JFTC adopted an informal approach to enforcing the AML. It relied on cooperation rather than a confrontational approach that stressed its remedial powers.[99] For this reason, it is somewhat misleading to rely solely on the number of formal actions initiated by the JFTC during this period to make judgments about the effectiveness of Japanese competition policy. For example, there is evidence that the JFTC's approach had a positive impact on the number of *keiretsu* relationships.[100] Competition policy (once completely ignored in the pursuit of industrial policy) now had some effect, although the effect should not be overstated—it still remained quite limited. The manner in which competition policy was administered remained very much in keeping with the dominant regulatory process of cooperation and persuasion.

D Post 1989: an uncertain future

1 External pressure

During the 1980s, Japan's trade balance with the US and Europe continued to grow rapidly in favor of Japan. US manufacturers and service providers claimed that the reason for the trade imbalance was that Japan sustained, directly and indirectly, significant barriers to imports. US complaints were taken seriously by MITI and by the LDP as they threatened to jeopardize the engine room of the Japanese economy. Business, on the other hand, was generally hostile to making any concessions.[101]

In 1989, the US forced Japan to enter into wide-ranging talks—the Structural Impediments Initiative (SII)—aimed at effecting structural changes to the Japanese economy to make it more open to foreign products. Of the six areas of US concern identified by SII, four involved competition policy: exclusive trade practices, distribution agreements, *keiretsu*, and pricing mechanisms. Among a raft of solutions, the US urged Japan to increase its competition enforcement, including an increase in JFTC investigators, greater use of remedial powers, publicity about enforcement activities (naming offenders), an increase in the surcharge, and an overhaul of the provisions relating to private damages.[102] Japanese policymakers were receptive to the idea of strengthening competition enforcement because they preferred that to managed trade.[103] MITI, in fact, took the lead for Japan in the SII talks.[104]

As a result of foreign pressure (*gaiatsu*), the AML was strengthened. The surcharge rate was lifted in 1991 to 6 percent of turnover in the relevant product.[105] The JFTC also increased its enforcement activity.[106] Private enforcement, on the other hand, remained virtually non-existent.[107]

Foreign pressure on Japan to open its markets and restructure its economy diminished as circumstances changed. First, as US producers achieved increased access, US interest waned. The trade lobby is invariably interested only in outcomes (increased market access). Competition policy can be employed to further that object but, once increased market access is achieved, competition policy is no longer needed. In fact, it often becomes an obstacle as the trader's preference moves to blocking access for others. As US interest waned, so did Japanese interest. For MITI and the other Japanese policymakers, the issue was always one of protecting trade, not competition.[108] Business, of course, remained hostile to *gaiatsu*. Second, the Japanese "bubble economy" burst in the early 1990s and was followed by years of economic stagnation (interrupted occasionally by periods of recession). While the Japanese economy performed poorly during the 1990s, the US economy boomed. This took further heat out of US efforts to force open Japanese markets.

Thus, while external pressure clearly had some influence on the application of competition policy in Japan, its effect should not be overstated. In particular, there is no reason to think that by itself external pressure would have permanently altered the shape of Japanese competition enforcement. Nevertheless, external influences (on both state and non-state actors) will continue to have some role to play. Globalization forces will continue to affect the preferences of Japanese businesses and administrators. Japanese administrators, for example, played a significant role in initiating debate on competition policy at the World Trade Organization.[109] The JFTC is an enthusiastic participant in the international competition network.[110]

2 Internal factors

As the economic slump continued into the second half of the 1990s, Japanese administrators came under strong internal pressure to protect ailing firms.[111] Competition policy—revived by *gaiatsu* in the early 1990s—was again marginalized[112] until resurrected as part of the reform packages implemented by the Koizumi government.[113] In 2005, the Koizumi government made significant amendments to the AML. The amount of the surcharge increased from 6 percent of turnover to 10 percent (and 15 percent for repeat offenders), and new criminal investigation powers were given to the JFTC.[114] At the same time, a leniency program was introduced and the JFTC's resources increased.[115] These amendments brought the AML and competition policy theoretically closer to their original intent. Whether the legislative changes are translated into greater competition enforcement remains to be seen.

3 A realignment of political economic forces?

The forces that shaped Japan in its development (high-growth) years have changed. Japan now has a significant number of globally successful firms. To remain internationally competitive, many of these firms have had to move their production offshore. The process of moving production offshore (called "hollowing out") has changed the relationships that underpinned Japan's industrial structure and, indirectly, its regulation. Japan's successful transnational enterprises no longer share the same interests as other sectors of Japanese society. They now have multinational concerns. For example, most of their labor force is no longer Japanese. The use of foreign labor does not fit the lifetime work ethic that united Japanese capital and labor during the 1950s and 1960s. Some *keiretsu* relationships have also come under strain as transnational enterprises source supplies on the basis of best price, not loyalty.[116]

While many of Japan's successful multinational firms no longer seek or require protectionism, this is not true of the rest of the economy. Much of the Japanese economy—the non-tradeables sector together with agriculture and many domestically traded products—still remains highly regulated, highly protected, and dependent on government support. Trade associations continue to be very powerful in most industries. Making changes that affect these entrenched interests will be very difficult, but possible. In 2005, the reformist Koizumi government managed, despite bitter hostility from large sections of the LDP, to push through a bill that commenced the privatization of Japan Post.

This diversification of the Japanese economy has had an effect on the power relationship between government and industry. MITI (now renamed the Ministry of Economy, Trade, and Industry) has lost much of its influence over the direction of Japan's industrial growth. It has lost control of Japan's multinational enterprises.[117] Its attempt to pick new export winners has not been a success. In a mature economy, it is probably no longer possible for MITI to play the planning, coordination, and facilitation role that it played in the 1950s and 1960s. Thus, MITI has seen its power base eroded by structural changes and by policy failures. Other ministries have suffered similar fates. The Ministry of Finance's reputation has been severely affected by its failure to solve Japan's financial ills and by a series of financial scandals. As industry policy faltered and the economic ministries were blamed, business has increased its power within the regulatory space.[118] However, business is no longer a unified force when it comes to competition policy. This combination of circumstances may yet see the JFTC assume a greater regulatory role.[119]

E Summing up—Japan

Japanese competition law was a US idea. It was originally intended to look and behave like an ideal version of US antitrust law. Japanese bureaucrats, however, were opposed to a competition law. Acting within the constraints imposed by their inferior bargaining position, they concentrated on changing certain administrative and remedial elements of the proposed law to better fit their conception of an appropriate regulatory process. This meant making the law less legalistic. Thus, when enacted, the AML was already something quite different to US antitrust law.

Immediately the Allied Powers left Japan, the AML was effectively discarded. Competition laws did not fit the Japanese context—government and business were united in their desire to make use of price and production cartels, the very activities that competition law prohibits. Although the AML was deeply and almost universally unpopular, it was never entirely removed from the statute books. Instead, substantial amendments were made in 1953 that enabled it to be ignored. Thus, the AML survived, although in a highly attenuated form. It owed its survival to the fact that it was largely irrelevant.

In the 1970s, the AML and the JFTC gave the first signs that they had some part to play in the economic regulation of Japan. The first criminal action was initiated. The AML was amended to make it stronger. However, this was no realignment in the political economy of Japan. The AML survived, but it lived on the periphery of the Japanese economy. The JFTC utilized techniques that were familiar to the Japanese bureaucracy and which fitted the mold of the Japanese administrative culture.

Competition enforcement was further renewed in the 1990s as a result of external pressure from the US. However, the renewal was weak. It dissipated in the late 1990s as external pressure eased and administrators inclined toward protectionism in the face of a non-performing economy.

The strengthening of the AML in 2005, coupled with an increase in resources for the JFTC, suggests some sort of shift toward a more market-driven system of regulation with the JFTC intervening to protect competition. Whether this is so or not will depend on the political economy of Japan. Japanese political economy is a contested arena. Scholars differ greatly over the historical and contemporary power and influence of the bureaucrats, the politicians, and business interests.

One story from postwar Japan has it that highly educated and largely independent bureaucrats created and orchestrated Japan's successful industry policy.[120] Business joined in this process because of the advantages that cooperation could bestow on them: government protection, subsidies, and a favorable regulatory environment.

This explanation is rejected by commentators who argue that the political economy of Japan is not so different from that of other capitalist democracies.[121] According to this view, Japanese economic policies resulted from political forces operating through a parliamentary democracy in response to electoral imperatives. In this process, the bureaucracy acted simply as the agent of the politicians.[122] Many of these critics also reject the notion that Japan's success was due to industry policy; in their opinion, Japan's economic success is attributable to orthodox market forces.[123]

A third perspective comes from those who emphasize the importance of the private sector and the role of self-regulation. These commentators reject the bureaucrat-dominated, development state theory because they believe it overstates the influence of the bureaucracy. They reject the revisionist view because they believe it overstates the role of parliamentary democracy. These critics tend to see Japanese regulatory development since World War Two in terms of an increasing devolution of regulatory power from the government and bureaucracy to the private sector.[124]

V Conclusion

Competition rules arrived in Australia and Japan by very different pathways. Whereas Australia borrowed US antitrust law, it was thrust upon Japan. In both cases, however, competition rules were soon marginalized in favor of an economic path that included the use of cartels to allocate resources and set prices. In Australia, this was facilitated by judicial conservatism. Business was able to communicate its preference for private ordering of markets (through the use of cartels and trading associations) without the need to remove the Act from the statute books and despite the presence of an attractive scheme of private enforcement.

The change in policy in Australia came from its economic isolation after World War Two. The economy was changing rapidly and the non-interventionist policies of the prewar years were viewed as inadequate by important elements within the policymaking community. Economists and lawyers, and eventually the economic and law ministries, were able to sell the idea of competition policy to business and the community so successfully that, by the end of the century, no one doubted the critical importance of stopping price and output cartels. Competition policy so successfully took over regulation of the Australian economy that the battle in the last few years has been for special interest groups (most notably small business) to regain some traction in the regulatory space.

In Japan, the bureaucracy took the lead in pushing back against foreign competition law. It did this because it wished to avoid a US-style legalistic regime based on the enforcement of fairly precise rules using court procedures. Japan's economic actors—the government, the bureaucracy, and business—were used to a quite different regulatory culture, one that emphasized regulation as a consultative process. In this regulatory space, state actors (in the main the bureaucracy) engaged with business representatives operating through well-developed networks (trade associations) to implement broad government policies. The emphasis was on contextual solutions. In this, there was little room for competition rules or for the courts.

As Japanese markets diversified and became far more complex, it was inevitable that the power balance between the relevant actors would shift. Despite a brief flirtation with the use of competition rules and court enforcement in the early 1970s and again in the early 1990s, the politicians and the public have generally been unwilling (or unable) to replace long-established regulatory norms. In the absence of a normative change, power has shifted to private actors (business). The modern economy is just too complex for the kind of state-led ordering that occurred in the 1950s.

The continuing failure of the Japanese economy to rise out of its slump may eventually trigger the kind of paradigm shift that would see Japan's industry policy give way to an invigorated competition policy. If this were to occur, business, rather than dealing with MITI, may find itself dealing with the JFTC and the courts. In that case, the AML will resemble something approaching its original design.

Notes

1 Mitsuo Matsushita, *International Trade and Competition Law in Japan*, Oxford: Oxford University Press, 1993, pp. 1–2.
2 See Matsushita, *supra*, note 1, p. 2.
3 Imelda Maher, 'Regulating Competition', in Christine Parker, Colin Scott, Nicola Lacey, and John Braithwaite, eds, *Regulating Law*, Oxford: Oxford University Press, 2004, pp. 195–97.
4 See Matsushita, *supra*, note 1, pp. 77–78.
5 See Article 46 of the *Havana Charter for an International Trade Organization* in United Nations Conference on Trade and Employment, *Final Act and Related Documents*, UN Doc E/CONF.2/78, 1948. The conditions for the entry into force of the Havana Charter, set forth in Article 103, were not fulfilled within the prescribed time limit. See American Bar Association, Sections of Antitrust Law and International Law and Practice, *Report on the Internationalization of Competition Law Rules: Coordination and Convergence*, 1999. See also John Braithwaite and Peter Drahos, *Global Business Regulation*, Cambridge: Cambridge University Press, 2000, p. 177.
6 See generally William E. Kovacic and Carl Shapiro, 'Antitrust Policy: A Century of Economic and Legal Thinking', *Journal of Economic Perspectives* 43, 2000.
7 Bruce G. Donald and John D. Heydon, *Trade Practices Law*, Sydney: Law Book Company, 1978, p. 5.
8 Criminal proceedings required authorization from the Attorney General.
9 Ray Steinwall, 'Tensions in the Development of Australian Competition Law', in Ray Steinwall, ed., *25 Years of Australian Competition Law*, Sydney: Butterworths, 2000, p. 10. Much of the drive for the Act came from Hugh McKay, Australia's largest manufacturer of farming equipment, who claimed that US manufacturers had pirated his designs and were dumping cheap imports in Australia.
10 D.J. Stalley, 'Federal Control of Monopoly in Australia', *University of Queensland Law Journal* 2, 2000, pp. 262–63.
11 Herbert Hovenkamp, *The Antitrust Enterprise: Principle and Execution*, Cambridge, MA: Harvard University Press, 2005, p. 41.

12 Hovenkamp, *supra*, note 11, pp. 39–42.

13 Hovenkamp, *supra*, note 11, p. 39.

14 The Act also included anti-dumping provisions.

15 NSW enacted similar legislation. See generally Stalley, *supra*, note 10.

16 Maher, *supra*, note 3, pp. 189–92.

17 *The Adelaide Steamship Company, Limited v. Attorney-General of the Commonwealth of Australia* (1912) 15 CLR 65 (High Court); *Attorney-General of the Commonwealth of Australia v. The Adelaide Steamship Company, Limited* (1914) 18 CLR 30 (Privy Council).

18 See *Nordenfelt v. Maxim Nordenfelt Guns & Ammunition Co* [1891–94] All ER 1; *Mogul Steamship Co. v. McGregor, Gow* [1892] AC 25.

19 Stalley, *supra*, note 10, p. 283.

20 J.E. Richardson, 'The 1965 Bill: The Legal Framework', in J.P. Nieuwenhuysen, ed., *Australian Trade Practices: Readings*, Melbourne: Cheshire, 1970.

21 Alex Hunter, 'Restrictive Practices and Monopolies in Australia', in Nieuwenhuysen, *supra*, note 20; J.P. Nieuwenhuysen, 'Recent Light on Trade Practices in Australia', in Nieuwenhuysen, *supra*, note 20; Neville Norman, 'Concentration Ratios and Trade Practices in Australia', in Nieuwenhuysen, *supra*, note 20.

22 Independent Committee of Inquiry into National Competition Policy (Hilmer Committee) AGPS, 1993, p. 9.

23 J. Hutton and J.P. Nieuwenhuysen, 'The Tribunal and Australian Economic Policy', in Nieuwenhuysen, *supra*, note 20.

24 See Maureen Brunt, 'Legislation in Search of an Objective', in Nieuwenhuysen, *supra*, note 20, p. 240.

25 Hutton and Nieuwenhuysen, *supra*, note 23, p. 266.

26 Hutton and Nieuwenhuysen, *supra*, note 23, p. 266.

27 See Stalley, *supra*, note 10, p. 288.

28 In 2007, Richard Pratt, a leading businessman and philanthropist, was unanimously condemned by the media for the price-fixing activities of his Visy Group of companies.

29 See particularly the decisions in *Aluminium Company* (1945) 148 Fed. 2d. 416 and *American Tobacco Co. v. US* (1945) 328 US 781.

30 See, for example, Hunter, *supra*, note 21. See also Steinwall, *supra*, note 9, p. 16.

31 See Brunt, *supra*, note 24, p. 231. Also generally Richardson, *supra*, note 20.

32 Hunter, *supra*, note 21.

33 Brunt, *supra*, note 24, p. 235.

34 See Brunt, *supra*, note 24, p. 231, citing Sir Garfield Barwick, *Trade Practices in a Developing Economy*, G.L.Wood Memorial Lecture, 1963, p. 21.

35 Steinwall, *supra*, note 9, p. 17.

36 Alan Ransom and Warren Pengilley, *Restrictive Trade Practices: Judgments, Materials and Policy*, Sydney: Legal Books, 1985, pp. 340–41.

37 Nevertheless, by 1972, over 13,000 agreements had been registered. Most had not been examined. See Steinwall, *supra*, note 9, p. 19.

38 Brunt, *supra*, note 24, pp. 231–32.

39 Brunt, *supra*, note 24, p. 234.

40 Brunt, *supra*, note 24, p. 233. Of course, a case can be made that this was a legitimate administrative compromise. The dilemma facing the creators of a competition regime can be stated as follows: it is almost impossible for parliament to lay down precise competition rules to cover all situations (for the reason that it is inherent in the nature of restrictive trade practices that what is on one occasion anti-competitive may on another occasion be pro-competitive). Therefore, it makes sense to delegate broad powers to some authority handling day-to-day cases. On the other hand, to give the judiciary broad powers of interpretation is to make the judiciary, rather than parliament, the law-making authority. See Sir Garfield Barwick, *Administrative Features of*

Legislation on Restrictive Trade Practices, Robert Garran Memorial Oration, 1963. Those looking back at the Coal Vend case would understand this problem.

41 Pengilley, 1973, cited in Michael Blakeney, *Law and the Regulation of Market Behaviour*, Sydney: Legal Books, 1983, p. 3.

42 Some of the constitutional hurdles that had ensured the demise of the Australian Industries Preservation Act 1906 had been swept away by the High Court in *Strickland v. Rocla Concrete Pipes Ltd* (1971) 124 CLR 468.

43 Blakeney, *supra*, note 41, p. 4.

44 Blakeney, *supra*, note 41, p. 3.

45 Georgina Murray, *Capitalist Networks and Social Power in Australia and New Zealand*, Aldershot, Hampshire: Ashgate Publishing Co., 2006, ch. 6.

46 *Melway Publishing Pty Ltd v. Robert Hicks Pty Ltd* [2001] HCA 13; *Boral Besser Masonry Ltd v. ACCC* [2003] HCA 5; *Rural Press Ltd v. ACCC* [2003] HCA 75.

47 See Explanatory Memorandum accompanying the Trade Practices Revision Act 1986 (Cth). See also the Second Reading Speech of the Attorney General in respect of the Act.

48 Eleanor M. Hadley, *Antitrust in Japan*, Princeton: Princeton University Press 1970 p. 4.

49 See generally Hadley, *supra*, note 48, pp. 3–19. See also Hiroshi Iyori and Akinori Uesugi, *The Antimonopoly Laws and Policies of Japan*, New York: Federal Legal Publications, 1994, p. 12.

50 Hadley, *supra*, note 48, p. 4.

51 Hadley, *supra*, note 48, p. 8.

52 The Trade Association Law (TAL) was enacted in 1948. Under the TAL, trade associations were prohibited from engaging in a range of activities, including price fixing, and were required to obtain the approval of the Japan Fair Trade Commission (JFTC) before engaging in other activities. See Ulrike Schaede, *Cooperative Capitalism: Self Regulation, Trade Associations, and the Antimonopoly Law in Japan*, Oxford: Oxford University Press, 2000, pp. 76–78.

53 Responsibility for US antitrust law is actually divided between the independent Federal Trade Commission and the Antitrust Division of the Department of Justice.

54 Harry First, 'Antitrust in Japan: The Original Intent' *Pacific Rim Law and Policy Journal* 9, 2000, p. 1.

55 In fact, the provisions were more interventionist than US law.

56 It is possible to bring a damages claim under the general tort provisions of the Civil Code. The plaintiff must show negligence or intent to injure.

57 First, *supra*, note 54; Richard Schwindt and Devin McDaniels, 'Competition Policy, Capacity Building, and Selective Adaptation: Lessons from Japan's Experience', *Washington University Global Studies Law Review* 7, 2008, p. 35.

58 See J.M. Ramseyer, 'The Costs of the Consensual Myth: Japanese Antitrust Enforcement and Institutional Barriers to Litigation in Japan', *Yale Law Journal* 94, 1985, p. 604, arguing that the Japanese reluctance to sue is not solely the result of a non-litigious culture. Rather, important institutional barriers deter all but the most intrepid plaintiff.

59 Akinori Uesugi, 'Recent Developments in Japanese Competition Policy—Prospect and Reality', Speech delivered to the International Antitrust Forum, American Bar Association, 24 January 2005.

60 Schaede, *supra*, note 52, p. 91.

61 Ibid., pp. 92–93.

62 Iyori and Uesugi, *supra*, note 49, Part I; Schaede, *supra*, note 52, pp. 69–96.

63 Hadley, *supra*, note 48, p. 11; Hiroshi Iyori, *Antimonopoly Legislation in Japan*, Federal Legal Publications, 1969, p. v.

64 Kenji Sanekata and Stephen Wilks, 'The Fair Trade Commission and the Enforcement of Competition Policy in Japan', in G. Bruce Doern and Stephen Wilks, eds, *Comparative Competition Policy: National Institutions in a Global Market*, Oxford: Clarendon Press, 1996.

65 See Matsushita, *supra*, note 1, p. 76.
66 Iyori and Uesugi, *supra*, note 49, p. 4.
67 Ibid., p. 5.
68 See Matsushita, *supra*, note on pp. 59–73.
69 Christopher A. Ford, 'The Indigenization of Constitutionalism in the Japanese Experience', *Case Western Reserve Journal of International Law* 28 (1), 1996, p. 51.
70 Iyori and Uesugi, *supra*, note 49, p. 15.
71 Hadley, *supra*, note 48, p. 12.
72 See Tetsuji Okazaki, 'Government–Firm Relationship in Postwar Japan: Success and Failure of the Bureau-Pluralism', Discussion paper, April 2000. Available from http://www.e.u-tokyo.ac.jp/cirje/research/dp/2000/2000cf69.pdf (accessed 25 March 2008).
73 See Matsushita, *supra*, note 1, p. 69.
74 Schaede, *supra*, note 52, p. 79.
75 Kenji Suzuki, *Competition Law Reform in Britain and Japan: Competitive Analysis of Policy Networks*, London: Routledge, 2002, p. 22.
76 Schaede, *supra*, note 52, pp. 93–97.
77 Suzuki, *supra*, note 75, p. 22.
78 Iyori and Uesugi, *supra*, note 49, p. 35.
79 Ibid., p. 36.
80 Schaede, *supra*, note 52, p. 90.
81 Ibid.
82 The LDP derived around 60 percent of its funds from donations by business. See Suzuki, *supra*, note 75, p. 69.
83 Ibid.
84 Ibid.
85 There was a strong "near institutional" personal network between business and the bureaucrats. Ibid., pp.72–73.
86 Steven K. Vogel, 'Can Japan Disengage? Winners and Losers in Japan's Political Economy, and the Ties that Bind Them', *Social Science Japan Journal* 2 (3), 1999, p. 6.
87 Iyori and Uesugi, *supra*, note 49, p. 43.
88 Ibid., p. 44.
89 See Matsushita, *supra*, note 1, p. 82.
90 Schaede, *supra*, note 52, pp. 97–100; Iyori and Uesugi, *supra*, note 49, pp. 250–53; See Matsushita, *supra*, note 1, p. 147.
91 See Matsushita, *supra*, note 1, p. 147.
92 Schaede, *supra*, note 52, p. 100.
93 Suzuki, *supra*, note 75, p. 44.
94 Ibid., pp. 24–26.
95 John O. Haley, 'Antitrust Sanctions and Remedies: A Comparative Study of German and Japanese Law', *Washington Law Review* 59, 1984, p. 486. In addition, the interventionist chairman of the JFTC, Takahashi, was succeeded by a more conservative figure in Chairman Sawada. See Michael L. Beeman, *Public Policy and Economic Competition in Japan*, London: Routledge, 2002, p. 62.
96 Sanekata and Wilks, *supra*, note 64, pp. 112–13; Frank K. Upham, 'Privatized Regulation: Japanese Regulatory Style in Comparative and International Perspective', *Fordham International Law Journal* 20, 1996, p. 440.
97 Sanekata and Wilks, *supra*, note 64, p. 104.
98 G. Bruce Doern and Stephen Wilks, 'Conclusions: International Convergence and National Contrasts', in G. Bruce Doern and Stephen Wilks, eds, *Comparative Competition Policy: National Institutions in a Global Market*, Oxford: Clarendon Press, 1996, p. 327.
99 Iyori and Uesugi, *supra*, note 49, p. 56.
100 Ibid., pp. 58–59.
101 Suzuki, *supra*, note 75, p. 103.

102 Iyori and Uesugi, *supra*, note 49, p. 62. The Final Report of SII was delivered in 1991.
103 Sanekata and Wilks, *supra*, note 64, p. 9.
104 Suzuki, *supra*, note 75, p. 120.
105 Harry First, 'Antitrust Enforcement in Japan', *Antitrust Law Journal* 64, 1996, pp. 158–59.
106 First, *supra*, note 105. First estimated that, in 1991 and 1992, the JFTC's enforcement activity was only slightly less than that by US agencies. This, however, may overstate the situation. See Suzuki, *supra*, note 75, pp. 128–29.
107 First, *supra*, note, p. 161. The US, of course, relies considerably on private actions.
108 Suzuki, *supra*, note 75, p. 117.
109 See Eleanor Fox, 'Competition Law', in Andreas F. Lowenfeld, ed., *International Economic Law*, Oxford: Oxford University Press, 2002, pp. 379–83.
110 Japan hosted the Seventh Annual Conference of the International Competition Network in April 2008.
111 Suzuki, *supra*, note 75, p. 165.
112 Ibid., p. 165.
113 In 2005, the Koizumi government, despite bitter hostility from large sections of the LDP, pushed through a bill that commenced the privatization of Japan Post. This was a direct attack on the old Japan.
114 See Sadaaki Suwazonon, 'The Features of the Newly Revised Anti-Monopoly Act – Japan's Experience of Making Competition Policy Stronger', Paper delivered to APEC Competition Policy Deregulation Group at Jeju, Korea, 24 May 2005.
115 See Akinori Uesugi, 'A Leniency Program A La Japonnaise – How is it going to be Enforced?', Speech delivered to Fifth Annual Fall Forum, Section of Antitrust Law, American Bar Association, 16 November 2005.
116 Ulrike Schaede, 'Globalization and the Japanese Subcontractor System', in David Bailey, Dan Coffey, and Philip Tomlinson, eds, *Crisis or Recovery in Japan*, Cheltenham: Edward Elgar, 2007.
117 Keith Cowling and Philip Tomlinson, 'Transnational Monopoly Capitalism, the J-mode Firm and Industrial "Hollowing Out" in Japan', in Bailey, Coffey, and Tomlinson, *supra*, note 116.
118 Suzuki, *supra*, note 75.
119 See Beeman, *supra*, note 95, arguing that the role of the JFTC has already increased significantly.
120 Chalmers Johnson, *MITI and the Japanese Miracle*, Stanford: Stanford University Press, 1982.
121 See, for example, Dick Beason and Dennis Patterson, *The Japan That Never Was*, Albany: State University of New York Press, 2004.
122 Beason and Patterson, *supra*, note 121.
123 Beason and Patterson, *supra*, note 121. For the view that Japan's growth depended largely on competition, see Michael E. Porter and Mariko Sakakibara, 'Competition in Japan', *Journal of Economic Perspectives* 18, 2004, p. 27. For an analysis of the literature on the causes of Japan's growth, see David Coates, 'The Rise and Fall of Japan as a Model of "Progressive Capitalism"', in Bailey, Coffey, and Tomlinson, *supra*, note 116.
124 Upham, *supra*, note 96; Schaede, *supra*, note 52.

6 Resistance, revision, and retrenchment in the transition to a competitive market economy in China

Randall Peerenboom

China has generally benefited from globalization, particularly in the economic area, and Chinese citizens know it. For years, China has been one of the largest recipients of foreign direct investment in the world. Much of its growth has been driven by exports and imported technology. Also, it has benefited from an international economic order that has created peaceful mechanisms for avoiding trade wars, and from a global order that has allowed it to develop peacefully, despite fears that a rising China could pose a military threat to the existing world order. Little wonder then that, in a poll of eighteen countries, 87 percent of Chinese respondents maintained that "globalization is mostly good." This was the highest proportion in the survey, and contrasts sharply with the 41 percent in Russia and 54 percent in India who also viewed international trade favorably.[1]

China, for its part, has been one of the most open developing countries. The general trend since economic reforms began in 1978 has been toward greater openness and a more competitive market economy.

However, China never blindly followed the principles of the Washington Consensus, particularly with respect to the relationship between the domestic and the international economy. Rather, it has acted in many ways like other successful East Asian developmental states.

Moreover, Chinese government officials and citizens are now much more acutely aware of the many practices adopted by rich countries to pursue their own national economic interests and to protect their own domestic companies. As a result, there are now signs of a retrenchment in China, including a greater emphasis on industrial policy, the development of a regulatory regime to review the impact of foreign investment projects on national economic and security interests, the reliance on anti-dumping and other measures to protect domestic industries, and, perhaps, the beginning of a more assertive stance in World Trade Organization (WTO) disputes.

Part I of this chapter provides an overview of China's economic policies, highlighting the differences between Beijing's development strategy and the Washington Consensus; the recent policy shift away from a myopic focus on aggregate growth to greater concern for sustainable development, social justice, and the creation of a harmonious society; and the increase in protectionism.

Part II takes a closer look at various areas in which there has been resistance to economic globalization, or signs of retrenchment, including WTO compliance, intellectual property rights (IPR) enforcement, merger and acquisition (M&A) regulation, anti-monopoly law, labor law, and dispute resolution patterns in securities, bankruptcy, and anti-dumping.

Part III concludes with an explanation of why the pushback on economic globalization has occurred, and why, nevertheless, the general trend is still toward greater openness and an increasingly competitive market economy.

I An overview of development strategies and the commercial regulatory framework

Pragmatic approach to reforms and modification of the Washington Consensus

China's policymakers have adopted a pragmatic approach to reforms, adopting some aspects of the Washington Consensus (WC) and rejecting or modifying others.[2] In particular, they have adopted most of the basic macroeconomic principles of the WC for the domestic economy. The government generally followed the WC with respect to fiscal discipline. It has managed inflation reasonably well, despite brief periods of high inflation, and increased the authority and capacity of the People's Bank of China (PBOC) as the central bank to manage macroeconomic policy. It has carried out significant reforms to the tax system and broadened the tax base, with collection rates rising from 11 percent of gross domestic product (GDP) in 1995 to 20 percent in 2004. And it has built up large surpluses of foreign exchange, which has allowed it to pump money into the economy at the first signs of a slowdown and to bail out banks burdened with non-performing loans.

However, China's policymakers resisted the neoliberal aspects of the WC that would greatly reduce the role of the state in reducing poverty. On the whole, China has done reasonably well in addressing poverty, meeting basic health needs, increasing longevity rates, and ensuring that most of its population is literate. Since reforms began in 1978, 150–400 million people have been lifted out of poverty, depending on how poverty is measured. From 1978 to 2001, the real income per capita increased more than five times for rural residents and four times for urban residents. And from 1975 to 2002, China posted a 55 percent improvement in the Human Development Index, which measures life expectancy, adult literacy, school enrolments, and standard of living.

The government also modified the prescribed WC relationship between the domestic and global economy by gradually exposing the domestic economy to international competition while offering some protection to key sectors and some support to infant industries. Accordingly, the government resisted the WC prescription to rapidly privatize and deregulate. The government has sold off most small and medium-sized state-owned enterprises (SOEs) as well as some large ones, and allowed investors to obtain a minority share in others. However, it did so over time, and still controls the majority shares of many large SOEs. On the controversial issue of industrial policy, China has allowed limited competition in key sectors such as telecommunication, insurance, and banking, although the government still controls or supports key sectors directly or indirectly.

Despite various restrictions on foreign investment, China has been remarkably open for a developing country. China's average tariff rate of 10 percent is much lower than that of Argentina (32 percent), Brazil (31 percent), India (50 percent), and Indonesia (37 percent). Its ratio of imports to GDP is almost 35 percent, compared with 9 percent for Japan.[3] China has also been more open, and relied more heavily on foreign direct investment, than South Korea, Japan, or Taiwan. In 2003, the ratio of the stock of foreign investment to GDP was 35 percent in China, compared with 8 percent in Korea, 5 percent in India, and 2 percent in Japan.[4]

Over time, there have been new forms of investment, including various ways of participating in China's debt and equity markets, such as through Qualified Foreign Investment Institutions and renminbi (RMB)-denominated corporate debt issued in Hong Kong, and new types of business entities, including partnerships, franchises, and branch offices.

The government has also taken other steps to create a more investment-friendly environment. The approval and licensing system has been overhauled as a result of State Council-initiated reforms and the passage of the Licensing Law, although most projects still require numerous licenses. The Legislation Law, China's WTO accession agreement, and other regulations have led to increased public participation in the processes of making, interpreting, and implementing laws and regulations. There has been an increase in the number of public hearings and opportunities for public comment prior to the passage of key laws and regulations, a trend that will be further strengthened with the passage of the Administrative Procedure Law, currently being drafted.

These reforms are reflected in empirical surveys. China ranked thirty-fourth out of 131 countries in the 2008–9 World Economic Forum's Global Competitiveness Index,[5] and fifty-seventh out of 127 countries on the Business Competitiveness Index. In 2008, the World Bank ranked China ninety-second out of 178 countries for doing business overall.[6] Reflecting the considerable investment in institution-building, China now outperforms the average in its income class on the World Bank's indexes for government effectiveness, regulatory quality, and rule of law.[7]

To be sure, many problems remain, as these rankings indicate. Security markets are dominated by firms in which the state continues to hold a majority share, which has hampered the development of corporate governance and a legal regime to protect minority rights.[8] Starting a business is time consuming and difficult, with numerous approvals and licenses required. Despite some improvements, including a recently passed public information act, transparency of government policymaking remains an issue.[9] Corruption also continues to be a problem, with China only slightly outperforming the average in its income class in 2006.[10] There are also continued concerns about excessive bureaucracy, poorly drafted and inconsistently implemented regulations, intellectual property violations, and human resources constraints, including a shortage of managerial level professionals and growing labor costs.[11]

Foreign investors have relied mainly on lobbying to address these issues, arguing generally that reforms are in China's own national interests (although administrative litigation and other mechanisms also provide disgruntled parties with avenues for challenging government acts).[12] Lobbying by the business community is frequently combined with bilateral and multilateral pressure. However, the two processes are not always in lock-step, as when the US Congress publicly reprimanded the American Chamber of Commerce for opposing labor-friendly provisions of the 2007 Labor Contract Law.[13]

In some cases, foreign businesses joined forces with domestic businesses when their interests coincided. Thus there have been joint efforts, for example to promote intellectual property protection and establish standards in consumer products.[14] In general, both foreign and domestic businesses also have an interest in institutional reforms that fall under the umbrella of the promotion of rule of law and good governance, although in some cases domestic businesses may benefit from close relationships with the authorities.[15] Interests collide most directly, however, when domestic industries face increased competition from foreign companies.

From aggregate growth to sustainable growth and a harmonious society

The Deng–Jiang focus on aggregate economic growth led to rising inequality and severe environmental degradation. While pumping money into infrastructure development needed to support rapid growth, the government was ignoring other pressing social needs. The government's public spending on education and health as a percentage of GDP had been among the lowest in East Asia. The reduced spending, combined with a turn toward market forces in education and health, and the lack of a sound welfare system had exacerbated the plight of the most vulnerable members of society and heightened social tensions.

With greater rights consciousness and higher expectations, Chinese citizens were turning to the courts, government agencies, and Party organs to address their needs. When those channels proved inadequate, they took to the streets in increasing numbers. There were 538,941 multiparty suits in 2004, up 9.5 percent from 2003.[16] The number of petitions to government entities rose dramatically until 1999, before starting to decline. Even with the decline, in 2005, the letters and visits offices received a total of 12.7 million complaints.[17] According to one survey, 63.4 percent of those who eventually brought their complaints to the central authorities in Beijing had first sought resolution in the courts.[18]

The number of mass protests and large-scale demonstrations also rose rapidly, from 58,000 in 2003 to 74,000 in 2004, and 85,000 in 2005. According to the state media, over 1,800 police were injured and twenty-three killed during protests in the first nine months of 2005 alone.

The government viewed these protests as a threat to social stability, and thus a threat to sustained economic growth. Much of the Chinese Communist Party (CCP)'s legitimacy is based on its ability to ensure social stability and improve people's living standards. Understandably, the Hu–Wen administration announced a major new policy initiative.[19]

The new policy shifted away from the Deng–Jiang focus on aggregate growth, emphasizing instead high-quality sustainable growth, social justice, and the need to create a harmonious society. The goal is now efficient resource use, environmentally friendly development, and "green GDP." The harmonious society platform also pays more attention to income inequality, with greater efforts to stimulate growth in less developed regions through reallocation of state assets and new incentive programs as part of the Go Inland Campaign, the Great Western Development Strategy, and the Revitalize the Northeast Campaign. In addition, the government has sought to address the plight of farmers by eliminating the agriculture tax. It has promised more affordable medical care in rural areas. And it has vowed once again to eliminate school fees that prevented children from poor families from attending public schools.

Industrial policy: retrenchment amidst a general long-term trend toward openness

China's policymakers are adjusting economic policies in light of an increasingly protectionist global economy, domestic pressures, a rising nationalism, and national development goals, although the general direction of reforms remains unchanged. Signs of retrenchment include new restrictions on automobile manufacturers to encourage local brands and stimulate domestic product development; restrictions on foreign banks' expansion of retail branches; limits on large-scale retail outlets; telecommunication rules that make it difficult for foreign companies to control Internet content providers established in China through an offshore vehicle; the push to establish unions in foreign invested enterprises; and the refusal to cave in to foreign pressure to revalue the RMB significantly.

Adding fuel to the fire, in 2006, the State Council announced that seven industries were to remain under "absolute" state control: armaments, electricity, oil, telecommunications, coal, civil aviation, and shipping. In addition, several others would remain under "relatively strong" state control, including manufacturing, automobiles, electronics, architecture, steel, metallurgy, chemicals, surveillance, science, and technology. The objective was to produce thirty to fifty globally competitive enterprise groups.

In addition, the government is developing a system similar to that in the US to investigate the impact of economic transactions on national security, and to investigate and retaliate against trade barriers in other countries.[20] The Ministry of Commerce (MOFCOM) now also prepares annual reports that assess the openness of foreign markets and set out China's concerns about unfair trade practices.

The American Chamber of Commerce in China (AmCham) struck a cautious note regarding the prospects for foreign investors in its 2007 report:

> AmCham expects more focus on developing internal demand and promoting domestic industry. China is already emphasizing development in poorer inland and old rust-belt regions (e.g. central and northeast China). China will also seek "high quality" foreign direct investment (FDI), rather than welcoming all investment. Preferential treatment for foreign-invested companies, such as preferential taxation for foreign-invested enterprises (FIE), will be eliminated. There will also be more laws aimed at protecting Chinese

companies and consumers, such as those for fair trade and antimonopoly, and enforcement of unionization laws with respect to foreign companies. As China tries to move up the value-added chain, there will be measures to encourage innovation …

Yet not all is bad news for free-traders and foreign investors. On 31 October 2007, the National Development and Reform Commission and the Ministry of Commerce jointly promulgated the new Foreign Investment Industrial Guidance Catalogue (2007 Amendment). On the whole, the new catalogue reflects the long-term trend toward greater openness. The new catalogue relaxes restrictions on foreign investments in commercial services, finance, and various forms of manufacturing in accordance with China's WTO commitments. There is also a clear emphasis on encouraging green manufacturing and other energy-efficient, environmentally friendly businesses.

Some industries did not get the relief they were hoping for, and a few are subject to more restrictions, including real estate. The enhanced restrictions in real estate reflect the government's efforts to cool speculation. In addition to tightening regulatory control, the government has raised interest rates repeatedly, and imposed taxes on the transfer of land and housing within five years of purchase. Foreign nationals must also be resident in China for more than one year to purchase a house, and may only buy one.

The new guidelines also make it clear that the government intends to maintain tight control over publishing, media, and the Internet, although the motivation is primarily political stability rather than economic protectionism.

In short, as throughout the entire reform period, the government continues to adopt a gradualist approach, driven by pragmatic experimentalism rather than neoliberalism or any other clearly defined economic ideology.

II Sectoral analysis of resistance and retrenchment

WTO compliance and IPR enforcement

China has by and large lived up to its WTO commitments. It has revised its laws to make them consistent with the principle of national treatment in most areas. It has reduced tariffs and quotas as required. It has increased market access in key industries such as banking, insurance, and financial services. Although not all of these changes were completed exactly in accordance with the stipulated time schedule, some delays are to be expected given the enormity of the task and the size of China. In September 2006, Pascal Lamy, the WTO's Director General, gave China an "A+" for fulfilling its WTO undertakings.[21]

Nevertheless, there are still concerns. China has not always issued implementing regulations needed to clarify essential operational issues. It has also passed regulations opening certain sectors such as telecommunications and construction, but then imposed high registered capital or eligibility requirements or imposed other non-tariff barriers.[22]

In terms of institutional development, there is as yet no central repository for all trade-related legislation. Although foreign parties are now often given more opportunities to comment on laws and regulations, the practice has yet to be institutionalized, and detailed procedures are still lacking. Meanwhile, central–local conflicts, regional protectionism, interagency conflicts, and weak institutions continue to complicate policymaking and hinder implementation.

There has been some progress with respect to the protection of intellectual property rights as a result of high-profile campaigns to crack down on counterfeiting, greater reliance on criminal prosecutions, and institutional changes, including the establishment of complaint centers for reporting intellectual property violations in fifty cities. Among foreign investors who cited intellectual property protection as a major problem, 44 percent agreed that there was overall improvement in the last two years, with 51 percent citing improvement in public security enforcement, and 43 percent noting improvement in customs enforcement.[23]

Nevertheless, enforcement is still weak. Counterfeiters are willing to take the risk, viewing the confiscation of goods and fines should they be caught as just part of doing business. Noting that counterfeiters generally violate several laws at once, AmCham has pressed the Chinese authorities to adopt the US practice of combining several charges into a single proceeding to increase the total fine. AmCham has also pushed for lower thresholds and evidentiary requirements for criminal prosecution.

However, higher fines and more criminal prosecutions are unlikely to be a sufficient deterrent given the systematic obstacles to more rigorous enforcement. As is now widely recognized, enforcement problems are largely due to difficulties in the political economy typical of developing countries. For instance, the inability of the central government to control local governments given an incentive structure that emphasizes economic growth and stability as key criteria for promotion, as well as various administrative obstacles, including organizational politics, institutional structures, administrative hierarchies, overlapping jurisdictions, and competing agency interests.[24]

Significant progress is likely to come when the overall benefits of greater protection to the political economy of China outweigh the costs. The experiences of other countries, including the US and European countries, as well as other successful East Asian states, would suggest that the tipping point is generally at a higher level of development than China's current GDP/capita of just over US$2,000.

On the other hand, intellectual property is increasingly important to China's domestic economy. Domestic companies now have intellectual property worth protecting. The overwhelming majority of patent applicants are Chinese parties, as are the overwhelming majority of parties seeking administrative or judicial remedies for IP violations. China is now one of the leading exporters of technological goods among developing countries.[25] And the government has realized that sustained economic growth requires innovation and a continuous climb up the value chain toward more high-tech manufacturing and services. In January 2006, for instance, the government announced The Guideline for Planning Mid- and Long-Term National Science and Technology Development.

Given the increasingly global nature of trade, China may be reaching the tipping point where the domestic political economy cost–benefit balance favors stronger protection of IP rights faster than other countries have. There now appears to be a ratcheting up of the efforts to address the administrative obstacles to enforcement. The State Intellectual Property Office (SIPO) has been working on a national IPR strategy since 2005 under the direction of the Leading Group for National IP Strategy Formulation, which represents more than twenty People's Republic of China (PRC) ministries and agencies. And in contrast to many other government reports, SIPO's 2007 work plan assigns responsibility for each task to a specific SIPO office.

Although China has generally complied with WTO requirements reasonably well and made some progress on IP enforcement, there are increasing signs that China is beginning to take a more aggressive and protectionist stance in other areas, including WTO dispute resolution. China's accession to the WTO was widely criticized domestically as the modern-day equivalent to the late nineteenth-century unequal treaties forced on China by foreign powers. China assumed a number of obligations that no other country had ever assumed, including the translation of all laws into an official WTO language; national treatment not just for goods but for foreign companies doing business in China; treatment of China as a non-market economy in anti-dumping cases; and a reduced standard for invoking surge protection mechanisms, with the safeguard measures allowed to continue longer than generally allowed, and China's rights to impose countervailing duties in case of violations limited. Many of these provisions run counter to the basic WTO commitment to "free trade." Adding insult to injury, the deal was also pushed through without much consultation with key industrial constituents. A certain amount of pushback is perhaps to be expected.

One sign of a tougher approach is China's unwillingness to provide detailed written responses to questions from other countries as part of the review process. Unlike other countries, China is subject to review of its trade policies every year for the first eight years, and then a final review no later than ten years after accession. China has bridled at the extensive list of queries and the time commitments required to respond to them.

More substantively, government agencies have adopted narrow interpretations of China's WTO obligations in some cases. For instance, the Ministry of Information (MII) adopted a restrictive interpretation of which value-added services (VAS) are to be liberalized, claiming that its obligations extend to only those services specifically identified in the WTO schedule of commitments. However, the rapid pace of technological change has rendered many of the listed services commercially unattractive, while new, more profitable areas are not open to foreign investors. The approval authorities have also approved only a limited number of VAS joint ventures, blocked access to the most sought-after services already provided by Chinese companies, placed some services in the more restrictive "basic service" category, and required foreign investors to meet vague qualification requirements such as having a "sound track record and operational experience."[26]

Perhaps even more worrisome for foreign companies is the creation of indigenous technical standards. In 2003, China announced that all wireless devices sold or imported into China were required to use WLAN Authentication and Privacy Infrastructure, a proprietary encryption standard for wireless communications. Although China backed down under pressure from the US in that case, future conflicts are looming regarding a wide range of indigenous technical standards for mobile TV, wireless Internet access, audio/video encoding, and EVD, an alternative to DVD technology.

While foreign companies see these as a barrier to trade, developing countries such as China argue that the mandatory adoption of international standards favors rich countries with the resources to spend on R&D, and involves considerable costs in terms of royalties and other payments.[27]

Furthermore, although foreign business associations tend to portray the issue as a battle between foreign and domestic companies, with the latter aided by government policies that are driving the process, the reality is more complicated. The old system in which the government took the lead in setting standards, where the process was meant to be open, cooperative, and conducive to the public good, has given way in the face of rapid technological change, increased market competition, and the high value of intellectual property rights in new technologies.[28] The standard-setting process is now driven by industry, rather than the government. Moreover, there may be competing domestic standards supported by different business alliances, with the alliances composed of a combination of foreign and domestic companies, including both SOEs and private companies.

Dispute settlement is another area where China may be adopting a more aggressive stance.[29] Immediately after accession, China was quick to settle any disputes. China settled the first case against it within three months, after the US contested a refund of value-added tax on integrated circuits to domestic companies. It then settled two disputes before they were taken to the WTO.

In the first, China announced in January 2004 that it would limit coke production because of pollution concerns, and reduce the coke export quota to ensure adequate supplies for domestic needs. The European Union (EU), which relies heavily on coke from China, threatened to bring a complaint to the WTO. In May 2004, China compromised, despite strong legal arguments supporting its policy, and reached an agreement with the EU that ensured EU countries would receive no less coke than in previous years.

The second dispute involved an anti-dumping claim of unbleached kraft linerboard against US companies. In September 2005, MOFCOM issued its determination, finding both dumping and injury. The US government asked MOFCOM to reverse its finding and amend its anti-dumping regulations to address a variety of procedural issues. When MOFCOM refused, the US notified China that it would take its complaint to the WTO the following week. That very same weekend, MOFCOM rescinded the decision on procedural grounds.[30]

In early 2006, the EU, US, and Canada challenged China's policy with regard to duties on auto parts. This time, despite a weak legal case, China did not fold during consultations. A panel was established in October 2006. The panel issued a preliminary report finding against China in early 2007, with a final report expected to follow later in the year. Whether China will appeal, thus buying more time for the domestic auto industry, remains to be seen.

In September 2007, China initiated a WTO complaint against the US regarding the levying of countervailing duties against imports of Chinese coated paper. Previously, the US had never applied countervailing duties to imports from non-market economies. As a result of the decision, the US now treats China as a non-market economy for anti-dumping purposes and a market economy for countervailing duty purposes.[31]

China may have no choice but to adopt a more aggressive position. The US raised three additional complaints against China in 2007 alone, plus another in early 2008. In February 2007, the US and Mexico challenged measures granting refunds, reductions, or exemptions from taxes to enterprises in China if they purchase domestic goods or meet export performance criteria.

In April, the US requested consultations with China concerning certain measures pertaining to the protection and enforcement of intellectual property rights in China. The US alleged that: (i) the thresholds that must be met in order for certain acts of trademark counterfeiting and copyright piracy to be subject to criminal prosecution are too high; (ii) confiscated goods should not be released into the market following removal of their infringing features; (iii) the scope of coverage of criminal procedures and penalties for unauthorized reproduction or unauthorized distribution of copyrighted works should be expanded; and (iv) China should provide copyright protection to creative works, sound recordings, and performances that have not been authorized for publication or distribution within China.

In the same month, the US challenged measures that gave designated SOEs the right to import films, audiovisual home entertainment products, and publications, while imposing market access restrictions or discriminatory limitations on foreign companies.

In March 2008, the US and EU challenged 2006 rules that gave Xinhua control over foreign financial business news providers.

Some of the issues raised are in accordance with China's own development goals, and thus more readily resolvable. For instance, China has long contemplated eliminating preferential tax treatment to encourage exports, many of which go to foreign invested enterprises, including US companies established in China. Thus it is not surprising that China moved quickly to resolve that dispute by eliminating the subsidies. Similarly, it may be willing to move more aggressively to protect IP rights, including lower thresholds for criminal punishment. And the 2006 financial information rules were never enforced to begin with.

But some of the complaints directly challenge China's industrial policies and the role of the state in promoting or subsidizing certain companies or sectors. Others, such as those involving the distribution of audiovisual products, raise concerns about China's ability to restrict unwanted cultural influences and to maintain control over information deemed politically sensitive.[32] These complaints raise the controversial issue of how much policymaking space is to be left to sovereign states, particularly developing ones.

Chinese trade officials have responded with tougher talk, vowing that China will defend its interests by fighting cases to the bitter end and initiating WTO dispute settlement procedures where necessary. In June 2006, for example, Chinese Commerce Minister Bo Xilai stated that China has the right to use the WTO dispute settlement system and would not hesitate to resort to the system when needed.[33] In April 2007, then Vice-Premier Wu Yi stated that "the Chinese government is extremely dissatisfied about [the US intellectual property complaints]" and "will proactively respond according to the related WTO rules and see it through to the end."[34]

Mergers and acquisitions

Acquisition of Chinese companies has become an important market entry and growth strategy for foreign companies. By some estimates, foreign company acquisition of Chinese companies amounted to US$20 billion in 2006, or one-third of all FDI.[35] The regulatory structure for M&A, which has developed in a piecemeal fashion over the years, was complicated, fragmented, and conflicting. In August 2006, new M&A regulations were issued in an attempt to bring some coherence to the area.

The new regulations sought to address two substantive concerns. The first was that many domestic investors were establishing companies offshore, transferring cash and other assets from China into the company, and then using the cash and assets to establish FIEs in China in order to obtain the preferential tax treatment afforded FIEs. The offshore company is listed or sold to foreign investors, bypassing the approval process in China that would be required if the foreign investor acquired the FIE itself. The government has attempted to subject these offshore M&A deals to regulatory control.

The second concern addressed is the growing nationalist concern that foreign companies are acquiring too many important Chinese companies in key sectors.

Foreign investors have praised the new regulations for establishing a unified, simple, and relatively transparent regulatory environment for foreign acquisition transactions. However, AmCham also "noted with regret" the following:[36]

[T]he M&A Regulations establish significant new barriers to foreign M&A activity that directly discriminate against foreign companies in normal acquisition transactions. These new discriminatory barriers include:

1. Special restrictions on foreign M&A activity in unspecified "key industries" or on acquisitions of leading Chinese companies without listing such industries and companies or providing criteria for their identification

2. Special restrictions on acquisition transactions on the vague and unspecified grounds of "possibly imposing a material impact on the economic security of the State"

3. Special review procedures for the acquisition of companies that have "well-known trademarks or Chinese historical brands" without providing a list of such brands

4. The added power of MOFCOM to review and approve any foreign acquisition transaction or to reverse such a transaction at its own discretion and without right of appeal

5. Anti-monopoly review of acquisitions by foreign companies that have extensive operations in China or that would gain more than 25 percent market share as a result of an acquisition or that meet a number of other threshold criteria in terms of the size of their operations or their market positions

6. The ability of "domestic competitors, relevant authorities, or industry associations" to petition MOFCOM and SAIC [State Administration of Industry and Commerce] for an anti-monopoly examination of an acquisition transaction, even in cases in which the acquisition and the acquiring company do not meet the thresholds for such an examination.

Anti-Monopoly Law

The Anti-Monopoly Law (AML) was a long time in the making: more than thirteen years. The drafting process involved several drafts and extensive comments and suggestions from international donor agencies such as the World Bank and Asian Development Bank, trade representatives from various countries, academics both foreign and Chinese, antitrust lawyers, and industry groups.

The passage of the AML has given rise to numerous concerns. Most fundamentally, Mark Williams has argued that an essential precondition for the successful implementation of a competition law is an ideological commitment to a market economy. He claims that such a commitment is lacking, pointing to continued government intervention in the market, numerous policies that favor SOEs, and the existence of administrative monopolies in key sectors. He concludes that the adoption of an anti-monopoly law at this stage of development is inappropriate and may actually impede the development of a market economy, as the law may be "selectively or mendaciously employed as a trade weapon to protect domestic markets or domestic producers" by those in authority who see competition law "as part of an overarching industrial policy to promote national champions by mercantilist means."[37]

The concern that law will be used against foreign companies for protectionist purposes is a common one. Domestic companies and foreign companies are subject to the same rules. However, foreign company mergers and acquisitions of a Chinese company may also be subject to a national security review. The bigger worry is that foreign and domestic companies will be treated differently, despite similar rules.

Fueling that concern, the AML appears to exempt SOEs in key industries, although it is possible that the AML could be interpreted as applying to such companies. Article 7 provides that the state shall protect the legitimate business activities of undertakings in "industries that are dominated by the state-owned economy and that have a direct bearing on national economic wellbeing and national security, as well as industries that conduct exclusive and monopolistic sales in accordance with law." The state will supervise such firms, adjusting and controlling their business operations and the prices of their products and services in order to safeguard the legitimate interests of consumers and promote technological progress.

Another concern has been administrative abuse of power. Abuse comes in two forms. The first refers to national-level administrative monopolies. The second refers to regional protectionism, where local governments have set up barriers to trade. Article 8 provides that administrative agencies and organizations shall not abuse their administrative powers to eliminate or restrict competition. Article 32 adds that administrative agencies and organizations shall not abuse their administrative powers to mandate any entities or persons to operate, buy, or use only the products supplied by the undertakings designated by them. However, this is subject to the limitations of Article 7 for key industries.

Articles 33–35 expressly prohibit administrative agencies or organizations from using their administrative powers to impede the free flow of products across regions, specifically banning a number of the most common means used by local governments to protect their own companies, including the imposition of additional licensing requirements and higher technical requirements, and the erection of checkpoints to keep out products from other regions, or failing to publish requirements.

However, the enforcement provisions are weak. According to Article 51, the superior agency shall order an agency that abuses its power to correct its errant ways, and responsible persons shall be subject to disciplinary sanctions "in accordance with law." The Anti-Monopoly Enforcement Authority is only given the power to make proposals to the relevant superior agency about the problems, remedies, and discipline.

It is much too early to tell how the law, effective from 1 August 2008, will be implemented. Much depends on how the law is interpreted, and the status of the Anti-Monopoly Committee and the Anti-Monopoly Enforcement Authority.[38] Implementing rules are now being discussed that will help to clarify some of the key provisions.

While the final law reflects the input from foreign advisors, it also clearly reflects China's own circumstances. Most notably, it covers both private and public abuses of power.[39] At the same time, the provisions for controlling administrative monopolies were considerably weakened in the final law compared with earlier drafts, reflecting the compromise needed to have the law passed. The failure to specify the administrative rank of the Committee and Enforcement Authority also suggests that turf battles between MOFCOM, the National Development and Reform Commission, SAIC, and industrial ministries are far from over.

More generally, the enforcement of the AML will inevitably require tough choices regarding conflicting policy goals of economic efficiency, consumer welfare, and the protection of small and medium-sized businesses, as in other countries. In addition, China will have to reconcile the desire for growth with the desire to protect infant industries and maintain social stability by safeguarding weaker SOEs.

Labor law

In recent years, China has passed a number of laws to clarify and enhance the rights of workers, including the Trade Union Law, the Employment Promotion

Law, and the Labor Contract Law. The laws are the result of a conflux of forces, including rampant labor abuses, international and domestic pressure to increase labor protections, lobbying by labor non-governmental organizations (NGOs) and organizations, the arguments of new left intellectuals, and the government's desire to create a harmonious society. At the same time, the drafters had to contend with opposition from domestic and foreign companies, and arguments from the new right that many of the proposed reforms, while motivated by good intentions to help workers, would actually hurt them, impede growth, and make China less competitive in the world marketplace. Political concerns about the role of unions in destabilizing regimes also influenced the outcome. The result has been a compromise where no faction obtained all it wanted.

The Labor Contract Law, effective from 1 January 2008, reflects these compromises. The law was initially drafted by labor organizations and then made publicly available for comments. A second draft was also circulated for comments before the final law was issued. During the process, the rights of laborers were increasingly pared down, particularly with respect to the role of unions.

The first public draft for comments provided unions (or worker representatives if the company did not have a union) with remarkable powers, giving them the right to approve all company regulations and policies that were directly related to the vital interests of employees. If a company decided a matter without first obtaining union approval, the employer's decision would be invalid, and the matter would be handled as proposed by the trade union. This represented a radical departure from the status quo, where unions are given the right to be consulted and offer an opinion, which can then be ignored at will by the employer.

Foreign business associations vehemently objected to this provision.[40] The final law drastically cut back the powers of unions, returning to the status quo, which essentially leaves it up to individual employers how seriously they will take union opinions in termination cases or on other matters that affect employees.

Foreign business associations also objected to shortened probationary periods. The first draft provided for probationary periods of one month for non-technical employees, two months for technical employees, and six months for senior technical and professional employees. Foreign businesses argued that these periods were too short to properly assess employees, and recommended that parties be allowed to stipulate the period, not to exceed six months. They also objected that the distinctions between employees were vague and hard to draw in practice.

The second draft abandoned the distinction between types of employees, providing probationary periods of one month for a one-year contract, two months for contracts of more than one year and less than three years, and six months for contracts of three years or more. AmCham countered with a proposal of three months for contracts of less than two years, and six months for contracts of more than two years. AmCham also worried that the evidentiary standard to demonstrate an employee was incompetent (and thus could be fired during the probationary period) was not clear. The final law prohibited probationary periods for contracts of less than three months but retained the rest of the periods in the second draft.

The first draft sought to protect dispatched (temporary) employees by requiring the employer to hire them on a fixed-term basis if they worked for the company for one year, and preventing the employer from terminating that person and hiring another temporary worker for the same job. AmCham argued that companies would hire fewer people, and warned that they would change the job description to avoid the rules and continue to hire temps. The final law rather vaguely provided that the employer shall not conclude several short-term contracts to cover a continuous period of work.

The second draft also provided that the employer had to provide an open-ended contract after the second fixed contract expired, if the employee so requested. AmCham wanted the law revised to clarify that the provision only applied to short-term fixed contracts of less than six months, so that the employers could enter as many multiple contracts over six months as they desired, and also to allow the employer the right to renew the contract, not the employee. The final law did not incorporate AmCham's recommendations.

AmCham also pushed for greater rights to terminate employees, arguing that the employer should be able to terminate fixed-term employees as well as non-fixed-term employees subject to one month's notice or one month in pay, if the employee had a non-work-related illness or injury, is incompetent and cannot be retrained, or there has been a "major change" in circumstances such that the contract could no longer be carried out. The final version incorporated this recommendation.

The draft also required union consent when the company proposed laying off more than fifty employees, and that terminations should be based on seniority. AmCham objected to the need to obtain union consent and the preferential treatment based on seniority, dramatically claiming that the latter would be a return to the era of the "iron rice bowl." It also argued that the standard should be based on a percentage of employees rather than a number, given that the size of companies varies widely. It suggested 30 percent.

The final law eliminated the requirement to obtain union consent, changed the standard to twenty employees or 10 percent of the workforce if fewer than twenty, and provided preferential treatment based on seniority and whether the employee was responsible for the support of parents or children and the only one in the family employed.

AmCham also objected to the payment of severance pay when the labor contract expires. The draft would apparently have required compensation even when the employee chose not to renew the contract. AmCham wanted no severance pay even when the contract was not renewed by the employer. They then suggested in the second round that severance pay be limited only to fixed contracts entered into after the new law went into effect. The final law provided for severance if the contract is not renewed by the employer, but not by the employee.

The draft law also limited non-competition clauses to two years (compared with the prevailing three years), imposed geographical limitations, required that the employer pay one year's salary to the employee on severance, and limited liquidated damages paid by the employee in case of breach to three times their annual salary.

Foreign business groups objected to all these provisions. The final law maintained the two-year limit, but left all the other terms to be agreed by the parties.

The draft law also provided that companies could recover training costs from employees for full-time training programs of six months if they left before their contract expired. This was considered unreasonable, as many companies provide training for shorter periods, including on-the-job training. The final law left the matter to be decided by contract between the parties, provided that liquidated damages could not exceed training costs adjusted on a pro rata basis for the amount of time left on the contract.

AmCham also suggested that employers be allowed to enter into contracts with highly compensated senior executives and professionals without being subject to the default rules for compensation, termination, and severance pay. However, the final version did not incorporate this recommendation.

In the end, businesses were able to cut back the power of the unions, which was their main concern, and also improved their situation from earlier drafts in terms of termination of fixed-term employees who are sick or injured, recovery of training expenses, and non-competition clauses. However, workers gained more protection with respect to probationary periods, job security after the second fixed-term contract, restrictions on layoffs, and severance pay if their contracts were not renewed. Several issues were left to the parties to settle. Such provisions will tend to benefit highly qualified employees, who are in short supply, and work against unskilled laborers, who are all too plentiful in most parts of the country.

The legislative history demonstrates the complexities of the policymaking process today. The government received almost 200,000 pages of written comments in response to the 2006 draft. As in other areas, factions formed based on interests rather than nationality: foreign companies joined with Chinese companies, while international labor organizations and even the US Congress criticized foreign business groups for harming the interest of Chinese workers.[41]

Dispute settlement patterns in securities, bankruptcy, and anti-dumping: the interplay between litigation and government policy

A comparison of dispute settlement patterns in securities, bankruptcy, and anti-dumping shows the continued importance of government policy and administrative means of resolving disputes in some areas, and how China has moved at its own pace, resisting the pressure to conform to a particular developmental model or to adopt the prescriptions of the agents of global capital.

The general trend in the commercial area has been for an increase in litigation with an expansion of the range of justiciable disputes, while mediation has decreased and arbitration has remained relatively stable and limited.[42] Between 1983 and 2001, economic disputes increased by an average of 18.3 percent a year, an increase twice the rate of civil disputes, and four times the rate of criminal cases.[43] Contract disputes are the major cause of litigation.[44]

Nevertheless, the utility of litigation to protect commercial actors is affected by many factors, including limitations on the right to sue, the use of other means to achieve similar ends, conflicting policy goals, and the strength and independence of the courts. These factors affect certain areas of law and types of cases more than others.

For instance, until recently, shareholder rights were mainly protected through criminal sanctions and fines.[45] The 1993 Company Law appeared to limit private shareholders to injunctive relief rather than damages. In 2001, the Supreme People's Court (SPC) issued an interpretation preventing shareholders from bringing suits and then, four months later, issued another interpretation allowing shareholders the narrow right to sue for misrepresentation where the China Securities Regulatory Commission had issued a report finding misrepresentation. The restrictions were justified on a variety of policy grounds, including that the judges lacked experience in handling such cases, jurisdictional rules had yet to be worked out that would prevent different courts from issuing different awards for suits arising out of the same cause of action but brought by shareholder plaintiffs located in different areas, and large damage awards against listed SOEs would result in significant loss of state assets.

In 2003, the SPC issued a third, much more detailed interpretation. Although the interpretation did not expand the subject matter for litigation, it did clarify a number of procedural and evidentiary issues. After experience had been gained from further study of the issues and the handling of several cases, the Company Law was amended in 2005 to strengthen the rights of minority shareholders to bring suit. Courts have now begun accepting suits for reasons other than misrepresentation, and the SPC appears to be set to issue another interpretation based on the experience gained from these cases.

Bankruptcy provides another example of the interplay between litigation and government policy.[46] The Enterprise Bankruptcy Law passed in 1986 was limited to SOEs, and not very effective in practice. There were on average only 277 bankruptcies a year from 1989 to 1993. Banks objected to provisions that gave priority to workers; local government officials were worried about social unrest from laid-off workers; judges lacked independence and specialized training in bankruptcy proceedings; and the support network of trained accountants, lawyers, and bankruptcy specialists was lacking.

Rather than relying on creditor-initiated bankruptcy proceedings to resolve the problem of insolvent SOEs, the government opted for an administrative approach, with the State Council encouraging the merger of weaker SOEs with stronger ones, and carefully allowing selected SOEs to go bankrupt based on a regional quota that allowed government officials to factor in the likelihood of social unrest in deciding which companies could enter bankruptcy proceedings. The government also reversed the preference for workers by reassigning the priority for the proceeds from the sale of secured land use rights to the secured parties, in most cases People's Republic of China (PRC) banks.

Over time, the vast majority of SOEs were sold off, with many of the remaining ones less of a burden on the state, having been exposed to increasing competition. More generally, the private sector (including collective enterprises) played an increasingly dominant role in the economy. These changes were reflected in the

2006 Enterprise Bankruptcy Law (EBL), which applies to both state-owned and non-stated-owned companies, except for 2,116 SOEs that are either at particular financial risk or in a sensitive industry, and small unincorporated private businesses. The courts will oversee bankruptcies, aided by the private professions of lawyers, accountants, and other bankruptcy specialists.

While the government's role has been diminished, there are still various opportunities for the government to intervene to pursue non-economic policy goals, such as social stability. These include special approvals for certain SOEs and financial companies to commence bankruptcy proceedings, possible pressure on courts from local governments to decide that companies are not technically insolvent or to simply refuse to accept the case, and government pressure on banks to issue policy loans to prop up ailing SOEs. Nevertheless, the 2006 EBL provides creditors with the means to initiate bankruptcy proceedings and, on the whole, represents a large step forward in clarifying and strengthening their rights.

Whereas the general trend in securities litigation and bankruptcy proceedings has been to provide a more rule-based system that strengthens the hand of private actors, anti-dumping remains an area that is much more politicized and dependent on administrative discretion.[47] China is one of the most frequent targets of anti-dumping claims, and appears to pay a rising-power premium.[48] On the other hand, China has increasingly turned to anti-dumping actions against others doing business in China. By the end of 2006, China had initiated 150 anti-dumping actions, with ninety-one anti-dumping enforcement measures in place, affecting imports from twenty-one countries and seventeen ongoing anti-dumping investigations. There are currently seven cases against the US, mainly in the petrochemical industry.

MOFCOM is charged with both investigating the existence of dumping and determining the amount of injury. Anti-dumping proceedings remain shrouded in mystery. Parties are not allowed access to confidential information subject to protective order, to staff reports in particular cases, or even to MOFCOM's standards used for calculating the dumping margin and industry damage.

Although MOFCOM reversed its decision in response to the US challenge in the kraft linerboard case on procedural grounds, it has yet to substantially revise the rules. While MOFCOM is under pressure from foreign trade governments and business associations to adopt rules that would make the process and standards more transparent and consistent with international standards, domestic companies have lobbied hard to modify the rules to make anti-dumping cases easier to initiate and win by lowering the standards of evidence to prove dumping.[49] As in other countries, anti-dumping decisions appear to be driven by domestic political concerns to protect certain vulnerable industries rather than by principles of free trade or legal considerations, and it seems likely that this will continue, even if the rules are changed to incorporate "international best practices."

On the other hand, the diversification of the economy, along with China's national economic interests, complicate the situation. For instance, China's steel industry is on the whole inefficient. Not surprisingly, large SOE producers have lobbied aggressively in favor of anti-dumping duties to slow imports from more efficient foreign producers.[50] Between 1999 and 2002, they initiated three anti-dumping cases against eight countries, and also lobbied the government to initiate a WTO challenge to the US invocation of safeguard measures to protect the US steel industry. While the government imposed duties of 50 percent in all three cases, the victory was, if not hollow, decidedly less than complete, as many products were exempted. Foreign companies, joining forces with the Chinese companies that bought their products, lobbied hard. They argued successfully that the foreign products were necessary for sustained growth and domestic companies either could not produce them or could not produce them as cheaply and with the same high quality.

III Conclusion

The pushback on globalization is the result of several factors. One is China's non-ideological, pragmatic approach to reforms, which has led China to reject parts of the WC in favor of a model of development similar to that followed by other successful East Asian countries.[51] The model also explains the tighter restrictions on civil and political liberties and delayed democratization, the most notable areas of resistance to the prevailing international wisdom. But then East Asia is the only regional exception to the otherwise gloomy results to promote economic growth, rule of law, good governance, and ultimately democracy and the protection of human rights. Moreover, the model appears to work for reasonably large countries without oil or the benefits of being tax-haven islands with large tourist revenues. With an average annual growth rate of 10 percent since 1978, the results in China, at least thus far, have been impressive.

A second and related factor is the realization that the policies, rules, standards, institutions, and practices that work in developed countries are not always appropriate or useful in developing countries. Moreover, rich countries did not get where they are by following the same policies they are now prescribing for developing countries.

A third factor is the increasing pluralism of Chinese society and an increase in lobbying pressure from domestic interest groups. Foreign businesses, who also engage in extensive lobbying, must now operate in a policymaking arena crowded with increasingly assertive domestic interest groups pushing their own agenda, including large SOEs and private companies, representatives of labor, consumers, NGOs, and single-issue interest groups. As in other countries, there is also a notable trend toward a rising nationalism seeking to push back globalization.[52]

A fourth factor is the government's growing concerns over socio-political stability, which has led to the new harmonious society policy. The new policy rejects the neoliberal emphasis on a small state and the alleged trickle-down benefits of economic growth in favor of greater protection of disadvantaged groups who have lost out during the process of globalization and the transition to a market economy.

Perhaps the biggest factor fueling the backlash, however, is the rise in global protectionism, much of it directed at China. Critics of globalization point to the failure of the Doha round to address the imbalances in the international trade regime that have contributed to the widening income gaps between rich and poor countries.

The average income in the twenty richest countries is thirty-seven times that of the poorest twenty countries, with the spread doubling in the last forty years.[53]

Developing countries have argued for a trade regime that provides access to patented drugs, protects cultural artifacts and local know-how not recognized under Trade-related Aspects of Intellectual Property Rights (TRIPS), abandons the WTO single-undertaking approach in favor of an intellectual property regime more tailored to the different level of development and circumstances in developing countries, avoids the protectionist and discriminatory use of anti-dumping and safeguard mechanisms to limit imports of textiles and other products from developing countries, and perhaps most importantly, eliminates agricultural subsidies in developed countries and relaxes restrictions on immigrant workers from poor countries.

As residents of a developing country, Chinese citizens are sympathetic to these arguments. However, as noted, Chinese citizens realize that, for the most part, they have benefited from economic globalization. What upsets them most are unfair trade practices that target China specifically.

Noting the parallel to the demonization of Japan in the 1980s, Bown and McCulloch describe "unprecedented" discriminatory policies against China by the US that protect domestic industries and favor China's competitors. For example, Chinese companies face the most anti-dumping actions, are the most likely to have duties imposed, and suffer the highest duties—a "China premium" of an additional 80 percent—making China "public enemy number one."[54]

In addition to anti-dumping cases, the US and EU have invoked surge mechanisms to protect US and European industries from imports of Chinese textiles and other products. The US government has also scrutinized PRC investments in the US for their impact on national security (Lenovo/IBM, Hutchinson/ports), and prevented a PRC company from acquiring the oil company Unocal. Other complaints include foreign pressure to let the RMB appreciate further, the limits on dual-use technologies, and the widespread attention to defective products from China even though China is not the largest source of defective imports in the US and many of the problems were the result of design defects.[55]

As if that were not enough, the US Congress is currently considering a slew of bills that would lower evidentiary thresholds for imposing anti-dumping, anti-subsidy, and China-specific safeguard duties; revoke China's "most favored nations" status (in effect the normal trade status); treat currency manipulation as a subsidy subject to countervailing duties and impose a 27.5 percent tariff on all goods from China unless the RMB appreciates by an amount to be determined by Congress; subject imports from non-market economies such as China to higher rates of duty; require the President to pursue concrete measures to achieve greater trade balance with countries that have persistent trade surpluses with the US; and expand trade adjustment assistance programs to cover people who have lost jobs in the services sector due to outsourcing.[56] While many of these bills are election-year chest-pounding, they fuel the image of China as a cut-throat mercantilist power, which may long survive the 2008 Presidential elections.

On the other hand, there are numerous reasons to believe that the general trend is likely to be toward more openness and an increasingly competitive market economy.

First, China's overall geopolitical strategy is to maintain a non-aggressive international profile and focus on development and resolving domestic issues.[57] In particular, China places great importance on its relationship with the US, which it does not want to antagonize. Nor does it want to antagonize its neighbors or other developing countries, particularly resource-rich African and mid-Eastern states. It needs good relations with these countries to balance US power, provide the raw materials to keep China Inc. running, and provide export markets for Chinese products.

Moreover, the Chinese Communist Party is heavily dependent on continued growth for legitimacy, which is essential if China is going to be able to address pressing social issues, including rural–urban inequality, the lack of an adequate social welfare system or medical care, and environmental degradation.

There is also a general consensus among government officials and citizens alike that the only way to sustain growth is through continued reforms toward a more competitive market economy. One survey found that even 24 percent of laid-off workers thought the reforms were right while another 53 percent thought the reforms were right for the state but not for the workers.[58]

Policymaking is now much more contested. There is domestic pressure from domestic interest groups, including many companies that benefit from reforms. It is difficult for any particular group or industry to capture the process and maintain support for protectionist measures that harm other domestic constituencies for long. As noted, the steel industry victory in a series of anti-dumping cases was limited by domestic demand for high-quality imported steel. And the final forms of the Property Law, Bankruptcy Law, and Labor Contract Law all represent victories for foreign investors, banks, developers, creditors, and other champions of global capitalism, notwithstanding new left arguments about the need to protect socially vulnerable laborers and the victims of land takings, or the government's promises to establish a harmonious society.

The policymaking process belies the stereotypical image of an omnipresent authoritarian party deciding industrial policy in top-down fashion based on a narrow interpretation of China's national economic interests. Rather, the government is riding a tiger, trying to balance various goals, including sustaining rapid growth, realizing a harmonious society, placating different interest groups, and pursuing national development policies. The goals are internally inconsistent, and the political process heavily contested, ensuring that no single goal will drive regulatory development and economic policies. China may be too big to govern, but it is also too big for any given interest faction, whether foreign or domestic, to capture.

Notes

1 James Dorn, 'China in a vice grip', 14 June 2007. Available from http://freetrade.org/node/680.
2 For a more extended discussion, see Randall Peerenboom, *China Modernizes: Threat to the West or Model for the Rest*, Oxford: Oxford University Press, 2007.
3 Lee Branstetter and Nicholas Lardy, 'China's Embrace of Globalization', *Asia Program Special Report*, Washington, DC: Woodrow Wilson International Center for Scholars, 2005, p. 12.

4 Martin Wolf, 'China's rise need not bring conflict', *Financial Times* 14 September 2005. Available from http://www.FT.com.

5 The index is based on twelve pillars: institutions; infrastructure; macroeconomic stability; health and primary education; higher education and training; goods market efficiency; labor market efficiency; financial market sophistication; technical readiness; market size, business sophistication; and innovation. See http://www.weforum.org/pdf/GCR08/GCR08.pdf.

6 China fared better on some indicators than others, including enforcing contracts (20), registering property (28), trading across borders (31), closing a business (76), and protecting investors (86). Problem areas include the time required and difficulty in starting a business (128), dealing with licenses (175), and the amount and administrative burden of paying taxes (173).

7 D. Kaufmann, A. Kraay, and M. Mastruzzi, 'Governance Matters VI: Governance Indicators for 1996–2006', published 2007. Available from http://web.worldbank.org/WBSITE/EXTERNAL/WBI/EXTWBIGOVANTCOR/0,,menuPK:1740542~pagePK:64168427~piPK:64168435~theSitePK:1740530,00.html (accessed 24 November 2008).

8 According to the World Economic Forum, China ranked 115th and 114th out of 122 countries on efficacy of corporate boards and protection of minority shareholders rights. World Economic Forum, 'The Global Competitiveness Report 2007–8'. Available from http://www.weforum.org/en/initiatives/gcp/Global%20Competitiveness%20Report/index.htm (accessed 24 November 2008).

9 China ranked 99th out 122 countries on transparency of government policymaking. World Economic Forum, *supra*.

10 Kaufmann et al., *supra*.

11 Since 1999, foreign investor respondents in the American Chamber of Commerce (AmCham) surveys have cited the four biggest challenges for doing business in China as lack of transparency (major challenge for 41 percent of respondents), inconsistent regulatory interpretation (37 percent), unclear regulations (34 percent), and excessive bureaucracy (31 percent), followed by human resource constraints (29 percent) and IP infringements (26 percent). Interestingly, the top ten list of complaints from US–China Business Council (USCBC) members in 2007 was slightly different. Human resources topped the list, followed in descending order by administrative licensing, IPR enforcement, increased competition and overcapacity, transparency, standards, protectionism in China, logistics, access to China's services sector, and protectionism in the US.

    Almost 40 percent of AmCham respondents believe that there have been improvements in transparency over the last four years (versus 55 percent unchanged), 27 percent saw improvements in consistency of regulations (versus 63 percent unchanged), 34 percent thought regulations were clearer (versus 54 percent unchanged), and 37 percent felt the bureaucracy had improved (versus 60 percent unchanged). USCBC respondents cited significant improvements in logistics (55 percent), but 87 percent complained about a dramatic rise in *US* protectionism.

    For all of the complaints, 83 percent of USCBC respondents were profitable, with two-thirds enjoying profitability rates that met or exceeded their company's global rate.

    Looking forward, 33 percent of AmCham respondents cited a slowdown in the Chinese economy as the biggest risk for coming years, while 26 percent cited increased Chinese protectionism, 21 percent cited deterioration in Sino-US relations, and 20 percent cited labor costs. Nevertheless, over 90 percent of respondents from both surveys are bullish about their companies' future in China. See American Chamber of Commerce (AmCham), 'The Business Climate for US Firms in China', 2007. Available from http://www.amcham-china.org.cn/amcham/show/content.php?Id=2361&menuid=&submid=&PHPSESSID=11eade809492f6ad040c37af69cec8af (accessed 1 November 2007); US–China Business Council, 'US Companies' China Outlook: Continuing Optimism Tempered by Operating Challenges,

Protectionist Threats', 4 October 2007. Available from http://www.uschina.org/public/documents/2007/10/uscbc-member-survey-2007.pdf.

12 According to one survey, 71 percent of foreign companies have in-country staff dedicated to lobbying the government. The main tasks are management relationships, advocacy for specific projects, advocacy for regulatory and policy changes, followed by business development, image management, corporate social responsibility (CSR), and regulatory compliance. Only one-third of respondents were working on foreign corrupt practices compliance issues or environmental, health, and safety compliance issues. USCBC, 'Conducting Government Affairs in China', 30 October 2007. Available from http://www.uschina.org/public/documents/2007/10/survey-gov-affairs.pdf (accessed 1 November 2007).

See also Scott Kennedy, *The Business of Lobbying in China*, Cambridge: Harvard University Press, 2005. Looking at lobbying by both foreign and domestic companies, Kennedy found that business–government relations varied by sector in terms of the relative usefulness of business associations, the amount of direct contact with the government, the extent to which businesses adopted a cooperative or confrontational approach, and the transparency of the political process. In general, size matters: larger companies that account for a bigger share of the market or economy have more influence on the policy process. Moreover, size matters regardless of ownership form (SOE or private) or nationality (domestic or foreign). Associations are more likely to be active and effective when there is a high percentage of foreign and domestic private companies as opposed to a small number of large SOEs with a dominant market share. Associations may serve the purposes of smaller members, but may also serve the interests of the larger members.

13 The AmCham annual report contains a number of recommendations for the US government, including making visas more easily accessible for Chinese business people and government officials, relaxing export restrictions on dual-use technology and, most fundamentally, avoiding the politicization of trade issues by focusing on particular issues such as the trade deficit or by pressing for dramatic but counterproductive changes such as radical revaluation of the RMB. AmCham, *supra*.

14 Kennedy, *supra*.

15 Kennedy found that corporatism and clientelism have limited, and decreasing, explanatory power for government–business relations generally in China, and in the steel, consumer product, and consumer electronics industry in particular. Pluralism, while a better fit, overstates the influence of civil society on the policy process in China, notwithstanding that civil society's influence has increased across all sectors.

16 Supreme People's Court's 2005 Work Report. Available from http://www.court.gov.cn/work/200503180013.htm (accessed 1 November 2007).

17 Fu Hualing and Richard Cullen, 'From Mediatory to Adjudicatory Justice: The Limits of Civil Justice Reform in China', in M.Y.K. Woo, M.E. Gallagher, and M. Goldman, eds, *Chinese Justice: Civil Dispute Resolution in Contemporary China*, Cambridge, MA: Harvard University Press, 2009.

18 Yu Jianrong, 'Dui 560 mingjing shangfangzhe de diaocha [An Investigation on 560 Petitioners to Beijing]', *Falü yu senghuo* [Law and Life] 5, 2007, p. 14.

19 These measures were set out in the Harmonious Society platform and 11th Five-Year Plan.

20 See Chapter VII of the 2004 Foreign Trade Law. The Law calls for investigations of the impact of foreign trade on the competitiveness of domestic industries as well as national security, and contemplates such remedies as anti-dumping measures, countervailing duties, or safeguards. One of the advantages of being a latecomer to such protectionist measures is that China's legislators have been able to incorporate some of the most sophisticated and cutting-edge protectionist measures. See Henry Gao, 'China's Participation in the WTO: A Lawyer's Perspective', *Singapore Year Book of International Law* 11, 2007, pp. 1–34.

21 'Lamy: China Fulfilling WTO Commitments Well', *China Daily*. Available from http://english.cri.cn/3130/2006/09/06/262@135641.htm (accessed 1 November 2007).

22 USCBC, 2005, *supra*.
23 AmCham, 2007, *supra*.
24 For a discussion of the administrative obstacles to enforcement, see Andrew Mertha, *The Politics of Piracy: Intellectual Property in Contemporary China*, Ithaca: Cornell University Press, 2005.
25 Seven countries, including China, account for 70 percent of low-technology exports and 80 percent of high-technology exports from developing countries. United Nations Development Program, *Human Development Report 2005*. Available from http://hdr. undp.org/en/reports/global/hdr2005/ (accessed 24 November 2008).
26 AmCham, *supra*.
27 Christopher Gibson, 'Globalization and the Technology Standards Game: Balancing Concerns of Protectionism and Intellectual Property in International Standards', *Berkeley Technology Law Journal* 22 (1401), 2007.
28 Kennedy, *supra*, pp. 119–25, describes standard-setting in the consumer industry.
29 China has been a complainant twice and a respondent in eight cases arising out of five issues. The US was involved in the challenge to China on all five issues. China's first action was to challenge, along with the EU, Japan, and several others, US safeguard measures intended to protect the domestic steel industry in 2002. The Dispute Panel found against the US, as did the Appellate Body, and the US terminated the safeguard measures. However, China could have taken a much more aggressive approach under WTO rules, and imposed duties prior to the hearing, as the EU threatened to do. Indeed, the US encouraged countries to raise a WTO complaint rather than imposing duties directly. See Henry Gao, 'Taming the Dragon: China's Experience in the WTO Dispute Settlement System', *Legal Issues of Economic Integration* 34 (4), 2007. China's WTO cases are available at http://www.wto.org/english/tratop_e/dispu_e/ find_dispu_cases_e.htm#results
30 Wang Jiangyu, 'Rule of Law *and* Rule of Officials: Explaining the Different Roles Played by Law in Shareholders' Litigation and Anti-dumping Investigation in China', in Randall Peerenboom, ed., *Dispute Resolution in China*, Oxford: Oxford Foundation for Law, Justice and Society, 2008; Gao, *supra*, 2007.
31 Daniel Ilkenson, 'Growing Pains: The Evolving US–China Trade Relationship', *Free Trade Bulletin* 28, 7 May 2007. Available from http://freetrade.org/node/626 (accessed 1 November 2007).
32 Gao argues that China is likely to lose a legal battle in this case if it tries a cultural defense. Given that Beijing's real interest is political control, he suggests that China would be better off reaching a settlement. Henry Gao, 'The Mighty Pen, the Almighty Dollar, and the Holy Hammer and Sickle: An Examination of the Conflict between Trade Liberalization and Domestic Cultural Policy with Special Regard to the Recent Dispute between the United States and China on Restrictions on Certain Cultural Products', *Asian Journal of WTO & International Health Law and Policy* 2 (2), 2007, p. 313.
33 See People's Net, 'Bo Xilai Made Stern Warnings against Double Standards in Trade,' 3 June 2006.
34 'Wu: US Piracy Case Will Harm Trade Ties', 24 April 2007.
35 AmCham *supra*, 2007.
36 Ibid.
37 Mark Williams, 'Competition Policy and Law', in Randall Peerenboom ed., *Regulating Enterprise: The Regulatory Impact on Doing Business in China*, Oxford: Oxford Foundation for Law, Justice and Society, 2007.
38 The law contemplates an Anti-Monopoly Committee under the State Council, which is responsible for formulating competition policy and anti-monopoly guidelines policy, assessing the state of overall market competition, and coordinating enforcement work, which is to be handled primarily by the Anti-Monopoly Enforcement Authority.
39 International practice is divided on this issue and commentators have disagreed about the wisdom of including public abuse of power in China's law. Compare

Mark Williams, *Competition Policy and Law in China, Hong Kong and Taiwan*, Cambridge: Cambridge University Press, 2005, with Eleanor Fox, 'An Anti-Monopoly Law for China—Scaling the Walls of Protectionist Government Restraints', *Antitrust Law Journal* 74, 2007.

40 The following section draws on the position papers prepared by AmCham and USCBC. See American Chamber of Commerce People's Republic of China Comments on the Draft Labor Contract Law of the People's Republic of China, 19 April 2006; American Chamber of Commerce People's Republic of China Comments on the Second Deliberated Draft Labor Contract Law of the People's Republic of China, 12 February 2007; US–China Business Council Comments on the Draft Labor Contract Law of the People's Republic of China, 19 April 2006. The recommendations of the two organizations are consistent and largely overlapping.

41 Letter from Congress to the White House, 31 October 2006.

42 Zhu Jingwen, ed., *Zhongguo falü fazhan baogao (1979–2004)* [China Legal Development Report (1979–2004)], Beijing: People's University Press, 2007.

43 Donald Clarke, Peter Murrell, and Susan Whiting, 'The Role of Law in China's Economic Development', 2006. Available from http://ssrn.com/abstract=878672 (accessed 15 March 2008).

44 Zhu, *supra*, p. 221.

45 Wang Jiangyu, *supra*.

46 Terence Halliday, 'The Making of China's Bankruptcy Law', in Randall Peerenboom ed., *Regulating Enterprise: The Regulatory Impact on Doing Business in China*, Oxford: Oxford Foundation for Law, Justice and Society, 2007.

47 Wang Jiangyu, *supra*.

48 Chad Bown and Rachel McCulloch, 'US Trade Policy Toward China: Discrimination and its Implications', 2005. Available from http://ssrn.com/abstract=757124 (accessed 19 April 2006).

49 Kennedy, *supra*, p. 89.

50 Kennedy, *supra*, pp. 83–89.

51 Peerenboom, *China Modernizes, supra*.

52 The literature on nationalism in China is vast. See, for example, Peter Hays Gries, *China's New Nationalism: Pride, Politics, and Diplomacy*, Berkeley: University of California Press, 2004; Suisheng Zhao, 'We are Patriots First and Democrats Second: The Rise of Chinese Nationalism in the 1990s', in Edward Friedman, Edward and Barret McCormick, eds, *What If China Doesn't Democratize? Implications for War and Peace*, New York: M.E. Sharpe, 2000.

53 United Nations Development Programme, *Human Development Report 2005, supra*.

54 Bown and McCulloch, *supra*.

55 The Ministry of Commerce sets out a long list of what China considers to be discriminatory or unfair practices by the US, in Ministry of Commerce, *Foreign Market Access Report 2005*. Available from http://gpj.mofcom.gov.cn/table/2005en.pdf (accessed 1 June 2006).

56 Daniel Ilkenson, 'A new protectionism: dashed hopes and perhaps worse for US trade policy', 26 October 2007. Available from http://www.freetrade.org/node/784 (accessed 1 November 2007).

57 See, generally, Robert G. Sutter, *China's Rise in Asia*, Lanham: Rowman & Littlefield, 2005; Yong Deng and Fei-ling Wang, eds, *China Rising: Power and Motivation in Chinese Foreign Policy*, Lanham: Rowman & Littlefield, 2005.

58 Shujie Yao, *Economic Growth, Income Distribution and Poverty Reduction in Contemporary China*, London and New York: RoutledgeCurzon, 2005.

7 Regulatory learning and its discontents in China

Promise and tragedy at the State Food and Drug Administration

Dali L. Yang[1]

Throughout the reform era, China's reformers have actively considered international practices in domestic reforms. Whereas China's leaders have far from adopted wholesale Westernization, they have nonetheless become bolder in adopting international practices. The trend toward convergence hit a high note during the administration of Premier Zhu Rongji (1998–2003) with China's re-accession into the World Trade Organization (WTO) in 2001. Since then, as the results from a recent Chicago Council on Global Affairs survey of public attitudes suggest, China has become a poster child for globalization.[2]

The Zhu Rongji administration also stood out for remodeling various Chinese government agencies to resemble American counterparts. In restructuring the People's Bank of China (PBOC), the central bank, for example, the Chinese leadership replaced the PBOC's thirty-two provincial-level branches with nine regional branches to look, structurally, like the US Federal Reserve.

Another area that drew the central leadership's attention was regulation of the pharmaceutical industry and the promotion of drug safety. Here again, the Chinese reformers' model was the US Food and Drug Administration (FDA). The US has had the world's strongest pharmaceutical industry, and the US FDA is well known for setting the standard in drug regulation. In survey after survey, the FDA, along with the FAA (Federal Aviation Administration), have received positive performance ratings and are ranked as the top institutions the American public have come to trust.[3] Chinese reformers hoped that the move to emulate the US FDA would help provide the regulatory environment for the upgrading of China's own drug industry.

In 1998, China's own State Drug Administration (SDA) was born. In 2003, the SDA was also given oversight over food safety regulation and became the State Food and Drug Administration (SFDA). Chinese officials have not been shy in suggesting that the SFDA is modeled upon the US FDA and have used SFDA, the abbreviation of the agency's name in English translation, as the agency's web name (http://www.SFDA.gov.cn).

Yet the SFDA has turned out to be no US FDA at all. In this chapter, I provide an overview of the SFDA's first decade and describe how the SFDA has failed to live up to its promise so far. In particular, I discuss the SFDA's pursuit of much-needed reforms of the drug regulatory system and how each of these reforms has been riddled with corruption. In July 2007, Zheng Xiaoyu, the first SFDA commissioner until June 2005, was executed for bribe-taking and dereliction of duty. The SFDA's vicissitudes in its first decade thus offer a striking case for explicating the challenges of regulatory globalization in the Chinese context.

The politics of institution building

Historically, a regulatory state has tended to be associated with the expansion of markets and social transformation. It is now generally recognized that a modern regulatory state is essential to help overcome certain problems of coordination and collective action, and thus maintain market order.[4]

As China has made the transition from plan to market, most industrial ministries inherited from the pre-reform central planning era have been eliminated, while a long list of regulatory commissions, administrations, and bureaus have been established or reinforced. In addition to the regulatory commissions for banking, insurance, and securities, the list of regulatory agencies also includes the State Environmental Protection Administration, the General Administration of Industry and Commerce, the General Administration of Quality Supervision, Inspection and Quarantine, the State Intellectual Property Office (formerly the State Patent Bureau), the State Administration of Press and Publications (National Copyright Administration), the State Food and Drug Administration, and the State Administration of Workplace Safety. Working alongside the powerful National Development and Reform Commission as well as government ministries such as the Ministries of Finance, Construction, Land and Resources, the regulatory agencies are charged with the enforcement of state laws to protect the rights of consumers, workers, investors, and the state, as the case may be.

For the regulatory agencies to function well as modern regulators, they must be designed properly, in order to focus on the intended mission and be equipped with the appropriate resources (personnel and funds, as well as sufficient enforcement authority) to carry out that mission. In reality, regulatory agencies as organizations must contend with internal conflicts and cope with external pressures.[5] Good agency design may help to mitigate these internal and external complexities and motivate the agency to fulfill its mission, but that is only part of the story.

A review of Chinese regulatory developments in the reform era suggests that the regulatory institutions are often born with serious congenital flaws. The effects of these flaws are magnified by a volatile socio-psychological environment that has made many officials incapable of resisting the urge to seek self-enrichment at the expense of public interest. As a result, the regulatory agencies have not only found it difficult to be effective regulators, but have succumbed to widespread corruption. A history of Chinese regulatory developments in the reform era is thus a history of the struggle to cope with and overcome the various institutional flaws and to curb regulatory corruption.

The vicissitudes at the SFDA have sadly become Exhibit A for understanding the challenges of regulatory institution building in China. When China's leaders decided to strengthen regulation of the pharmaceutical industry and promote drug safety by establishing a drug regulator modeled after the US FDA, their goal was both clear and lofty. The leadership they installed at the SFDA also seemed determined to carry out the reforms needed.

To understand how the reforms at the SFDA went awry, we can begin with the role of Zheng Xiaoyu, the SFDA's founding commissioner until June 2005. The career and rise of Zheng Xiaoyu offer us an excellent vantage point for understanding the problems that have plagued the SFDA and the Chinese pharmaceutical industry, as well as the SFDA's continuing challenges to become a modern regulator.

Born in 1944 in Fujian Province, Zheng Xiaoyu graduated in 1968 from the Biology Department of the Shanghai-based Fudan University, one of China's best. Upon his graduation, Zheng was offered a job in neighboring Zhejiang province. For the next decade after his graduation, Zheng served as a technician at the state-owned Hangzhou First Pharmaceutical Factory, which was renamed the Hangzhou Minsheng Pharmaceutical Co. in the reform era. With the reforms, Zheng's talents began to shine and he rose steadily through the ranks to become the company's managing director and party secretary at Hangzhou Minsheng.

Not content with the world of enterprise management, Zheng sought a move into the world of rank and political privilege. In early 1991, Zheng moved from the business world to the Zhejiang provincial Federation of Labor Unions and became, successively, its vice chairman and chairman. Although the Labor Union was hardly at the center of political influence in China, Zheng's post as Labor Union chairman placed his name on the nomenklatura list and got him ready for further promotions.

When the central leadership searched for someone with subnational experience to head the State Pharmaceutical Administration (SPA), Zheng looked like a candidate with the right qualifications for the job. He had a good college education, possessed the right bureaucratic rank for appointment to the SPA, and had extensive industry experience in a province well known for its strengths in the pharmaceutical industry.

Yet Zheng didn't just wait for the appointment. After all, the possession of the right qualifications is no guarantee of promotion in the world of Chinese politics, particularly when national leaders can choose from a long list of potential candidates. Instead, Zheng actively lobbied for his appointment, armed with an "activities" fund contributed by his friends in the pharmaceutical industry, especially Zhejiang-based firms.[6] For these firms, it was an investment that would ultimately repay itself many times.

The State Pharmaceutical Administration, then subordinated to the State Economic and Trade Commission, was not a modern drug regulator. Instead, as a legacy agency from the era of central planning, it primarily acted as the central government's steward of the pharmaceutical industry and was considered the mother-in-law of China's leading pharmaceutical enterprises. As such, the SPA's mission included the formulation and implementation of policies on and strategies for pharmaceutical industry development, including participation in adjusting total output, responsibility for supervision of the finances and assets of state-owned firms directly under the SPA, and promotion of medical research and new product development. Nonetheless, the SPA had also gradually acquired certain regulatory functions that would fall under the rubric of a modern drug regulator, including supervision of the production and operation of pharmaceutical products, the right to approve licenses for the production and sale of medical devices, and the setting and implementation of national standards for medical devices, materials, machinery, and packaging.[7]

Yet the SPA's regulatory authority overlapped with that of the Ministry of Health. The Ministry of Health's main functions include the supervision of food, drug, and bio-medical products, as well as bio-materials and medical equipment. It also oversaw the State Administration of Traditional Chinese Medicine. The Ministry of Health's Drug Administration Bureau (DAB), in particular, had the authority to set and implement laws and regulations on drugs and bio-medical products and to set the standards for the same. It also had the key power to approve drugs and bio-medical products and to issue licenses for the production, sale, and in-hospital manufacture of drugs and bio-medical products.[8]

As is to be expected, the SPA and the Ministry of Health's overlapping regulatory authority was a source of constant friction. Because the Ministry of Health enjoyed a higher bureaucratic ranking than the SPA, it was natural for Zheng to feel somewhat overshadowed by the Ministry of Health.

The regulatory fragmentation, coupled with the burgeoning but "chaotic" pharmaceutical industry, cried out for rationalization. Zheng Xiaoyu, as Director General of the SPA, wrote or authorized various reports, based on trips abroad, advocating reforms of the drug regulatory system.[9] The model that continually evoked admiration among Chinese regulators and industry was the US Food and Drug Administration, which has overseen the world's largest and most innovative pharmaceutical industry. In January 1997, the Chinese Communist Party (CCP) Central Committee and State Council's decision on health reform and development called for "active exploration of drug administration reforms and gradually form a unified, authoritative, and efficient management system."[10]

In accordance with the above objective and as part of the sweeping government reorganization and rationalization in spring 1998, incoming Chinese premier Zhu Rongji chose to merge the regulatory functions over drugs (the DAB and part of the State Administration of Traditional Chinese Medicine) and medical devices (SPA) under one roof in a newly constituted State Drug Administration (SDA).[11] Because the SPA (and Zheng Xiaoyu) boasted a vice-ministerial rank and thus outranked the Ministry of Health's DAB headed by Shao Mingli, it was natural that Zheng Xiaoyu was appointed the new Commissioner and party secretary of the newly constituted SDA, while Shao was appointed Deputy Commissioner.[12] Zheng continued in these positions after the SDA took over responsibility for food safety regulation to become the SFDA in 2003. When Zheng retired in June 2005, Shao Mingli was his successor.

Zheng Xiaoyu was not only an advocate for the administrative reorganization that created the SDA but also a forceful Commissioner. Partly because the SDA is a newly constituted administration, Zheng had more leeway to shape it, especially because the Chinese SDA was a stand-alone agency in contrast to the US FDA, which is within the Department of Health and Human Services. Like the enterprise manager that he once was, Zheng put his stamp on the SDA by placing trusted lieutenants in key positions. During the transition to the SDA in 1998, Zheng first appointed Cao Wenzhuang, his former secretary and the former director of the SPA Labor and Personnel Bureau, to serve as the SDA Personnel Bureau Director, as well as head of the SDA General Office. The appointment of Cao Wenzhuang helped Zheng Xiaoyu to take firm control over personnel appointments in the SDA. In 2002, Zheng moved Cao Wenzhuang to direct the Drug Registration Bureau, the heart of the SDA. Another of Zheng's former secretaries, Hao Heping, previously the deputy director of the Bureau of Medical Devices Administration, assumed the directorship of the Bureau of Medical Devices at the SDA. Zheng thus had his two former secretaries in control of the two most important regulatory bureaus in the SDA.

The commissioners and deputy commissioners oversee work in different areas. Not surprisingly, Zheng Xiaoyu took on drug registration and approval—the core of any drug administration, even though his operational background in the pharmaceutical industry suggested that he would have been especially suited to assume oversight of production safety supervision. In contrast, he put Shao Mingli, who had dealt with drug approval at the Ministry of Health, to oversee production safety supervision. After Zheng fell from power, some insiders noted that Zheng placed his own people in the key posts on drug and medical devices registration and industry legislation, where they reported only to Zheng. They commented, "Those deputy commissioners who didn't come from the former SPA were almost idle," and "The first deputy commissioner Shao Mingli was always excluded from the circle of real decision makers."[13]

Zheng Xiaoyu's reform initiatives

With these personnel appointments and other maneuvers, Zheng Xiaoyu took firm command of the SDA as its first commissioner and pursued an aggressive reform agenda. The reform initiatives launched during Zheng's tenure included the nationalization of standards for drugs, the reform of drug registration, as well as the promotion and adoption of good practices for manufacturing (GMP), research (GLP), and sales (GSP). Had this agenda been realized, it would have had an enormously positive impact on the development of China's pharmaceutical industry. As it transpired, however, every one of the major reform initiatives launched on Zheng's watch went awry. An examination of how this happened helps to illuminate the promise and pitfalls of efforts to quickly spread regulatory norms globally.

The conversion to national standards

The replacement of local with national standards was a much needed reform. It would have been impossible to have a unified drug regulatory regime if each provincial unit in China could set its own pharmaceutical standards and keep them secret as they had done to that point. It was thus natural that Zheng Xiaoyu put the promotion of national standards high on his reform agenda shortly after the SDA was formed.

In 1999, Zheng Xiaoyu decided to recentralize the right to approve new drugs in the national drug administration. To sort out the local standards, the SDA itself set up a temporary office in the Drug Registration Bureau to assess whether the locally approved drugs met the national standards as set forth by the Chinese Pharmacopoeia Commission (药典委员会), which reports to the SDA.[14]

Whereas the replacement of local with national standards greatly enhanced the SDA's power of approvals, the process for the re-registration of existing drugs was not one welcomed by the pharmaceutical firms or local drug administrations. It was well known that various local administrations had adopted lower standards to make it easier for firms within their jurisdictions to secure drug approvals and accelerate production. If the SDA firmly adhered to the more rigorous national standards, it would have to revoke many drug approvals that were based on local standards. This would in turn cause many pharmaceutical firms to suspend production and alienate most local authorities.

In practice, the SDA re-certification of drug approvals based on local standards faced a major logistical obstacle. The entire SDA headquarters had only a modest authorized staff size of 120 (although supplemented by temps or others on secondment). Simply put, unlike the US FDA, which once enlisted the help of the National Science Foundation to help it deal with the backlogs of drug applications, the State Drug Administration, even if it could have mobilized the entire headquarters staff, simply did not have the personnel to do a good job of vetting the local drug licenses in a reasonable time period.[15] In fact, the special office for the upgrade to national standards had a staff of less than twenty.

Rather than holding the local drug licenses to the more rigorous national standards, however, what transpired in the review process amounted to an abdication of responsibility by the SDA. Faced with intense lobbying by firms and local administrations, the SDA eventually offered national status to existing local drug approvals. In one three-month period, the Drug Registration Bureau certified 147,900 locally registered drugs as meeting national standards.[16] Rather than elevating existing drug approvals to the rigors of national standards, the review process essentially devalued the drug approval standards to the pre-existing local standards. Eventually, prosecutors would charge Zheng Xiaoyu and Cao Wenzhuang with lowering drug approval standards, endangering the public, and lowering the credibility of a government agency.[17]

The re-certification process also turned into a rent-seeking process. Some pharmaceutical companies simply would not have met the national standards (that necessitated experiments and trials) but nonetheless obtained drug approvals with faked data and bribes to the Drug Registration staff.[18] Most remarkably, some members of the Pharmacopoeia Commission turned the re-certification into a lucrative venture for themselves. Prior to the re-certification, the local standards were not public information. In the process of converting to national standards, local administrations were required to submit their local standards, including confidential information regarding production processes (生产工艺) and quality specifications (质量标准) to the Pharmacopoeia Commission. The Pharmacopoeia Commission should have kept all this information confidential but a company based in Jilin province obtained the entire package of local production processes and quality specifications by bribing Wang Guorong, executive vice secretary general of the Pharmacopoeia Commission, and others, to the order of 8 million yuan. After obtaining this cache of information, the firm selected over 100 injection products and bribed personnel at the Jilin provincial drug administration into giving the company backdated (pre-1996) approvals for these products. Equipped with the backdated local approvals and supporting materials, the company was able to convert the local approvals into national approvals (药品批准文号) for over 200 products, even though the company had not done research on these drug products on its own.[19]

Drug registration

In light of how the conversion to national drug standards was handled, it comes as no surprise that drug registration and approval would continue to fall short. Before we discuss the problems that afflicted drug registration and approval, however, it is useful to note that government regulation of drug prices in China has created powerful incentives for drug makers. More specifically, the National Development and Reform Commission (NDRC), in its efforts to placate public complaints about rising medical costs, has intervened vigorously to cap the prices for commonly used drugs. To get around the NDRC's drug price caps, a drug maker must work hard to secure approvals for new drugs for which the drug maker is more at liberty to set the price. Meanwhile, the SFDA worked with a broad definition of new drugs, and drug manufacturers could generally secure approval for new drugs that are essentially old drugs in new formulations, for example by making tablets into injections or by adding innocuous new ingredients. In essence, the SFDA became the institutional gatekeeper for getting around the NDRC's price controls.

Once the pharmaceutical standards were "nationalized" and the authority to approve new drugs centralized in the SFDA, the SFDA essentially became a rent-collecting machine under Zheng Xiaoyu. Cao Wenzhuang, as director of the Drug Registration Bureau, wielded enormous power over the pharmaceutical companies. In the absence of well-designed processes, the regulators had much discretion. For drug companies, their livelihood entirely depended on whether or not Cao gave approval to their new drug applications and how fast the approvals were given. To get the approvals speedily, the companies would seek to bribe Cao. Likewise, Zheng Xiaoyu's oversight over the Drug Registration Bureau offered him much influence. Both Zheng and Cao were later found to have taken bribes for approving drug registrations.

It is with a deep sense of irony and sadness that I write the above. For the SDA had started with a system of expert review panels to mitigate corruption in the approval process, and Zheng Xiaoyu was himself behind the expert review panel. In December 1998, the first group of 591 national drug evaluation experts

(国家药品审评专家) were elected to form China's national expert bank for drug evaluation. The move was hailed as a major measure of corruption prevention. According to the original design, a drug maker would first make an application for a new drug to the provincial drug administration and, following the initial review by the provincial drug administration, pass the file on to the SFDA national headquarters. The SFDA would then convene a panel of experts, composed of seven or eight experts chosen randomly from the bank of national drug evaluation experts, to review the case, in particular with a technical review of the clinical trial data, and then provide technical evaluations.

Yet the expert review system failed to make a dent on corruption during Zheng Xiaoyu's tenure as commissioner. According to Huang Jun, an expert who had participated in the drug application reviews, each time the experts chosen would gather at a hotel and be shown the application materials. As the experts did not visit the applying firm's production facilities, they had no way of knowing if the application was faked. Sometimes, even when the experts' assessment was not very favorable and they had issued reservations, their assessment was used as reference only. The SFDA official could go to someone else for a different and more favorable opinion and could even discard the negative opinion. Such discretion meant that the experts' opinion had relatively little impact on the outcomes of drug applications.[20] The situation was made even worse because, according to Ba Denian, a member of the Medicine and Health Group of the Chinese People's Political Consultative Conference, some of the experts took bribes from the pharmaceutical firms.[21, 22]

In 2004, the SFDA processed 10,009 applications for new drug approvals. To process these applications, the SFDA would have had to go through and decide on more than thirty-eight applications each business day. This would be an impossible job to perform adequately for the small staff at the Drug Registration Bureau in light of the size and complexity of each of the applications. In effect, the Drug Registration Bureau processed the applications like an assembly line. Even in 2006 (the year Zheng retired), when the situation had become more routine at the SFDA, the SFDA approved 1,426 applications for new drug clinical trials, 1,803 applications for the production of new drugs, and 5,958 applications for the production of drugs on state standards (generics).[23] In contrast, in a fairly typical year, the US FDA, whose Center for Drug Evaluation and Research had a staff of more than 1,700, approved seventy-eight new drugs and 321 generic versions of already marketed drugs in 2002.[24]

With the likes of Cao Wenzhuang, the SDA (SFDA) became a magnet for lobbyists and mediators. Various companies emerged near the SDA (SFDA) headquarters that touted their identities as drug registration agents or purveyors of medical information. They were supposed to help pharmaceutical companies to prepare the complex applications that were needed to comply with the regulations and procedures for new drug applications or for the approval of medical devices. Yet it was understood that some of these entities had "special access" to help acquire approvals for new drugs or medical devices (新药批号或药械使用批文). In their quest for profits, pharmaceutical companies paid handsome sums for such special access.[25] In the words of one pharmaceutical company executive, "[If you] go to them, [you'll] have to bring money. Money quickens the approval process; [you're made] to wait if you don't bring money. [They] won't say [you're] not qualified, or that there's a need for additional materials. Anyway, [you] just have to wait and wait."[26] Money became the essential lubricant for smoothing the approval process.

The corruption that infested the drug approval process went far beyond using money to speed up approvals. Some pharmaceutical companies even purchased the application materials and passed drugs from established manufacturers as their own samples to go with the applications, to secure approvals and thus the right to manufacture the drugs.[27] Because of the rampant issuance of new drug approvals, many firms had the approvals but would not go to the length of producing the drugs. In fact, there was a virtually open market for drug approvals (licenses), with some firms transferring some approvals, for a profit, to others to produce.[28]

Indeed, as the whistle-blower Gao Chun and others found out, it was not simply the pharmaceutical companies that committed outright fraud in the process of drug registration and production. Most remarkably, some of the personnel working at the drug registration bureau sold copies of application documents supplied by legitimate companies, including foreign companies, to other Chinese pharmaceutical companies, who then used dressed-up versions of these documents to get similar drug approvals.[29] Some of the drug registrants (新药注册专员), including both retired drug administration staff in the provinces and in the SDA (SFDA) and even staff still working at the SFDA, made huge sums in the process.[30] When a company can quickly secure approval for a new drug using someone else's documents, what incentive is left for China's own pharmaceutical companies to invest in research and development?

The forced march to GMP compliance

With the formation of the SDA in 1998, Zheng Xiaoyu also made the promotion of good manufacturing practices (GMP) a key mission of the SDA. GMP, which governs the documentation of the manufacturing process and the certification of all manufacturing and testing equipment, is a set of industry standards designed to ensure the quality of the manufacturing process for foods and pharmaceutical products. Like the nationalization of drug standards, the adoption of GMP, which has spread worldwide in both developed and developing economies, is a highly desirable goal for China's pharmaceutical industry. It is, nonetheless, a technical and highly complex, as well as costly, process, and thus demands substantial regulatory capacity.

Initially, GMP certification was centralized in the SDA, but was voluntary for drug manufacturers. This made sense because the SDA had a small staff and it was impossible for the SDA staff to undertake a lot of certifications at any one time. From 1999 to 2002, about 1,000 pharmaceutical firms passed GMP certification.

Then Zheng Xiaoyu was seized with the idea of industry-wide GMP compliance. In August 2001, Zheng, in his desire to upgrade the profile of China's pharmaceutical industry and that of the SDA (SFDA), decided to mandate all drug manufacturers to become GMP compliant by 1 July 2004. Those manufacturers who failed to achieve GMP compliance would essentially have to stop production and lose their business.

Zheng's forced march to GMP compliance immediately aroused vociferous complaints from the pharmaceutical companies that had yet to comply as well as the local authorities worried about firms in their jurisdictions not being able to become GMP compliant and thus facing suspension of production.

Confronted with tremendous pressure from the localities and confronted with the possibility that he might have to eat his own words on the deadline for GMP compliance, Zheng relented. In 2003, the SFDA delegated the responsibility for GMP certification to the provincial-level drug administrations; the provincial-level administrations only needed to file the certifications with the SFDA headquarters for record (省局审批、国家备案的两级联审). As the delegation of GMP certification authority to the provinces was not accompanied by adequate training of staff in the provinces or the standardization of certification processes, it quickly led to the relaxation of standards for GMP compliance simply because the provincial administrations had strong incentives to let the firms in their own jurisdictions gain certification.

Not surprisingly, the delegation of GMP certification authority to the provinces dramatically accelerated the pace of GMP certification. In the space of a year, the local food and drug administrations certified nearly 5,000 pharmaceutical firms for GMP compliance. By the deadline of 1 July 2004, some 6,000 pharmaceutical firms had been certified as being GMP compliant.[31] It was a contemporary version of China's Great Leap Forward in the pharmaceutical industry.

In practice, given the drive to undertake the GMP certification in a relatively short time period, the attention of regulators easily focused on improved equipment rather than management of manufacturing processes. Even in the best circumstances, the local drug administration often failed to crack down on local firms that were important to the local economy. Amid the campaign to certify pharmaceutical firms, GMP certification had become a mere formality as long as the applicant pharmaceutical firm possessed the right pieces of equipment and submitted the reams of data needed.

Most egregiously, it appears that the GMP certification process became a massive rent-seeking exercise for some local regulators and a giant sales opportunity for equipment makers and sellers. According to a survey by the Chinese Pharmaceutical Enterprise Management Association of 140-plus firms that passed GMP certification, the average cost to upgrade equipment and improve management to pass the GMP certification was 31 million yuan (about US$3.7 million).[32] This was a significant sum and a heavy financial burden, especially as many firms were starved of capital at that time and needed to borrow heavily from banks to keep operating. Many Chinese pharmaceutical firms continue to be saddled by the bank loans they took out to pass GMP certification.

Fraud was also not unusual, however, and there was little double-checking of data submitted. The SFDA had simply withdrawn from the actual certification process. Some pharmaceutical companies would systematically fake the data needed for GMP certification by filling up the required forms for over half a year with fake data. With the right connections and perhaps money to lubricate the wheels of approval, they would become GMP certified with little difficulty.[33]

The SFDA did close some pharmaceutical firms for their failure to become GMP certified. Yet Zheng clearly overstated the SFDA's regulatory prowess. One reporter estimated that Zheng's speeches and reports at the time implied that more than 4,000 firms had been closed, but this was simply a gross exaggeration designed to falsely emphasize the significance of the reforms.[34] In fact, there were 6,984 pharmaceutical companies in China in 1998 and more than 6,600 as of early 2007. During that time, some of the firms were closed, others were merged, still others were new, and the suggestion that thousands of firms had to close as a result of the SFDA's drive to promote GMP certification was simply false.

Corruption, whistle-blowing, and disciplinary failure

As noted earlier, the various reforms launched on Zheng Xiaoyu's watch became corrupted by bribery and rent-seeking. Much of the corruption involving SFDA officials occurred through their family members, many of whom also worked in the pharmaceutical industry. In connection with the trials of Zheng Xiaoyu, Cao Wenzhuang, Hao Heping, and others, the Chinese media have reported on some of the corrupt dealings, although they undoubtedly did not have the full story. For a short time, Zheng Xiaoyu's two defense lawyers released the key court documents connected with the case and thus revealed the major charges brought by the government.[35]

Even a cursory review of the Zheng Xiaoyu case would help to illuminate how the personal failings of Zheng and his associates undermined the regulation of drug safety even as they took on the role of champions for regulatory reforms. Most of the bribes Zheng Xiaoyu took were for approval of new drug applications and collected through his wife Liu Naixue (刘耐雪) and son Zheng Hairong. Ultimately, Zheng was charged with taking bribes totaling 6.5 million yuan.

Zheng Xiaoyu's wife Liu Naixue accompanied Zheng from Zhejiang to Beijing and became a highly compensated employee at the Beijing Jinsaishi biotech company. In at least one case, Jinsaishi appeared to have gained access to a drug application by another company then pending (and stalled) at the drug administration.[36] It seems reasonable to speculate that Liu's influence helped Jinsaishi gain access to confidential information that it was not supposed to have and that the drug administration was not supposed to disclose. The indictment states that Zheng received more than one million yuan from the head of the research institute where Liu Naixue worked.[37]

Zheng Hairong, Zheng Xiaoyu's son, also got into the medical industry. Hao Heping, director of the Bureau of Medical Devices, was instrumental in helping Zheng Hairong make profits from registering medical devices. In fact, under Hao Heping, it was relatively easy (and, relative to drug registration, relatively inexpensive) to obtain registration and approval for medical devices. Around Hao, besides Zheng Hairong, various other retired SFDA officials set up or controlled registration agencies (注册代理公司). Hao dominated the approval process and overrode the technical assessments by experts.[38]

For Zheng Hairong, however, it was much easier to collect money just by being the son of Zheng Xiaoyu. Between 2000 and 2006, Zheng Hairong was paid 730,000 yuan in salaries by a Guangdong company even though he never worked there. The same company also covered the costs of home decorations for Zheng Xiaoyu that were worth 250,000 yuan.[39] During his trial, Zheng Xiaoyu stated, "I have come to realize that the bosses of pharmaceutical companies took different approaches to bribe me. They gave stocks and money to my wife and son. I didn't object but gave my tacit approval (予以默认). This was taking bribes."[40]

In his official capacity, Zheng Xiaoyu did pay some lip service to the need to combat corruption and fraud, especially in the early days of the SFDA. Yet the behavior of Zheng and his lieutenants obviously told a different story. Zheng's relationship with the whistle-blower Gao Chun, a pharmaceutical researcher responsible for research and new drug registration at the Hunan pharmaceutical company Yueyang Zhongxiang Kangshen (湖南岳阳中湘康神药业集团), reveals a striking portrait of personal willfulness and institutional arrogance at the SDA.

Between 1995 and 2003, Gao Chun visited the SDA (and its predecessor the SPA) a total of thirty-five times. In 1995, Gao reported fraud at one Hunan pharmaceutical company directly to Zheng Xiaoyu. In 1999, Gao complained to the SDA that the Hunan provincial drug administration was shielding companies committing fraud. For nine years, Gao tried to blow the whistle on fraud at that company and others to Zheng Xiaoyu and other top SDA regulators, but Gao's efforts had no effect on the behavior of either the firms or the regulators. Indeed, the SDA officials and staff grew increasingly dismissive of Gao, at one time even threatening him with custody. Frustrated that Zheng and other SDA officials were not taking action on his reports, Gao Chun sued the SDA for its failure to fulfill its administrative duties (行政不作为) at the Beijing First Intermediate Court in 2003.[41] Sadly for Gao, the court decided in 2004 that it had no jurisdiction over the case.

In contrast, some of the firms that committed fraud were downright ferocious in dealing with their critics. Zhang Zhijian, then a pharmaceutical researcher at a Hainan pharmaceutical company, found this out the hard way. On 20 March 2006, Zhang re-posted an essay written by someone else that mentioned corrupt dealings between Haikou Kangliyuan and SFDA officials including Cao Wenzhuang.[42] A month later, Kangliyuan got the local police and prosecutors to have Zhang taken into custody on charges of defaming the reputation of a commercial enterprise. Had not Zheng Xiaoyu himself been taken into custody and put on trial, and had Kangliyuan not been among the firms that had bribed Zheng, Zhang Zhijian would most likely have continued to languish in custody. On 6 February 2007, the procuracy withdrew the lawsuit against Zhang Zhijian, saying that that "the evidence has changed."[43] For his ten-month ordeal, Zhang received state compensation of 24,000 yuan from the Longhua District Procuracy of Haikou city.[44]

The consequences and implications of regulatory corruption

Even though Zheng was ultimately executed for bribery and dereliction of duty, some industry insiders nonetheless believed that the Chinese drug administration "underwent quite obvious reforms and made progress."[45] Indeed, each of the reforms called for more strict and uniform regulation even though actual implementation fell short of the desired objectives. And the GMP certification did force most pharmaceutical companies to upgrade equipment, even if its effect on manufacturing processes was more limited. Yet where the regulators had no discipline and succumbed to venal temptations, every certification or approval process became an opportunity for rent-seeking and bribery, and therefore a potential safety hazard, with grave consequences.

First, in light of the large number of drugs approved, and because of the substantial corruption and outright fraud in the approval and GMP certification processes and the relatively small regulatory staff available to inspect and ensure drug safety, it is to be expected that safety issues would emerge. This is all the more the case because the SFDA has been criticized for having simply abandoned its regulatory duty beyond drug registration. It is thus no exaggeration to say that the SFDA on Zheng Xiaoyu's watch had essentially approved various time bombs. It was only a matter of time before some of these time bombs would explode.

And explode they did. By the time of Zheng Xiaoyu's retirement, China was confronted with a spate of major drug safety disasters, including the Qiqihaer No. 2 Pharmaceutical Factory case and the Xinfu case ('齐二药' 事件, '欣弗' 事件). In each case, the problem came to light only after patients had suffered from serious adverse reactions and some had died.[46] These events focused attention on the SFDA and made the corruption cases at the SFDA especially egregious for putting lives in jeopardy.

Second, the proliferation of defective drug approvals has also been a major setback for the ambitions of China's pharmaceutical industry. The proliferation of new drug approvals lowered the barriers to entry into the pharmaceutical industry. Seeing the ease with which one could obtain approvals to produce copies of existing drugs and make money, even some real estate developers decided to shift gears and get into the pharmaceutical industry, although their sole purpose for entering the industry was to make quick profits and they did not tend to have a long-term vision.[47] In the end, the lower regulatory barriers to entry served to drive down profit margins, especially because the "new" drugs being approved were typically versions of existing drugs. This left the Chinese pharmaceutical industry in a vicious cycle. Precisely because it was easy to gain regulatory approval for "new" drugs, firms resorted to bribery and other means to get more and more versions of the same drug approved as "new drugs." There was little incentive to become truly innovative.

There is a great irony in this state of affairs. To some extent, the regulators could mass approve large numbers of "new" drugs partly because they knew that these were copies of drugs that had already been tested in other countries. In the wry comment of one industry veteran, "If you really come up with a breakthrough drug, the SFDA may not dare to approve it [so quickly for fear of the safety implications]."[48]

Third, the rampant corruption and regulatory failure in the SFDA were signs of the limited efficacy of China's discipline and anti-corruption system. To be sure, Zheng and a substantial number of SFDA officials, as well as pharmaceutical entrepreneurs, have gone to jail and been executed in the case of Zheng, but the punishment occurred only after Zheng and his cronies had caused great harm over many years.

Zheng and his associates' behavior would not have gone as far had there been more effective supervision. The SFDA is part of the State Council line-up but is ranked below ministerial rank and does not enjoy cabinet status. Part of the reason why Zheng Xiaoyu rushed the various reforms was believed to be his desire to show quick results and thus to get the bureaucratic ranking of the SFDA and his own raised to ministerial level like the other regulatory administrations.

While each of the regulatory administrations is overseen by one of the vice premiers or state councilors, the CCP and the government monitor the ministries and administrations through a discipline and supervision system (the Central Discipline Inspection Commission (CDIC) and the Ministry of Supervision). Typically, one of the deputy secretaries in each ministry or administration is to represent the CDIC/Ministry of Supervision. Yet in the past, the discipline inspection person tended to become "captured" by the organization in which he or she was embedded. This was clearly the case at the SFDA, where the presence of Yang Baoxiang, officially the team leader of the SFDA Discipline and Inspection Team and a member of the Party Group, was ineffective in curbing the rampant corruption in the SFDA.

In recognition of the tendency toward capture, the CDIC began to introduce reforms to the discipline inspection system. In March 2006, Qu Shuhui, formerly director of the Supervision Office of the Supreme People's Court, was brought in to replace Yang Baoxiang. Yang Baoxiang was more like a member of the SFDA, while Qu Shuhui's reporting relationship was more oriented toward the CDIC. As an outsider, Qu became an effective player and reportedly played a significant role in the Zheng Xiaoyu case.[49] The arrest of some SFDA officials encouraged others to come forward as informers. In the first half of 2006, the Discipline Inspection team at the SFDA received 886 letters and visits from informers to report on cases of abuse of power and corruption and on problems of fraud and failure to comply with laws and regulations in drug research, registration application, and production.[50]

The quest for regulatory prowess in the aftermath of Zheng Xiaoyu

On 24 January 2007, Premier Wen Jiabao convened a State Council executive meeting, attended by the vice premiers and State Councilors, to discuss the case of Zheng Xiaoyu. Most significantly, the meeting was also attended by the secretary and deputy secretary of CDIC, Wu Guanzheng and He Yong. The meeting came to the conclusion that this was a serious case of dereliction of duty and corruption. The SFDA had clearly become the poster child for regulatory corruption and incompetence in China. In the words of Vice Premier Wu Yi, "The SFDA is a typical case and [the problems that afflicted it] may more or less exist in other government departments."[51] At a time when the Chinese leadership sought to decrease the number of death penalties, Zheng became the first ministerial-level official to be executed since 2000 and only the fourth in the reform era.[52]

The arrest and trial of Zheng Xiaoyu and other SFDA officials as well as local drug administration officials did not solve the problems at the SFDA, but merely marked the beginning of a new phase. Now Commissioner Shao Mingli had to face up to the daunting challenge of cleaning up the mess at the SFDA. Not surprisingly, there was much soul-searching as well as personnel replacements within the SFDA. Besides rotations within the SFDA itself, key positions at the Drug Registration and Medical Devices bureaus went to outsiders, with Zhang Wei, formerly deputy director of the Beijing municipal FDA, taking over as director of the Drug Registration Bureau, and Wang Baoting, formerly deputy director of the Shandong Provincial Health Bureau, assuming the directorship of the Medical Devices Bureau. Under great pressure, Shao Mingli launched intense study sessions among staffers to learn about and reflect on the purposes (For whom do we regulate?) and mechanisms (How to regulate?) of regulation.[53] With much fanfare, the SFDA announced a list of eight prohibitions banning regulatory staff from various activities such as receiving gifts from drug firms.[54] In 2007, the SFDA severed links with twenty-two firms that were set up by ten SFDA affiliate units. SFDA staff gave up more than 3.5 million shares in drug stocks and more than 2.6 million yuan in gifts of cash and securities.[55]

The SFDA has also introduced a series of institutional mechanisms designed to mitigate the incidence of corruption. These mechanisms include separation of regulatory duties (case acceptance, technical assessment, and administrative evaluation and approval), collective responsibility for administrative approval, enhancement of regulatory transparency including greater use of web-based processing, and the rotation of regulators within the SFDA.[56]

Yet the Zheng Xiaoyu administration has left a massively flawed legacy that cannot be easily corrected. One statistic alone underscores the magnitude of the challenge. According to Zhang Wei of the SFDA Drug Registration Bureau, some 150,000 legacy approvals—the bulk of the existing drug registrations—were issued without adequate data from clinical trials and pharmaceutical evaluations.[57] In other words, the Chinese public has good reason not to trust the safety of most drugs manufactured by drug makers based in China.

As discussed earlier, many of the problems on Zheng Xiaoyu's watch arose when he set ambitious deadlines for various reforms but, lacking the resources to undertake the reforms at the SFDA headquarters, simply lowered the standards and thus defeated the goals of reform. Under Shao Mingli, there has been no campaign or forced march. Espousing the motto of "scientific regulation," which is a reference to General Secretary and President Hu Jintao's emphasis on the scientific outlook of development, the SFDA under Shao has taken a multipronged approach to drug regulation.

In drug registration, the pace of drug approvals at the SFDA has slowed down dramatically, to a virtual standstill as far as many drug firms are concerned, as the SFDA refocused its attention on quality rather than quantity. Numerous firms that had submitted drug approval applications voluntarily withdrew their applications for fear that their applications would not pass muster in light of the SFDA's newly found emphasis on safety. According to one report, the number of withdrawn applications in the first half of 2007 amounted to 6,441 or 22 percent of the total.[58] To deal with the large number of legacy drug approvals, the SFDA announced in fall 2006 that all existing drug approvals would need to be re-evaluated and re-registered over time as they come up for renewal five years after the initial approval, with special emphasis on safety. It will be about 2011 by the time the SFDA will have re-examined all the drug approvals issued during the Zheng Xiaoyu era.

While the re-evaluation of existing drug approvals continues, the SFDA has stepped up initiatives to upgrade the overall regulatory environment for drug safety by amending the regulations on drug registration, GMP inspections, supervision of drug sales, and of drug advertising in 2007. It also issued new regulations on drug recalls.

Of particular import have been the SFDA's efforts to enhance post-drug approval regulation. To begin with, the central government budget allocation for food and drug regulation rose to 3.7 billion yuan in 2006–7, compared with about 2.85 billion for the 1998–2005 period. The funding increase has enabled the SFDA to upgrade facilities and equipment for analysis and detection.[59]

Armed with more resources, the SFDA has turned to random inspections and onsite inspectors to keep pharmaceutical companies on their best behavior, especially with respect to GMP compliance. The dedicated onsite inspectors are first dispatched to drug manufacturers deemed to be potentially high safety risks, including makers of blood products, vaccines, injected drugs, and certain special drugs. By the end of 2007, some 1,300 inspectors were already at work.[60] To mitigate the risk of the inspectors being bought off by the drug makers they are monitoring, the SFDA has devised an elaborate set of rules to ensure the inspectors do not take any payment or other forms of benefits from the drug makers. Moreover, the inspectors are to be rotated every two years, again to mitigate the possibilities of capture.[61] For certain classes of drugs (narcotic drugs and anti-psychotic drugs), a dedicated regulatory information network was set up to monitor the entire production and sales processes.[62]

Yet even random inspections have their limits. Software companies have produced software to help pharmaceutical companies cope with the stricter SFDA regulations and reportedly even provide periodic upgrades to the software. According to one pharmaceutical executive, such software can help pharmaceutical companies cook their data to deal with SFDA random inspections and are even designed to trick the software packages that the SFDA inspectors use to conduct the inspections.[63] In this respect, the SFDA drive to conduct inspections may have only limited effect on the conduct of certain companies bent on deceit. Ultimately, entrepreneurs must internalize the ethics and rules of the regulators before China's drug industry can be truly cleaned up. Before that happens, however, what is needed is regulatory implementation with teeth that really bite.

Under tremendous pressure from the national leadership and the media, the SFDA has begun to show some backbone. During the 18-month drive in 2006–7 to improve drug regulation, the SFDA revoked twenty-seven licenses for the production of drugs and medical devices and cancelled 157 GMP certifications. The SFDA also cancelled 1,210 operational licenses for drug wholesalers or retailers and closed 1,719 that operated without a drug-sale license.[64] Drug recalls, some following the lead of the US FDA, have also become a well-accepted practice.

Whereas previously the Zheng Xiaoyu administration had tended to cave in to local and industry pressures and not uphold the policy aims and standards set earlier, the SFDA under Shao Mingli has chosen to stick to its guns. In one important area, the SFDA has displayed remarkable toughness. In 2004, the SFDA issued an order on promoting GMP compliance among producers of prepared herbal pieces (中药饮片). The order stipulated that all manufacturers of prepared herbal pieces must become GMP compliant by 1 January 2008. By the end of 2007, however, only 300 of the 1,100 firms making herbal pieces had been certified as being GMP compliant, while most others balked at the high costs of GMP certification and took a wait-and-see attitude.[65] Rather than postpone the deadline for compliance, however, the SFDA took a hard-line stance and decreed that the original order must be honored and those firms that violated it would be dealt with as if they were manufacturers of fake medicine. This means they can be fined and prosecuted for a criminal offense (PRC Drug Administration Law: Article 74).[66]

In handling the string of drug safety incidents since 2006, the SFDA has also cut a more vigorous and professional profile. Take the case of Hualian, a unit of the Shanghai Pharmaceutical Group. Hualian was a manufacturer of several anti-cancer drugs, including methotrexate, a drug commonly used to treat leukemia. In 2007, nearly 200 Chinese cancer patients were seriously harmed and even paralyzed after using the anti-leukemia drug produced by Hualian. After reports of the adverse effects came to light, Shanghai Pharmaceutical tried to play down the problem as that of side-effects. The Shanghai Food and Drug Administration, together with a joint investigation team from the State Food and Drug Administration and the Ministry of Health, launched their own investigation and concluded that this was a case of serious contamination. In a failure to follow GMP operating procedures, a technician contaminated multiple batches of methotrexate, as well as another drug cytarabine hydrochloride, with vincristine sulfate, an anti-cancer compound. The SFDA accused Hualian's managers of "systematically covering up violations of production procedures." The defective drugs were recalled. In response to the results of the investigation, the Shanghai Food and Drug Administration revoked Hualian's drug production license, rescinded all 119 drug approvals held by Hualian, confiscated its earnings from the defective drugs, and imposed the largest fine allowed by the Drug Administration Law. The SFDA revealed that the responsible individuals at Hualian had been arrested and would be prosecuted for criminal responsibility.[67]

Proposals for further institutional reforms

Whereas the SFDA under Shao Mingli has acquired more vigor, as well as rigor, as a regulator, the SFDA's failings under Zheng Xiaoyu have nonetheless prompted calls for thorough reforms. These calls have continued to reverberate in China.

The default option for the SFDA would be to respond to the problems uncovered and strengthen itself along the model of the US FDA. After all, the US FDA has historically had its crisis moments, and it was by politicians and the agency responding to the crises that the US FDA gradually acquired its good institutional reputation.[68] Unlike the drug regulators in the US and other developed economies, however, the SFDA can model itself on its counterparts and thus should find it easier to enhance its regulatory capability. Advocates for this trajectory have called for the SFDA to adopt full national integration (vertical administration) to curb local influences and thus enhance the agency's integrity. This is especially important in remote areas in China's interior, where the local administrations tend to be underfunded and may be asked by the provincial government to help attract business investment and thus divert themselves from their regulatory mission.[69] Nonetheless, increased central government funding since 2006 has to some extent alleviated the budgetary pressures on the local administrations.

Others, however, contend that SFDA's regulatory portfolio, covering food and pharmaceuticals, is too large to be managed effectively in the Chinese context. One proposal, mooted in the *China Daily*, would separate food regulation from the SFDA into a separate agency to allow for greater attention to food safety regulation. Another option was to separate drug approval and drug production safety regulation into separate agencies, with the remainder of the severely weakened SFDA being put into another ministry, such as the Ministry of Health.[70]

Still others in China have called for empowering non-governmental organizations (NGOs), including consumer organizations, patient groups, pharmaceutical enterprise associations, hospitals, and the media to serve as monitors, so that it would be extremely difficult for regulators to buy off all of them.[71] In light of the travails the few whistle-blowers have suffered, such proposals are not likely to go far without significant improvements in press freedom and the protection of civil society groups.

In the end, no institutional tinkering is adequate without more robust supervision of the SFDA's administrative powers. Unlike the US FDA, which is part of the Department of Health and Human Services and watched intently by Congress, the SFDA gained great autonomy in setting its agenda and had relatively little supervision, whether from the State Council or the National People's Congress. Some analysts in China attribute the SFDA's institutional autonomy to the professional nature of drug regulation. Yet, as we know, the mess at the SFDA on Zheng Xiaoyu's watch occurred precisely because Zheng enjoyed a dominant position. Zheng himself warned against exactly the problems that he caused and benefited from at various times. Against this background, the government restructuring plan, approved by the National People's Congress in March 2008, placed the SFDA under the fold of the Ministry of Health, much as the US FDA is in the Department of Health and Human Services. Shao Mingli received a concurrent appointment as vice minister of Health. At the time of writing, it is not yet clear how the revamped "super-ministerial" administrative set-up will work. The Ministry of Health will likely be in charge of overall policy formulation on food and drug regulation while the SFDA is likely to focus on regulatory implementation, thereby providing some check on the SFDA.

Conclusion

The pharmaceutical industry is not just about profits but about the safety of drugs and medical devices, and the protection of people's health. Because it comprises thousands of widely dispersed firms engaged in diverse and highly technical production, it has been especially challenging to raise the regulatory standards and the quality of regulatory enforcement. Seen from this perspective, the Chinese initiatives to centralize drug regulation in one regulatory agency and the efforts by the SFDA to unify drug standards and promote GMP and other international standards did not come one moment too soon. Seeking to emulate the US FDA, these Chinese initiatives symbolize China's eagerness for globalization.

Sadly, the SFDA's efforts during the Zheng Xiaoyu administration have not led to a straightforward elevation of standards but have instead produced a contorted and corrupt regulatory apparatus, even by Chinese standards. The entire drug regulatory system became distorted and the reforms were twisted beyond recognition and became tools for rent-seeking and personal profiteering. And the consequences of the SFDA's failure go far beyond the agency in this case, as they have undermined the development of an industry and resulted in harm to the health and safety of the public, including the loss of lives.

This analysis of the tortuous development of the SFDA over the past decade thus does not condemn the reformist goals, which were highly desirable and well intended. It speaks instead to the complexities of globalization and, especially in this case, of how institutional development does not occur in a political vacuum, but is often the result of negotiations and compromises. The tragedy of Zheng Xiaoyu is that he set lofty goals and accelerated deadlines even though the SFDA did not possess the requisite funds and personnel to meet the targets on time and, unlike the US FDA, had no recourse to the Academy of Sciences. Even worse was the profound lapse in judgment and moral integrity shown by Zheng and his colleagues as they sought to meet the publicly announced deadlines. In GMP certification, for example, Zheng could have accepted the reality he faced and set more modest objectives (such as phasing in GMP compliance based on certain priorities and perhaps even enlisting international help including third-party certification). Instead, the vanity of simply having met a deadline—a common practice during the days of central planning—took hold of Zheng and his lieutenants, at the expense of the SFDA's mission of protecting people's health.

One could argue that the problems with the SFDA reforms were over-determined because of the socio-political context in which Zheng and his colleagues had to function. While the SFDA's regulatory scope may be short of the FDA's (25 cents of every consumer dollar spent), it nonetheless oversees thousands of firms in the pharmaceutical industry alone, and these firms are often seen as vital to the local economy by local governments. The SFDA's reforms under Zheng stepped on the toes of powerful local and industrial interests and, given the pressures these interests exerted, it was not too surprising that Zheng—the quintessential man of the pharmaceutical industry—would cave in to these pressures and lower regulatory standards. Yet, ultimately, it was Zheng himself who was responsible for the key decisions regarding the nationalization of drug standards and the promotion of GMP. The socio-political structure was a major influence, but Zheng was a key agent who could have chosen to act differently, even though doing so would have exposed him to tremendous pressure (but, in retrospect, would have saved him from the death penalty).

Zheng's execution on 10 July 2007 marked a milestone in the institutional development of the SFDA. Despite Zheng's execution, the deleterious impact of the corruption that infested the drug approval and GMP certification processes during the Zheng era will not disappear overnight. The drug safety incidents at Shanghai Hualian and others are symptoms of the problems that have accumulated during the Zheng era with lax GMP certifications and inspections. For now, however, the SFDA has yet to emerge from its darkest hour. Nonetheless, it appears that the initiatives that have been taken in the post-Zheng era, whether in raising the standards for drug approvals, strengthening GMP inspections, or regulatory enforcement in cases of safety incidents, will gradually help the SFDA, now in the Ministry of Health, to gain the sort of institutional credibility that China can be proud of.

Notes

1 I am indebted to John Gillespie and Randy Peerenboom for their helpful suggestions.
2 'The United States and the Rise of China and India: Results of a 2006 Multination Survey of Public Opinion', Chicago: Chicago Council on Global Affairs, 2006.
3 See, for example, The Pew Research Center for the People and the Press, 'Performance and Purpose: Constituents Rate Government Agencies', 12 April 2000. Available from http://people-press.org/report/41/ (accessed 24 November 2008).
4 Karl Polanyi, *The Great Transformation*, Boston: Beacon, 1957; Cass Sunstein, *After the Rights Revolution*, Cambridge, MA: Harvard University Press, 1990.
5 For comparative perspective on these issues, see, for example, John Huber and Charles Shipan, *Deliberate Discretion?: The Institutional Foundations of Bureaucratic Autonomy*, Cambridge: Cambridge University Press, 2002.
6 赵何娟 [Zhao Hejuan], '郑筱萸腐败路线图 [Zheng Xiaoyu fubai luxiantu]', 第一财经日报 [Diyi caijing ribao], 10 April 2007. Available from http://finance.sina.com.cn/g/20070410/02353485549.shtml.
7 中国政府机构名录 [Zhongguo zhengfu jinggou minglu], Beijing: Xinhua Chubanshe, 1, 1996, pp. 25–27.
8 中国政府机构名录 [Zhongguo zhengfu jinggou minglu], Beijing: Xinhua Chubanshe, 1, 1996, pp. 209–15.
9 刘薇 郭爱娣 [Liu Wei and Guo Aidi], '药监历经改革权力扩大 [Yaojian lijing gaige quanli kuoda]', 京华时报 [Jinghua shibao], 8 March 2007. Available from http://finance.sina.com.cn/g/20070308/07533387009.shtml.
10 '中共中央、国务院关于卫生改革与发展的决定   [Zhonggong   zhongyang guowuyuan guanyu weisheng gaige yu fazhan de jueding]', 15 January 1997. Available from http://www.china.com.cn/chinese/zhuanti/yg/933900.htm.
11 For an overview of the 1998 reforms, see Dali Yang, *Remaking the Chinese Leviathan*, Stanford: Stanford University Press, 2004, pp. 37–58.
12 I have followed the official SFDA translation by using the word "commissioner." Chinese and foreign media reports have generally translated Zheng's post as director, but this makes it difficult to distinguish his position from those held by the directors of the various bureaus within the SFDA.

13 罗昌平 张映光 [Luo Changping and Zhang Yingguang], '郑筱萸罪与罚 [Zheng Xiaoyu zui yu fa]', 财经 [Caijing], 18 April 2007. Available from http://finance.sina. com.cn/g/20070418/11223513657.shtml.

14 The website for the Chinese Pharmacopoeia Commission is at http://www.chp.org.cn/.

15 For a history of the US FDA, see Philip Hilts, *Protecting America's Health: The FDA, Business, and One Hundred Years of Regulation*, New York: Knopf, 2003.

16 李欣悦 [Li Xinyue], '药监局原药品注册司长曹文庄被控受贿200万 [Yaojianju yuan yaopin zhuce sizhang Cao Wenzhuang beikong shouhui 200 wan]', 新京报 [Xinjingbao], 21 May 2007. Available from http://news.sina.com.cn/c/l/2007-05-21/044213034442. shtml. For details on the investigation into the Cao Wenzhuang case, see 吴珊 [Wu Shan], '一抓住刘玉辉 曹文庄就蔫了 [Yi zhuazhu Liu Yuhui, Cao Wenzhuang jiu yanle]', 新京报 [Xinjingbao], 25 December 2007. Available from http://www.the beijingnews.com/news/deep/2007/12-25/011@072955.htm.

17 李欣悦 [Li Xinyue], '药监局原药品注册司长曹文庄被控受贿200万 [Yaojianju yuan yaopin zhuce sichang Cao WenZhuang beikong shouhui 200 wan]', 新京报 [Xinjingbao], 21 May 2007. Available from http://news.sina.com.cn/c/l/ 2007-05-21/044213034442.shtml.

18 孙晨 [Sun Chen], '郑筱萸双规激荡药监新政 药监局内部凸显大换班 [Zheng Xiaoyu shuanggui jidang yaojian xinzheng, yaojianju neibu tuxian da huanban]', 中国经营报 [Zhongguo jingying bao]. Available from http://finance.sina.com. cn/g/20070108/16063226153.shtml.

19 王强 [Wang Qiang], '药监设租之祸 [Yaojian shezu zhihuo]', 商务周刊 [Shangwu zhoukan], 22 January 2007. Available from http://finance.sina.com. cn/g/20070122/15553270240.shtml.

20 刘薇 [Liu Wei], '政协委员钟南山: 郑筱萸案源于监督缺失 [Zhengxie weiyuan Zhong Nanshan: Zheng Xiaoyu an yuanyu jiandu queshi]', 京华时报 [Jinghua shibao], 8 March 2007. Available from http://news.sina.com.cn/c/2007-03-08/021811361410s. shtml.

21 Ibid.

22 State Food and Drug Administration, '2006 年统计数据年报 [2006 nian tongji shuju nianbao]', 2007年10月11日. Available from http://www.sfda.gov.cn/WS01/ CL0108/25441.html.

23 Ibid.

24 These data are quoted from http://www.fda.gov/opacom/factsheets/justthefacts/3cder. pdf. For discussion of FDA staff size and drug approvals, see Daniel Carpenter, Michael Chernew, Dean Smith, and Mark Fendrick, 'Approval Times for New Drugs: Does The Source of Funding for FDA Staff Matter?', *Health Affairs* 13 December 2003, pp. W3/618–24. Available from http://content.healthaffairs.org/cgi/reprint/ hlthaff.w3.618v1.pdf.

25 罗昌平 张映光, '郑筱萸罪与罚', 财经, 18 April 2007. Available from http://finance. sina.com.cn/g/20070418/11223513657.shtml.

26 Quoted in 仇玉平, '药监新政使医药行业走出信任危机阴影', 法制与新闻, 6 August 2007. Available from http://news.sina.com.cn/c/2007-08-06/113013603509.shtml.

27 罗昌平 张映光 [Luo Changping and Zhang Yingguang], '郑筱萸罪与罚 [Zheng Xiaoyu zui yu fa]', 财经 [Caijing], 18 April 2007. Available from http://finance.sina. com.cn/g/20070418/11223513657.shtml.

28 厉林 [Li Lin], '国家药监局反思审批之乱 [Guojian yaojianju fansi shenpi zhiluan]', 中国经营报 [Zhongguo jingying bao], 28 August 2006. Available from http://www. p5w.net/news/cjxw/200608/t488469.htm (accessed 24 November 2008)

29 Personal interview with a foreign pharmaceutical executive.

30 王刚 [Wang Gang], '他只是一个人在战斗 [Ta zhishi yigeren zai zhandou]', 中国新闻周刊 [Zhongguo xinwen zhoukan], 9 March 2007. Available from http:// news.sina.com.cn/c/2007-03-09/111712473728.shtml.

31 罗昌平 张映光 [Luo Changping and Zhang Yingguang], '郑筱萸罪与罚 [Zheng Xiaoyu zui yu fa]', 财经 [Caijing], 18 April 2007. Available from http://finance.sina.com.cn/g/20070418/11223513657.shtml.

32 何忠洲 蒋明倬 [He Zhongzhou and Jiang Mingzhuo], '一个部门损害一个行业 [Yige bumen sunhai yige hangye]', 中国新闻周刊 [Zhongguo xinwen zhoukan], 19 March 2007.

33 仇玉平 [Qiu Yuping], '药监新政使医药行业走出信任危机阴影 [Yaojian xinzheng shi yiyao hangye zhouchu xinren weiji yinying]', 法制与新闻 [Fazhi yu xinwen], 6 August 2007. Available from http://news.sina.com.cn/c/2007-08-06/113013603509.shtml.

34 何忠洲 蒋明倬 [He Zhongzhou and Jiang Mingzhuo], '一个部门损害一个行业 [Yige bumen sunhai yige hangye]', 中国新闻周刊 [Zhongguo xinwen zhoukan], 19 March 2007.

35 '郑筱萸案行贿人曝光令人震惊 [Zheng Xiaoyu an xinghui ren puguang lingren zhenjing]', 中国金融网 [Zhongguo jinrong wang], 23 July 2007. Available from http://news.zgjrw.com/News/2007723/News/092669132400.html.

36 陈小莹、沈玮、左志坚 [Chen Xiaoying, Shen Wei, and Zuo Zhijian] '亲友称郑筱萸落马与年幼时家庭贫困有关 [Qinyou cheng Zheng Xiaoyu luoma yu nianyou shi jiating pinkun youguan]', 21世纪经济报道 [Ershiyi shiji jingji baodao], 8 February 2007. Available from http://www.southcn.com/news/china/zgkx/200702080332.htm.

37 '郑筱萸案行贿人曝光令人震惊 [Zheng Xiaoyu an xinghui ren puguang lingren zhenjing]', 中国金融网 [Zhongguo jinrong wang], 23 July 2007. Available from http://news.zgjrw.com/News/2007723/News/092669132400.html.

38 丘敏 赵何娟 [Qiu Min and Zhao Hejuan], '郑筱萸之子办公司报父亲名号 受郝和平支持敛财 [Zheng Xiaoyu zhizi bangongsi bao fuqin minghao, shou Hao Heping zhichi liancai]', 第一财经日报 [Diyi caijing ribao], 7 February 2007. Available from http://finance.sina.com.cn/g/20070207/02423318579.shtml.

39 '郑筱萸获极刑背后 [Zheng Xiaoyu huo jixing beihou]', 中国经营报 [Zhongguo jingying bao], 14 July 2007. Available from http://news.sina.com.cn/c/2007-07-14/152713446956.shtml.

40 杨昌平 张勇杰 [Yang Changping, Zhang Yongjie], '郑筱萸涉嫌受贿640万元案开庭审理 [Zheng Xiaoyu shexian shouhui 640 wanyuan an kaiting shenli]', 北京晚报 [Beijing wanbao], 16 May 2007. Available from http://news.sina.com.cn/c/l/2007-05-16/144613003020.shtml.

41 王刚 [Wang Gang], '他只是一个人在战斗 [Tao zhishi yigeren zai zhandou]', 中国新闻周刊 [Zhongguo xinwen zhoukan], 9 March 2007; 李宗陶 [Li Zongtao], '高纯: "郑筱萸, 你是天下第一贪" [Gao Chun: Zheng Xiaoyu, nishi tianxia diyitan]', 人物周刊 [Renwu zhoukan], 11 February 2007. Available from http://www.nanfangdaily.com.cn/rwzk/20070211/sz/200702280031.asp; 高纯 [Gao Chun], '我的中国梦 [Wo de zhongguo meng]'. Available from http://www.bokerb.com/logshow.asp?id=5439 (accessed 16 March 2007).

42 康力元(集团)涉嫌巨额行贿SFDA曹文庄等 [Kangliyuan (jituan) shexian ju'e xinghui SFDA Cao Wenzhuang deng]. Available from http://my.clubhi.com/bbs/661473/16/31253.html (accessed 30 June 2007; no longer available).

43 刘伟 [Liu Wei], '揭露郑筱萸网民张志坚: 中纪委让我放心讲真话 [Jielu Zheng Xiaoyu wangmin Zhang Zhijian: Zhongjiwei rangwo fangxin jiang zhenhua]', 新京报 [Xinjingbao], 9 April 2007. Available from http://news.sina.com.cn/c/2007-04-09/011512728481.shtml.

44 杨燕生 [Yang Yansheng], '男子揭发郑筱萸被关近10个月获国家赔偿 [Nanzi jiefa Zheng Xiaoyu bei guanya jin 10 ge yue huo guojia peichang]', 法制日报 [Fazhi ribao], 23 July 2007. Available from http://news.sina.com.cn/c/l/2007-07-23/081613505986.shtml.

45 孙晨 [Sun Chen], '郑筱萸双规激荡药监新政 [Zheng Xiaoyu shuanggui jidang]', 中国经营报 [Zhongguo jingying bao]. Available from http://finance.sina.com. cn/g/20070108/16063226153.shtml.

46 王亦君 [Wang Yijun], '专家态度: 药监部门不能认证后就当 "甩手掌柜" [Zhuanjia taidu: yaojian bumen buneng renzheng hou jiudang shuaishou zhanggui],' 中国青年报 [Zhongguo qingnian bao], 7 August 2006. Available from http://news.sina.com. cn/o/2006-08-07/07289676745s.shtml.

47 蒋明倬 何忠洲 [Jiang Mingzhuo and He Zhongzhou], '谁来保证我们的药品安全 [Sheilai baozheng women de yaopin anquan]', 中国新闻周刊 [Zhongguo xinwen zhoukan], 9 March 2007. Available from http://news.sina.com.cn/c/2007-03-09/ 111712473735.shtml.

48 安库雷 [An Kulei], '谁来监督药监局 [Shei lai jiandu yaojianju]', 人物周刊 [Renwu zhoukan], 11 February 2007. Available from http://www.nanfangdaily.com. cn/rwzk/20070211/sz/200702280032.asp.

49 '国家药监局成腐败重灾区中纪委整顿派驻机构[Guojia yaojianju cheng fubai zhongzai qu, zhongjiwei zhengdun paizhu jigou]', 21世纪经济报道 [Ershiyi shiji jingji baodao], 14 February 2007. Available from http://news.sina.com.cn/c/ 2007 -02-14/104312316581.shtml.

50 蒋明倬 何忠洲 [Jiang Mingzhuo and He Zhongzhou], '谁来保证我们的药品安全 [Sheilai baozheng women de yaopin anquan]', 中国新闻周刊 [Zhongguo xinwen zhoukan], 9 March 2007.

51 '郑筱萸的典型性腐败 [Zheng Xiaoyu de dianxingxing fubai]', 中国新闻周刊 [Zhongguo xinwen zhoukan], 9 March 2007.

52 Joseph Kahn, 'China Executes Former Food and Drug Regulator', *New York Times* 11 July 2007. Available from http://www.nytimes.com/2007/07/11/business/ worldbusiness/11execute-web.html.

53 While Shao Mingli has distanced himself from the Zheng Xiaoyu regime and been portrayed as a victim of Zheng's dominance, it is an open question whether he was corruption free during a period of massive bribery and rent-seeking at the SFDA. In private conversation, one Chinese reporter even suggested to me that Shao could not possibly be.

54 '食品药品监管局发布食品药品监管工作人员八禁令 [Shipin yaopin jianguanju fabu shipin yaopin jianguan gongzuo renyuan ba jinling]', 28 March 2007. Available from http://www.gov.cn/gzdt/2007-03/28/content_564367.htm.

55 曾利明[Zeng Liming], '国家药监局07年清退药企股票350多万股 [Guojia yaojianju 07 nian qingtui yaoqi gupiao 350 duo wangu]', 中国新闻网 [Zhongguo xinwen wang], 30 January 2007. Available from http://news.sina.com.cn/c/2008-01-30/ 165514864034. shtml.

56 曾利明 [Zeng Liming], Ibid.

57 何忠洲 蒋明倬 [He Zhongzhou and Jiang Mingzhuo], '一个部门损害一个行业 [Yige bumen sunhai yige hangye]', 中国新闻周刊 [Zhongguo xinwen zhoukan], 19 March 2007.

58 苏永通 赵蕾 邓江波 [Su Yongtong, Zhao Lei, Deng Jiangbo], '中国药监系统 "刮骨疗毒" [Zhongguo yaojian xitong guagu liaodu]', 南方新闻网 [Nanfang xinwen wang], 17 August 2007. Available from http://news.xinhuanet.com/legal/2007-08/17/ content_6549685.htm.

59 吕诺 [Lü Nuo], '中央财政对食品药品监管两年投入37亿元 [Zhongguo caizheng dui shipin yaopin jianguan liangnian toulu 37 yiyuan]', 新华网 [Xinhuawang], 31 January 2008. Available from http://news.xinhuanet.com/newscenter/2008-01/31/ content_7533998.htm.

60 '药监局约束派驻药企监督员行为 [Yaojianju yueshu paizhu yaoqi jianduyuan xingwei]', 1 January 2008. Available from http://www.china.com.cn/policy/txt/ 2008-01-01/content_9464328.htm.

61 '派驻监督员管理暂行规定[Paizhu jianduyuan guanli zanxing guiding]', 18 December 2007. Available from http://www.sfda.gov.cn/WS01/CL0288/27213.html.

62 '国家食品药品监督管理局召开例行新闻发布会 [Guojia shipin yaopin jiandu guanliju zhaokai lixing xinwen fabu hui]', 1 February 2007.

63 孙晨 [Sun Chen], '药监反腐面临 "深度严查" [Yaojian fanfu mianlin shendu yancha]', 中国经营报 [Zhongguo jingying bao], 4 June 2007.

64 李亦菲, 杨俊坚 [Li Yifei, Yang Junjian], '国家药监局鼓励药企兼并重组 [Guojia yaojianju guli yaoqi jianbing chongzu]', 南方都市报 [Nanfang dushi bao], 7 February 2008.

65 贺民 [He Min], '中药饮片距标准之路还有多远 [Zhongyao yinpian ju biaozhun zhilu haiyou duoyuan]?' 中国产经新闻 [Zhongguo chanjing xinwen], 18 November 2007.

66 '关于加强中药饮片生产监督管理的通知 [Guanyu jiaqiang zhongyao yinpian shengchan jiandu guanli de tongzhi],' 1 February 2008. Available from http://www.sfda.gov.cn/WS01/CL0055/27837.html.

67 '上海华联制药厂被依法吊销药品生产许可证 [Shanghai hualian zhiyaochang bei yifa diaoxiao yaopin shengchan xukezheng]', 13 December 2007. Available from http://www.sfda.gov.cn/WS01/CL0051/26941.html; 叶洲 [Ye Zhou], '上海华联药厂批号全被注销 [Shanghai hualian yaochang pihao quan bei zhuxiao],' 京华时报 [Jinghua shibao], 12 April 2008. Available from http://finance.sina.com.cn/chanjing/b/20080412/01294739270.shtml; Nicholas Zamiska and Avery Johnson, 'China Drugs: A Cautionary Tale', *Wall Street Journal* 31 January 2008. Available from http://online.wsj.com/article/SB120171630877229197.html; Jake Hooker and Walt Bogdanich, 'Tainted Drugs Linked to Maker of Abortion Pill', *New York Times* 31 January 2008. Available from http://www.nytimes.com/2008/01/31/world/asia/31pharma.html.

68 Daniel Carpenter and Gisela Sin, 'Policy Tragedy and the Emergence of Regulation: The Food, Drug, and Cosmetic Act of 1938', *Studies in American Political Development* 21, Fall 2007, pp. 149–80.

69 蒋明倬 何忠洲 [Jiang Mingzhuo and He Zhongzhou], '谁来保证我们的药品安全 [Sheilai baozheng women de yaopin anquan]', 中国闻周刊 [Zhongguo xinwen zhoukan], 9 March 2007.

70 'Anti-graft campaign hits drug watchdog', *China Daily* 5 February 2007. Available from http://www.chinadaily.com.cn/china/2007-02/05/content_800730.htm.

71 孙晨 [Sun Chen], '郑筱萸案: 中国 "治人救药" [Zheng Xiaoyu an: Zhongguo zhiren jiuyao]', 中国经营报 [Zhongguo jingying bao], 18 May 2007. Available from http://finance1.jrj.com.cn/news/2007-05-18/000002249718.html.

8 Unacknowledged legislators

Business participation in lawmaking in Vietnam

John Gillespie and Bui Bich Thi Lien

Introduction

Over the last decade, Vietnam has accelerated the harmonization of its domestic legal systems with global regulatory regimes (e.g., World Trade Organization (WTO) and bilateral trade agreements).[1] Yet in borrowing global scripts, regulators face a conundrum. How do they reconcile global legal rules, principles, and processes (global scripts) with diverse domestic regulatory interests and practices that straddle profound economic, urban–rural, and ethnic divides? The way in which state and non-state actors interact with each other to influence the adaptation and implementation of global scripts will shape the regulatory trajectory for decades in this economically dynamic country.

Evidence considered in this chapter suggests that Vietnamese lawmakers are enacting a commercial legislative framework that primarily reflects international treaty provisions and the interests of an elite group of state-owned enterprises (SOEs) and foreign investors. Most domestic businesses, on the other hand, struggle to communicate their preferences to lawmakers.[2] Some commentators believe an unbridgeable gulf is emerging between legislative expectations and the standards and practices that order everyday business transactions.[3] Others are more open to transplanted legal change, but argue that, in Vietnam's bifurcated regulatory landscape, many domestic businesses believe imported commercial laws are overly complex or simply irrelevant.

To examine how state and business actors in Vietnam come together to shape the domestic application of global scripts, this chapter draws on the analytical framework developed by Gillespie (Chapter 2 in this volume). Gillespie uses the notion of the "regulatory space"[4] to open analysis to the possibility that law and formal state authority may not always play a determining role in ordering global scripts. The regulatory space is occupied by both state and non-state actors that may variously collaborate or compete with each other. He identifies three regulatory regimes in which state and non-state actors may influence global scripts. They are constitutional, self-regulatory, and deliberative regulation.

In the first regulatory regime, the state uses legislation, bureaucratic regulation, and court judgements to order the adoption and implementation of global scripts. But

constitutional processes also give non-state actors opportunities, through representative democracy, referendums, and litigation, to voice their concerns about
globalization. This chapter will explore whether electoral processes in Vietnam
sensitize policymakers to the concerns of businesses. It will also briefly discuss
whether the state is prepared to allow non-state actors to enlist the state power exercised by the courts to influence the interpretation and implementation of global
scripts.

   In the second regulatory regime, non-state actors develop self-regulatory
regimes that (with or without the state) shape the adaptation and implementation
of global scripts. This study will use case studies to explore how self-regulatory
networks have joined with state actors to regulate global scripts. It will also
explore the ways in which non-state actors bypass the state and directly engage
global scripts.

   In the third regulatory regime, state and non-state actors use deliberative
exchanges that take place outside formal institutions and hierarchies of law to
influence policymakers.[5] This study will map discourse in public and private
forums. It aims to understand how dialogical exchanges set the limits to state and
non-state regulation of global scripts. A key inquiry is whether asymmetrical public discourse enables one social group to gain a deliberative advantage within the
regulatory space. Discourse studies illuminate the linkages between the regulatory
preferences of state and non-state actors to underlying social forces.

Local actors in a global space

Before considering how state and non-state actors interact with each other in
the "regulatory space," it is necessary to first describe the non-state actors under
consideration.

Non-state actors: businesses

The term "business actor" used in this chapter denotes a broad range of commercial
entities in Vietnam, including unincorporated firms, domestically owned companies, SOEs, and foreign investment firms. Most domestic firms and companies are
small and medium-sized enterprises (SMEs). According to the World Bank, about
7.4 million household businesses (unincorporated firms) operated in the non-farm
sector in 2006.[6] There are now approximately 150,000 companies formed under
the Enterprise Law 2005.[7] This is the fastest growing business sector.[8]

   SOEs are more difficult to categorize, as some remain under full state ownership,
while others have been partially privatized. The number of SOEs has decreased
sharply from 12,000 a decade ago to around 2,100 in 2007.[9] The foreign investment
sector is equally diverse. Investors from East Asian and Western countries have
very different understandings about the role of businesses in influencing lawmakers. For example, a study of businesses in northern Vietnam (the Business Study)[10]
suggests that Western and, to a lesser extent, Japanese multinational investors are
familiar with global scripts.[11] They prefer an operational environment governed

by legal transparency, codified legal standards, and judicially defined boundaries between state and private interests. In contrast, investors from other East Asian countries, and especially overseas Vietnamese, tap into local business networks and are much less enthusiastic about global scripts.

All this suggests that the business community in Vietnam is polarized. At one end of the continuum, large numbers of SMEs employ fewer than fifty staff each, but in aggregate employ more than twice as many people as the state and foreign sectors combined.[12] At the other end of the continuum, a small number of foreign, domestic, and state-owned large enterprises (LEs) employ on average more than 1,000 people each and account for most of the economic activity in the country. The following discussion investigates why SMEs have been unable to leverage their numerical strength and growing economic importance to shape legislative policy regarding global scripts.

International donor agencies

The picture would be incomplete without mentioning the role of international donor agencies. Since the early 1990s, many international donor agencies (both multi- and bilateral) collaborated on law reform programs in Vietnam.[13] According to the United Nations Development Programme (UNDP), sixteen multinational and bilateral donors have provided legislative support to Vietnam.[14] Most projects support specific legislative drafting initiatives in the commercial area. For example, the United States Agency for International Development (USAID)-funded Support for Trade Acceleration (STAR) project from 2001 to 2006 supported various Vietnamese agencies to draft seventy-two laws and sublaws in the commercial field.[15]

This chapter marshals evidence that international agencies play a leading role as agents for global change. Working closely with like-minded state officials and local consultants, they are slowly eroding decades of socialist antipathy toward private legal rights and, in the process, supporting global scripts that protect the interests of LEs such as foreign investors and SOEs. Their influence on elite thinking is reshaping the domestic regulatory regime.

The first regulatory regime: constitutional processes

The preoccupation in the "law and development" literature with placing representative democracy and other constitutional processes at the center of state–society interaction has been widely criticized as describing idealized rather than actual practices.[16] Not only does much state–society interaction fail to conform to constitutional prescriptions, there are many ways of influencing regulatory policy that are not intended or even capable of being formalized into constitutional processes. These problems multiply in some developing East Asian states such as Vietnam where constitutions are only slowly transforming from documents that announce and legitimize party policy into binding legal texts.

Collin Scott suggests that constitutional prescriptions make little sense if they are limited to positivist discussions about the legislature, executive, and judicial branches.[17] He suggests placing constitutional processes in a broader regulatory framework that goes beyond traditional constitutional discourse to take in the state and non-state structures that steer the exercise of public power. This decentered approach broadens the analytical focus to embrace the negotiations taking place at the periphery of constitutional institutions.

Representative democracy in Vietnam

Representative democracy is potentially important because it can give ordinary people a say in shaping state regulatory policy. It has the potential to give Vietnam's 7.4 million household businesses voting power to persuade legislators to localize global scripts. For this to happen, however, SMEs need some say over the selection and election of delegates to the National Assembly (NA), as well as deliberative channels to communicate their preferences to the NA.

Business influence in the National Assembly

Some commentators find progress toward representative democracy in the increased numbers (from 10 percent to 25 percent) of full-time NA delegates. Further movement toward representative democracy is implied by party efforts to encourage delegates to maintain close contact with their constituents. Media scrutiny of plenary debates has also undoubtedly raised public expectations that the NA is a representative body.

The potential for these reforms to make delegates more responsive to voters should be understood in the broader context of official narratives about representative democracy. For decades, the NA was regulated by "socialist democracy" (*dan chu xa hoi chu nghia*), an organizational principle that sharply contradicts democratic liberal notions of representative government.[18]

Although official policy now stresses the procedural trappings of electoral representation, more than 90 percent of delegates remain party members.[19] The Fatherland Front guides democracy by selecting most candidates to fill predetermined class and ethnic minority quotas.[20] As the party decides the electorates in which delegates stand, the election of self-nominated entrepreneurs is far from certain. In this context, SMEs have few opportunities to influence the selection and election of candidates sympathetic to their views.

The few delegates from the private sector are reluctant to voice their opposition to state policy out of a well-grounded concern that their comments might excite reprisals from the authorities.[21] In contrast, politically connected SOEs are better represented in the NA.

Influencing National Assembly delegates

Private businesses not only have limited opportunities to participate in the electoral system, their influence over elected delegates is similarly attenuated. The rules governing voter interaction with NA delegates are vague. Although delegates meet constituents in gatherings organized by the Fatherland Front during and after elections,[22] informants say that organizers use agendas to control what issues are discussed. Individual voters are rarely permitted to debate concrete matters, much less voice concerns outside those announced in the agenda.[23] Reports prepared by organizers that summarize proceedings are distributed to interested mass organizations and authorized entrepreneurial associations such as the Vietnam Chamber of Commerce and Industry (VCCI) for comment.

Deliberation within the National Assembly

Some commentators believe that NA delegates are acting more like legislators in debating and codifying social issues.[24] They point to debates that precipitated amendments to various draft bills (e.g., press, labor, and land laws) as evidence that delegates are becoming more responsive to public discourse. Further corroboration is found in the increasing length of NA deliberations, reforms aiming to professionalize delegates, and the increased oversight powers of NA committees.[25] Closer analysis suggests a more complex interaction in which delegates rarely manage to introduce unorthodox and contentious views into lawmaking discourse.

NATIONAL ASSEMBLY PROCEDURES

Delegates wishing to speak at plenary sessions must give the NA chairperson a written summary before the session starts. The chairperson controls debate by pre-arranging the order in which delegates speak and by limiting speaking time for those presenting unorthodox or dissenting opinions. Few delegates speak during NA plenary sessions. It is estimated that fewer than twenty-five out of almost 500 delegates address sessions during its thirty-day annual sitting time. Discussions are dominated by fewer than ten speakers from NA committees (particularly the Standing Committee).

Procedures designed to limit individual discourse in plenary sessions are not as rigorously enforced during smaller group (*thao luan o to*) sessions.[26] There is more scope for sustained negotiation, learning, and preference convergence on sensitive policy issues. Senior party and state officials nevertheless promote the party's viewpoint during these sessions.[27] Group reports about draft laws are compiled by the session secretary into "forms for requesting delegates' opinions" (*phieu xin y kien dai bieu*).

CONSTITUTIONAL AND LEGISLATIVE DISCOURSE

It is not enough for delegates to simply participate in NA debates. They need to communicate their ideas in a manner that is easily converted into statutory language. What is missing in Vietnam are abstract constitutional, as opposed to political, "ground rules" for converting everyday concerns and practices into the legal and constitutional language used by lawmakers.

The style of presentation by delegates in the NA warrants comment. Delegates present set speeches or interventions that either make general comments about the "spirit of the law" or deliberate minutiae such as the placement of punctuation or grammar. In the few hours reserved to discuss each bill, there is little exchange of ideas through debate. Speeches in general stand alone and rarely respond to ideas presented by other speakers.

Occasionally, debates erupt in NA sessions when issue-oriented coalitions invoke (usually without success) political and emotional rhetoric to block certain laws. For example, 36 percent of delegates voted unsuccessfully to oppose the ratification of the US–Vietnam Bilateral Trade Agreement. Equally large minorities could not stop the Enterprise Law 1999 from stripping away local discretionary powers and introducing overly complex corporate governance provisions.[28]

Nevertheless, in some cases, minority votes have successfully blocked imported legislative provisions. Ministry of Justice drafters imported the "incorporation doctrine" into the draft Law on the Promulgation of Legal Documents, which was submitted to the NA in 2002. The doctrine would have made market access treaties ratified by the government automatically binding in domestic law. In opposing the bill, some delegates recited passages from the preamble in the Constitution about Vietnam's independence struggle to excite nationalistic opposition to the bill. Once conceived in political and emotional terms as an attack on national sovereignty, delegates equated the "treaty incorporation" doctrine with foreign intervention.[29] Without constitutional "secondary codes" to guide them, delegates could not reconcile political arguments about power struggles with legal arguments raised by the drafting committee that civil law countries such as Vietnam follow the "treaty incorporation" doctrine. Delegates struggled to codify their political and emotional objections to the bill into legal principles that could guide the application of the legislation. As a compromise, they instructed state authorities to decide on a case-by-case basis whether treaties are automatically binding. This ad hoc approach was incorporated into Chapter V of the Law on the Conclusion, Accession to, and Implementation of Treaties 2005.

Although delegates occasionally surprise party leaders by using political and moral arguments to challenge imported commercial law, more generally, deliberations lack the sustained and relatively unmediated discourse required to develop agreed positions about the adaptation of global scripts. As a consequence, lawmaking rarely progresses beyond blocking imported rules to proposing amendments that adjust legal imports to underlying social practices.

Court litigation

There is some evidence that Vietnam is undergoing a limited form of judicialization in which the state is allowing businesses to submit new social and economic problems to courts. This transformation may enable businesses to harness state power to change global scripts. Verification for this reform is found not only in the increasing number of commercial cases, but also in the broad range of business transactions brought before the courts. Coming from a low base, commercial cases increased by about 35 percent between 1999 and 2005.[30] But the rate of litigation increased sharply in 2006 and 2007.

Increased litigation rates coincide with reforms to the Civil Procedure Code that have given litigants more opportunities to submit evidence and raise legal arguments in the courtroom.[31] Structural changes to judicial practice cannot be achieved quickly. In the inquisitorial tradition, judges were responsible for framing outcomes that reconciled litigants' claims to the state benefit and sent ideologically correct educational messages to the people.[32] Reforms that give lawyers rights to advocate their clients' interests, even if this means opposing state interests, run into obstacles set up by recalcitrant judges who, by training, habit, and temperament, are not disposed to arguments predicated on private legal rights. It is too early to assess accurately whether procedural changes will overcome deeply ingrained attitudes, but a party resolution in 2005 urging judges to take legal arguments into account when writing decisions, if rigorously implemented, may go some way toward convincing judges to take the initiative in reconciling imported commercial legislative framework with local conditions.[33]

The second regulatory regime: self-regulation

The second regulatory regime consists of self-regulatory regimes formed by non-state actors (with or without the state) that shape the adaptation and implementation of global scripts.

Market support networks

The composition and operation of market support networks in capitalist economies, such as advertising, insurance, industry standards associations, accountants, and lawyers, shape the regulatory space by establishing the standards and procedures governing professional services, market information, and access to insurance and finance.[34] Although market support networks are rarely mentioned in the literature about legal globalization, they profoundly influence the domestic operation of property, contract, and company laws. Laws designed to operate in specific networks, it follows, will not necessarily induce similar economic behavior in new markets governed by different "rules of the game" and institutions.[35]

Market support networks regulate the way in which states engage with global scripts by shaping the way that entire markets are structured. This in turn constrains the regulatory options available to the state. The argument goes something like this: networks control market entry and the way transactions are structured, financed, and enforced. They create a regulatory environment that controls the demand for legal services, insurance, quality standard organizations, and other institutions associated with law-based marketplaces. In order to remain relevant, states must respond to a particular version of network capitalism.

After twenty years of economic reform, market support organizations are still poorly developed in Vietnam. For example, a recent study suggests that, although there are between 150 and 200 business consultancy firms, their services are used by less than 1 percent of the business community.[36] Large foreign-owned companies are the main users of services such as marketing and branding, and management, financial, and accounting support. A similar pattern has been observed in the use of legal and banking services.

The Survey[37] found that, although most SMEs were aware of market support services, they found the advice offered irrelevant to their business practices. Market support services are generally provided by Western-educated professionals imbued with law-based notions about market behavior. For example, management consultants assume that businesses are internally organized in accordance with the corporate governance principles in the Enterprise Law. Research, on the other hand, suggests that most SMEs remain embedded in a relational transactional environment that is indifferent toward law-based standards and processes. According to John McMillan and Christopher Woodruff, relational connections provide the "rules of the game" for many domestic business transactions in Vietnam.[38] They concluded that "Vietnamese private firms do not yet have a formal legal system to fall back on" and rely on community norms, trade associations, and market intermediaries in place of state-based rules.[39]

The Business Survey also found that the SMEs rarely use corporate governance rules to organize themselves and instead transact business through networks based on personal relationships. The highly selective use of market support services in Vietnam suggests a fragmented regulatory space where foreign companies ground their decision-making on law-based criteria. Small Vietnamese businesses remain embedded in a relational transactional environment that has little use for market support services that assist businesses to comply with formal laws. In discussing the failure of transplanted market laws to take root in Russia, Carol Rose observed "capitalist property has a kind of moral and cultural infrastructure that we may have mistakenly thought was simply natural, whereas in fact it is learned through sustained commercial practice."[40] In Vietnam, SMEs have not learned to base their decisions on legally structured markets.

Adoption of global standards by domestic firms and business networks

As discussed by Gillespie (Chapter 2 in this volume), business actors supervise and, in some cases, regulate the way in which states respond to globalization. This is most likely to occur in societies where the state acknowledges that in fragmented markets no one actor, including the state, has sufficient knowledge to solve complex regulatory problems. Where Western states have come to accept a regulatory role for non-state actors, new forms of regulation have emerged based on a "responsive" or "reflective" relationship between the state and non-state actors that places increased reliance on self-regulating organizations and regimes of self-regulation. This "new governance" has opened more regulatory space for non-state regulators such as business actors.

There is some evidence that the Vietnamese state is experimenting with "new governance" regulatory techniques. In one example, the Ha Nam Department of Industries (DoI) adopted the International Standards Organization (ISO) 9001:200 protocol to "improve the quality of and efficacy of its public services as well as the state governance."[41] The DoI is responsible for drafting policy and regulation on industrial development in Ha Nam. Complaints were made that it had made administrative errors in failing to base regulatory policy on reliable data. Due to systemic errors DoI was forced to withdraw some regulations after their promulgation. In order to improve the policymaking process, GTZ, a German-funded donor, was asked to train officials in ISO 9001:200 quality management protocols. Over the course of the project, a local government department adopted data management standards derived from a global template.

In another example, the Ministry of Finance recently authorized the Vietnam Association of Accountants and Auditors to formulate professional standards and registration procedures for the accounting profession.[42] In a similar vein, Vietnamese private businesses have taken the lead in promoting European agricultural standards. To increase their market share in Europe, Vietnamese food producers have turned to the European Good Agricultural Practices standards (EurepGAP, later renamed GLOBALGAP). Similar to ISO protocols, GLOBAL-GAP sets standards for the certification of agricultural products around the globe.

Although foreign donor agencies initially played a key role in introducing EurepGAP into Vietnam, domestic organizations, including private businesses, have taken over this function. Two domestic firms, Hung Thien Company, an organic vegetable grower, and Bao Thanh Company, an exporter of dragon fruit, promote EurepGAP standards. These companies saw the importance of importing globally recognized quality standards into domestic business methods.[43]

In another development, supply chain agreements entered into between international buyers and Vietnamese manufacturers are changing local attitudes about global scripts. In one representative case, Nike contractually bound a Vietnamese footwear manufacture (Maxsport) to adopt labor standards that exceeded domestic requirements. Maxsport was also required to implement a logistics management regime that tracked every stage of manufacture to ensure that production met quality standards and delivery schedules.

Maxsport now acts as a node in a network. It imports the new organizational thinking through the supply chain agreement and then spreads this knowledge internally and externally to subcontractors and suppliers. The new organizational thinking bypasses state institutions and stimulates domestic firms to create novel ways of dealing with each other.

In each case example, global ideas circumvented the constitutional mechanisms discussed in the first regulatory regime. Instead, business actors in these cases deployed global knowledge for their own business purposes. Although local authorities in some cases maintained an involvement in the dissemination of ideas, they were seen as facilitators rather than the prime regulator.

Reflective regulation

Business actors may also influence the domestic implementation of global scripts by forming reflective regulatory relationships with government authorities. Reflective regulation alters the role of government from a dictator of rules to a facilitator of agreements with stakeholders. Government becomes one of many interest groups and is discouraged from exercising a determining judgment about what the public interest involves and how best to achieve it.

There are tentative signs that Vietnamese authorities are prepared to experiment with reflective regulation. For example, a fishery co-management project near Hue brought local commune officials and fish farmers together to design a regulatory plan and co-manage the environmental impact of this industry.

The third regulatory regime: deliberative regulation

As the Vietnamese economy becomes more globally integrated, the state cannot simply enforce its will upon society. It needs to ground its selection and adaptation of global scripts on a specific reservoir of knowledge based on discourse with state and business actors. Deliberative theory adds to our understanding of such exchanges by directing our attention toward the forums and processes in which lawmaking discourse takes places.[44] As we shall see, much discourse takes place outside constitutionally defined mechanisms and pathways, and it is in these semi-formal and informal forums that elite business actors influence the regulatory space. This section not only examines actors within the regulatory space, but also the reasons that prevent SMEs from fully participating in the deliberative arena.

The forums in which institutions, agencies, groups, activities, and individuals discuss lawmaking may be spontaneous bottom-up networks, sustained interactive discussions, or highly structured gatherings organized by the state, trade unions, business associations, or law reform commissions.[45] Although deliberative theory is a debated concept with many subthemes, it is possible to identify three core assumptions about what constitutes effective deliberation between business actors and lawmakers:

- Business actors are willing to and capable of engaging in reasoned and reflective ("rational") debate with lawmakers.
- Deliberation promotes shared understandings (or preference convergence) about the nature of regulatory problems and the appropriate legislative responses.
- Business actors have the political space to organize and deliberate state policy and regulation.

Although these assumptions may not apply in their entirety to Vietnam, at minimum they offer a framework in which to place and analyze lawmaking discourse. They anticipate Vietnamese regulatory patterns by recognizing that formal state authority may not always play a determining role in localizing global scripts and that the regulatory arena can be occupied by major and minor players that may variously collaborate or compete with each other in some way.

State policy and legislative support for public participation

It is important to examine the social understandings that determine who is entitled to participate in lawmaking discourse. Such notions decide who constitutes the public, whether the public should participate in lawmaking, and "who should speak on their behalf."[46]

Ben Kerkvliet argues that civil society in contemporary Vietnam is not a source of state opposition because the party and the state use their extensive powers to co-opt and suppress public opposition.[47] Certainly, political discourse is partially sealed off from public debate and trespassing can provoke serious reprisals. Although the state uses various tactics to discourage discussion about "sensitive" (*te nhi*) topics, with the exception of obviously taboo subjects such as multiparty democracy or Ho Chi Minh's life, it is often unclear what commentary is permissible.[48] This leads to public discourse that is often vague and figurative, a socially accepted way of approaching potently "sensitive" topics. Balanced and reasoned discussion, on the contrary, is considered in bad taste as it shines too brightly on delicate matters.

Recently, the Vietnamese government has promoted public participation in policymaking as a means of bringing laws closer to the people.[49] This reform needs to be viewed in the broader context of Vietnamese constitutional and organizational principles. Democratic centralism (*tap trung dan chu*), for example, stresses the vertical integration of administrative ranks where the "minority yield to the majority, lower ranks obey upper ranks and localities obey the centre."[50] It is designed to entrench party leadership over the state. Democratic centralism might work against public participation by discouraging lawmakers from seriously considering public comments that contradict explicit party policy.

Within the boundaries set by these principles, the state has demonstrated support for public participation in lawmaking as a means of "bringing the law into real life."[51] Various scholars maintain that public participation will excite "people's sovereignty" and ensure that "laws reflect the common will of society."[52] But they also insist that the state should lead public participation by stimulating "legal consciousness" and discrediting "false" opinions and ideologies. This pragmatic approach to lawmaking uses public participation as a way of increasing the effectiveness of laws, government services, and official accountability, without necessarily enlarging the public space for businesses to organize and advocate their interests. As party policy is often broad and hortatory, lawmakers have considerable latitude to learn from, and respond to, business concerns about globalization.

The legislative basis for public participation in lawmaking has also been gradually broadened over the past two decades. The Law on the Promulgation of Legal Instruments 1996 (amended 2002) formalized this policy by establishing procedures for businesses to *tham gia* (participate) in lawmaking. Article 26 requires drafting agencies to "organize public comment" from those affected by draft bills,[53] but gives regulatory authorities the discretion over what legislation requires public comment and which "people's opinions" to solicit.[54] In addition, drafting agencies are required to consolidate comments received from the public into a report that is sent together with the draft law to the government for approval.[55]

A central question in determining the effectiveness of public consultation is whether lawmakers believe they have an obligation not only to consult, but also to reflect "people's opinions" (*y kien nhan dan*) in laws. Reports suggest that most drafting committees treat public consultations as a mere formality—a process that must be followed, but can then be disregarded. The Office of Government accused some drafting committees of "being conservative, refusing to accept comments from enterprises, generally compartmentalizing their thinking, and favoring the state's interests over private interests."[56] More recently, the VCCI concluded that "a 'closed circle' within state agencies, including drafting committees, drafting procedures, and gathering criticisms and opinions, does not involve different groups within society."[57] Further limiting their involvement, private businesses worry that critical comments may provoke interference with their commercial interests.[58]

Although there is currently no express right for entrepreneurs to comment on legislation, the legislative framework is moving closer to this position.[59] In 2003, the government approved a large research project aiming to improve the mechanism for public participation in legislative making. Policy recommendations made by project researchers have stressed the importance of including entrepreneurs and business associations in public consultation.[60] Encapsulating these concerns, some commentators argue for an inversion of the party slogan "bring policy into real life" (*dua chinh sach vao cuoc song*) to read "bring real life into policy."[61]

Amendments proposed by the Ministry of Justice to the decrees implementing the Law on the Promulgation of Legal Instruments 1996 will, for the first time, give the public a positive right to comment on draft legislation. In addition, the amendments will create a duty for lawmakers to "seriously absorb" public opinion and explain why comments were not incorporated into legislation. In another bid to implement WTO commitments, the Prime Minister ordered government ministries and provincial authorities to post draft legislation (except those categorized as state secrets) on to websites for public comment.[62] If these policies are properly implemented, they will create a legislative platform for SMEs to convey their views about draft legislation. However, as the discussion in the following section implies, such initiatives will not necessarily give LEs and SMEs equal opportunities to enter and influence the deliberative space.

Emerging pressure groups in Vietnam

There are signs that deliberative space is emerging outside the state for pluralistic social groups such as business associations.[63] This section considers whether SMEs are given the social space to organize and communicate their concerns to legislative drafters.

Business associations in Vietnam

Official narratives in Vietnam about social organization were influenced by collective mastery (*lam chu tap the*), a doctrine that rejected civil society (*xa hoi dan su*) or individual space outside state and collective orbits as bourgeois individualism.[64] During the high socialist period (1945–86), the views of "the masses" were transmitted through party and mass organizations to legislative drafters. Following *doi moi* (renovation) reforms in 1986, the party cautiously granted social actors, especially businesses, more autonomy to form associations. With the exception of groups that engage in overtly political activity, state authority has generally tolerated—if not encouraged—the activities of revitalized organizations and newly formed associations.

After years of debate and numerous redrafts, Decree No. 88 ND–CP Providing for the Organization, Operation, and Management of Associations was passed in 2003. It attempts to reconcile the party's desire for associations that promote economic and social development with concerns that business organizations may oppose party and state policies.[65] On balance, however, the Decree reflects the state's intention to retain strict "management" (*quan ly*) over associations.

Recent attempts by NA deligates to upgrade the Decree into a Law on Associations have so far been blocked by unresolved debates about to whom associations should be accountable—the state, members, or society?[66] Pressure by the Ministry of Home Affairs to bring associations further under state management is opposed by groups within the party that want a diversity of associations to represent the interests of citizens and society.[67]

Although "state management" of business associations remains strong, the government has been under pressure to relax its control over business associations in certain key service sectors. For example, senior officials at the Ministry of Trade acknowledge the need to reduce state interference and to promote the role of business associations.[68]

Member-directed business associations in Vietnam

The diversity and growing number of business associations conveys the erroneous impression that businesses interact with legislative drafters through many channels.[69] A recent study[70] claims, on the contrary, that businesses convey their views to lawmakers through a small number of member-directed, industry-based associations and country-based chambers of commerce. Some industry-based associations have successfully used political networks to lobby state regulators. Industry-based associations operating in key industries, such as textile, footwear, seafood, coffee, and tea, are often dominated by SOEs. They enjoy close political connections with the supervising ministries (*bo chu quan*) that determine regulatory policies within their economic sector.[71] As one commentator put it, "many business associations are joining government agencies in a choir" (*hiep hoi doanh nghiep cung "hat be" voi co quan Nha nuoc*).[72]

Politically connected industry associations can directly influence regulatory decision-making. Consider the Vietnam Steel Association. It draws on the financial resources and political connections of its forty-nine state and foreign members to protect domestic production from foreign competition.[73] The association benefits from a close working relationship with the Vietnam Steel Corporation (VSC); it uses premises supplied by the VSC and is led by former senior officials from the VSC. Regulatory policy in this area heavily protects domestic steel producers against foreign imports, overriding protests about high steel prices from the construction and steel processing industries.[74]

In the financial service sector, the Vietnam Association of Financial Investors (VAFI) is an emerging member-directed association. In addition to large state-owned banks and insurance companies, members of this association include seven departments from the Ministry of Finance—the country's financial regulator. Former and current senior government officials, such as the Vice Chairman of the Economy and Budget Committee of the NA and the former advisor to the Prime Minister sit on the VAFI Executive Board.

The VAFI has commented on draft legislation including the investment law, corporate law, tax law, and securities law. It generally argues for greater legal protection for private rights by increasing transparency and predictability, deregulating licensing, and increasing market access.[75] The VAFI has considerable opportunities to leverage its political connections to influence regulators. Its views are sought by like-minded state officials to counterbalance state management policies advocated in government circles.[76]

There are encouraging signs that public debate is emerging within some industry-based associations. For example, SME members of the Vietnam Fertilizer Association (VFA) opposed the association's campaign for value added tax (VAT) exemption for fertilizer imports on the grounds that this would give SOEs a competitive advantage.[77] The SMEs manufacture fertilizer locally, while the VFA is chaired by the General Director of the state-owned Vietnam Chemical Corporation, a large fertilizer importer.[78]

Also joining the regulatory space, foreign investors use country-based chambers of commerce such as AmCham and Euro Cham to request changes to policies and laws. Many of the changes to the Law on Investments 2005 are attributable to submissions made by foreign chambers of commerce.[79]

In contrast, SMEs have been unable to form associations that effectively convey their interests to lawmakers. Despite its name, the Association of Vietnamese SMEs mainly acts as a conduit for government policy rather than a member-directed business association.[80] More generally, SMEs believe that business associations are the "playing field" of SOEs and seldom advocate the interests of SMEs.[81] Consequently, most SMEs join associations to enhance their public profile and form business contacts, but not to influence government regulatory policy.[82]

Even broadly constituted business associations such as the VCCI, the Vietnam Young Entrepreneurs Organization (VYEO), and the Union of Association of Industry and Commerce (UAIC) seldom represent SMEs.[83]

Take, for example, the VCCI—the largest and most active business association in Vietnam. There is conflicting evidence whether it fulfills its mandate to "solicit opinions from its members" and acts as a "representative" (*dai dien*) organization.[84] According to the VCCI's former Vice President, the relationship between the state and business associations is a "partnership" in which the state assists private firms to follow party and state socio-economic policy.[85] Some commentators maintain that the VCCI is slowly disaggregating from the party and state,[86] while others claim that the VCCI remains a semi-governmental top-down organization.[87]

The VCCI has many SME members; however, they are generally small in size compared with the numerically fewer but financially larger and more influential SOEs and foreign members. SME members are skeptical that a body receiving approximately 30 percent of its revenue from the state can meaningfully disengage from party and state organs and communicate unorthodox or controversial ideas to lawmakers. They argue that the VCCI is more interested in inculcating party and state policies than in advocating member interests.

The role played by the VCCI in drafting the Enterprise Law 1999 (amended in 2005) supports this assertion. On one hand, the VCCI took on powerful adversaries to champion greater market access for its private sector members.[88] On the other hand, the VCCI ignored opposition from SMEs to imported corporate governance rules.[89] Rather than fearlessly championing its members' interests, the VCCI joined together with the Central Institute of Economic Management (CIEM)—the principal drafter of the Law—and like-minded government agencies in a "palace war" against ministries trying to retain lucrative licensing powers over entrepreneurs. The VCCI and the CIEM selectively represented entrepreneurial views that supported market liberalization, while ignoring opposition to complex corporate governance provisions. Consultative workshops were organized to collect members' opinions on the draft Law, but these gatherings were tightly controlled by the VCCI and prevented the open exchange of ideas needed to persuade lawmakers to consider the views of SMEs.

Making matters worse, SMEs lack the resources to employ lawyers to convert their business concerns into the abstract legal language understood by lawmakers. Unlike better resourced and more commercially sophisticated foreign investors and SOEs, SMEs rarely provide evidence-based policy positions to counter the view expressed in government policy and draft laws. As a consequence, their exchanges with lawmakers lack depth and rarely propose ways to localize imported commercial laws.

Lawmakers made more effort to solicit comments from businesses when the draft Unified Enterprise Law was released for public discussion in 2005. Nevertheless, public consultations still overwhelmingly focused on concerns raised by foreign investors, international donor agencies, and law firms. Lacking resources and access to member-directed business associations, SMEs had few opportunities to express their opposition to complex internal organizational practices that supported the organizational structures used by their large-scale competitors. Throughout the drafting process, the VCCI remained remarkably silent about the growing unease among its SME members regarding the draft Law and the broader legal harmonization project that aimed to give foreign companies greater market access.

In sum, the VCCI and the CIEM strategically deployed the storylines collected from entrepreneurs to promote neoliberal deregulation. But the VCCI did not act as a member-directed organization and communicate opposition by SMEs to complex corporate governance rules. At the same time, political and legal controls over social organizations prevented SMEs from forming member-directed associations to convince lawmakers to bring imported global scripts closer to local business precepts and practices.

The influence of business forums on drafting committees

We have seen that SMEs have been unable to use business associations to express their views. This section considers whether SMEs can use deliberative channels such as the Vietnam Business Forum (VBF) to convey their message to lawmakers.

Following the initiative adopted at the Vietnam Consultative Group (CG) meeting in Tokyo in 1997, the Private Sector Forum (later renamed VBF) was created to open communication channels between the private sector and government. Members of the Forum comprised representatives from foreign and domestic enterprises, various business associations and chambers, and government counterparts.[90]

Despite its name and mandate, the VBF primarily serves the interests of foreign investors. Different working groups of the VBF hold frequent meetings with government authorities to discuss ways to improve the legal framework governing foreign investment. Working groups first liaise with members to formulate policy options and then instruct lawyers to translate economic preferences into a legal language that lawmakers can easily codify into new and amended legislation.

Although the government only adopts a relatively small number of the VBF's proposals, this forum is among the most active and effective of the advocacy groups. In fact, over the last decade, it has become the main force pushing for the adoption of global scripts, especially those that promote foreign investment. For example, the Manufacturing and Distribution Working Group within the VBF produced a comprehensive position paper and a proposal for reforming the Labor Code. Some of these recommendations were eventually adopted into the amended Code, including the provisions on hiring local staff, overtime working limits, dismissal, and termination of labor contracts. The amendments reflect global labor policies and overturned deeply entrenched socialist views that the state should protect labor against capital. The Forum has also provided extensive comments on other draft laws and regulations, such as the 2005 Unified Enterprise Law, draft technology transfer law, and the draft decree implementing real estate business law.

The deliberative space granted to, and arrogated by, the VBF has given the Forum a platform to discuss issues with lawmakers in a reflective and relatively unmediated environment that encourages preference convergence. This fruitful relationship has attracted support from foreign donors and the diplomatic community.

Efforts to promote the active participation of domestic players in the VBF have not yielded positive results. Selected SMEs are invited to observe VBF semi-annual meetings, but otherwise they play a minor role in VBF dialogs.

It is interesting to ponder why the government appears to be more receptive to foreign rather than domestic concerns. One possible explanation is that foreign backing for global scripts seems to be disconnected from politically sensitive domestic issues. The concerns expressed by SMEs, on the contrary, are often enmeshed in domestic power struggles that threaten deeply entrenched hierarchical orders. Another reason is that foreign investors present their preferences in a legal language that is easily cognizable by lawmakers. In contrast, SMEs rarely synthesize highly contextual and figurative information about "how global scripts affect me" into abstract commercial and legal principles that can inform policy debates.

Informal deliberative pathways

The Business Study shows that many businesses do not consider public participation an effective way to influence legislative policy. Rather than participating in public debate, SMEs have traditionally organized mutual assistance (*tuong tro lan nhau*) networks to influence the implementation of law by state officials. As David Marr opined, "Vietnamese active in the public sphere do not generally see themselves as asserting civic power against state power. Rather, they prefer to infiltrate the state, find informal allies, and build networks that may conceivably be seen as fulfilling state, public, and private objectives simultaneously."[91]

However, a recent report implies that the percentage of firms that regularly submit comments on draft legislation to business associations has increased from 29 percent in 2001 to 39 percent in 2006.[92] Although many of these firms are LEs, the report concludes that societal attitudes toward lobbying (*chay lo thu tuc*) lawmakers are rapidly changing.

Informal deliberation by LEs

Informal and secretive dialogical exchanges are naturally difficult to research. Lawyers observing the strategies used by their Vietnamese clients to influence legislative policy describe two types of exchanges.[93] LEs use every possible informal channel, such as sporting clubs, parties, or other types of social gatherings, to convince state officials to change specific regulatory norms and practices. In addition, they employ intermediaries such as lawyers and business consultants to communicate specific requests to lawmakers and regulators.

Lawyers and business consultants broker agreements between LEs and lawmakers. They leverage personal relationships with state officials that give LEs relatively unmediated access to policy and lawmakers. For example, during negotiations for permits and other trade concessions, lawyers try to show officials how regulators in other systems use laws to balance private and state interests. They explain how legal doctrines invest commercial laws in Western or East Asian (typically Singapore or Hong Kong) legal systems with standardized meanings. They also arrange training courses and study trips to shed light on international regulatory practices. In building trust through personal relationships, lawyers assist officials to adjust inflexible globalized legal principles to local business conditions. Incrementally, these interventions are beginning to weave a protective web around the private legal rights that secure the interests of LEs.

Informal exchanges may also persuade regulators to "fence break" (*xe rao*) and directly violate central laws. This phenomenon most commonly occurs at local administrative levels. The Ministry of Justice reported recently, for example, that over sixty statutes issued by forty-two provincial authorities gave preferential treatment to investors that overreached limitations set by national laws. Benefits included tax holidays, land allocations, and financial support from the state budget.[94]

Informal influence is not merely directed toward local-level authorities. Consider the regulation of private banking in Ho Chi Minh City. Central regulators "manage" joint stock banks by ensuring that the boundaries separating lawful and unlawful activities are never clearly understood.[95] Contradictory and poorly disseminated State Bank lending provisions and vague bank licensing conditions make it virtually impossible to predict the limits of regulatory power. Compounding the problem, provincial and even central bank officials cannot provide advice, because ministers and/or deputy prime ministers decide lending policy at the political level.

Lacking the political networks available to the large state-owned banks, joint stock banks are compelled to form personal relationships with state officials to avoid legal violations that may incur criminal penalties. Bankers approach ministerial advisors or other senior bureaucrats obliquely through "professional" mediators. They lobby ministers to issue official letters that clarify the lending practices that are permitted by the state. This privileged information allows them to expand their business into new and profitable areas, conferring a competitive advantage over rival banks. The purpose of these exchanges is not to encourage the rights-based transactional environment favored by foreign investors. On the contrary, joint stock banks thrive on secretive (and frequently corrupt) privileges negotiated with regulatory authorities.

In contrast to much public deliberation, discussions in informal deliberative settings are sustained and relatively unmediated. These are the conditions that are most conducive to compromise and agreement. But unlike public debate, these exchanges aim to secure narrow personal advantage and only inadvertently reconcile imported global scripts with broadly based domestic concerns.

The influence of international development agencies on Vietnamese legal reform

Legal assistance programs in Vietnam aim to perfect constitutional institutions by encouraging representational democracy, improving legislative drafting, strengthening the courts, and expanding legal training.[96] They advocate neoliberal legal teachings that promote rights-based regulation, but dismiss government initiatives to ameliorate the harm caused by deregulated international trade as market interference. In advocating global scripts and solutions, legal assistance programs find domestic relational norms and practices that regulate most SMEs unbounded, inefficient, and potentially anarchic.[97]

The penetration of neoliberal ideas into elite thinking in Vietnam is shown by party resolutions that now endorse rule of law ideas, such as entrepreneurs can conduct any business not proscribed by law and "user pays" "socialization" policies.[98] But neoliberal legalism is not uncontested. Rather than embracing these ideas en masse, there are small but influential cliques within the lawmaking elite in sympathy with this thinking. They cluster around the collaborative structures that bind foreign donors/lawyers, Vietnamese consultants, and state officials in law reform projects. These communities inculcate neoliberal regulatory ideas by bringing foreign advisors into a close working relationship with local legal consultants, who frequently remain employed as state officials.[99]

Most officials working on donor projects have received a Western education, or at least training, and are well acquainted with the neoliberal legal canon. They are encouraged to follow stylistic and methodological approaches prescribed by foreign donors. The professionalization of domestic consultants is inferred by standardized report writing styles and structures, and their advocacy of neoliberal legalism implies agreement with the donors' regulatory objectives. These epistemic clusters should not be thought of as communities in a physical sense, but rather as abstract bonds with the potential to generate cooperation and shared understandings and responses to lawmaking.

Members of neoliberal orientated epistemic communities are rather heterogeneous in their use of language and ideas. This epistemological flexibility reflects their need to reconcile competing values between the various epistemic communities—based on the party, state, and family—to which they belong. CIEM officials, for example, deployed neoliberal legalism strategically to avoid offending power brokers within the Ministry of Planning and Investment. But they used well-scripted neoliberal solutions to regulatory problems to gain a rhetorical edge over rival drafters who were trying to reconcile socialist "state management" practices with market conditions.

As international economic integration gained momentum, members of neoliberal epistemic communities grew in status and their ideas penetrated further into organizational hierarchies. In a sense, neoliberalism is an "unintended consequence" of the party's international integration policy.[100] CIEM and other state institutions faithfully carry out this policy, and the party leaders tolerate some of the ideas that make international integration possible (i.e., neoliberalism). At the same time, however, the party is divided, and among its members are those who belong to neoliberal communities.

The media

The media constitute another deliberative channel for businesses. Despite party and state's efforts to promote media and business collaboration as "fellow travelers" (*ban dong hanh*), both sides remain skeptical of each other. According to a recent survey conducted by the VCCI and the Vietnam Journalists Association, 40 percent of businesses surveyed were concerned about low levels of capacity and lack of professionalism in the media, while 20 percent viewed the media as a possible threat to their interests and therefore wanted no involvement with it.[101] Some businesses, however, saw the media as a useful source of information on market and consumer demands and party and state policies and laws.[102]

There is some evidence that businesses use the media to communicate their concerns to the government about problems caused by globalization. Recent reports on WTO implementation imply frustration by domestic business about the lack of government protection from foreign competition.[103] Businesses routinely place stories in the media. For example, the *Thoi Bao Kinh Te Sai Gon* (*Saigon Economic Times*) has a business forum that regularly publishes articles written by businesses complaining about specific regulatory problems. However, business concerns are raised on a case-by-case basis and do not establish a sustained discourse that seriously challenges general media support for the government's policy of international economic integration.

Although reporting about the commercial regulatory framework has become more multifaceted—there are now approximately 600 newspapers and 250 news websites—controversial issues concerning regulatory policy are rarely debated.[104] Instead, media reports focus on technical issues. For example, articles about Vietnam's accession to the WTO are educative rather than analytical. They explain how it works and what changes are required to Vietnam's legal system to comply with WTO rules and standards. In a similar vein, reports about trade disputes, for example barriers to catfish exports to the US and shoe exports to the European Union (EU), are documented, but not analyzed in a broader regulatory perspective. As a consequence, the media rarely deliberate the key policy issues concerning international economic integration and the implication of importing global scripts into the domestic legal system.

Further complicating the picture, the state retains a considerable level of control over the media. The Press Law requires the media to act as the spokesperson or literally "spoke agency" (*co quan ngon luan*) of the party, government authorities, and mass organizations.[105] According to the Minister of Culture, Sport, and Tourism, "the media's function is to propagate Party policies and state laws, and to reflect public wishes back to the Party and the state." He warned the press about politically sensitive reporting that might negatively affect socio-economic development.[106] The Chief Editor of the *Vietnam Economic Times*—a popular commercial newspaper—admits that he must reconcile the needs of the business community with party and state policies on economic development.[107] Unsurprisingly, businesses are reluctant to approach the media to publish views that contradict established state policy and laws on economic integration.

To summarize, LEs are better equipped than SMEs to negotiate the hurdles that inhibit public deliberation in Vietnam. Even so, most communication between businesses and state regulation of global scripts takes place in highly structured forums or, more frequently, in private and secretive discussions. As a consequence, deliberative channels are easily transformed into clientelist and essentially corrupt relationships that aim to benefit particular business interests.

Conclusion

This chapter shows that SMEs in Vietnam have been unable to leverage their growing economic and social importance to influence the way in which the state adapts global scripts to local conditions. They have not mobilized their numbers to use representative democracy to communicate their concerns to lawmakers. Unquestionably, the contest between SMEs and LEs the world over to influence globalization is unequal. But the struggle is arguably more difficult in Vietnam because state controls over social organization and public discourse discourage SMEs from forming member-directed business associations and participating in formal deliberative forums. Unlike politically connected LEs, SMEs lack the relational and political connections needed to convey personal preferences to lawmakers. Further constraining their participation in lawmaking, elite-level lawmakers attuned to globalized legal debates are reluctant to recognize value in the commercial practices followed by the vast majority of domestic businesses.

Most commercial law in Vietnam has been imported over the past two decades and has not evolved from a long-term codification of underlying commercial practices. There is little correlation between global scripts and underlying political, economic, and social practices. According to systems theory, global scripts are unlikely to move out of legislation into daily life unless they have "co-evolved" and correspond to the domestic subsystems relevant to regulation—the political, legal, social, and economic systems. A problem with bringing global scripts closer to underlying regulatory practices is that there are few sustained exchanges between SMEs and state regulators to develop a common regulatory language. Until this happens, most SMEs are likely to continue viewing global scripts as alien and imposed.

Excluded from the state-dominated regulatory space, SMEs rely on self-regulation and personal relationships with state officials to construct their own market support networks. Some self-regulatory networks are not completely isolated from global scripts. For example, some SMEs bypass the state and adopt global scripts embedded in transnational supply chain agreements or transmitted by foreign lawyers.

Vietnam appears to be undergoing several types of regulatory transformation simultaneously. The state is cautiously experimenting with "new governance" techniques to implement global scripts. At the same time, most small- and medium-scale businesses self-regulate with little reference to the state, although they are increasingly prepared to adopt transnational "soft law" such as ISO standards. A bifurcated regulatory space is emerging in which LEs and SMEs follow different regulatory scripts about how commercial transactions should be negotiated, structured, and adjudicated.

Finally, it is useful to conclude by speculating about how the government can expand the regulatory space to reconcile global scripts and domestic business practices. This change requires the government to acknowledge that, in a fragmented and rapidly globalizing market, imported legislation cannot provide all the regulatory solutions to commercial problems. Lawmakers need to respect and learn from domestic business practices. To bring global and local regulation into communication, the government needs to relax its control over public deliberation and the formation of business associations. In practical terms, this means allowing SMEs to form member-directed associations and establishing public forums where businesses can publicly debate their regulatory preferences without fear of trespassing in "sensitive" areas. It also requires the government to behave more like a mediator or facilitator in developing regulatory policy in collaboration with business actors. In short, regulation should stimulate dialogical exchanges that reconcile global scripts with a broad range of domestic precepts and practices. Without this shift, most businesses are likely to continue to prefer self-regulation to state-based regulation.

Notes

1 See John Gillespie, *Transplanting Commercial Law Reform: Developing a 'Rule of Law' in Vietnam*, Aldershot: Ashgate, 2006.
2 See Pham Van Chuc, 'Dang Co Chang Mot Toan Cau Hoa Cho Moi Nguoi' (Is There Now a Globalization for all People?), *Tap Chi Cong San* 12, 2002, p. 33.
3 See Pham Duy Nghia, 'Phap Luat Thuong Mai Viet Nam Truoc Thach Thuc Cua Qua Trinh Hoi Nhap Linh Te Quac Te' [Commercial Law Faces the Challenges of International Economic Integration], *Nha Nuoc va Phap Luat* 6, 2000, p. 9, pp. 16–18.
4 See generally Colin Scott, 'Analysing Regulatory Space: Fragmented Resources and Institutional Design', *Public Law* 2001, p. 329.
5 See Jurgen Habermas, *Structural Transformation of the Public Sphere: An Inquiry into a Category of Bourgeois Society*, trans. Thomas Burger, Cambridge, MA: MIT Press, 1991; John Dryzek, *Deliberative Democracy and Beyond: Liberals, Critics and Contestations*, Oxford: Oxford University Press, 2000.
6 See World Bank, *Vietnam Development Report: Business*, Hanoi: World Bank, 2000, p. 5.
7 At the end of 2003, sole proprietors had on average fifteen employees, whereas limited liability and joint stock companies had on average thirty-eight and fifty-three employees respectively; Ibid., p. 8; Tran Huu Huynh and Dau Anh Tuan, 'Draft Report Business Associations', (unpublished), Hanoi: VCCI, 2006.
8 The number of SMEs being set up in Ho Chi Minh City is about 230 on a weekly basis. See 'Nong Nhu Cau Tu Van, Ho Tro Doanh Nghiep' [Heat in Demand for Business Consultancy and Support Services], Vietnam Media website, 12 January 2007. Available from http://www.vnmedia.vn/newsdetail.asp?NewsId=78177&CatId=31 (accessed 10 October 2007).
9 See World Bank, *Vietnam Development Report: Aiming High*, Hanoi: World Bank, 2007, p. 59.
10 The foreign and domestically owned firms operated in five industries: copper wire, car battery, and sunglasses trading, and computer and garment manufacturing. Approximately half the interviews were conducted with the assistance of Vietnamese lawyers (N.H. Quang and Associates and Investconsult); others were conducted with the assistance of research assistants.
11 The term "global scripts" refers to the globalization of norms, standards, principles and rules that govern a broadly conceived understanding of commerce.
12 See Markus Taussig, 'Domestic Companies in Vietnam: Challenges for Development of Vietnam's Most Important SMEs', The William Davidson Institute, Policy Brief No. 34, Ann Arbor, MI: University of Michigan, 2005, p. 5.
13 Information about international donors was gleaned by the authors while working on numerous international development assistance projects between 1994 and 2007 with the Australian International Development Agency (AusAid), Canadian International Development Agency (CIDA), Danish International Development Agency (DANIDA), Foreign Investment Advisory Service (FIAS), International Finance Corporation (IFC), United Nations Development Programme (UNDP), and the World Bank.
14 See UNDP, 'Assistance for the Implementation of Vietnam Legal System Development Strategy to 2010', Hanoi: UNDP Newsletter No. 3, 2005, pp. 14–17.
15 See USAID, 'Report of STAR-Supported Technical Assistance Programs', Annex I, Hanoi: USAID, 2006, pp. 1–5.
16 John Morison, 'The Case against Constitutional Reform', *Journal of Law and Society* 25 (4), 1998, pp. 510–35.
17 Colin Scott, 'Regulating Constitutions', in Christine Parker, Colin Scott, Nicola Lacey, and John Braithwaite, eds, *Regulating Law*, Oxford: Oxford University Press, 2004, pp. 226–45.

18 See Duong Xuan Ngoc, 'Social Democratisation According to Socialist Orientation', *Vietnam Social Sciences* 3, 1996, pp. 36–40.
19 See Nhan Dan, 'Rights to Vote and Stand for National Assembly Election', *Nhan Dan* 14 September 2002.
20 See The Gioi, 'Tenth Legislature of the National Assembly of the Socialist Republic of Vietnam', *Vietnam's Urgent Issues* March, 2002, pp. 73–74.
21 Huy Duc blog. Available from http://blog.360.yahoo.com/blog-Q78P6g5br89WVUa77q C3PG4?p=27 (accessed 5 September 2007).
22 See Legis, 'The National Assembly in a Nutshell', *Tap Chi Nghien Cuu Lap Phap* (English edn, No. 1), 2001, p. 60.
23 See Matthieu Salomon, 'Power and Representation at the Vietnamese National Assembly: The Scope and Limits of Political Doi Moi', in Stephanie Balme and Mark Sidel, eds, *Vietnam's New Order: International Perspectives on the State and Reform in Vietnam*, New York: Palgrave Macmillan, 2007, p. 213.
24 See Mark Sidel, 'Analytical Models for Understanding Constitutions and Constitutional Dialogue in Socialist Transitional States: Re-Interpreting Constitutional Dialogue in Vietnam', *Singapore Journal of International and Comparative Law* 6, 2002, p. 42, Salomon, *supra*, pp. 207–10.
25 See Khanh Van, 'Democracy in the National Assembly', *Tap Chi Nghien Cuu Lap Phap* [Legislative Studies], January, 2003, pp. 6–7.
26 See Legis, *supra*, p. 60.
27 See Tran Ngoc Duong, 'Noi Dung va Phuong Thuc Lanh Dao Cua Dang Doi Voi Quoc Hoi O Nuoc Ta Hien Nay' [Leadership of the Communist Party Over the National Assembly in Vietnam – Content and Method], *Tap Chi Nghien Cuu Lap Phap* 2, 2005, pp. 17–23.
28 See VNS, 'Constitutional Debate Heats Up', *Vietnam News*, 21 September 2001, pp. 3, 4.
29 See Dinh Ngoc Vuong, 'Van De Sua Doi Bo Sung Quy Dinh Cua Hien Phap 1992 Ve Ky Ket Quyet Dinh Viec Phe Chuan Gia Nhap Bai Bo Dieu Uoc Quoc Te' [Problem of Amending and Adding Stipulations to the 1992 Constitution on Signing, and Deciding to Ratify and Abrogate International Treaties], *Nha Nuoc va Phap Luat* 9, 2001, p. 43, pp. 44–47.
30 Average annual increases in litigation are difficult to estimate because litigation rates have not increased steadily. For example, over 1,280 new cases were filed in 1999, only 598 new cases were filed in 2002, but the litigation rate rose to 1,260 new cases in 2005. Civil litigation rates are rising much faster. There were approximately 25,000 cases in 1994 rising to over 50,000 in 2005. See Toa An Nhan Dan Toi Cao, 'Bao Cao Tong Ket Cong Tac Toa An Nam 2005 va Phuong Huong Nhiem Vu Cong Tac Toa An Nam 2006' [Report on 2005 and the Plan for 2006 Supreme People's Court], Hanoi: Supreme People's Court, 2005.
31 Interview, Hanoi Provincial Court Judges, Hanoi, 13 July 2007. See Nguyen Phu Son, 'Bo Luat To Tung Dan Su Can The Hien Tinh Than Cai Cach Tu Phap' [Civil Procedure Code Should Express the Spirit of Judicial Reform], *Tap Chi Nghien Cuu Lap Phap* 4, 2004, pp. 24–31.
32 Le Trung Ha, 'Chuyen Huong To Chuc Cua Cac Toa An Nhan Dan Dia Phuong De Dap Ung Voi Tinh Hinh va Nhiem Vu Moi' [Changes in Local Court to Meet the Requirements of the New Conditions and Requirements], *Tap San Tu Phap* 8, 1965, pp. 1, 2.
33 Party Resolution No. 48, NQ/TW, 24 May 2005 on Perfecting the Socialist Oriented Economy and *Nha Nuoc Phap Quyen* [Law-based State].
34 See Michael Burawoy, *The Politics of Production: Factory Regimes under Capitalism and Socialism*, London: Verso, 1985, pp. 5–20; Gunther Teubner, 'Legal Irritants: How Unifying Law Ends Up in New Differences', in Peter Hall and David Soskice, eds, *Varieties of Capitalism: The Institutional Foundations of Comparative Advantage*, Oxford: Oxford University Press, 2003, pp. 417–41.

35 Personalistic relationships regulate commerce in every society; what distinguishes societies is the composition of such relationships. See Curtis Milhaupt and Katharina Pistor, *Law and Capitalism: What Corporate Crises Reveal about Legal Systems and Economic Development around the World*, Chicago: University of Chicago Press, 2008, pp. 116–120; Boaventura de Sousa Santos, 'On Modes of Production of Law and Social Theory', *Journal of Sociology and Law* 13, 1996, p. 299, pp. 320–39.

36 Nguyen Van Lan and Nguyen Phuong Quynh Trang, 'Management Consultancy: The Emerging Business Service for Private Businesses in Vietnam', Hanoi: MPDF, 2004, pp. 6–9.

37 Ibid., pp. 23–24.

38 See John McMillan and Christopher Woodruff, 'Interfirm Relationships and Informal Credit in Vietnam', *Quarterly Journal of Economics* 114 (4), 1999, p. 1285.

39 John McMillan and Christopher Woodruff, 'Private Order under Dysfunctional Public Order', *Michigan Law Review* 98, 2000, pp. 2421–58. Only 9 percent of Vietnamese entrepreneurs trusted courts to enforce contracts, as opposed to 87 percent in Romania and 56 percent in Russia.

40 Carol Rose, 'Propter Honoris Respectum: Property As the Keystone Right?', *Notre Dame Law Review* 71, 1996, pp. 329 and 354.

41 Vu Tuan Anh and Tran Ngoc Trung, 'Case Study Public Administrative Reform: Implementation of Quality Management System at Ha Nam Department of Industries by Introducing a Quality Management System based on ISO 9001:200' (unpublished paper), Hanoi, September 2005, p. 3.

42 See Circular No. 72/2007/TT-BTC, dated 27 June 2007. This is a part of the commitment between the government of Vietnam and international financial organizations including the IMF, Asian Development Bank (ADB), and the World Bank. See also Vietnam Net, 4 April 2005. Available from http://www.vnn.vn/kinhte/taichinhnganhang/2005/04/410943/ (accessed 21 September 2007).

43 Interview with Ton Nhat Quang, program officer at Vietnam Competitiveness Initiatives project, Hanoi, September 2007. See also Vietnam Net, 5 November 2005. Available from http://www.nguoivienxu.vietnamnet.vn/chuyenquenha/2005/11/507840/ (accessed 10 October 2007).

44 John Dryzek, 'Discursive Democracy vs. Liberal Constitutionalism', in M. Saward, ed., *Democratic Innovation: Deliberation, Representation and Association*, London: Routledge, 2000, pp. 78–89.

45 Maarten Hajer, 'A Frame in the Fields: Policy Making and the Reinvention of Politics', in M. Hajer and H. Wagenaar, eds, *Deliberative Policy Analysis: Understanding Governance in the Network Society*, Cambridge: Cambridge University Press, 2003, pp. 1–20.

46 Carolyn Hendriks, 'Participatory Storylines and their Influence on Deliberative Forums', *Policy Science* 38, 2005, pp. 1 and 5.

47 See Benedict Kerkvliet, *Getting Organized in Vietnam: Moving In and Around the Socialist State*, Singapore: Institute of Southeast Asian Studies, 2003.

48 See Patrick Raszelenberg, 'Why Do We Look at Political Discourse in Vietnam?', in Claudia Derichs and Thomas Heberer, eds, *The Power of Ideas: Intellectual Input and Political Change in East and Southeast Asia*, Copenhagen: NIAS Press, 2006, pp. 166–71.

49 See Pham Duy Nghai, 'Nguy Co Cua Chung Ta: Mot Nha Nuoc Thieu Nang Luc Phan Ung' [Our Danger: A State of Limited Pensiveness], *Nha Nuoc va Phap Luat* 6, 2006, pp. 3–5.

50 C. Dixon, 'State, Party and Political Change in Viet Nam', in Duncan McCargo, ed., *Rethinking Viet Nam*, London: RoutledgeCurzon, 2004, pp. 15–26.

51 See *Lay Y Kien Cac Van Ban Quy Pham Phap Luat* [Obtaining Comments on Legal Documents], Official Letter No. 2012/VPCP-PC, 27 May 1998.

52 See Nguyen Dang Dung, 'Phap Luat Khong Chi La Cong Cu Cua Nha Nuoc' [Law is Not Only the Instrument of the State], *Tap Chi Nghien Cuu Lap Phap* 11, 2001, pp. 53–57.
53 See Thanh Nien, 'Direct Democracy for Public Issues', *Thanh Nien* 19 August 2004, p. 3, trans. Development Vietnam, Intellasia News Service, p. 19.
54 See Article 27 (3) Decree No. 161/2005/ND-CP, 'Making Detailed Provisions and Providing Guidelines for Implementing Certain Articles of the Law on the Promulgation of Legal Instruments and the Law Amending and Supplementing a Number of Articles of the Law on Promulgation of Legal Instruments'.
55 Article 31 Decree No. 161/2005/ND-CP, 'Implementing the Law on Promulgation of Legal Instruments'.
56 Office of Government, 'Study Report to Improve the Quality of Laws and Ordinances Drafted by the Government to be Submitted to the NA and the NA Standing Committee', unpublished report, Working Delegation No. 804, Hanoi, 5 December 2003.
57 See Tran Huu Huynh and Dau Anh Tuan, *supra*, pp. 29–30
58 Tieu Phong, 'Doanh Nghiep Ngai Xay Dung Luat' [Enterprises are Reluctant to Participate in Law Making], *Nguoi Dai Bieu Nhan Dan* (People's Representative). Available from http://www.nguoidaibieu.com.vn/pPrint.aspx?itemid=23998 (accessed 13 September 2007).
59 Speech by Hoang The Lien, Vice Minister of Justice, 'Public Participation in Commercial Policy and Lawmaking Workshop', Thanh Hoa, 31 March 2007.
60 See Decision No. 909/QD-Ttg, dated 14 September 2003.
61 Vu Quoc Tuan, 'Van Dong Chinh Sach: Mot So Van De Tu Thuc Tien' [Policy Advocacy: Some Practical Issues] (unpublished paper), Conference on Policy Advocacy: Practice and Law; Hanoi: VCCI and SPERI, 7 December 2007.
62 See Official Letter No. 732/TTg-TCCB, dated 11 June 2007.
63 See Joe Hannah, 'Civil-Society Actors and Action in Vietnam: Preliminary Empirical Results and Sketches from an Evolving Debate', in Heinrich Böll Foundation, ed., *Towards Good Society: Civil Society Actors, The State, and The Business Class in Southeast Asia – Facilitators of or Impediments to a Strong, Democratic, and Fair Society?*, Berlin: Heinrich Böll Stiftung, 2005, pp. 101–10.
64 See Do Sang and Dui Hanh, *Ve De: Lam Xa Hoi Chu Nhgia bang Nha Nuoc* [On the Use of the State to Realise Socialist Collective Mastery], Hanoi: Nha Xuat Ban Phap Ly, 1986, pp. 11–12.
65 The state manages public association by giving the Ministry of Home Affairs licensing powers to control the office bearers, funding sources, fields of operation, and *nghiep vu* (operating skills) of business associations in Decree No. 88 ND-CP Providing for the Organization, Operation, and Management of Associations, 2003. See Mark Sidel, *Law and Society in Vietnam: The Transition from Socialism in Comparative Perspective*, Cambridge: Cambridge University Press, 2008, pp. 155–63.
66 Interview with Dau Anh Tuan, Legal Office, VCCI, Hanoi, March 2007, about the draft Law on Associations prepared by the Vietnam Union of Science and Technology Associations.
67 See Nguyen Chi Dung, '"Van Dong Hanh Lang" Trong Hoat Dong Lap Phap Cac Nuoc va Xu Huong O Viet Nam' [Lobbying in Global Lawmaking and the Trend in Vietnam], *Tap Chi Nghien Cuu Lap Phap* 9 (83), 2006, pp. 51–57.
68 Ministry of Finance website. Available from http://www.mof.gov.vn/Default. aspx?tabid=612&ItemID=21860 (accessed 12 September 2007).
69 There are approximately 90 national and 200 provincial business associations (Nguyen Ngoc Lam, 2007, p. 31).
70 Tran Huu Huynh and Dau Anh Tuan, *supra*.
71 Nam Nguyen, 'Vai Tro Cua Cac Hiep Hoi Doanh Nghiep Vietnam Trong Thoi Hoi Nhap Quoc Te' [Role of Vietnamese Business Associations in the Context of Global Integration], Radio Free Asia website. Available from http://www.rfa.org/vietnamese/

in_depth/2007/05/10/Business_associations_in_Vietnam_NNguyen/ (accessed 10 September 2007).

72 Author unknown, 'Y Kien Ve Van Dong Chinh Sach Cua Hiep Hoi Doanh Nghiep Van Dong Chinh Sach' [Some Opinions on Policy Advocacy by Business Associations] (unpublished paper), Conference on Policy Advocacy: Practice and Law; Hanoi: VCCI and SPERI, 7 December 2007.

73 VNS, 'Steel Producers Feeling Threatened by Chinese Imports', *Viet Nam News* 12 March 2007, pp. 15 and 16.

74 Nam Nguyen, 'Thep Trung Quoc Mang Thuong Hieu Viet Nam, Loi va Hai?' [Chinese Steel Bearing Vietnamese Brand Name: Advantages and Disadvantages?], Radio Free Asia website. Available from http://www.rfa.org/vietnamese/in_depth/2007/04/07/DomesticPressReview_NNguyen/ (accessed 13 March 2008).

75 Vietnam Association of Financial Investors. Available from http://www.vafi.org.vn/2006/category.php?id=8&PageNum=3 (accessed 15 September 2007).

76 Ministry of Finance. Available from http://www.mof.gov.vn/Default.aspx?tabid=82&ItemID=5821 (accessed 15 September 2007).

77 D. Duong and G. Hy, 'Vao Hiep Hoi Cho … Vui' [Joining Associations for … Fun], *Nguoi Lao Dong* [The Workers] Available from http://www.nld.com.vn/tintuc/kinh-te/138273.asp (accessed 13 September 2007).

78 See also Hung Van, 'Khong Tha Noi Gia Phan Bon' [No Floating Price for Fertilizer], *Thoi Bao Kinh Te Vietnam* [Vietnam Economic Times]. Available from http://www.vneconomy.vn/?home=detail&page=category&cat_name=19&id=b433bcef0b8813 (accessed 20 October 2007); and Decision No. 80/2007/QD-BTC, dated 2 October 2007.

79 Interview with a member of the Law on Investments 2005 drafting committee, Hanoi, March 2006.

80 Quynh Lam and Nguyen Minh, 'Doanh Nghiep Nho Va Vua Khong Man Ma Voi Hiep Hoi' [SMEs Are Not Passionate about Association], *Thoi Bao Kinh Te Vietnam* [Vietnam Economic Times], 23 August 2007. Available from http://www.vneconomy.vn/?home=detail&page=category&cat_name=05&id=419cd1fba0fed9 (accessed 10 September 2007).

81 Nam Nguyen, *supra*, p. 28.

82 D. Duong and G. Hy, *supra*, p. 33.

83 VCCI claims 5,270 members, the VYEO claim 5,600 members, and the UAIC has approximately 1,800 members; see World Bank, *Vietnam Development Report: Business*, Hanoi: World Bank, 2006.

84 Decree No. 161/2005/CP Providing Details and Guidelines on the Implementation of the Law on the Promulgation of Legal Instruments.

85 Interview with Pham Chi Lan, Vice President VCCI, Hanoi, March 2003.

86 See Jonathon Stromseth, 'Business Associations and Policy-Making in Vietnam', in B. Kerkvliet et al., eds, *Getting Organized in Vietnam: Moving In and Around the Socialist State*, Singapore: Institute of Southeast Asian Studies, 2003, pp. 88–92.

87 See Thomas Finkel, 'Public Private Dialogue in the Making of the Enterprise Law and Investment Law 2005: The Case of Vietnam', Paris: International Workshop on Public Private Dialogue, 2005.

88 Stromseth, *supra*, pp. 88–92.

89 See John Gillespie, 'Localizing Global Rules: Public Participation in Lawmaking in Vietnam', *Law and Social Inquiry* 33 (3), 2008, pp. 673–707.

90 Vietnam Business Forum. Available from http://www.vbf.org.vn/ (accessed 20 September 2007).

91 David Marr, 'The Vietnam Communist Party and Civil Society', unpublished paper, Australian National University, Canberra, November 1994.

92 See Tran Huu Huynh and Dau Anh Tuan, *supra*, p. 15.

93 Comments concerning informal deliberative exchanges are based on numerous interviews with Hanoi-based law firms, VILAF, Leadco, Bizconsult, Investconsult, and

N.G. Quang and Associates, from March 2002 until October 2006. See also Martin Gainsborough, *Changing Political Economy of Vietnam: The Case of Ho Chi Minh City*, London: RoutledgeCurzon, 2002, pp. 29–39.

94 VietnamNetwebsite.Availablefromhttp://www.vnn.vn/chinhtri/doinoi/2005/08/483894/ (accessed 15 September 2007).

95 Duong Xuan Minh, 'Viec Hinh Su Hoa Quan Le Giua Ngan Hang va Doanh Nghiep Rat Nang Ne' [Heavy Criminalisation of Relationships between Banks and Businesses], *Dau Tu* 18 September 2001, pp. 1–2.

96 See Mark Sidel, *Law and Society in Vietnam: The Transition from Socialism in Comparative Perspective*, Cambridge: Cambridge University Press, 2008, pp. 204–10. See also Brian Quinn, 'Legal Reform and Its Context in Vietnam', *Columbia Journal of Asian Law* 15 (2), 2002, pp. 235–60; Carol Rose, 'The "New" Law and Development Movement in the Post-Cold War Era: A Vietnam Case Study', *Law and Society Review* 32 (1), 1998, pp. 126–35.

97 See John McMillan and Christopher Woodruff, 'Private Order under Dysfunctional Public Order', *Michigan Law Review* 98, 2000, p. 2422.

98 Politburo Resolution No. 48 NQ/TW on The Strategy for the Development and Improvement of Vietnam's Legal System to the Year 2010 and Direction for the Period up to 2020, 24 May 2005.

99 Investment consultant firms such as Investconsult, Galaxy, Leadco, N.H. Quang, Vietbid, and Concetti, as well as foreign law firms, work closely with foreign investors and donors in providing research and strategic advice in law reform projects.

100 Politburo Resolution No. 07, dated 27 November 2001.

101 VCCI, unpublished report, Hanoi, October 2007.

102 Vu Duy Thai, President of Hanoi Association for Industry and Commerce, presented at Workshop on Media–Business Relations, Hanoi, October 2007.

103 See Decree No. 23/2007/ND-CP, dated 12 February 2007, and Circular No. 09/2007/TT-BTM, dated 17 July 2007.

104 See Ta Ngoc Tan, 'Some Current Issues of Press Development in Vietnam' *Tap Chi Cong San* 1 June 2007. Available from http://www.tapchicongsan.org.vn/print_preview.asp?Object=29152838&news_ID=163 (accessed 15 April 2008).

105 See Article 1 of Press Law, dated 12 June 1999.

106 Le Doan Hop, 'Quan Ly Bao Chi Trong Su Nghiep Doi Moi Dat Nuoc Hien Nay' [Press Management in the Period of Renovation], *Tap Chi Cong San* [Communist Review], 15 August 2006. Available from http://www.tapchicongsan.org.vn/details.asp?Object=4&news_ID=18652313 (accessed 21 September 2007).

107 Dinh Nam, 'Bao Chi va Doanh Nghiep: De Cung Nhau Boi Ra Bien Lon' [Press and Businesses: To Swim Together Towards The Ocean], *Thoi Bao Kinh Te Vietnam* [Vietnam Economic Times], 13 October 2007. Available from http://www.vneconomy.vn/?home=detail&page=category&cat_name=05&id=5e22229e3f28e7 (accessed 14 October 2007).

9 Pushing against globalization

The response from civil society groups in Thailand

Jakkrit Kuanpoth

Introduction

Globalization has brought benefits to developing countries. A globalized market enables the international regulatory system to move toward greater liberalization and better regimes for world trade and cross-border business transactions. It also spreads ideas and values that strengthen a respect for the rule of law, and increases political and social rights. Despite the overall positive perceptions of globalization and its potential benefits, globalization has had three major adverse impacts on national development in developing countries. First, it affects national economic policies in terms of the forms of economic system and attitudes toward politics, law, and bureaucracy. Globalization requires a country to have a market-based economy, where the market has a significant influence over the government, and where the state has a limited ability to regulate the market. In order to increase capital accumulation, the government is prohibited from interfering with private economic activities, and is required to amend its policies that affect cross-border trade, such as price distortions in domestic commodity markets. Second, globalization creates a system that allows supranational organizations to impose more restrictions on national governments. International trade law brought about by the World Trade Organization (WTO), for example, is based on a process of exchange embodying minimum standards of treatment, which reduce national rights to regulate in the public interest. Third, globalization helps to create economic inequality in developing nations and perpetuate an elite and middle class who are in tune with and trapped by Western consumer culture and ideals.[1]

The globalization of the world economy provides ample opportunities for some states to force the negative consequences of their domestic policies on other states, in the form of multilateral rule-making through multilateral agreements of the WTO or the World Intellectual Property Organization (WIPO), and also through bilateral or regional trade agreements. Like many other countries, Thailand, as a response to international pressures resulting from globalization, has had to reform its laws and regulations in several areas, including agriculture, natural resources, trade, services, intellectual property protection, and so on. The external pressures seem to have a more significant influence on the law and economic policy of Thailand than the domestic push for reform.

However, revolt against globalization has continued to grow in Thailand. There are a number of groups of non-governmental organizations (NGOs), academics, and community leaders in Thailand, which were formed to monitor recent economic and social changes. The non-state sector has warned the Thai government about the direct and indirect effects of globalization. On several occasions, they also had a chance to be involved in the development and implementation of national legislation. This chapter describes forms of local resistance and the unity of local power against the economic globalization of corporate power in Thailand. It will devote particular attention to the movement of civil society groups in Thailand. The first part of the chapter primarily explores factors that have influenced legal reform in Thailand. The second part focuses on the impacts of globalization on Thailand's agricultural sector and natural resources. The final part examines the revolt against the globalization process by civil society groups and networks in Thailand, with a view to determining whether it holds out any real hope of addressing and effectively redressing the imbalance in the world's economic system.

1 Factors contributing to legal and economic reform in Thailand

Like many other developing countries, Thailand has, to varying degrees, been influenced by the political, economic, social, and cultural heritage of Western countries. Although it has never endured colonial rule and its legal system was not directly influenced by the West through colonization, Thailand still adopted Western forms of law and judiciary. Five factors in particular have influenced the legal system in Thailand, including:

- attempts at modernizing the legal and judiciary systems in the early twentieth century;
- social and economic planning advised by the World Bank;
- accession to the WTO;
- the economic crisis that led Thailand to enter the reform program of the International Monetary Fund (IMF); and
- political and economic pressure from Western countries.

(a) Modernization of legal and judicial systems

The early twentieth century, while Thailand was under the absolute monarchy of King Rama V, could be regarded as the era in which Thailand tried to create a modern nation-state. The modernization of Thai law and judicial administration was considered essential to being perceived as a civilized nation.[2] Law reform also resulted from Thailand's attempt to retain its sovereignty, avoiding colonization by Western powers.

In the late nineteenth century, colonization was a huge threat in the Southeast Asian region, and Thailand's sovereignty was threatened by two colonial powers, Great Britain and France. It was believed that Westernizing and modernizing all aspects of Thai society, including its legal and judicial systems, would allow Thailand to maintain its independence. The modernization and reform of law would presumably help Thailand to do away with the extraterritoriality it had previously ceded to foreign powers, particularly under the Bowring Treaty B.E. 2398, which Siam signed with Great Britain in 1855.[3] This was proved to be the case, as Thailand regained complete judicial sovereignty from the Western countries in 1925 after the reform program was completed.

The reform helped to modernize national law and brought the legal system of Thailand in line with Western-style legal systems. It led to the promulgation of several law codes, including the Penal Code, the Civil and Commercial Codes, the Civil Procedure Code, and the Criminal Procedure Code. The laws of countries such as France, Germany, Switzerland, England, Italy, and Japan were used as a model for drafting the four codes of Thailand. In addition, a number of legal institutions were established based on the Western-style system, including courts, prosecutor offices, and the council of state. During that time, the first law school was set up under the Ministry of Justice.

(b) Policy and plan for economic development

Thailand started its open door policy during the government of Field Marshall Sarit Thanarat. The government adopted the country's first national economic development plan (NEDP) in 1961.[4] It also established the National Economic Development Council and the National Economic Development Board to implement the NEDP. With the advice of the World Bank, one of the institutions of the Washington Consensus, the NEDP focused on market-oriented development strategy that dominated the world, especially during the 1980s. The World Bank and Thailand's elites tried to impose these ideas on the country. The national plan, which was based on neoclassical theory, viewed the problems of underdevelopment as resulting from the intervention of the government in the market. In order to sustain growth and stability, government controls needed to be removed and replaced by liberalization and openness. Since the first NEDP, the Thai economy has been mainly driven by the private sector and market mechanisms, and the country has devoted its attention to developing infrastructure and industrialization.[5]

The Thai government attempted to accelerate economic growth and industrial development. This required heavy capitalization, more sources of financing, and modern technology. The government implemented deregulation to encourage private foreign investments, which are widely regarded as the major driving forces behind the rapid development of many business sectors in Thailand. It also provided a number of incentives to firms investing in areas considered to be of high priority, defined in terms of development objectives, most of which were in manufacturing businesses.[6]

It may be noted that Thailand's economic growth increased dramatically during the sixth NEDP (1987–91), particularly under the Chatichai Choonhavan government, which aimed to turn Thailand into an industrialized country. Thailand became one of the fastest growing economies in the late 1980s.[7] In 1988 and

1989, the Thai economic growth rate reached a remarkable figure of 11 percent.[8] The main factor contributing to the high rate of economic growth was the boom in exports of both goods and services.[9] Promotion of tourism and export of labor to other countries also assisted growth. On the internal side, a very important positive factor was the government's foreign exchange policy of maintaining the value of the baht at an appropriate level, compared with the currencies of the country's trading partners and rivals. In addition, the Chatichai government's policy calling for the development of an old war zone into a marketplace has stimulated trade along the borders with neighboring countries (i.e., Cambodia, Laos, and Burma). This has led Thailand, due to its geographical location, to become a manufacturing base for many companies intending to market their products in Indo-China.

Neoliberalism has recently become less popular in Thailand. The prevailing conventional economic theory of international trade and comparative advantage has been greatly criticized. Its unrealistic assumptions of efficient markets and resource allocation that a country would achieve through market liberalization have proven unworkable in the context of Thailand. Although the market mechanism generates economic growth for Thailand, the growth is not sustainable and has not helped alleviate the poverty of the poorest in society.[10] There has also been a serious problem of income and wealth distribution.[11] For example, government spending was centered on Bangkok and other major cities, which created deficiencies in the infrastructure (e.g., roads, water and electricity supply, telecommunications, and so on) within rural areas.[12]

(c) Economic crisis

The economic crisis in Thailand started in the mid-1990s when the Thai government decided to liberalize the financial sector. From 1990 to 1994, the government accepted the obligations of Article VIII of the Agreement of the International Monetary Fund, which demanded the complete deregulation of current account transactions and the removal of restrictions on payments and transfers of capital. It also deregulated the exchange controls and adopted a series of further liberalization measures, which resulted in less control over the flows of foreign currencies in and out of the country.

The Thai government loosened restrictions on capital flows, but it poorly regulated and mismanaged the financial sector.[13] The financial market was allowed to grow rapidly without control, which brought more money into the economy. However, the money was unscrupulously and wrongly spent, such as on property speculation or on projects that lacked justifiable investment opportunities such as construction where real estate was already oversupplied. This affected the Thai corporate sector's ability to compete and to do business.[14] In 1997, the Bank of Thailand attempted to defend the value of the baht by spending huge sums of money to bolster an overvalued currency. By doing this, it committed almost all its foreign reserves. The Thai government eventually decided to devalue the baht, which caused the currency to lose half its value and consequently doubled the cost of foreign debt, creating financial pressure for many banks and businesses. More than half the foreign loans became non-performing, which led to the bankruptcy of fifty-six finance companies. All these factors contributed to the collapse of the Thai economy in 1997, which subsequently extended to other countries and became the Asian economic crisis.[15]

The economic crisis forced Thailand to seek a SDR 2.9 billion (about US$4 billion) rescue package from the IMF. The IMF's Stand-by Arrangement program demanded that Thailand cut spending and reform its financial and legal systems. In order to restore a competitive climate for foreign investment and stimulate investment flows, the IMF also required Thailand to establish a new bankruptcy court and reform bankruptcy and foreclosure procedures. Some property laws such as the Land Code, the Condominium Act, and the Property Leasing Act had to be amended to remove restrictions on foreign property ownership. Reform of foreign investment law was demanded by the IMF, which led Thailand to replace the Alien Business Law (ABL) of 1972 (National Executive Council Announcement No. 281) with new legislation. The IMF conditions demanded that Thailand open additional sectors to foreign investment, to increase total foreign equity investment up to 49 percent in certain sectors, and to privatize state-owned enterprises.

(d) Accession to the World Trade Organization

The trade that developed between Thailand and foreign nations led to the signing of a number of trade treaties, which later on became a major factor in the reform of Thai law and judicial system. The most important treaty was the Marrakesh Agreement, establishing the WTO, and the full package of multilateral Uruguay Round agreements.[16]

Thailand is one of 153 member countries of the WTO. In order to comply with its WTO commitments, Thailand had to reform its laws and regulations in several areas. It had to reduce the tariff rates on certain industrial and agricultural products, and convert non-tariff measures (e.g., quotas and other quantitative restrictions) to tariffs on certain agricultural products such as rice, corn, soybeans, sugar, garlic, and so on. In the area of foreign investment, the Agreement on Trade-Related Investment Measures (TRIMS) provided that Thailand may apply certain investment measures such as performance requirements and local content requirements, but such measures must not become barriers to trade or distort trade. The WTO General Agreement on Trade in Services (GATS) does not oblige member states to liberalize their service market, but it does require that they enter into negotiations with a view to liberalizing service trade under the principle of progressive liberalization.[17] Thailand made commitments with respect to financial services, banking, and insurance. It had therefore liberalized and amended the laws relating to those service sectors.

The WTO Agreement on Implementation of Article VI of the General Agreement on Tariffs and Trade (GATT) and Agreement on Subsidies and Countervailing Measures required member states to adopt rules dealing with dumping and subsidy. Thailand enacted the Anti-dumping and Countervailing Act B.E. 2542, which came into force in 1999. The Act provides a legal basis for anti-dumping and countervailing measures with regards to details of procedure, timeframe, and appeal process in compliance with WTO agreements.

The WTO obligations that require significant reform of law are those under the Agreement on Trade-Related Aspects of Intellectual Property Rights (TRIPS).[18] The TRIPS Agreement requires Thailand to substantially eliminate intellectual property (IP) infringements and to bring the country's IP laws up to the TRIPS standards. This includes amending patent, trademark, and copyright laws and adopting new laws to protect geographical indications, trade secrets, and layout designs of integrated circuits. Thailand introduced a major overhaul of its IP systems in accordance with its obligations under the TRIPS Agreement and as a result of bilateral pressure that the US was exerting on Thailand.[19]

It may be noted that Thai local industries have been split on the issue of WTO accession. The push to join the WTO did not come only from outside Thailand. Some local industries (e.g., textiles, leather products, electronics, and so on) saw advantages in pursuing trade liberalization. When Thailand entered the WTO, its export companies enjoyed savings from the elimination of customs duties and improved market access. Although Thailand-based exporters may have to brace themselves for a new set of rules and may increasingly face international competition, their exported goods and services would benefit from the WTO rules of non-discrimination and national treatment (i.e., being treated like locals upon entering the WTO members' markets).

However, industries under more strict protection from the government (e.g., the automobile industry, the petrochemical industry, the pharmaceutical industry, and the agriculture industry) could be under serious threat from imported products and the penetration of multinational corporations. These local industries were very concerned about the consequences of Thailand's accession to the WTO. A good example is the pharmaceutical industry. The Thai pharmaceutical industry is directly affected when the country is required to comply with the WTO regulations on IP rights. According to the WTO/TRIPS Agreement, member countries are obliged to protect the invention of new medicine and pharmaceuticals. Because the majority of pharmaceutical patents in Thailand are foreign owned, it appears that the Thai manufacturers of generic medicine who have provided the country with essential medicines at cost price have been excluded from competition or would have to pay substantial amounts to patent-holding firms if they want to stay in the market.[20]

(e) Political and economic pressure for increased IP protection

Although the rapid developments in the IP law of Thailand may partly come from domestic demand, it was in fact external pressure which led to the rapid development of law in this area. The most controversial area of IP law is patents. A patent system was initially adopted as part of the economic policy of the Thai government, and was a result of Thailand's attempt to accelerate industrial production and trade expansion. However, the policy of Thailand on patents has been greatly influenced by external pressures, particularly those exerted by the US government.

As the US's growing trade deficit had an increasingly negative impact on the US economy, the US administration decided to use trade leverage against its trade partners, including Thailand. In 1989 and 1991, the United States Trade Representative (USTR) removed the Generalized System of Preferences (GSP) privileges from some export products from Thailand because of the country's alleged inadequate protection for copyrights on computer software and pharmaceutical patents. USTR also threatened Thailand with trade sanctions under Special 301 of the Omnibus Trade and Competitiveness Act of 1988.[21]

After being named as a priority foreign country subject for trade retaliation by the US, attempts were made by the Thai government to meet the demands in the hope of avoiding trade retaliation, because it realized that the US market was an essential part of Thailand's recent economic success. Thailand decided to modify its copyright, trademark, and patent laws in order to protect particular products such as pharmaceuticals, computer software, some forms of living organisms, and so on. It also extended the term of patent protection from fifteen years to twenty years and the copyright term to fifty years after the death of the author. It also revised its IP laws in order to tighten penalties and eliminate provisions designed to prevent the abuse of patent monopoly such as the price monitoring board for pharmaceutical products.[22] The Thai government also made a great effort to enforce the IP laws more vigorously. A number of cases of copyright and trademark infringement were successfully prosecuted, and the average penalties for such illegal practices have increased substantially.

It may be noted that IP protection generally focuses on the situations in developing countries, but ignores the fact that developed countries largely aid their own development by copying or imitating inventions—a process that they are preventing or disallowing developing countries from doing by imposing a proprietary IP rights regime. This does not take into account the needs and capacities of developing countries. Like many others, Thailand has found itself in the dual position of being both a promoter of IP as well as an infringer of IP rights. This is seen as a natural process of economic development, where industries in developing nations evolve from being "users" to "producers" of IP. They too begin to have a stake in IP protection and enforcement. The debate on IP protection therefore touches upon the impact and ability of local industries to use and produce new innovations. It is a matter of addressing issues of how to balance rights, limits, and interests at various stages of development.

In summary, after almost two decades of rapid growth since the 1980s, Thailand was severely affected by the Asian financial crisis in 1997, which led to internal restructuring and reforms in the economy. Political and economic pressures exerted by foreign governments and multilateral institutions such as the IMF are the major forces that have transformed Thailand into a market economy. However, the push to restructure the economy comes not only from external forces, but also from policymakers and the private sector within Thailand. These local interest groups have adopted the conventional wisdom that the market economy and neoliberal capitalism are the best routes for the development of competitive industries. These groups viewed the problems of underdevelopment as resulting from the intervention of the government and demanded the removal of commercial barriers to creating a free market to benefit Thailand in many ways. First, it would prepare Thailand for the liberalized trade in goods and services as required under the WTO multilateral agreements. The liberalization would also increase competition and thereby improve efficiency, which benefits both domestic consumers and the long-term growth of the overall economy. If economic growth is to be achieved, they argued, economic reform requires an increase in the role of the private sector and the introduction of market ideas to the economy.[23]

On the other hand, the idea of economic liberalization has been strongly opposed by some interest groups. Internal actors with vested interests frequently mount stiff opposition to the neoliberalization concept. Labor unions and employees of state-owned enterprises, for example, are the major opponents of privatization, as many workers could be made redundant and laid off under the control of private actors.[24] They view the attempt to privatize the public enterprises as effectively selling the country to foreign interests as local investors lack sufficient liquidity to purchase such enterprises when in competition with foreign spending power.[25]

Opposition also comes from consumer groups. Opponents view the government as better positioned than private enterprise to provide necessary services (e.g., electricity, transportation, and water supply). They claim that the control of public services by private interests will lower service standards and increase prices. Neoliberalism also prevents the government from subsidizing some of the public services, which will likely result in increased prices to consumers.

Such opposition became much more pronounced during the economic crisis in the late 1990s. The nationalist, anti-globalization sentiment surfaced not only in certain interest groups but also within the general population. Proponents of the nationalist ideal include some parliamentary members, NGOs, and academics. From 1998 to 1999, while the Chaun Leekpai government was preparing plans for the privatization of state-owned companies, the nationalists had successfully aroused economic nationalist passions to abolish the privatization plans. There were considerable protests and large-scale mass demonstrations in Bangkok and all major cities in Thailand by groups of farmers and labor unions against the IMF-dictated policy of privatization.[26]

Since the Thaksin Shinawatra government declared its financial independence from the IMF after having paid off the country's debts in 2003, it seems that Thailand has broken away from the neoliberalization concept. The populist/nationalist policy platform adopted by the Thaksin government (i.e., the government freezing repayments on rural debt, instituting government-financed universal health care, and giving each village one million baht to spend on a special project) had turned Thailand further away from neoliberalism. The anti-globalization sentiment has become more intense, particularly when the "Sufficiency Economy Philosophy" was bestowed by the country's popular monarch, His Majesty King Bhumibol Adulyadej, on the people of Thailand. The Sufficiency Economy is an inward-looking concept that stresses self-reliance at the grassroots and the creation of stronger ties among domestic economic networks. This philosophy focuses on the quality of people's lives as the ultimate agenda in development. It requires the government to focus its economic and development policies on improving the wellbeing of the people, along with the growth of the economy in a sustainable environment. The concept of Sufficiency Economy has offered a new paradigm of development and conveyed new ideas for Thailand in dealing with the globalization concerns. The government of Thaksin Shinawatra and the military-supported government of Surayud Chulanont cleverly used the Sufficiency Economy to gain popularity and to legitimize their rule. No doubt all these factors combined have made globalization unpopular in Thailand today.[27]

2 Perceived impacts of globalization on the agriculture and natural resources of Thailand

The basic development philosophy promoted by the international donor agencies such as the World Bank and the Food and Agriculture Organization (FAO) was that the rapid modernization of the agricultural sector would create general wealth that would eventually trickle down to the poor.[28] The agricultural policy of Thailand shifted from production for domestic consumption to export-oriented production, with the majority of total production exported. It was believed that, if Thailand could achieve income from the export trade, its capacities for economic development would be increased.

(a) Green Revolution policy

New agricultural policy, known as the Green Revolution, introduced modern farming practices to Thailand. The policy, which aims to significantly increase crop production, is based on the use of modern farming techniques such as stronger pest-resistant and high-yield varieties of crops, modern farm machinery, and chemical fertilizers and pesticides. This type of farming tends to be monocrop and commercial, for export.[29]

Under the Green Revolution policy, the Ministry of Agriculture encouraged the expansion of export cash crops such as cassava, maize, jute, pineapples, oil palm, and sugar cane. Developed hybrid varieties were distributed to farmers by government agencies or agribusiness companies. Farmers have been pushed to invest in export-oriented agriculture by using high-cost inputs with credit provided by the state-run Bank for Agriculture and Agricultural Cooperatives.

Modern agricultural policy has had adverse effects on Thailand. The farming practices have consumed a vast amount of natural resources. In order to expand irrigated areas, a number of dams were built, notably Bhumiphol Dam, which was the first large dam in Thailand. It was built in 1964 with the support of the World Bank. The international granting agencies such as the World Bank and the Asian Development Bank (ADB) have successfully promoted the construction of numerous dams in Thailand, causing the destruction of the environment and loss of livelihoods of millions of people.[30] Trees were cut down. Forest areas have been legally and illegally converted into agricultural farmlands and cash crop monoculture plantations. As a result of the expansion of the cultivated area, it has been estimated that more than half of all forests in Thailand have been destroyed.[31]

From 53.3 percent of the country's total area in 1961, the forest areas substantially declined to 25.62 percent in the early 1980s.[32]

Modern agricultural policy demands that Thai farmers turn their fields to growing food for export. This has plunged the farmers in Thailand into crisis. By adopting monoculture farming, the small-scale farmers required farm inputs (i.e., inorganic fertilizers, pesticides, and machinery), the prices of which were beyond their means. A large number of farmers do not have sufficient access to the quantities of land and water that are essential for commercial agricultural systems. In addition, the farmers are price-takers as they have very limited bargaining power to get a fair return from their agricultural products due to unstable yields of agricultural produce and marketing problems. Some have an oversupply of their produce and then drop the price drastically. The liberalization of the world trade in agricultural products as required by the WTO Agreement on Agriculture (AOA) and various free trade agreements (FTAs) and fluctuating prices due to the vagaries of the global commodities market have exacerbated the problem. Furthermore, agricultural subsidies provided by governments of developed countries have encouraged farmers in the West to produce more crops, which creates an oversupply.[33] The oversupplied and cheap (subsidized) products are then dumped on to world markets, affecting the livelihoods of small-scale farmers and their families in developing countries.

Free farm trade as promised by trade rules of the WTO/AOA or FTAs seems to benefit Thailand, which is one of the major exporters of agricultural products. But there is also the question of wealth and income distribution. The benefits of the expansion of Thai agricultural exports are likely to go to large agribusiness companies, rather than small-scale farmers. Compared with the heavily subsidized agricultural sectors in Europe and the US, the farming sector in Thailand does not obtain adequate support from the government and is not in a position to compete in the world market or in the domestic market against subsidized imports, which are dumped below cost price or sold at such low prices that local farmers cannot compete.

Modern agricultural practices have led farmers in Thailand into debt. Many farmers have found themselves heavily indebted, bankrupt, and then landless. Farming communities have lost their livelihoods. Many impoverished farmers are forced to sell their land, and have been driven to migrate into urban areas to be available as cheap labor. It has become common for most Thai farmers to dream of getting out of farming to do something else.[34]

In addition, despite the promise that modern agriculture would increase food supply to adequately feed Thailand's rapidly increasing population, Thailand still faces an ongoing malnutrition problem. Large numbers of Thai people are unable to access sufficient quantities of food.[35] This is so despite the fact that Thailand is the world's largest food-exporting country. Food scarcity in Thailand is not a result of inadequate production levels but more a factor of inequitable distribution of food. Instead of guaranteeing food security, export-oriented agriculture has sustained the inequitable food distribution, the unjust distribution of farm land, resources, and income.

Rural farming communities are the custodians of their traditional knowledge, wisdom, and cultures. Many indigenous knowledge systems are at risk of becoming extinct because of the intrusion of foreign technologies and practices. As a result of the focus on commercial agriculture, native plant species were either ignored or given low priority, and many of them have been replaced with new monoculture high-yield varieties. The loss of indigenous varieties, together with indigenous (traditional) knowledge, has environmental effects as these native resources and traditional practices are fundamental for *in situ* conservation and the development of biodiversity and genetic resources.

(b) Bio-piracy

As one of the biodiversity-rich countries, Thailand has suffered several experiences involving "bio-piracy," in which biological resources were claimed, patented, and commercially exploited by a person or company to the detriment of the source country.[36] Among the famous cases is the patenting of extracted substances of Thai herbs, Plao Noi (*Croton sublyratus*), by a Japanese pharmaceutical company, Sankyo Corporation.[37] Plao Noi is a traditional medicinal plant in the South Asian region; its leaves and stem bark have been used by Thai traditional healers to treat ulcers for several hundred years. The medicinal properties of the herbal plant have been inscribed in the ancient palm leaf herbalist book for centuries. Yet Sankyo Corporation has successfully patented the use and the compounds of Plao Noi in several countries, including Japan, the US, and Thailand. Plaunotol, the purified Plao Noi extract, is marketed in tablet form under the brand name "Kelnac," with annual sales in Thailand alone of 800 million baht (US$20 million).

Another case of bio-piracy concerns the well-known Thai jasmine rice. The rice is regarded as the highest quality rice available. The variety was originally only found in a certain part of Thailand. Its origin was in the eastern part of Thailand, Chachoengsao. Having been promoted by Thailand's Department of Agriculture since 1959, the rice became popular and is now grown nationwide. Currently, jasmine rice exports have been growing, and it is considered one of Thailand's most important export products. Thailand exports around 4–6 million tonnes of rice to the world markets per year, of which over 25 percent is jasmine rice.[38]

In September 1997, Rice Tech Co., a company based in Texas, sought to register a trademark "Jasmati" in several countries. It then marketed its rice product under "Jasmati." The product's package says it is a "Texas-grown copy of jasmine rice from Thailand." Rice Tech's "Jasmati" rice has nothing to do with jasmine and basmati rice, a variety of aromatic rice grown only in India and Pakistan, except for a similar name on the packaging.[39] Presumably, by using the name "Jasmati," Rice Tech can lure people to believe its product is a cross between jasmine and basmati rice. This kind of practice is a tort under US unfair competition law because the use of the "Jasmati" brand is intended to mislead consumers into thinking that their product is Thai rice. This practice could generate adverse effects for Thailand and might imperil Thailand's market share in jasmine rice exports. Inevitably, Rice Tech is capitalizing on the reputation of other products.[40]

In November 2001, a US researcher, Chris Deren, publicly admitted that he had undertaken a project to genetically modify the Thai jasmine rice variety for planting in the US. The researcher works at the Everglades Research and Education Center at the University of Florida under the "Stepwise Program for Improvement of Jasmine Rice." The project, which is sponsored by the US Department of Agriculture, has the aim of developing a new strain of early maturing jasmine rice that needs little sunshine and is short enough to be harvested easily by machines. It could thus be planted throughout the flatlands of the US. If the US scientist is successful in developing a new variety of jasmine rice, international markets for the famous rice would almost certainly be affected, as a competitive product would enter the market. The large-scale planting of jasmine rice in the US could damage Thailand's rice exports and jeopardize the economic livelihoods of millions of poor Thai farmers.

(c) Genetically modified organisms

Genetically modified organisms (GMOs) are defined as organisms that have had any of their genes or genetic material modified by means of an artificial technique. It has been promoted as part of the second Green Revolution. In Thailand, the keeping and use of GMOs are strictly regulated in order to protect human health and to prevent or minimize damage or harm to the environment.[41] The commercial release of GMOs has been prohibited until it has been proved that they have no detrimental effects on the environment and people's health. As Thai law also imposes a ban on open-field production of GMO field trials, it is almost impossible to produce genetically modified food and products in Thailand.

Despite the ban, illegal cultivation of transgenic crops has occurred in some parts of the country. These genetically modified plants were smuggled into the country and illegally introduced to Thai farmers. The cultivation of genetically modified crops has expanded rapidly to other parts of the country. For example, Bt cotton and maize, which were found to be illegally grown in the southern province of Phetchaburi, are cultivated in the northeastern region. Law enforcement is a major problem for Thailand. The government has proven unable to take any action to eradicate the illegal cultivation of genetically modified crops. The introduction of transgenic crops has increased the biotech industry's control over the production chain of crops and food, but it poses a potential risk to human health and the environment in Thailand. In addition, as consumer resistance to GMOs has increased in many parts of the world, the expansion of GMOs would threaten the market image of Thai agricultural products and potentially undermine the capacity for Thai producers to compete in export markets.[42]

(d) Mega projects and resource management

Forests are a contested resource, with many different values and functions for different people. Thailand has used the centralized technocratic system of resource management, whereby the state exerts monopoly control over access to and use of the country's forests and mountainous lands. Thailand's forest policy has been based on national security and on the notion that local forest users were ignorant and destructive.[43] Any use of state forests, particularly in conservation areas, is prohibited, except where authorized by the Forestry Department.

The Thai government has ordered the creation of vast conservation areas in many parts of the country. Once forests are declared as conservation areas, local communities and community members who have lived off the forest for generations become, in the eyes of the state at least, enemies of the forest and are evicted from those areas. Also, people have been removed from their homelands for the establishment of development projects such as concession logging, large dams, or tourist developments. The story of the Karen (W'wa K'nyaw) people is a case in point. The Karen indigenous communities in Thailand live in the highlands and have developed highland cultivation systems and community-managed forests over generations. Many of these forest-dwelling communities in the northern provinces were evicted from their lands after the lands were designated reservoir areas and construction sites for dams.[44]

The system of state appropriation and control of the forests was imposed on Thailand through development agencies such as the World Bank and the FAO. In addition, international financial agencies such as the ADB and IMF have imposed legally binding conditions on debtor countries such as Thailand to have their natural resource management systems restructured. For example, Thailand adopted eleven economic laws as part of the IMF Standby Agreement. The commitments included allowing foreign investors to purchase lands and lease the land for up to ninety-nine years.[45] This has a tremendous impact on Thailand, on both food security and land tenure systems.

Like many other developing countries, Thailand passed laws to arrogate forests and the lands of local communities to the state, and then portions out rights to exploit the natural resources to private interests. This resource management policy has led to the wholesale trade of the forests for the sake of industrial forestry interests and development projects. The result has been forest degradation and destruction, displaced people, and the loss of local livelihoods and cultures. Traditional forest dwellers and local communities are excluded from their traditional lands despite the fact that they are the most interested parties in the sustainable management of the forests as these are their source of sustenance. In addition, these people know how the forest ecosystem functions better than anyone else. There is now also a growing concern to preserve what is left of the country's and the world's forests. One of the solutions proposed by civil society groups in Thailand was to adopt the community-based management of natural resources, which will be discussed in detail below.

3   Revolt against globalization by civil society groups

It can be seen from the foregoing discussion that external factors, such as globalization and modernization, have a significant influence on Thailand's law and policy. However, revolt against globalization has continued to grow in recent years. There are a number of groups of NGOs, academics, and community leaders in Thailand that were formed to monitor the recent economic and social changes. These groups have so far been very critical of the way in which the national development and decision-making processes are made, particularly under the influence of corporate-led globalization.

The pro-democratic movement of 1973, when a large number of students protested, demanding political freedom and democracy, was regarded as a turning point in the non-state sectors' movement in Thailand. The successful student-led uprising in October 1973 introduced a new period in Thai politics. Since then, a great number of pro-democratic groups have been formed. These groups, which eventually evolved into NGOs, began to expand their work in politics to social development work. NGO networks have been growing and broadening their alliances with other pro-democratic groups. They started working as individual organizations, but later on they formed coordinated and consolidated networks based on issues of interest, such as child development, women's issues, public health, education, religions, labor, human rights, natural resources, and the environment.

The work of Thai NGOs has had a significant impact on society. Through advocacy work, they perform some of the key roles in civil society, which include articulating public interests. NGOs represent the citizens' interests by building participation and checking the state but, unlike political parties, their works are based on non-partisan civic engagement aiming at social, economic, and development issues rather than specifically political ones. However, these NGOs share some similarities with political groups as they aim to win public support, and their advocacy and civic education are activities that seek to influence public opinion and therefore have a direct impact on political development.[46]

There are several factors contributing to the rise in civil society organizations and social movements in Thailand, particularly during the 1980s. First, shifts occurred in the understanding of the "governance" concept. The 1973 political uprising led to the belief in Thailand that public governance was no longer the domain of governments alone, but could involve contributions from other political actors and stakeholders. Apart from the established channels for public participation such as elections, there could be other less formal ways for citizens to engage in decision-making about the management and distribution of resources.[47] Second, another factor that has given rise to the people's movement in Thailand was the growth of social networks at the international level. The growing power of non-democratic and non-accountable supranational institutions such as the World Bank, the IMF, and the WTO was responsible in part for the emergence of NGOs. Third, the past two decades witnessed significant shifts in ideas and strategies fighting for the development and implementation of policies. With the collapse of communism, any violence or threat of violence against a government agent had lost much of its credibility as a method for implementing change. Advocacy and civic education had become a viable alternative to the use of violence.[48]

The following are instances of civil society movements that have had impacts on Thailand's law and public policy.

(a) The People's Constitution

The political, social, economic, and legal systems of Thailand took a very significant turn in 1997 when the Constitution of the Kingdom of Thailand B.E. 2540 was promulgated. It was called the "People's Constitution" as it was the first to be written by an assembly that was elected by popular vote. The constitution had a substantial impact on the reorganization of political, legal, and judicial systems in Thailand.[49] It established the Constitution Court and the Administrative Court, which work in parallel with the Court of Justice. A series of independent watchdog bodies were established, including the Election Commission, the Human Rights Commission, and the National Counter-Corruption Commission. The constitution also reformed parliamentary and electoral systems, and structurally changed the cabinet, the bureaucracy, local administration, education, telecommunications, health care, welfare, state-owned enterprises, and so on.

The 1997 constitution was introduced as a result of the political crisis in 1992 when the military-supported prime minister was forced to resign after the army suppressed a middle-class uprising. The incident led to a vigorous campaign for political reform and drafting of a new constitution. Civil society organizations directly and indirectly played key roles in drafting the constitution. Several NGO leaders were elected to the Constitution Drafting Assembly. During the drafting of the constitution, the NGO networks mobilized to exert pressure on the drafting agenda. Together, NGO leaders and academics proposed constitutional requirements that promoted basic human rights, social welfare, educational opportunities, and so on. They also made submissions that addressed development issues, including environmental protection, land distribution, government support for agricultural production and distribution, and community rights to manage natural resources.[50] Without the people's movement, many provisions that guaranteed people's rights, liberty, freedom, and welfare would not have been adopted.

The 1997 constitution, which was considered Thailand's best constitution, was abolished on 19 September 2006 when a military coup d'état was staged against the government of Thaksin Shinawatra. Despite its relatively short life, the constitution has set the template for the Thai political and social systems. Most of the clauses that guarantee the people's freedom and liberty have been incorporated into the newly adopted constitution of 2007.

(b) Natural resources management: the case of the Community Forest Bill

Conflicts involving access to and control of natural resources are becoming the most common source of national conflict. Civil society organizations and academics have played an important role in influencing public policy and inciting change. These groups have successfully raised public awareness on the deterioration of the country's natural resources and the environment. They often lead mass public demonstrations on issues relating to bio-piracy, natural resource management, community forestry, and similar issues, and have been able to enroll considerable public and political interest. In 1997 alone, there were more than 1,200 mass demonstrations demanding government attention to issues relating to natural resources and agriculture.[51]

Among other things, the NGO networks demanded the shift from state to more community-based management, as recognized in Articles 46 and 56 of the 1997 constitution. The NGOs called for new directions for improved management of the country's natural resources based on self-sufficiency, conservation of biodiversity, and traditional knowledge. They believe that failure to involve local communities in the formulation of policies and laws regulating access to and use of natural resources has led to conflicts and mismanagement of the resources. The involvement of local communities in the country's resource management is crucial if sustainable development is to be achieved. Local communities, who are major stakeholders, must have the right to be consulted and involved in decision-making and the implementation of those decisions, as well as having the right to seek redress.

NGOs proposed the Community Forestry Bill, along with bills for plant varieties protection and for the protection of Thai traditional medicinal knowledge. The Community Forest Bill was proposed under Article 170 of the 1997 constitution that allows the public to propose legislation with the support of 50,000 signatures.[52] Under the draft bill, the focus is mainly placed on the community-based forest management system that seeks to guarantee access and control over forest resources to the communities living in them. The local communities benefiting from the bill are those who depend on the forest to satisfy their economic, social, cultural, and spiritual needs.

While the bill was still being negotiated, local communities and NGOs developed community forest management plans to support their demands. In the plans, they claimed that the new model, if adopted, would ensure forest conservation. The community-based forest management would eliminate the direct and underlying causes of deforestation by returning responsibility for forest management to the communities who inhabit them, as those communities are the ones primarily concerned with the conservation of the forest resources. The NGO-supported plans cited a number of examples of appropriate forest management, in which environmentally sustainable use is assured while benefiting local communities. It was claimed that more than 8,000 community forests all over Thailand were being used, protected, and managed by local communities.[53]

The Forestry Department's government officials and some conservation groups have consistently opposed the draft bill, particularly on the establishment of community forests inside protected forest areas.[54] The debate on the Community Forest Bill heated up in 2005 when a senate-selected committee scrutinizing the bill voted in favor of a proposal by the Natural Resources and Environment Ministry to set up "special forest zones" where human activities, including the establishment of community forests, were prohibited, and all human settlements in these forest zones had to be relocated. This clearly subverted the original objective of the bill that intended to involve communities living in protected forest areas in the management of forest resources.

Since it was proposed to parliament in early 1993, the bill has been deadlocked until parliament was abolished by the coup in 2006. However, attempts to enact the Community Forestry Bill by civil society groups are a good example of how domestic forces within a nation-state shape the way in which government regulators localize global legal texts.

(c) The country's position at the international level

Thai NGOs have played integral roles in setting standards and formulating Thailand's position in international negotiations on various issues. The following is a summary of the work of NGOs on various issues:

- Under pressure from NGOs, the Thai government made use of the exception clause under Article 27.3(b) of the Agreement on TRIPS that allows for the exclusion of animals, plants, and biological processes from patentability. NGOs also successfully put pressure on the Department of Intellectual Property that administers the Patent Office not to authorize patentability of GMOs and transgenic animals or plants.
- Based on experiences with Plao Noi and jasmine rice, NGOs exerted pressure on the Thai government position in the WTO to adopt the international regime on access and benefit-sharing as submitted by a group of developing countries led by India and Brazil. The Thai government called for an amendment to Article 29 of TRIPS that will incorporate into the international patent rules of TRIPS the principles of mandatory disclosure of origin, benefit-sharing, and prior informed consent.
- Faced with huge political pressure from NGOs and civic groups, the Thai government took a strong position on access and benefit-sharing and traditional knowledge in FTA negotiations with the US. Together, FTA Watch and the Human Rights Commission were pushing for a binding text on genetic resources and traditional knowledge, and for the tight control of GMOs.
- Thailand's position on the protection of geographical indications (GI) at the WTO/TRIPS Council was the result of pressure exerted by a group of NGOs and academics. In GI negotiations, Thailand supported the extension of GI protection to agricultural goods and products other than wines and spirits.
- The Thai government yielded to demands made by civil society groups by not ratifying the International Convention for the Protection of New Varieties of Plants (UPOV)[55] and the FAO's proposed International Treaty on Plant Genetic Resources for Food and Agriculture (ITPGRFA). The rejection of the UPOV Convention is based on the idea that patent-like monopoly privileges granted to plant breeders under UPOV would lead to far-reaching claims over living nature and would monopolize the local seed markets. Thailand also declined to join the FAO treaty that established the multilateral regime on access and benefit-sharing of plant genetic resources. The government agreed with the NGOs that the treaty does not recognize farmers' contributions to the conservation of plant genetic resources, but would facilitate access to the resources and thus increase corporate control and monopoly power over seeds.
- NGO and civic groups have recently staged mass demonstrations against the FTAs being negotiated by Thailand and its trade partners, notably the Thai–US FTA. These groups raised concerns that FTAs would generate socio-economic impacts on Thailand in many ways. In response to the plethora of

bilateral FTAs, an NGO group called FTA Watch was established in 2003. The group comprises academics, lawyers, environmentalists, social activists, trade unions, and other interest groups such as the Alternative Agriculture Network, the Thai Network of People Living with HIV/AIDS, and the Consumer Network. The NGO network on FTA is well coordinated and has three primary activities: (i) advocacy work; (ii) civic education; and (iii) political lobbying.[56] The group has successfully raised public awareness of FTA negotiations. Their education campaign has increased public concern about trade liberalization issues and the development impact of the FTAs.

(d) Protection of traditional knowledge and genetic resources

As part of TRIPS requirements, in 1999, the Thai government developed *sui generis* legislation for the protection of plant varieties, the Protection of Plant Varieties Act B.E. 2542 (PVP). The Thai government and parliament responded to the concerns raised by NGOs and civic groups by incorporating into the PVP Act provisions on the protection of wild varieties, traditional plant varieties, and plant genetic resources. The law also adopts the systems of prior informed consent and benefit-sharing, and a mechanism that prevents the environmental impacts resulting from the invasion of genetically modified plants. In addition, based on the alleged bio-piracy episodes and misappropriations of genetic resources in Thailand and other countries, the Thai Ministry of Public Health, with the collaboration of the NGO networks on health, proposed a bill to parliament in 1999 that was adopted as the Act on Protection and Promotion of Thai Traditional Medicinal Intelligence B.E. 2542.

Before the two laws were adopted, a great variety of proposals were debated to protect ethnobotanical knowledge, traditional medicines, biological resources, traditional plant varieties, landraces, herbs, folklore, cultural property, and so on. With regard to the PVP law, at an early stage, two draft bills were prepared by government agencies: the Ministry of Agriculture and the Department of Intellectual Property under the Ministry of Commerce. The two bills did not contain substantially different contents, but were modeled from the 1978 and the 1991 UPOV Acts.

It is worth noting that the attempts of the two ministries to adopt the PVP law were attacked by many interested domestic groups, including farmers and academics, on the grounds that the bills provided excessive protection for multinational seed companies at the expense of farmers. The law, if introduced, would cause adverse effects to indigenous plant breeders and the wellbeing of poor farmers.

Owing to the political pressure exerted by a highly vocal NGO community acting with farmers' groups and academics, the Thai government appointed the Drafting Committee for Plant Variety Protection Bill, comprising representatives of farmers, plant breeders, companies, and academics. It was the first time in Thailand that local communities have had the opportunity to participate in decisions regarding the use of their traditional knowledge as well as the development of legal frameworks for the protection of traditional knowledge. While government officials and representatives of the seed companies demanded strong plant breeders' rights, the groups of NGOs and academics had argued for an "effective *sui generis*" system within the WTO/TRIPS, containing provisions relating to farmers' privileges, broad exemptions, compulsory licensing, protection of traditional plant varieties, and mechanisms of access, benefit-sharing, and prior informed consent. Finally, the Committee combined the two bills drafted by the ministries into one single bill. A political compromise was also reached by which the bill would grant plant breeders' rights and strong farmers' rights at the same time.

In the same year, a draft bill for the protection of traditional medicines was prepared by the Ministry of Public Health. The proposed bill aimed to protect the genetic resources of medicinal plants for their sustainable use. The bill was adopted partly as a result of political debates relating to Thailand's ratification of the Convention on Biological Diversity (CBD). The Ministry of Public Health, NGOs, and some academics resisted ratification without proper regulation in place.[57] The opponents pointed out that the CBD lacked international mechanisms controlling the cross-border movement of genetic resources. They also argued that a rush to ratify the Convention without any law to protect Thai local wisdom and genetic resources would cause an adverse impact on the country's resources and allow foreign scientists and multinational corporations to use natural resources and possibly to patent local genetic sources. Therefore, they would like to delay ratification until the government approved the draft bill, which was then under scrutiny by a parliamentary committee.

Eventually, the two bills that purported to protect traditional knowledge were approved by parliament.[58] The two laws of Thailand for the protection of traditional knowledge (i.e., the Plant Varieties Protection Act, B.E. 2542, and the Act on Protection and Promotion of Thai Traditional Medicinal Knowledge, B.E. 2542) are clearly the work of NGOs and civic groups.

Conclusion

At the early stage of Thailand's national development, public participation was not part of the planning and decision-making process. Political power was controlled by state officials and middle-class elites. External factors such as globalization and internationalization have affected the county's decision-making and the implementation of new development policies. However, since the political changes toward democracy in the late 1970s, the Thai government authorities have come to realize the significance of public participation in the national development process, and have included a cross-section of civic groups in policy processes. The appearance of the civil society sector has been one of the most striking political events in Thailand. It reflects not only increased concern about globalization and its impacts on the economy, but also a transformation in Thailand's political economy, which has brought civic organizations and people networks closer together to represent rural demands.

The movements of civil society in Thailand are a classic rural struggle over rights to resources of land, forests, water, and local wisdom. The severe social and economic impacts resulting from globalization and development processes, together with a growing public discontent with those holding political power, have motivated the people to struggle for their rights, creating an anti-globalization movement in Thailand. Thai civic groups have now become lobby-style organizations that can exploit opportunities opening up in parliamentary politics. They were formed to provide not only a basis for cooperation among dispersed local movements but also a mechanism for bargaining with the state. Their works have expanded from urban areas to rural villages and from an individual issue to network-based issues of interest. NGOs in Thailand now enjoy a wide policy window allowing them to be involved not only in development planning but also in the development and implementation of national legislation.

If a national development plan is to be a success, the public must be entitled to participate in the political arena. The involvement of these people's groups must be promoted at all levels and in all legislative processes, government operation, and public policy planning. At the same time, they must be free to determine their future, and independent to choose whatever economic, cultural, and knowledge systems they wish to live by.

Notes

1 See Joseph Stiglits, *Making Globalisation Work: The Next Steps to Global Justice*, London: Allen Lane, 2006.
2 Abha Bhamorabutr, *The Chakri Dynasty*, Bangkok: Panya Thamavit, 1983.
3 Matthew Clarke, *Is Economic Growth Desirable?: A Welfare Economic Analysis of the Thai Experience*, unpublished PhD Thesis, Centre for Strategic Economic Studies, Victoria University, 2003, p. 36.
4 Pasuk Phongpaichit and Chris Baker, *Thailand: Economy and Politics*, Oxford: Oxford University Press, 1995, pp. 140–41.
5 Ibid.; Chris Dixon, *The Thai Economy. Uneven Development and Internationalism*, London: Routledge, 1999.
6 Dixon, Ibid., p. 80.
7 Karel Jansen, *External Finance in Thailand's Development*, London: Macmillan, 1997.
8 Phongpaichit and Baker, *supra*, p. 151.
9 Dixon, *supra*, p. 122.
10 Nanak Kakwani, *Income Inequality and Poverty: Methods of Estimation and Policy Applications*, Oxford: Oxford University Press, 1980.
11 Although the inequality of wealth is the country's political problem, the unequal distribution usually goes hand-in-hand with globalization, as the biggest problem with inequality relates to who has the political power and who benefits from openness (trade/finance) and direct foreign investment. There is strong evidence that it is the rich who benefit from openness and that globalization accelerates inequality and widens the gap between rich and poor. See Branko Milanovic, 'Can We Discern the Effect of Globalisation on Income Distribution? Evidence from Household Surveys', *World Bank Economic Review* 19 (1), 2005, pp. 21–44.
12 Peter Warr, *Poverty Reduction and Sectoral Growth: Evidence from Southeast Asia*, Paper presented for the WIDER Development Conference Growth and Development, Helsinki, 25–26 May 2001.
13 Dixon, *supra*, p. 239.
14 Ammar Siamwalla et al., *Foreign Capital Flows to Thailand: Determinants and Impact*, Bangkok: Thailand Development Research Institute, 1999.

15 Ammar Siamwalla, *Anatomy of the Thai Economic Crisis*, Bangkok: Thailand Development Research Institute, 2000; John Laird, *Money Politics, Globalisation, and Crisis: The Case of Thailand*, Singapore: Graham Brash, 2000.

16 John H. Jackson, *The World Trading System*, 2nd edn, Boston: MIT Press, 1997; Ernst-Ulrich Petersmann, 'How to Constitutionalise International Law and Foreign Policy for the Benefit of Civil Society?', *Michigan Journal of International Law* 20, 1998, p. 1.

17 Joel Trachtman, *Lessons for GATS Article VI from the SPS, TBT, and GATT Treatment of Domestic Regulation*, Working Paper, Social Science Research Network, 29 January 2002. Available from http://papers.ssrn.com.

18 Peter Drahos and Ruth Mayne, eds, *Global Intellectual Property Rights*, Basingstoke: Palgrave-Macmillan/Oxfam, 2002.

19 Jakkrit Kuanpoth, 'Political Economy of the TRIPS Agreement', in Ricardo Meléndes-Ortis and Graham Dutfield, eds, *Trading in Knowledge: Development Perspectives on TRIPS, Trade and Sustainability*, London: Earthscan, 2003, pp. 45–56; Jakkrit Kuanpoth, 'Thailand', in Christopher Heath, ed., *Intellectual Property Protection in Asia*, The Hague: Kluwer Publishing International, 2002, pp. 337–62.

20 Jakkrit Kuanpoth, 'Intellectual Property Rights and Pharmaceuticals: A Thai Perspective on Prices and Technological Capability', *Intellectual Property Quarterly* 2, 2007, pp. 185–214.

21 Gerald J. Mossinghoff, 'Drug Trade Seeks Leverage on Patents', *Chemical Marketing Report* (IAC) October, 1990, p. 5.

22 This price control mechanism was removed from the law in 1999 as a result of pressure from the US. Jakkrit Kuanpoth, 'Major Issues in the Thai Patent System', *Thai Bar Law Journal* 50 (1), 1994, pp. 55–84. Available from http://www.thailawforum.com/articles/jakpat1.html.

23 Chatrudee Theparat, 'IMF Gets a Drubbing as National Plan Discussed', *Bangkok Post* 10 April 1999, p. B1

24 Watcharapong Thongrung, 'Bangchak Club Seeks to Buy 50,000 Shares', *The Nation* 6 July 1999, p. 7.

25 Suvicha Pouaree, 'The Winners and Losers from Privatization', *Bangkok Post* 21 September 1997, p. B1.

26 Thongrung, *supra*.

27 Walden Bello, 'The Asian Financial Crisis, Neoliberalism and Economic Miracles', *Foreign Policy in Focus* 30 July 2007.

28 World Bank, *Attacking Poverty – World Bank Development Report 2000/2001*, Washington, DC: World Bank, 2001; Dani Rodrik, 'Globalisation, Social Conflict and Economic Growth', *World Economy* 21 (2), 1998, pp. 143–58.

29 Food and Agriculture Organization, *The State of Food and Agriculture 2005: Making Trade Work for the Poor*, Rome: Food and Agriculture Organization, 2005.

30 Chris Lang et al., *Dams Incorporated: The Record of Twelve European Dam Building Companies*, London: The Corner House, 2000. Available from http://www.thecornerhouse.org.uk/item.shtml?x=52008.

31 Guy Trebuil, *Pioneer Agriculture, Green Revolution and Environmental Degradation in Thailand*, Paper presented at the Fifth International Conference on Thai Studies, School of Oriental and African Studies, University of London, 5–12 July 1993.

32 Department of Forestry, *Forestry Statistics of Thailand*, Bangkok: Department of Forestry, 1996.

33 OECD, *Agricultural Policies in OECD Countries: Monitoring and Evaluation 2002*, Paris: OECD, 2002; Judith Goldstein, 'The Impact of Ideas on Trade Policy: The Origins of US Agricultural and Manufacturing Policies', *International Organisation* 43, 1989, pp. 44–46; Jon G. Filipek, 'Agriculture in a World of Comparative Advantage: The Prospects for Farm Trade Liberalization in the Uruguay Round of GATT Negotiations', *Harvard International Law Journal* 30, 1989, p. 135.

34 David R. Lewis, *Impact of Development on the Thai Rural Population*, Southeast Asia Studies Program, Ohio University, 1995 (unpublished monograph).

35 UNDP, *Thailand Human Development Report 2007: Sufficiency Economy and Human Development*, Bangkok: UNDP, 2007.

36 The Crucible Group, *People, Plants and Patents: The Impact of Intellectual Property on Biodiversity: Conservation, Trade and Rural Society*, Ottawa: IDRC, 1994.

37 Daniel F. Robinson, *Governance and Micropolitics of Traditional Knowledge, Biodiversity and Intellectual Property in Thailand*, Geneva: UNCTAD/ICTSD, 2005. Available from http://www.iprsonline.org/resources/docs/Final%20HRC%20Micropolitics%20Report%20Mar%202005.pdf.

38 Ministry of Commerce, Bangkok, 1997; Jakkrit Kuanpoth, 'Closing in on Biopiracy: Legal Dilemmas and Opportunities', in Ricardo Meléndes-Ortis and Vicente SÁnches, eds, *Trading in Genes: Development Perspectives on Biotechnology, Trade and Sustainability*, London: Earthscan, 2005, pp. 139–52.

39 Pennapa Hongthong, 'Rice Copycat Faces Wrath of Thailand', *The Nation* 1 May 1998.

40 BIOTHAI, 'Thai Peoples' Movements Mobilise To Protect Jasmine Rice', *BIOTHAI Information Release* 26 April 1998.

41 Ruud Valyasevi et al., *Current Status of Biosafety of Genetic Modified Foods in Thailand*, Bangkok: National Center for Genetic Engineering and Biotechnology, 2003. Available from http://home.biotec.or.th/newscenter/Uploads/WE_pic/radF9579.pdf.

42 Apinya Wipatayotin, 'Exporters want GM-free pledge', *Bangkok Post* 17 October 2006.

43 Chai-Anan Samudavanija and Kusuma Snitwongse, *Environment and Security: Security for the State, Insecurity for the People*, Bangkok: Institute of Security and International Studies, Chulalongkorn University, 1992 (in Thai).

44 Chupinit Kesmanee, *Capacity of Karen People in Natural Land, Water and Forest Resource Management: A Preliminary Analysis*, Chiang Mai: Tribal Research Institute, 1996, pp. 1–4; Prasert Trakarnsupakorn, 'The Wisdom of the Karen in Natural Resource Conservation', in Don McCaskill and Ken Kampe, eds, *Development or Domestication?*, Chiang Mai: Silkworm Books, 1997.

45 Laird, *supra*.

46 Gordon White, 'Civil Society, Democratisation and Development: Clearing the Analytical Ground', *Democratisation* 1 (3), 1994; Kumi Naidoo, *Civil Society Accountability: 'Who Guards the Guardians?'*, Lunchtime address delivered at UN Headquarters, New York, 3 April 2003. Available from http://www.impactalliance.org/ev02.php?ID=7548_201&ID2=DO_TOPIC.

47 Kumi Naidoo, Ibid.

48 Ji Giles Ungpakorn, 'Challenges to the Thai NGO Movement from the Dawn of a New Opposition to Global Capital', in Ji Giles Ungpakorn, ed., *Radicalising Thailand: New Political Perspectives*, Bangkok: Institute of Asian Studies, Chulalongkorn University, 2003, pp. 289–318.

49 'All things considered', *The Economist* 28 February 2002.

50 Witoon Lianchamroon, 'Community Rights and Farmers' Rights in Thailand', *Biotechnology and Development Monitor* 36, 1998, p. 9–11.

51 NGO–COD, *Alternative Country Report: Thailand's Progress on Agenda 21 Proposals for Sustainable Development*, Bangkok: The Thai Working Group on the People's Agenda for Sustainable Development, 2002, pp. 130–34.

52 The Community Forest Bill was presented to Parliament in 2000 with 52,698 signatures.

53 Noel Rajesh, 'Thailand: Community Forest Bill', *WRM's Bulletin* 99, October 2005. Available from http://www.wrm.org.uy/bulletin/99/Thailand.html.

54 Office of Natural Resource and Environmental Policy and Planning, *Biological Diversity: What the World Does, and What We Should Do*, Bangkok: Ministry of Science, Technology, and Environment, 2003 (in Thai).

55 The acronym UPOV is derived from the French name of the organization, which is "Union Internationale pour la Protection des Obtentions Végétales."
56 Robinson, *supra*.
57 Tunya Sukpanich, 'Repelling the Biological Pirates', *Bangkok Post* 16 May 1999.
58 Jakkrit Kuanpoth, 'Legal Protection of Traditional Knowledge: A Thai Perspective', *Asia Pacific Tech Monitor* 24 (2), 2007, pp. 34–41.

10 Globalization and Japanese regulation

A commercial dispute case study

Veronica L. Taylor

Introduction

Japan has undergone extensive legal and regulatory reform since 1989, when Japan's "bubble economy" collapsed. Since then, Japanese government and industry have embarked on deregulatory policy and economic restructuring, in the process explicitly turning to formal law, legal institutions, and lawyers as regulatory mechanisms.[1] As a result, we have seen a surge in rule-based, hierarchical controls in Japan, including more regulatory law but, at the same time, the emergence (or reshaping) of informal forms of regulation such as industry practices and codes of conduct and ethics. I call this process the "re-regulation" of Japan.[2]

My approach to understanding the last two decades of regulatory reform in Japan owes much to Haley's theories of the Japanese legal system.[3] Haley argues that, despite having a highly developed legal system, the Japanese state has relied heavily on informal social ordering and norm enforcement in order to achieve its policy goals. Moreover, he argues, the mix of formal and informal legal sanctions is the result of strong historical continuity in the evolution of social, economic, and legal institutions in Japan.[4]

In his depiction of mutually interdependent formal and informal modes of ordering within Japan, Haley seems to anticipate the pluralism that is the focus of much contemporary regulatory theory.[5] However, he articulated this paradigm in *Authority Without Power*[6] at precisely the time that Japan's high-growth economy began to falter and as many of the modes of regulation thought to be distinctively Japanese started to unravel. What has followed is a series of debates across different disciplines about whether, and to what extent, Japanese regulation since the 1990s represents a paradigm shift, and if so, towards what. Within the field of law, Haley argues that the twenty-first-century legal and regulatory mechanisms of governance in Japan represent, on balance, continuity rather than a dramatic rupture with the past.[7]

In this chapter, I examine Haley's claim that we see more continuity than change, testing it against a case study: the failed banking merger between Sumitomo and UFJ financial groups (as they then were). The transaction breakdown made international headlines in 2004 when Sumitomo sought a court injunction to prevent UFJ from: (i) reneging on its formal agreement to negotiate with Sumitomo; and (ii) pursuing an alternative tie-up with the Mitsubishi Tokyo Financial Group.

When all Sumitomo's alternative avenues had failed, it then sued UFJ for breaching obligations under their agreement to negotiate, documented in a letter of intent. On appeal from that lawsuit in 2006, the parties settled, with Sumitomo gaining JPY2.5 billion (US$21 million) in damages.

I argue that, on one hand, the failed merger illustrates the salience of Haley's paradigm of Japanese law. Litigation between very large commercial entities in Japan is atypical—we would usually expect to see their differences settled behind closed doors, perhaps with the help of bureaucratic mediation. Sumitomo, in particular, draws on both the "formal" and the "informal" techniques of dispute resolution offered in the Haley paradigm, claiming the moral high ground, while at the same time pursuing all available strategies, including litigation. The courts, in turn, rely on familiar legal and social norms of transactional continuity as they frame the dispute. Consistent with Haley's thesis, we also see here a "private" commercial transaction overlaid with a "public" character because it involves the future shape of a key Japanese industry. Thus, the transaction acts as a lightning rod for a longstanding domestic debate about the appropriate form and pace of deregulation.

On the other hand, the transaction underscores the limitations of Haley's model when applied to a globalized, re-regulating Japan. All the parties in this transaction and dispute were large banking groups, subject to the regulatory effect of multiple levels of globalization. Their transactional breakdown plays out against a decade of glacial progress in banking reform, where the Ministry of Finance had been displaced as industry regulator by the Financial Supervisory (later Services) Authority (the FSA); global regulatory standards have become increasingly influential; and where government was urging industry to restructure itself using "the market." The ultimate shape of the restructuring was determined not by a tacit government–industry agreement, but in a public, contested arena among new regulatory players, including commercial lawyers as transactional intermediaries, foreign investors, and the courts as arbiters and—in effect—economic regulators.[8]

Haley's Japan

Haley's Japanese state is characterized by "authority without power," a state in possession of a highly developed system of legal rules, standards, and mechanisms for formal adjudication that nevertheless chooses to harness social norms and rely heavily on informal social ordering and norm enforcement in order to achieve its policy goals.[9]

> Legislators, bureaucrats, and judges may continue to articulate and apply, and thus legitimate, new rules and standards of conduct. The norms thus created and legitimized may have significant impact. To the extent that legal sanctions are weak, however, their validity depends upon consensus, and thus as "living" law, they become nearly indistinguishable from non-legal or customary norms.[10]

The corollary of this is "the myth of the reluctant litigant"—the state's deliberate rationing of formal legal adjudication and sanctions through institutional design.[11]

Haley presents the paradox of a highly credentialed and independent Japanese judiciary, procuracy, and bar whose size is deliberately constrained by the state so that their capacity to deliver formal sanctions and their accessibility to citizens are limited. This controlled mix of formal legal sanctions and informal social ordering represents, he argues, a strong historical continuity in the evolution of social and legal institutions in Japan. While stressing these historical antecedents, Haley also acknowledges that culture is fluid and that the norms underpinning these policy choices and institutional design choices are subject to change.

In his depiction of mutually interdependent formal and informal modes of ordering within Japan, Haley seems to anticipate the pluralist focus of contemporary regulatory theory.[12] However, his paradigm is also the product of its time; where it focuses on the (then) representative social institutions such as large corporations, lifetime employment, organized crime, and local community bodies, the snapshot is of Japan at the end of a prolonged high-growth period. This is an economy that is "internationalized" in the sense of being export-oriented and in which the "international" inputs—standards, labor, and capital—are controlled and controllable. Within the legal system, too, there is a strong sense of Japanese exceptionalism, reflected in the relatively small number of legal professionals, the minimalist design of contract transactions, and the relatively low levels of commercial litigation. Haley represents the duality thus:

> The demand for ways to reduce the risk and costs intrinsic to a volatile social and economic environment is also manifest in the prevalence of dependency and relational contracting. The oft-repeated Japanese penchant for informal, long-term contractual relationships, in which "goodwill" and personal trust are more important than written contacts, is symptomatic of transactional relationships in which the parties rely more on morals and markets than laws for enforcement … On the other hand, when contracting abroad within legal systems Japanese believe are likely to enforce their agreements, they negotiate and draft with extreme care. Similarly a Japanese firm will assiduously abide by adverse commitments to its contact partners in cases where sanctions—either informal, arising out of either their relative bargaining positions or the promise of an ongoing relationship, or formal, such as the likelihood of legal action—are perceived to be strong.[13]

However, as Japan's high-growth economy began to slump after the collapse of its economic "bubble" in 1989, many of these institutional arrangements and modes of regulation begin to unravel or become the subject of extensive rethinking by government, corporate, and professional elites.

Japan's legal and regulatory reform since 1989

The 1990s were called the "lost decade" by Japanese and foreign scholars of Japanese politics and economics because of the perceived failure by the governing triumvirate of the Liberal Democratic Party, career bureaucrats, and big business to deregulate a stalled economy.[14] Others argued that the deregulatory push in Japan, albeit fitful between the Nakasone (1982–87) and Koizumi (2001–6) cabinets, induced important and enduring institutional changes.[15] By 2008, many commentators agreed that the Japanese government and industry *had* significantly restructured key political, economic, and social institutions since 1989,[16] but they continued to disagree about the pace of regulatory reform and its effects. Recent studies in political science have argued that Japan has been "remodeled"[17] or "reprogrammed"[18] or has adopted "aggressive legalism"[19] in spheres such as industrial policy, technology, and trade.

My own hypothesis is that Japan is shifting from being a "developmental state" to being a "new regulatory state."[20] For the purposes of this chapter, I highlight three changes in policy and practice that seem to mark departures from earlier paradigms of the Japanese state and that seem to signal a new approach to legal regulation.

The first of these changes is the separation (and delegation) by the state of some of its traditional functions and services to private actors or quasi-state actors.[21] Although a core component of the "new regulatory state,"[22] the reliance of the state on private actors in Japan is not new. What changes in the 1990s, however, is both the mode of harnessing private actors and the language used to describe this. So, for example, in the commercial sphere in Japan, we see a downplaying of "administrative guidance" as top-down, albeit "informal," state direction. This is further undercut by changes to administrative law and jurisprudence that require more formal and more transparent signaling from the bureaucracy. At the same time, we see a host of induced enhancements of self-regulation for business, bolstered by legislative reform, court decisions, and government exhortation. The new modes of regulation are, for the most part, concepts and terms taken directly from American, British, and European discourse on corporate regulation.

Thus, "corporate governance" (*kooporeeto gabanansu*) is operationalized in Japan through extensive legislative reform to governance structures of corporations, the introduction of consolidated accounting, and the enhancement of the role of the statutory auditor. "Transparency" (*toransupeeranshii/tōmeika*) is bolstered in the commercial sphere by lowering court filing fees to permit shareholder actions against company directors and auditors, including demands for the production of documents.[23] "Contract" is now understood in Japan as a regulatory institution,[24] and we see considerably more formalization of high-value contracts through the intermediation of attorneys. We also see a clear normative clash between different modes of regulation: private law visions of freedom of contract collide with court-designed rules that embody established business customs and the courts' preferred social norms. These are both overlaid with new legislative intervention by the state, which emphasizes efficiency and formal dispute resolution forums.[25] "Due diligence" (*dyū dirijiensu*) is new and used, as in the case study below, in the context of a market in which merger and acquisitions (M&A) activity, both friendly and hostile, begins to intensify after a long period of relative corporate stability in Japan. "Risk management" (*risuku kanri*) has been embraced by Japanese corporations battered by record levels of corporate insolvency and facing new challenges that range from dependence on information technology to the aggressive use of intellectual property rights by US trade competitors. "Compliance" (*kompuraiansu*) is suddenly in vogue as corporations establish compliance departments to either supplement or stand for in-house legal departments. The primary driver here is an upsurge in legislation that has a direct impact on corporations or that, like the *Antimonopoly Law*, is being enforced more vigorously than was the case historically. Reinforcing this is a new line of corporate law cases that spell out the obligation for listed companies to implement internal corporate controls and what the financial consequences of not doing so are likely to be.[26]

This range of state and private, voluntary, and induced regulatory techniques is consistent both with Parker and Braithwaite's observation that post-industrial states tend to show pluralization of regulation[27] and with Haley's earlier work on the mix of formal and informal social ordering in Japan.

A second feature of the new regulatory state is the proliferation of players who compete for regulatory traction in what Scott has termed "the regulatory space."[28] The regulatory space metaphor is illuminating because it suggests a suspended sphere with multiple planes, rather than the vertical channel of state–citizen command and control regulation, or a purely horizontal axis of private player interactions. For Scott, the appeal of the regulatory space is that:

> [It] is capable of drawing in perspectives which question the capacities of instrumental law and regulation and envisage greater reflexivity or responsiveness in systems characterized variously as post-bureaucratic or post-interventionist.[29]

While it is not yet clear whether Japan is either "post-bureaucratic" or "post-interventionist," the emergence of new regulatory players seems to be forcing open the developmental state's "iron triangle" of decision-making that privileged politicians, bureaucrats, and big business. The newly prominent players include consumer advocates, non-governmental organizations (NGOs), lawyers, prudential regulators, shareholder activists, and electronic commerce networks.[30] Most of these players existed prior to 1989 but have benefited from, and have grown more prominent as a result of, enabling legislation and policy changes that endow them with a new status or the ability to organize more effectively.[31]

Significantly, as the *Sumitomo v. UFJ* case illustrates, the Japanese "regulatory space" has become porous and many of the new stakeholders are non-Japanese. Prior to 1989, mobilizing *gaiatsu* or "foreign pressure" was a standard play in Japanese regulatory politics, as was invoking the threat of foreign domination, takeover, or destruction.[32] What is different in the contemporary period, as I discuss below, is that foreign stakeholders—in this case shareholders—are now *inside* the regulatory space and likely to stay there.

A third systemic shift visible in post-1989 Japan has been the elevation of formal law and legal institutions as legitimized regulatory tools available to both the state and its citizens. This development departs from accounts of the Japanese state in which legislation, courts, independent regulatory agencies, and legal professions play a marginal role. In those narratives, bureaucrats dominate politicians or (in Ramseyer and Rosenbluth's agency theory) are controlled by them.[33] In either case, bureaucrats exercise "authority without power,"[34] harnessing informal social norms to achieve their desired regulatory objectives. Business is steered through administrative guidance and government-supported self-regulation[35] or "cooperative regulation,"[36] "cooperative capitalism"[37] or "communitarian capitalism."[38] Emphasizing the minimal traction of direct legal regulation on corporations, Hirowatari calls this policy setting "corporatism" or law restrained in the service of economic growth.[39]

Consistent with these accounts, Haley's paradigm suggests that litigation in Japan was designed to be a regulatory technique of last resort.[40] This immediately begs the question of how we account for a long and crowded history of active litigation of commercial, private, and public interest matters in Japan. Despite the apparent paradox, the history and the theory are not inconsistent. In a system of interlocking formal and informal controls that limits access to the courts, litigation can be a highly effective way of exposing lack of consensus or challenging government or powerful interests in a public way.[41] Nonetheless, it is the relative lack of litigation in Japan in comparison to Western industrialized states that is the dominant characteristic in the varieties of capitalism literature[42] and in comparative regulatory studies,[43] as well as in older literature such as Chalmers Johnson's account of the Japanese "developmental state."[44] Suddenly, however, after an apparently short policy gestation, the Japanese government announced in 2001 that it is, in fact, law and legal institutions—including litigation—that are the "final linchpin" in the restructuring of "the shape of our country."[45] On the streets, public slogans, campaigns, and banners announce that it is now formal regulation ("rules") that will now govern, in preference to informal social ordering ("manners").[46]

Without data, it is difficult to argue that Japan's regulatory patterns have changed in the twenty-first century or to pinpoint the degree to which they replicate or deviate from those of other industrialized states. In this chapter, I take the failed Sumitomo–UFJ merger of 2004 as my smallest unit of analysis—a single transaction—and try to discern whether it evidences any influence from a new regulatory mix in Japan, the emergence of new regulatory players, and/or a new turn to formal law.

The proposed Sumitomo–UFJ merger

The Sumitomo–UFJ merger agreement and the litigation that followed are widely recognized as one of the high watermarks in business disputation in Japan in the 2000s. The core transaction began as a consensual merger negotiation between two major financial institutions in Japan. It was a negotiation fraught with some pressure: UFJ was one of two city banks at the time that was severely undercapitalized (and possibly substantively insolvent), within a Japanese banking industry that had chalked up ten consecutive years of losses.[47]

Japan suffered a banking crisis in 1997 when three large financial institutions failed, including city bank Hokkaido Takushoku Bank, followed by the 1998 failures of the Long-Term Credit Bank of Japan and Nippon Credit Bank. This prompted the re-regulation of the industry through the creation of the Financial Supervision (later "Services") Agency (the FSA) in 1998 to replace the Ministry of Finance's jurisdiction over the industry. The FSA was charged with the application of stringent global standards including new accounting rules to implement the Basel capital adequacy requirements for banks. A wave of industry restructuring followed: between 2000 and 2002, seven mergers had occurred among major banks.[48] By 2004, Sumitomo and UFJ were looking for merger partners at the tail end of this process and within a market that analysts predicted could only support a finite number of truly global banks. Thus the stakes in the Sumitomo–UFJ transaction were high.

On 21 May 2004, Sumitomo announced its intention to purchase UFJ's trust banking unit. This was one of UFJ's only profitable operations at the time. The value of the transaction was JPY300 billion (US$2.76 billion).[49] This was underpinned by a letter of intent between Sumitomo Trust and Banking Co.[50] and the UFJ Holdings Group—as they then were—in respect of the UFJ Trust Bank (hereafter "Sumitomo" and "UFJ"). The letter of intent was a formally drafted agreement reviewed by the parties' attorneys. Article 8 of the agreement provided that each party was to negotiate in good faith to conclude a basic agreement on the detailed terms of the business integration by the end of July 2004 and conclude a final agreement on integration as soon as practicable. The duration of the negotiations contemplated by the agreement was reported as two years.[51]

Article 12 of the agreement further obliged the parties to (i) negotiate in good faith on matters stipulated in the letter of intent and any matters arising but not stipulated in the agreement and (ii) prohibited the parties from either directly or indirectly providing information to, or negotiating with, third parties in relation to any matters that were the subject of this agreement.[52] The undertakings to negotiate in good faith were, of course, applications of Civil Code Article 1 (2), "[R]ights must be exercised and … obligations be performed in good faith," which applies to all legal acts in Japan, whether explicitly incorporated in the terms of the agreement or not.

Significantly, the agreement contained no penalties for non-performance:

> "We suggested a breakup fee to Sumitomo Trust," says one lawyer who worked on the deal. "But they rejected it, saying the business must be based on trust."[53]

On 13 July 2004, UFJ unilaterally broke off merger talks with Sumitomo and, on 14 July, it entered into full merger talks with the Mitsubishi Tokyo Financial Group (MTFG, as it then was)[54] in which the latter would acquire UFJ group, including the UFJ Trust Bank, creating the world's largest bank with US$1.75 trillion in assets.[55] That merger took place in 2005, creating the Mitsubishi UFJ Financial Group (MUFG), of which the Bank of Tokyo–Mitsubishi UFJ, Mitsubishi–UFJ Trust, and Banking and Mitsubishi–UFJ Securities are subsidiary units.[56]

Sumitomo responded to this breakdown in negotiations by calling the press. UFJ's termination of the letter of intent was widely reported:

"They just told us all of a sudden," Sumitomo Trust spokesman Naoki Sugihara said. "We were shocked that they would cancel something so critical without at least consulting us first."[57]

On the same day, 14 July 2004, UFJ and Tokyo–Mitsubishi shares were suspended on the basis that they may be seeking a merger, and Sumitomo's share price subsequently fell by about 14 percent.[58] Two days later, on 16 July 2004, UFJ and Tokyo–Mitsubishi announced talks aimed at effecting a merger. Sumitomo issued a formal objection to this and, on the same day, sought an interim injunction from the Tokyo District Court restraining UFJ from both providing information to third parties and negotiating with third parties.[59]

Sumitomo's multitrack approach to the negotiation breakdown

Sumitomo responded to UFJ's termination of the negotiation by pursuing a multitrack strategy. First, it sought injunctive relief to prevent UFJ from proceeding with merger talks with Tokyo–Mitsubishi, a move that was successful in the short term but was overturned on appeal. Second, it sought to convince UFJ's shareholders, through media announcements, that the Sumitomo merger, including a one-for-one share exchange, represented better value for UFJ than the proposed rival merger.[60] This was significant because any merger of a business of this size would require a special resolution (two-thirds approval) by shareholders at a general meeting.[61] At the time, about one-third of UFJ's shares were reportedly owned by foreign investors.[62]

In support of its claim that it represented a better tie-up partner, Sumitomo launched a counteroffer to the Tokyo–Mitsubishi proposal on 9 August 2004, announcing that it was ready to offer a JPY500 billion (US$4.48 billion) tranche of fresh capital to help write off UFJ's bad loans, in addition to reserving management positions for UFJ executives in the new merged entity.[63] At the same time, Sumitomo Mitsui Financial Group announced on 7 October 2004 that they had purchased 300 shares in UFJ Holdings, "raising the prospect of a proxy fight at the weaker rival's annual meeting."[64] Part of this strategy was aimed at increasing foreign press opinion, foreign shareholder, and outside director pressure on UFJ to consider Sumitomo's counteroffer and recommence negotiations. This reportedly resulted in a letter-writing campaign from shareholders to UFJ management, asking them to consider alternative proposals to the Tokyo–Mitsubishi deal.[65]

UFJ was under intense financial pressure at this point. Having posted losses for three years in a row, it was carrying significant debt from bad loans, which accounted for 10.24 percent of its loan portfolio in August 2004.[66] Press reports speculated that UFJ would be subject to government pressure to resolve these problems quickly and seek a large capital infusion to prevent its capital levels from dwindling to dangerous lows.[67] In October 2004, it also became the target of a criminal complaint against UFJ's banking unit and former executives for allegedly obstructing an investigation by hiding and destroying documents, resulting in the suspension of some of its banking operations by regulators.[68]

When UFJ announced it plans to go with Tokyo–Mitsubishi, Sumitomo turned to a third strategy—consideration of a hostile takeover of UFJ. This in turn prompted a JPY700 billion (US$6.28 billion) capital injection into UFJ's commercial bank by Tokyo–Mitsubishi and, on 10 September 2004, UFJ issued a new class of preferred shares to MTFG, giving MTFG veto power over major business decisions by UFJ Bank—in effect, a poison pill defense.[69]

The fourth and final strategy employed by Sumitomo was litigation for damages for loss suffered during the breakdown of the negotiations and its protracted attempt to restart them.

The court injunction track

At the same time as the business strategies of the two parties were playing out, Sumitomo had initiated a parallel legal track seeking formal injunctive relief from the courts in order to force UFJ back to the negotiating table.

On 27 July 2004, the Tokyo District Court granted the injunctive relief sought by Sumitomo. The basis for that decision was that the parties had evidenced their agreement in writing and, therefore, in the absence of other compelling reasons, this should be treated as binding. Moreover, the draft of the letter of intent including the lock-in clause had been prepared by the applicant (Sumitomo) and had been reviewed by the lawyer for UFJ Holdings, modified by agreement of those responsible on behalf of the parties, and then signed and sealed by the parties' representative directors. It was, therefore, treated as legally binding. Clearly, if the respondent were to embark on negotiations with a third party, this would cause serious damage and immediate danger to the applicant[70] and, to avoid this, injunctive relief was necessary.

In response to UFJ's formal objection to the injunction, the Tokyo District Court confirmed its original injunction and issued an injunction for preservation on 4 August 2004.[71] UFJ appealed the original injunction to the Tokyo High Court, which set the injunction aside on 11 August 2004. Within hours, the boards of directors of MTFG and UFJ approved a merger of the two groups.[72]

In setting aside the injunction, the Tokyo High Court confirmed that Article 12 of the letter of intent was legally valid and could be the basis for a restraining injunction. Moreover, the declaration by UFJ dated 14 July 2004 that it was terminating the agreement had no legal basis. However, the court found that:

> In relation to the said agreement, the major precondition was a mutual trust relationship supported by good faith efforts to bring about a cooperative enterprise. When the applicants decided to overcome their difficult situation by setting aside the agreement [lit. returning the agreement to a blank piece of paper] and announced this publicly and when the respondent reacted by seeking the injunction and in that initial hearing and in this hearing both arguments have been in opposition, the trust relationship has significantly eroded and we are in a situation where it is difficult to bridge the parties' [differences]. As of today, viewed objectively, the trust relationship between the parties has already broken down; moreover, we have to assume that it is

already impossible for the parties to negotiate in good faith to reach a final agreement. Consequently, at the very latest, we would view the final day of the examination, August 10, 2004, as being the point at which the article in question, substantively has lost its prospective binding effect and that at this point there is no leeway to allow a restraining injunction.[73]

On further appeal by Sumitomo, the Supreme Court on 30 August 2004 affirmed the High Court decision to set aside the injunction.[74] First, the Supreme Court concurred with the High Court that the letter of intent was legally valid, could be the basis for an injunction, and that subsequent events did not cause it to lose its legally binding power. The Supreme Court then adopted almost identical wording to that of the Tokyo High Court decision in describing the breakdown of the parties' relationship as the reason for leaving no leeway to grant a restraining injunction. The Court then noted that, by this time, UFJ had announced a merger with Tokyo–Mitsubishi and a plan to complete that transaction by 1 October 2004.

On the question of whether the lock-in agreement had lost its legal effect, the Supreme Court held that the purpose of the clause was to make good faith negotiation possible, and thus it was intimately linked to the negotiation itself. Thus, when it was judged that the possibility of a final agreement no longer existed, the obligation underlying the article in question was extinguished. Reviewing the chronology of events to that point, the Court judged the likelihood of reaching a final agreement to be "low." However, the Court then continued:

> However, in light of the overall chronology in this case, it is not possible to say that all fluid factors have completely disappeared and so, from a social sense (*shakaitsūnen*) [lit. conventional wisdom of society] we cannot say that the possibility referred to above does not exist. Thus the obligation underlying the article in question must be treated as not having been extinguished.[75]

On the question of whether sufficient dispute existed between the parties to justify injunctive relief in order to avoid serious damage or immediate danger to one of the parties, the Court held that the letter of intent did not compel the conclusion of a final agreement, but only made possible the conditions for the negotiations that might have that result. Therefore, Sumitomo had only a hope of reaching a binding agreement. Consequently, any damage suffered to Sumitomo should not be assessed as resulting from the loss of profits or benefits that would have accrued from a final agreement. In light of the low likelihood of a final agreement being reached and the passage of time up until this point, the Court then found no serious damage or immediate danger sufficient to justify granting a restraining injunction.

UFJ and Mitsubishi finally concluded their contract of merger on 18 February 2005, becoming MUFG on 1 October 2005.

The litigated damages claim

Once it became clear that the transaction was dead and that the injunctive track was exhausted, Sumitomo then launched a suit for tort damages in the amount of JPY100 billion for breach of the duty of good faith in the letter of intent of 7 March 2005 and the failure to conclude a final agreement. The points at issue in the case were:

(a) Was there an obligation under the letter of intent to conclude a final agreement?
(b) Could Article 130 of the Civil Code be applied directly or analogously as the basis for an estoppel that required the UFJ group to conclude a final agreement?
(c) Did the UFJ group have an obligation to negotiate in good faith and exclusively with Sumitomo?
(d) Did UFJ group's obligation to negotiate in good faith and exclusively with Sumitomo expire on 13 July 2004, had they breached these obligations, and was there a non-performance of an obligation or a tort?
(e) If there was non-performance of an obligation or a tort, what was the amount of foreseeable damages?

The Tokyo District Court responded to these questions as follows:

(a) The letter of intent was concluded at a relatively early stage in the parties' negotiations, on the basis of limited information exchanged. It included no provision that clearly required a final agreement to be reached, and so the parties could not be treated as having assumed an obligation to conclude a final agreement. Moreover, this was something that could only be done as the result of a decision reached after further negotiation and due diligence.[76]
(b) As the content of a final contract was not determined and no final contract was validly created, the necessary prerequisite for the direct application or application by analogy of Article 130 of the Civil Code was lacking.
(c) The UFJ group was under an obligation to negotiate exclusively with Sumitomo and to negotiate in good faith.
(d) As the letter of intent was a process for forming a final agreement, when the possibility for creating a final contract through repeated negotiation between Sumitomo and the UFJ group no longer existed, then their obligations would also be extinguished; however, in the case where the UFJ group had—without negotiation or consultation—announced that it would set aside the letter of intent, it could not be said that no possibility of forming a final contract existed.[77] Thus, the obligation to negotiate exclusively and the obligation to negotiate in good faith could not be said to expire; moreover, when UFJ group unilaterally took merger discussions with the Mitsubishi Tokyo Financial Group (MTFG), in doing so they assumed the burden of breaching these obligations or committing a tort.
(e) To the extent that a final contract did not exist, a foreseeable relationship between the breach of the obligations to negotiate exclusively and to negotiate in good faith and the profit that would have arisen under a final contract could not be established and, as Sumitomo was unable to show or prove damages arising from the breach of obligation or the tort, the claim for damages was dismissed.

The Tokyo District Court dismissed Sumitomo's damages claim on 13 February 2006.[78] On appeal to the Tokyo High Court on 24 February 2006, Sumitomo reduced its claim to JPY10 billion. On 21 November 2006, Sumitomo and MTFG settled in the Tokyo High Court for JPY2.5 billion (US$21 million), payable by MTFG.

Significance of the litigation

Settlement during commercial litigation is a well-established pattern in Japan as it is in most industrialized economies' legal systems. Earlier studies of Japanese courts also suggest that the judge frequently takes an active role in encouraging settlement and in providing a clear indication of what the damages award is likely to be if the parties persist to judgment. Thus, although the appeal does not result in a damages award per se, it is likely to be read as a strong indicator of the court's stance in the case. The ultimate obligation to pay damages could not have been a surprise for UFJ and its takeover partner, Tokyo–Mitsubishi. Already in 2004, when Sumitomo succeeded in its injunction at first instance:

> [o]fficials at UFJ and Mitsubishi Tokyo said the most likely outcome would be for UFJ to try to strike some out-of-court deal with Sumitomo Trust, possibly involving payment of compensation.[79]

Their prediction was consistent with contract law jurisprudence in Japan on the Civil Code Article 1 (2) duty of good faith, which applies to all legal acts, regardless of whether the duty is directly referenced or documented by the parties. It is well established as applying to the pre-contractual negotiation period. Parties are at liberty to terminate a pre-contractual negotiation but, if they terminate unilaterally, in the absence of a serious reason for doing so that absolves them of fault, they will be liable for damages. What distinguishes *Sumitomo v. UFJ* as a decision in the first instance is that it makes clear that breach of a duty to negotiate exclusively under a letter of intent (the lock-in provision) is a breach of an obligation or a tort.[80]

As a commercial dispute, what made *Sumitomo v. UFJ* unusual at the District Court level, however, was the inability to reach an early settlement, coupled with the size of the parties, the size of the final settlement, and the question of how damages would be calculated in subsequent cases.

This was an atypical transaction in the sense that it is the first case in the post-war period in Japan (perhaps ever) in which one Japanese financial institution sued another for breach of good faith in negotiation and the failure to consummate a consensual merger. Even in the deregulatory decade and a half since 1989, Japan has had relatively little litigation around M&A activity and very few attempted hostile takeovers.[81] As Ahmadjian comments, there is still a strong sense of stigma about overtly aggressive pressure toward corporate targets in Japan, even among foreign investors:[82]

> The propensity of foreigners to take a gentle approach to governance and not to rely on legal recourse or aggressive shareholder activism seems more

a case of social norms than to [sic] institutional and legal barriers to action. Shareholder derivative suits were available for use, but though numbers of these suits had increased after a decrease in the filing fee in the early 1990s, foreign shareholders did not use them … foreign shareholders that I interviewed suggested that they were concerned about not appearing too aggressive and demanding … There was also, among foreign investors, especially the investment banks, a concern that over-aggressive behavior would be punished. A fear of government reprisal was likely one of the reasons that foreign investors remained low-key in their activism.[83]

Thus, at one level, *Sumitomo v. UFJ* provides an interesting twist on the perennial theme of Japanese litigiousness or lack thereof, with Sumitomo pressing forward with litigation that may or may not have been the direct preference of its foreign shareholders.[84]

Litigating commercial transactional breakdowns in a deregulating Japan, however, is not at all unusual. Injunctions are frequently used as a tool by commercial lawyers and their clients in Japan, although this pattern has not attracted much analysis by foreign scholars.[85] From 1989 onwards, Japanese case reports are full of contract termination litigation as the economy slid into a prolonged downturn.[86] A parallel body of commercial litigation is also propelled by personal bankruptcy and corporate insolvencies, which reached historically high levels during the same period.[87] It is also worth noting that *Sumitomo v. UFJ* is not the average unilateral termination case where a vulnerable injured party pleads breach of good faith as a way of invoking the protective paternalism of the court. Here, we have commercial banking groups: large entities operating in a global market, subject to a host of global and domestic regulatory standards and statutory controls, and accustomed to calculating transactional risk. This feature of the transaction is reflected in its formalism, also characteristic of the banking sector. Banks are accustomed to drafting and adopting legally binding agreements, as they did here with the letter of intent, notwithstanding the fact that it did not anticipate failure of the negotiation.

What is interesting about the courts' analyses in both the injunction claim and the damages claim, however, is the way in which they view the fundamental obligations of the parties in relational terms: to negotiate in good faith and build a trust relationship that would be the basis for the business integration. Thus, for example, although the transaction breakdown occurs at the beginning of a potential business tie-up (rather than midway through a continuing contract), the court acknowledges and weighs the duration of the extended period of the negotiation and the likelihood (however slight) of the relationship being resuscitated. As it weighs the nature of the relationship, the Supreme Court in its determination about injunctive relief makes a not unusual reference to social norms (*shakaitsūnen*). Here, we see the court preference for preserving commercial relationships (or encouraging the parties to do so) if at all possible. This is consistent with much contract jurisprudence in Japan and also consistent with the high value of this transaction and its significance for both the banking industry and the national economy.

Doctrinally, the case is unremarkable because the background statute (the Civil Code) and related case decisions are relatively clear; this is not a situation in which new regulatory law is being tested.[88] What contributes interest from a practice perspective is that the District Court's treatment of the damages claim raises some uncertainty about how those damages should be calculated.[89] The court seems to treat the calculation of damages as limited to Sumitomo's expectation interest in the to-be-negotiated "basic agreement" regarding the merger, probably because this was the basis on which the claim was argued. Predictably, the court finds neither an obligation to finalize that agreement, nor a high probability that the agreement could be reached, particularly as the negotiations and the parties' relationship began to unravel. A stronger basis for arguing the case would have been the plaintiff's reliance interest, or damage incurred as a result of entering into the negotiation and having it unilaterally terminated. Presumably, this was an element in the eventual settlement.

What also distinguishes this case is the parties' inability (or unwillingness) to settle at an early stage of the dispute. We see two large banks exercising choices about how to structure the contract and navigate its breakdown, using both formal legal and informal social strategies. This reliance on litigation is atypical for large corporations or financial institutions. While Sumitomo clearly suffered economic loss from the UFJ termination of the proposed merger, until recently, Japan has no history of shareholders punishing directors for losses that arise simply from the exercise of business judgment, as opposed to fraud or illegal acts.[90] Nevertheless, it seems as though the damages litigation was intended to have a prophylactic, as well as a substantive, effect. The social and economic significance of the case is analyzed below.

Regulation, reactions, and risk management

As we noted above, the regulatory backdrop to this failed merger was a decade of malaise in Japan's banking sector. While this is popularly attributed to the collapse of Japan's "bubble" economy in 1989 and the financial institution and corporate failures that were precipitated by bad loans, Hoshi and Kashyap argue that the causes were much older and deeper. They suggest that the Japanese banking industry has never been globally competitive and that its core features (lack of private capital; misallocation of credit and continuous renewal of non-performing loans; a sector that is too large to allow adequate returns; and an inability to make profit because of government restraints on types of financial products) have been visible since at least the 1980s. When Japan's economic downturn predictably resulted in bank failures and hollowing out of assets, the government's response was a "muddling through" strategy of forbearance, injections of public funds, and selective and intermittent application of global banking standards and procedures through the FSA.[91] The "informal" channel of regulation continued with extensive communication between banks and their regulator, with the government signaling its preferred results by, for example, offering public funds to buy subordinated debt and preferred shares of major banks.

The banks were not forced to recapitalize, but were strongly encouraged to apply for the funds. The banks, however, are expected to "return" the public funds eventually by accumulating enough internal funds to buy-back the shares and debt. Bank of Tokyo Mitsubishi and Sumitomo Trust and Banking have already bought-back the government's holdings of their subordinated debt.[92]

What these measures underscored, however, was the limits of regulatory turn-around for banks within the Japanese market, unless new sources of capital could be found or unless the economy improved dramatically and in a sustained way. Thus, foreign investment became important.

The three banking groups that feature in this case study were all globalized banks—all three traded in the US[93] and had significant foreign share ownership. As Ahmadjian notes in relation to Sumitomo Trust Bank's sister institution:

> In 2003, Goldman Sachs purchased $1.37 billion of preferred shares, convertible into regular shares in a number of years in Sumitomo Mitsui Bank. These more concentrated stakes by single funds suggested that foreign ownership would become increasingly influential over time.[94]

In the case of Sumitomo Trust Bank, its foreign ownership was reported as representing 30 percent of its issued shares at the time of the dispute.

Not surprisingly, then, we see in the media statements by Sumitomo and UFJ during this period an emphasis on shareholder value—a (then) relatively new corporate norm for Japan—and the impact of the failed transaction on foreign perceptions of the market:

UFJ said …"We have explained to the court that Sumitomo Trust and Banking's request for a provisional injunction has no legal basis and that our group, MTFG, and Japan's economy and financial markets would suffer greatly if an injunction was granted." The group's comments came in response to a claim from Atsushi Takahashi, Sumitomo's President, that trust in Japanese law and the country's economy would be undermined if UFJ was able to pull out of the sale.[95]

Clearly, these claims were aimed at foreign investors who were likely to be more mobile in the market, rather than at the banks' own domestic institutional investors or shareholders from their own industrial groups.

Foreign shareholdings in Japan in non-financial corporations remained at very low levels after the 1950s. At the time that Haley published *Authority Without Power*, foreign share ownership by market value of all listed companies in Japan was still in single digits: about 4.2 percent in 1990. By the time of our case study dispute, foreign ownership had climbed steadily so that it was 21.8 percent in 2004 and subsequently grew to 28.0 percent in 2008.[96]

As Ahmadjian points out, foreign shareholders exercise influence in multiple ways in Japan. She codes this influence in classic corporate governance terms, as "voice" or "exit." Ahmadjian argues that exit represented a powerful option for foreign investors in the 1990s, who "had an influence over Japanese share prices far in excess of their actual stakes."[97] They were far more likely to buy and sell than

Japanese investors and "propped up share prices at a time when banks and other long-term shareholders were selling their holdings." For banks in particular,

> [l]owered stock prices had an impact on banks' shareholdings—and if the share prices went too low, they threatened to affect their capital adequacy ratios.[98]

Foreign shareholders also exercise "voice" in different ways. A 2003 survey by leading legal publisher Shōji Hōmu found that foreign and "other" shareholders exercised their voting rights against management proposals in 43.7 percent of companies surveyed in 2003, compared with 19 percent in 1999.[99] Seldom, however, have foreign investors escalated that voice to the point of being protagonists in litigation such as derivative suits.[100] More typically, Ahmadjian found in interviews that foreign shareholders exercised informal voice in meetings with corporate chief executive officers (CEOs) and corporate investor relations departments, and through representative bodies such as the American Chamber of Commerce in Japan (ACCJ).[101]

If Ahmadjian's argument is accurate, it would suggest that Sumitomo's commitment to litigation, both at the injunctive relief stage and in the later damages claim, could be read as an attempted show of strength, possibly for the benefit of foreign investors and/or industry analysts.

Media reaction to Sumitomo's actions was divided both at home and abroad. In some quarters, Sumitomo's litigation was seen as vindication of a domestic deregulatory discourse, a symbolic marker of "a more confrontational and legalistic society."[102] In other circles, Sumitomo was castigated for seeking an injunction, because it opened the door to "court intervention" in what was potentially a more lucrative rival deal for UFJ. In this case, the first court treatment of a bank merger, some observers saw "court intervention" as arresting a shift from developmental state-style planning to market-driven transactions. Some questioned whether arresting this trend was an appropriate role for the court. Yet other observers saw Sumitomo's actions as immoral—bringing a banking industry transaction into the glare of public and legal scrutiny—a reaction that aligns with the Haley paradigm.[103]

Globalization and juridification as new regulatory elements in Japan

As we consider whether *Sumitomo v. UFJ* may signal a departure from the Haley paradigm of regulation in Japan, two new elements seem to stand out. The first is globalization and the second a turn to the courts—what we might call Japan's juridification.[104]

Globalization is defined in multiple ways and features in a range of legal and regulatory discourses within and outside Japan. At the meta level, Dowdle has characterized it as a mutual, cross-system of regulatory borrowing.[105] This resonates with the account of changes in Japanese law and society described by legal sociologist Shiro Kashimura.[106] But what Kashimura stresses is that "globalization" in

Japan represents a very different phenomenon from the "internationalization" of the 1980s. Twenty-first-century "globalization" means a faster, deeper integration of Japan into the global economy in ways that are not entirely controllable, with regulatory results that provoke intense anxiety.

The Sumitomo–UFJ transaction illustrates those multiple dimensions of globalization: global markets and regulators influenced the parameters of Japanese government policy action (for example inducing government to signal that major banks should merge); the parties were already subject to direct global regulation through international banking standards and their participation in the US stock market; global intermediaries such as transaction lawyers shaped the transaction design; and the parties devised their negotiating strategies in part with an eye to how they would play with global observers.

Tokyo M&A practitioner Steven Givens points out that the rush by UFJ to accept the MTFG proposal in preference to the original merger with Sumitomo was not based on exhaustive analysis.[107] Instead, when UFJ's fiduciary duty to its shareholders and the propriety of MTFG's attempt to block Sumitomo was questioned as being possibly illegal and invalid under Delaware law,[108] this was picked up in reports by Japan's leading financial newspaper, the *Nihon Keizai Shimbun*:

> [this] in turn led all three principals in the transaction to hire prominent US law firms and investment banks to educate them, in the context of a purely domestic Japanese merger, with respect to Delaware law. Ultimately SMFG withdrew from the contest, but not before its competing bid had driven the UFJ stock price up to a level that in effect forced MTFG to pay the same premium (in relation to the price before SMFG's bid) that SMFG had offered.[109]

In Givens' account, we see not simply an opportunistic or coincidental application of global legal standards (here Delaware corporations law), but an active—and successful—push from a key legal practitioner in the Japan market to expand the application of those standards to the domestic M&A market.

The second salient feature of the transaction is the deliberate use of litigation throughout. Both the District Court decision and the appellate court-brokered settlement in *Sumitomo v. UFJ* crystallize a vigorous normative debate in Japanese legal and business circles since the mid-1990s about what business and legal norms should govern contract termination.[110] The contract jurisprudence of the 1990s, particularly in relation to long-term or continuing contracts, penalized breach of contract by calibrating damages according to factors such as:

> the process of the termination of the basic agreement; [party] motive and objectives; the degree of bad [behavior]; what legal benefits were protected under the basic agreement, etc.[111]

The other side of the debate stresses that "free competition should be permitted," and asserts that large, established businesses have no need of this kind of court paternalism, as they are both capable of devising their own transactional norms and should be permitted to do so. Here, of course, the irony is that we see one of the banking market's larger players deliberately invoking the court's role as arbiter from an early point in the transaction.

Clearly, one race to the courthouse does not a legal system transformation make. Socio-legal scholars in Japan have long been fascinated by the phenomena of "legalization" and popular "legal consciousness" and the gap between the state's use of law and the prevalence of non-legal means of social ordering. A subset of this discourse deals with the modernity of Japanese contracts and contracting practices and the apparent contradiction between a society that achieved high economic growth on the basis of contractual relationships that were often relational, undocumented, insulated from the market, and not contested in formal legal settings. This body of writing is closely aligned to Weberian notions of modernization. An alternative account is Kagan's contrast between Japan and the "adversarial legalism" typical of the US.[112]

A further element of juridification is the way in which ordinary transactions (whether commercial or consumer) are now regulated to transform them into self-consciously "legal" transactions that require support from professional intermediaries, place cost and risk on the parties or the consumer, require a documentary output, and channel disputes to a formal legal institution, whether institutionalized mediation or civil litigation.

Adjusting the Japanese regulatory paradigm to emphasize law and legal institutions has the appeal of putting law and lawyers where they like to be—at the center of things. It also offers a new platform for comparative institutional studies between Japan and legal-centric states such as the US.[113] Thus, in 2004, I saw *Sumitomo v. UFJ* as:

> [Representing] a paradigm shift on the legal side … it shows a more legally aware business mindset in commercial dealing. The days of unspoken understandings underpinned by personal relationships are fading away.[114]

In retrospect, a more accurate characterization would be to say that it represents the expansion of the formal side of Haley's paradigm, a re-regulated Japan presents a broader menu of choices for—and a wider range of players to shape—dispute strategies and sanctions.

As Scott cautions, I think correctly, both legalization and juridification are "dead-end" concepts.[115] The danger of elevating legal rules, legal institutions, and legal professionals as the "new" governance element in Japan is that this may lead us into a fairly narrow reading of regulation being effected primarily through state law and state institutions—at precisely the time when the state seems to be diversifying its regulatory modes, a globalized Japanese market has become porous, and market actors have a wider range of norms and stakeholders to consider in formulating dispute resolution strategies. This, ultimately, is the new, post-Haley regulatory reality underscored by *Sumitomo v. UFJ*.

Notes

1 For an analysis of how Japanese governance changed in response to global geopolitical and economic shifts, see economist Naoki Tanaka, *Nihon no atarashii rūru* [*Japan's New Rules*], Tokyo: Kodansha, 2004.

2 Veronica L. Taylor, 'Re-regulating Japanese Transactions: the Competition Law Dimension', in Peter Drysdale and Jennifer Amyx, eds, *Japanese Governance: Beyond Japan Inc*, New York: Routledge, 2003.

3 John O. Haley, *Authority Without Power: Law and the Japanese Paradox*, Oxford: Oxford University Press, 1991. A related paradigm that has been highly influential and remains salient is Upham's focus on litigation as an avenue of social protest: Frank K. Upham, *Law and Social Change in Postwar Japan*, Cambridge, MA: Harvard University Press, 1987. See also Feldman's application of Upham's approach to the contemporary area of health policy: Eric Feldman, *The Ritual of Rights in Japan: Law, Society and Health Policy*, Cambridge: Cambridge University Press, 2000. The third dominant paradigm from the same generation of Japanese law scholars is, of course, Ramseyer's application of Chicago School economics to Japan. For his full bibliography, see http://www.law.harvard.edu/faculty/directory/facdir.php?id=54&show=bibliography. All three scholars employ slightly different normative stances and very different methodologies, with Ramseyer's preference for statistical data and regression analysis fitting neatly with trends in US political science that emphasize "big N" style research. This essay is not an intellectual history of the field and so I limit my analysis to the contours of Haley's thesis.

4 John O. Haley, *Authority Without Power: Law and the Japanese Paradox*, Oxford: Oxford University Press, 1991.

5 For a survey, see Christine Parker and John Braithwaite, 'Regulation', in Peter Cane and Mark Tushnet, eds, *Oxford Handbook of Legal Studies*, Oxford: Oxford University Press, 2002; Bronwen Morgan and Karen Yeung, *An Introduction to Law and Regulation: Text and Materials*, Cambridge: Cambridge University Press, 2007.

6 John O. Haley, *Authority Without Power: Law and the Japanese Paradox*, Oxford: Oxford University Press, 1991.

7 John O. Haley and Veronica L. Taylor, 'Rule of Law in Japan' in Randall Peerenboom, ed., *Discourses on Rule of Law in Asia*, London: RoutledgeCurzon, 2004.

8 For a discussion of negotiation in the shadow of the law in an insolvency context, see Chapter 11 by Oh and Halliday, in this volume.

9 John O. Haley, *Authority Without Power: Law and the Japanese Paradox*, Oxford: Oxford University Press, 1991.

10 John O. Haley, *Authority Without Power: Law and the Japanese Paradox*, Oxford: Oxford University Press, 1991, p. 169.

11 John O. Haley, 'The Myth of the Reluctant Litigant', *Journal of Japanese Studies* 4 (2), 1978, pp. 359–90.

12 Christine Parker and John Braithwaite, 'Regulation', in Peter Cane and Mark Tushnet, eds, *Oxford Handbook of Legal Studies*, Oxford: Oxford University Press, 2002; Bronwen Morgan and Karen Yeung, *An Introduction to Law and Regulation: Text and Materials*, Cambridge: Cambridge University Press, 2007.

13 John O. Haley, *Authority Without Power: Law and the Japanese Paradox*, Oxford: Oxford University Press, 1991, p. 181.

14 See, for example, Edward J. Lincoln, *Arthritic Japan: The Slow Pace of Economic Reform*, Washington, DC: The Brookings Institution, 2001; Luke Nottage and Leon Wolff, 'Corporate Governance and Law Reform in Japan: from the Lost Decade to the End of History?', *CLPE Research Paper* 3, 2005. Available from http://ssrn.com (abstract_830005), 2005.

15 Peter Drysdale and Jennifer Amyx, eds, *Japanese Governance: Beyond Japan Inc*, London: Routledge, 2003.

16 For example, Gregory Noble, 'Koizumi and Neo-Liberal Economic Reform', *Social Science Japan* 34, March 2006, pp. 6–9; Steven K. Vogel, *Japan Remodeled*, Ithaca: Cornell University Press, 2006.

17 Steven K. Vogel, *Japan Remodeled*, Ithaca: Cornell University Press, 2006.

18 Marie Anchordoguy, *Reprogramming Japan*, Ithaca: Cornell University Press, 2005.

19 Saadia M. Pekkanen, 'Aggressive Legalism: The Rules of the WTO and Japan's Emerging Trade Strategy', *The World Economy* 24 (5), 2001, pp. 707–37; Saadia M. Pekkanen, 'Japan's Aggressive Legalism: Law and Foreign Trade Politics Beyond the WTO', Stanford: Stanford University Press, 2008.

20 Christine Parker and John Braithwaite, 'Regulation', in Peter Cane and Mark Tushnet, eds, *Oxford Handbook of Legal Studies*, Oxford: Oxford University Press, 2002.

21 A key example in the field of regulatory studies is the regulatory pyramid employed in "responsive regulation": Ian Ayers and John Braithwaite, *Responsive Regulation: Transcending the Deregulation Debate*, New York: Oxford University Press, 1992. This encourages changes in state-initiated governance by building in a range of public and private stakeholders, providing mechanisms for each to monitor the other, and employing techniques such as enforced self-regulation.

22 Here, I describe the concept as it is used in the non-US literature cited for this essay; the academic discourse on "regulation" within the US has been quite different.

23 A counterpart public example is the successful use of litigation, for example in establishing bureaucratic liability for Japan's HIV epidemic: Eric Feldman, *The Ritual of Rights in Japan: Law, Society and Health Policy*, Cambridge: Cambridge University Press, 2000.

24 Hugh Collins, *Regulating Contracts*, Oxford: Oxford University Press, 1999.

25 Takashi Uchida and Veronica L. Taylor, 'Japan and the Era of Contract', in Daniel Foote, ed., *Law in Japan: A Turning Point*, Seattle: University of Washington Press, 2007. Pilot interviews that I conducted in 1996–97 with ten Japanese corporations suggested that the shape and norms of Japanese contracts were not immutable. Instead, they were affected by factors such as the parties' power differentials, perception of risk, new legislation (e.g., the then new Product Liability Law), the perceived threat of litigation, price fluctuations in the market, and interference from professional cohorts such as lawyers and insurers. This was particularly well illustrated in Visser't Hooft's study of distribution contracts in the luxury cosmetics sector, where contract and competition policy intersect: Willem M. Visser't Hooft, *Japanese Contract and Anti-Trust Law*, London: RoutledgeCurzon, 2002.

26 The explicit reference to internal corporate control is first made in the Daiwa Bank Case, discussed in Bruce Aronson, 'Reconsidering the Importance of Law in Japanese Corporate Governance: Evidence from the Daiwa Bank Shareholder Derivative Case', *Cornell International Law Journal* 36, 2003, p. 11, but is then applied in subsequent directors' liability cases.

27 For Parker and Braithwaite, the normative appeal of regulatory pluralism lies in its potential to create spaces for Dorf and Sabel's "democratic experimentalism"; Christine Parker and John Braithwaite, 'Regulation', in Peter Cane and Mark Tushnet, eds, *Oxford Handbook of Legal Studies*, Oxford: Oxford University Press, 2002.

28 Colin Scott, 'Analysing Regulatory Space: Fragmented Resources and Institutional Design', *Public Law* 2001, pp. 283–305.

29 Scott, *supra*, pp. 283–305.

30 For example, Robert Pekkanen, *Japan's Dual Civil Society*, Stanford: Stanford University Press, 2006.

31 In relation to non-profit organizations, see Robert Pekkanen, *Japan's Dual Civil Society*, Stanford: Stanford University Press, 2006.

32 John O. Haley, *Authority Without Power: Law and the Japanese Paradox*, Oxford: Oxford University Press, 1991, p. 179.

33 J. Mark Ramseyer and Frances Rosenbluth, *Japan's Political Marketplace*, Cambridge, MA : Harvard University Press, 1993.

34 John O. Haley, *Authority Without Power: Law and the Japanese Paradox*, Oxford: Oxford University Press, 1991.
35 For example, Mark Tilton, *Restrained Trade: Cartels in Japan's Basic Materials Industries*, Ithaca: Cornell University Press, 1996.
36 Veronica L. Taylor, 'Consumer Contract Governance in a Deregulating Japan', *Victoria University of Wellington Law Review* 27 (1), 1997, pp. 99–120.
37 Ulrike Schaede, *Cooperative Capitalism: Self-Regulation, Trade Associations and the Antimonopoly Law in Japan*, Oxford: Oxford University Press, 2000.
38 Marie Anchordoguy, *Reprogramming Japan*, Ithaca: Cornell University Press, 2005.
39 Seigo Hirowatari, 'Post-war Japan and the Law: Mapping Discourses of Legalization and Modernization', *Social Science Japan Journal* 3 (2), 2000, pp. 155–69.
40 John O. Haley, *Authority Without Power: Law and the Japanese Paradox*, Oxford: Oxford University Press, 1991.
41 Frank K. Upham, *Law and Social Change in Postwar Japan*, Cambridge, MA: Harvard University Press, 1987; Eric Feldman, *The Ritual of Rights in Japan: Law, Society and Health Policy*, Cambridge: Cambridge University Press, 2000.
42 Peter A. Hall and David Soskice, *Varieties of Capitalism: The Institutional Foundations of Comparative Advantage*, Oxford: Oxford University Press, 2001.
43 For example, Robert Kagan, *Adversarial Legalism: The American Way of Law*, Cambridge, MA: Harvard University Press, 2001; Robert Kagan and Lee Axelrod Lee, *Regulatory Encounters: Multinational Corporations and American Adversarial Legalism*, Berkeley and Los Angeles: University of California Press, 2000.
44 Chalmers A. Johnson, *Japan: Who Governs? The Rise of the Developmental State*, New York : W.W. Norton, 1995.
45 Justice System Reform Council, *Recommendations of the Justice System Reform Council – For a Justice System to Support Japan in the 21st Century*, 12 June 2001. Available from http://www.kantei.go.jp/foreign/judiciary/2001/0612report.html; and in Japanese as: Shihōseido kaikaku shingikai, *Shihōseido kaikaku shingikai ikensho: 21 seiki no nihon o shihaeru shihōseido* (Heisei 13 nen 6 gatsu 12 nichi), 2001.
46 For example, Chiyoda-ku, *Anzen de kaitekina chiyodaku no seikatsu kankyō no seibi ni kansuru jôrei*, Heisei 14nen6gatsu25nichi jôreidai53gô [Ordinance on providing a safe and comfortable living environment in Chiyoda-ku, 25 June 2002, Ordinance No. 53]. Available from https://www3.e-reikinet.jp/cgi-bin/chiyoda/D1W_login.exe.
47 Takeo Hoshi and Anil K. Kashyap, 'Solutions to Japan's Banking Problems: What Might Work and What Definitely Will Fail', Paper prepared for the US–Japan Conference on the Solutions for the Japanese Economy, November 2004. Available from http://www.ier.hit-u.ac.jp/~iwaisako/solutions/TokyoAgenda.html.
48 Kaoro Hosono, Koji Saki, and Kotaro Tsuru, 'Consolidation of Banks in Japan: Causes and Consequences', National Bureau of Economic Research NBER Working Paper Series, Working Paper 13399, September 2007, p. 10. Available from http://www.nber.org/papers/w13399.
49 UFJ Hits Back as Sumitomo seeks injunction, *Financial Times* 21 July 2004, p. 18.
50 Sumitomo Trust and Banking Co (http://www.sumitomotrust.co.jp/IR/company/index_en.html) was, and remains, a separate entity from Sumitomo Mitsui Financial Group (http://www.smfg.co.jp/english/aboutus/profile/), although both are part of the Sumitomo corporate group.
51 Martin Fackler and Henny Sender, 'Court Blocks Japan Bank Merger Talks', *Wall Street Journal* 28 July 2004, C5. Compare this with the Tokyo District Court reference to one year and eight months: Hanrei tokuh?: UFJ shintaku ginko kyōdōjigyōkajiken daiisshinhanketsu [UFJ Trust Bank Merger Decision of First Instance], *Hanrei Jihō* 1928, 2006, p. 4.
52 Hanketsu sokuhō: UFJ gurūpuno keieitōgō o meguru karishobunjiken kettei, [Decision on Interim Injunctions Concerning UFJ Group Integration] *Shōji Hōmu* 1708, (22–25), 15 September 2004, p. 24.

53 Martin Fackler and Henny Sender, Court Blocks Japan Bank Merger Talks, *Wall Street Journal* 28 July 2004, C5.

54 Confusingly, after the initial merger that created this bank, it was known in Japanese as Mitsubishi–Tokyo Bank and so is reported as such during this failed merger, but is officially known in English as the Bank of Tokyo–Mitsubishi.

55 Martin Fackler and Henny Sender, 'Court Blocks Japan Bank Merger Talks', *Wall Street Journal* 28 July 2004, C5.

56 http://www.mufg.jp/english/.

57 Martin Fackler and Henny Sender, 'Court Blocks Japan Bank Merger Talks', *Wall Street Journal* 28 July 2004, C5.

58 Martin Fackler and Henny Sender, 'Court Blocks Japan Bank Merger Talks', *Wall Street Journal* 28 July 2004, C5.

59 The injunction was sought by Sumitomo Bank against UFJ Holdings, UFJ Trust Bank, and UFJ Bank.

60 'Final Ratio will determine Victor in Battle for the Banks', *Financial Times* 16 February 2005, p. 16.

61 Commercial Code.

62 Andrew Morse, 'Sumitomo Mitsui Raises Heat on UFJ', *Asian Wall Street Journal* 8–10 October 2004, p. 3.

63 Andrew Morse and Martin Fackler, 'Rival Offer for UFJ Might Go Public', *Wall Street Journal* 9 August 2004, A3.

64 Andrew Morse, 'Sumitomo Mitsui Raises Heat on UFJ', *Asian Wall Street Journal* 8–10 October 2004, p. 3.

65 Andrew Morse, 'Sumitomo Mitsui Raises Heat on UFJ', *Asian Wall Street Journal* 8–10 October 2004, p. 3.

66 Andrew Morse and Martin Fackler, 'Rival Offer for UFJ Might Go Public', *Wall Street Journal* 9 August 2004, A3.

67 Andrew Morse and Martin Fackler, 'Rival Offer for UFJ Might Go Public', *Wall Street Journal* 9 August 2004, A3.

68 Andrew Morse, 'Sumitomo Mitsui Raises Heat on UFJ', *Asian Wall Street Journal* 8–10 October 2004, p. 1.

69 Andrew Morse, 'Sumitomo Mitsui Raises Heat on UFJ', *Asian Wall Street Journal* 8–10 October 2004, p. 2; 'Scramble for UFJ, Sumitomo Mitsui Seen at Dead End', *Nikkei Business* 20 September 2004, cited in Curtis J. Milhaupt, 'In the Shadow of Delaware? The Rise of Hostile Takeovers in Japan', *Columbia Law Review* 105 (7), November 2005, p. 2171. In substance, this was a defensive measure dubbed a poison pill defense by the media, but it was adopted ahead of those actual poison pill defenses later used by other Japanese takeover targets and in advance of formal court consideration and ratification of these poison pill defenses in Japanese corporations law. For an extended discussion, see Curtis J. Milhaupt, 'In the Shadow of Delaware? The Rise of Hostile Takeovers in Japan', *Columbia Law Review* 105 (7), November 2005, p. 2171; Cristina Alger, 'The Livedoor Looking Glass: Examining the Limits of Hostile Takeover Bids in Japan', *NYU Journal of Law and Business* 3, 2006, p. 309.

70 This repeats the language of Article 23 (2), Civil Preservation Act [*Minji Hozen Hō*]: "The court may issue an order to establish a provisional status, when it is necessary to issue an order so as to avoid the extreme damage or imminent danger to be suffered by the oblige with a disputed right."

71 Pursuant to the Civil Preservation Act [*Minji Hozen Hō*].

72 Curtis J. Milhaupt, 'In the Shadow of Delaware? The Rise of Hostile Takeovers in Japan', *Columbia Law Review* 105 (7), November 2005, p. 2178. Presumably, this was a directors' resolution subject to confirmation at a later shareholders' meeting.

73 Hanketsu sokuhō UFJ gurūpuno keieitōgō o meguru karishobunjiken kettei, 1708 *Shōji Hōmu* 22–25, 15 September 2004, p. 23 (author's translation).

74 The original decision was reported in 58–6 *Minsh?*, p. 1763, and reproduced in: Hanketsu sokuhō UFJ gurūpuno keieitōgō o meguru karishobunjiken kettei, 1708 *Shōji Hōmu* 22–25, 15 September 2004, p. 22.

75 Hanketsu sokuhō UFJ gurūpuno keieitōgō o meguru karishobunjiken kettei, 1708 *Shōji Hōmu* 22–25, 15 September 2004, pp. 22 and 25.

76 The decision uses the legal neologism *dyū dirijiensu*.

77 The court also noted the relatively long period provided for the negotiation: the letter of intent was valid for a year and eight months.

78 1928 *Hanrei Jihō* 3.

79 Martin Fackler and Henny Sender, 'Court Blocks Japan Bank Merger Talks', *Wall Street Journal* 28 July 2004, C5.

80 1928 *Hanrei Jihō* 3, p. 4

81 Curtis J. Milhaupt, 'In the Shadow of Delaware? The Rise of Hostile Takeovers in Japan', *Columbia Law Review* 105 (7), November 2005, p. 2171; Cristina Alger, 'The Livedoor Looking Glass: Examining the Limits of Hostile Takeover Bids in Japan', *NYU Journal of Law and Business* 3, 2006, p. 309.

82 Christina Ahmadjian, 'Foreign Investors and Corporate Governance in Japan', in Masahiko Aoki, Gregory Jackson, and Hideaki Miyajima, eds, *Corporate Governance in Japan: Institutional Change and Organization Diversity*, Oxford: Oxford University Press, 2007, Chapter 4.

83 Christina Ahmadjian, 'Foreign Investors and Corporate Governance in Japan', in Masahiko Aoki, Gregory Jackson, and Hideaki Miyajima, eds, *Corporate Governance in Japan: Institutional Change and Organization Diversity*, Oxford: Oxford University Press, 2007, Chapter 4, p. 138.

84 See, for example: Eric A. Feldman, 'Law, Culture and Conflict: Dispute Resolution in Postwar Japan', in Daniel H. Foote, ed., *Law in Japan: A Turning Point*, Seattle: University of Washington Press, 2007, Chapter 3.

85 Presumably because the dispute settles, the case is not important enough to warrant case reporting, or the injunction is a very minor part of the overall litigation strategy.

86 Willem M. Visser't Hooft, *Japanese Contract and Anti-Trust Law*, London: RoutledgeCurzon, 2002.

87 This accounts for much of what Ginsburg sees as a surge in voluntary litigation during the same period: Tom Ginsburg and Glenn P. Hoetker, 'The Unreluctant Litigant? An Empirical Analysis of Japan's Turn to Litigation', 8 September 2004. Available from http://ssrn.com/abstract=608582. I tend to view bankruptcy-propelled civil litigation as somewhat involuntary.

88 In the wake of a series of attempted hostile takeovers of non-banking corporations that followed this case, and the spread of deliberate poison pill defenses, the government did develop a 2004 Takeovers Code, drafted by a Ministry of Trade, Economy and Industry Study Group, and corporations law jurisprudence developed on the poison pill defense. See Ken'chi Osugi, 'What is Converging? Rules on Hostile Takeovers in Japan and the Convergence Debate', *Asian Pacific Law and Policy Journal* 9 (1), Winter 2007.

89 The doctrinal aspects of this case are discussed in a forthcoming article by Doshisha University Law School scholar, Koji Takahashi, *'Walford v. Miles* in Japan: lock-in and lock-out agreements in *Sumitomo v. UFJ*, accepted for publication in *Journal of Business Law* (forthcoming).

90 Updated lists of the major shareholder derivative suits in Japan are published regularly (in Japanese); for the list current at the time of this dispute, see: 'Shuyō na kabushu daihyō soshō jiken ichiranhyō' [Major shareholder representative suits at a glance], *Shiryoban Shōjihōmu* 256, July 2005, pp. 41–51.

91 Takeo Hoshi and Anil K. Kashyap, 'Solutions to Japan's Banking Problems: What Might Work and What Definitely Will Fail', Paper prepared for the US–Japan Conference on the Solutions for the Japanese Economy, November 2004, especially p.25. Available from http://www.ier.hit-u.ac.jp/~iwaisako/solutions/TokyoAgenda.html.

92 Takeo Hoshi and Anil K. Kashyap, 'Solutions to Japan's Banking Problems: What Might Work and What Definitely Will Fail', Paper prepared for the US–Japan Conference on the Solutions for the Japanese Economy, November 2004, p. 11. Available from http://www.ier.hit-u.ac.jp/~iwaisako/solutions/TokyoAgenda.html.

93 Martin Fackler and Henny Sender, 'Court Blocks Japan Bank Merger Talks', *Wall Street Journal* 28 July 2004, C5.

94 Christina Ahmadjian, 'Foreign Investors and Corporate Governance in Japan', in Masahiko Aoki, Gregory Jackson, and Hideaki Miyajima, eds, *Corporate Governance in Japan: Institutional Change and Organization Diversity*, Oxford: Oxford University Press, 2007, Chapter 4, p. 130.

95 Barney Jopson, 'UFJ Hits Back as Sumitomo Seeks Injunction', *Financial Times* 21 July 2004, p. 18.

96 Tokyo Stock Exchange Fact Book, 2008, p. 61. Available from http://www.tse.or.jp/english/index/html.

97 Christina Ahmadjian, 'Foreign Investors and Corporate Governance in Japan', in Masahiko Aoki, Gregory Jackson, and Hideaki Miyajima, eds, *Corporate Governance in Japan: Institutional Change and Organization Diversity*, Oxford: Oxford University Press, 2007, Chapter 4, p. 133

98 Christina Ahmadjian, 'Foreign Investors and Corporate Governance in Japan', in Masahiko Aoki, Gregory Jackson, and Hideaki Miyajima, eds, *Corporate Governance in Japan: Institutional Change and Organization Diversity*, Oxford: Oxford University Press, 2007, Chapter 4.

99 Christina Ahmadjian, 'Foreign Investors and Corporate Governance in Japan', in Masahiko Aoki, Gregory Jackson, and Hideaki Miyajima, eds, *Corporate Governance in Japan: Institutional Change and Organization Diversity*, Oxford: Oxford University Press, 2007, Chapter 4, p. 135, citing the Shōji Hōmu survey in the text but not giving the citation to this in the bibliography.

100 Christina Ahmadjian, 'Foreign Investors and Corporate Governance in Japan', in Masahiko Aoki, Gregory Jackson, and Hideaki Miyajima, eds, *Corporate Governance in Japan: Institutional Change and Organization Diversity*, Oxford: Oxford University Press, 2007, Chapter 4.

101 Christina Ahmadjian, 'Foreign Investors and Corporate Governance in Japan', in Masahiko Aoki, Gregory Jackson, and Hideaki Miyajima, eds, *Corporate Governance in Japan: Institutional Change and Organization Diversity*, Oxford: Oxford University Press, 2007, Chapter 4, p. 139.

102 Martin Fackler and Henny Sender, 'Court Blocks Japan Bank Merger Talks', *Wall Street Journal* 28 July 2004, C5.

103 Interview with Bank of Tokyo Mitsubishi employee, Seattle, 2004.

104 Gunther Teubner, 'Juridification: Concepts, Aspects, Limits, Solutions', in G. Teubner, ed., *Juridification of Social Spheres: Comparative Analysis in the Areas of Labor, Corporate, Antitrust and Social Welfare Law*, Berlin: European University Institute/de Gruyter, 1987. Juridification is not really a regulatory theory per se, but it may be a useful conceptual tool for exploring the ways in which formal law and formal dispute resolution processes are being deployed and understood by a range of regulatory players in Japan.

105 Dowdle, Chapter 3 in this volume.

106 Shiro Kashimura, 'Legal Dynamics: A Multi-Disciplinary Inquiry into Law in the Era of Globalization', in Shiro Kashimura and Akira Saito, eds, *Horizontal Legal Order: Law and Transaction in Economy and Society*, Singapore: LexisNexis, 2008.

107 Steven Givens, 'Corporate Governance and M&A', in Gerald McAlinn, ed., *Japanese Business Law*, Amsterdam: Wolters Kluwer, 2007, p. 160.

108 Steven Givens, 'Corporate Governance and M&A', in Gerald McAlinn, ed., *Japanese Business Law*, Amsterdam: Wolters Kluwer, 2007, p. 160.

109 Reporting Givens' own article, Steven Givens, 'Derawea-shū saikōsai de attara, konkai UFJ Horudingusugawa ga totta gappei tōgō bōshisaku ni taishite, dono yōna

shihōhandan wo kudashita de arō ka?' [What Judicial Decision would have been handed down if the Defensive Measures adopted by UFJ Holdings were before the Delaware Supreme Court?], 32 *Kokusai Shōji Hōmu* 1295, 2004.

110 Key essays from this period include: Takashi Uchida, 'Zadankai: gendai keiyakuho no aratana tenkai to ippan jōkō' [Roundtable: New Developments in Contemporary Contract Law and General Clauses], *NBL* 515, 1993, p. 14; Noboru Kashiwagi, 'Nihon no torihiki to keiyakuhō: kyōdō kenkyu – keizokuteki torihiki o kangaeru' [Japanese Transactions and Contracts: Joint Research – Continuing Contracts Considered], *NBL* 500, 1992, pp. 22–23; Hiroyasu Nakata, *Keizoku baibai no kaish? [The Termination of Continuing Sales Contracts]*, Tokyo: Yuhikaku, 1994.

111 *Hanrei tokuhō: UFJ shintaku ginko kyōdōjigyōkajiken daiisshinhanketsu* [UFJ Trust Bank Merger Decision of First Instance], *Hanrei Jihō* 1928, 2006, p. 4.

112 The changes to formal legal institutions in Japan that we are seeing at present may be both a response to and a partial embrace of Kagan's adversarial legalism, but we need time and empirical data to track this. One example is the field of intellectual property, where we see new IP courts being established as a direct response to the patent litigation strategies being adopted in the US.

113 Milhaupt and West argue, approvingly, that this elevation of law is also mirrored in the shifting career choices of professional elites, many of whom now choose to become practicing lawyers rather than bureaucrats: Curtis J, Milhaupt and Mark D, West, 'Law's Dominion and the Market for Legal Elites in Japan', 14 June 2002. Available from http://ssrn.com/abstract=316120.

114 Martin Fackler and Henny Sender, 'Court Blocks Japan Bank Merger Talks', *Wall Street Journal* 28 July 2004, C5.

115 Colin Scott, 'Analysing Regulatory Space: Fragmented Resources and Institutional Design', *Public Law* 2001, pp. 283–305.

11 Rehabilitating Korea's corporate insolvency regime, 1992–2007

Soogeun Oh and Terence C. Halliday

In 2005, Korea comprehensively revised insolvency laws that had been in effect since the 1960s. These far-reaching reforms brought to culmination both a domestic impetus for change that had gathered pace during the 1990s and urgent international pressures for reform in the wake of the Asian financial crisis. We employ this case to explore the interchange between the global and the local, the intersection between Korean trajectories and international pressures for reform.

An intensive case study presents a necessary foundation on which to construct convincing answers to key questions of national law reforms in a global context. We propose that a valuable methodology for appraising the interplay of the global and local is to proceed systematically, in a single area of law, through four possible permutations of global–local encounters.

First, the null hypothesis, as social scientists style it, of global impact should be that the global has impinged on the local not at all. Here, we should entertain the plausible theory that legal change has deep indigenous roots that are not readily shaken loose. From the side of legal history, this hypothesis takes seriously the cultural embeddedness of legal families. It anticipates the "transplant effect" of failed grafting of laws nurtured in other soils.[1] From the side of historical institutionalism, this hypothesis is consistent with the powerful inertial effect of path dependency—that the conditions of an institution's founding, and the expectations, interests, and structures that come to sustain it, constrain any kind of change, not least that from alien legal soil.[2]

A second hypothesis, the mirror of the first, will be that global legal norms[3] inevitably penetrate deeply into any national laws, the more so if a domain of law is salient to global markets. Hyper-globalizers variously propose that a combination of market power, pressure on nation-states to integrate into the global economy, the impact of multinational corporations, and the manifest benefits of local conformity to global standards will bring rapid adaptation of the local to the global.[4] Hence, we should expect swift national responses by rational lawmakers to global standards in direct proportion to a country's integration into global markets. Of course, the stronger a commitment to this view, the less respect is given to the inertial conditions of a country's distinctive history and legal institutions that are imbued with history's lingering grip.

A third, and intermediate, proposition does not discount global influences, but it expects them to be resisted, attenuated, and unevenly adopted.[5] Globalization is a negotiated process that relies heavily on intermediaries, its fates closely linked to the relative balance of power between global and local actors. Its structural and discursive penetration of a country's laws depends on a wide variety of factors, some domestic, some international, with the result that its eventual impact on a country's legal practice remains highly indeterminate.[6] Indeed, it is easy to overestimate the impact of global influences because national policymakers may adopt practices not to conform to global standards but because domestic reforms have a functional affinity with domestic needs.

A fourth permutation of the global–local engagement helps to set the limits of global impact. We can expect situations, and indeed must find instances, where global pressures have been rejected. Unlike the first hypothesis, this is less a case of legal development following its domestic path relatively unmindful of foreign influences. It is rather a case of direct or perceptible global influences that are recognized for what they are, appraised by national policymakers, and repudiated.

In an account of legal change, we can expect that these four configurations of the global and local can exist side-by-side, even in a single domain of law. In fact, we shall show that, within insolvency law itself, there are examples of each configuration. Insolvency law at this time therefore melds at least four distinct trajectories of reforms that continue to unfold in dynamic and not always predictable ways. In order to explicate these interweaving patterns of legal change, however, it is critical to make a distinction between two manifestations of the local. Drawing on a broader theory of legal change in a global context,[7] we distinguish between the politics of enactment and the politics of implementation. The politics of enactment involve putting formal law (statutes, cases, regulations, presidential decrees) on the books. They are the point at which maximal international pressure is likely to be most effective, particularly on presidential decrees and statutory reforms. The politics of implementation involve the translation of formal law into practice. They are the point at which local actors, from government regulators to professionals and regulated subjects, are able to redress any asymmetry of power between the global and the local. This is deeply embedded in local conditions and is thus most difficult for global agents of change to penetrate. Pushing back on globalization can be found most ubiquitously in the phase of implementation. But it is also the most difficult to observe and thus to record. It is for this reason, among others, that estimates of globalization tend to be overestimates. Without knowing how broadly, deeply, and with what impact the global has penetrated the local,[8] we do not know the resiliency and imperviousness of national streams of practice.

Our chapter tackles these issues in three steps. First, we illustrate four configurations of insolvency reforms since the early 1990s: those developed domestically; those where there were global pressures and local acceptance; those where global norms initially brought rejection, and then eventual acceptance; and a case where global norms were explicitly rejected. Second, we reflect analytically on these reforms by tracking forms of global influence, by demonstrating Korea's capacities to manage various degrees and types of pressure, and the politics of the state and professions that were interwoven through these patterns of change. Third, we conclude with some general theoretical questions that continue to require attention in Korea and elsewhere if we are to comprehend the interplay of local and global politics in commercial law reform.

Korean insolvency reforms

Overview

The broad arc of Korean insolvency reforms since the early 1990s occurs in three sites of lawmaking: statutory reforms through the National Assembly; agreements among market actors brokered by the Ministry of Finance and Economy; and cases and regulations from the Korean Supreme Court and local district courts (Table 11.1). The sweep of reforms begins domestically, becomes tightly engaged with the International Monetary Fund (IMF) and the World Bank after the 1997 crisis, and slowly returns to domestic priorities after the retreat of international financial institutions after 2003–4.[9]

From the 1960s until 2005, bankruptcy in Korea was governed by three statutes—the Corporate Reorganization Act, the Composition Act, and the Bankruptcy Act—all enacted in 1962. In fact, however, the three statutes were rarely used. Corporate restructurings, mergers, and liquidations were handled administratively, most notably for major corporations by the Economic Planning Board and Blue House (Korea's Presidential office), which had driven Korea's state development model of economic growth. From 1990 to 1996, for instance, as economic difficulties started to emerge in the domestic economy, the number of companies that availed themselves of the Corporate Reorganization Act totaled only 42 in 1990, 80 in 1991, 101 in 1992, 71 in 1993, 86 in 1994, 104 in 1995, and 79 in 1996.[10]

Beginning in 1992, the Supreme Court responded to domestic criticism of political influence in bankruptcies, excessive delay, and low recovery rates for creditors by issuing guidelines intended to make reorganizations cleaner, faster, and more effective. On the eve of the crisis, as corporate failures loomed in large numbers, the Ministry of Finance and Economy (MOFE) pushed through an agreement among banks, the Anti-*Budoo* Accord, which permitted the issuer, the debtor company, to continue bank transactions even though it had insufficient funds to pay the promissory note or checks. Moreover, to forestall a chain reaction of company failures, MOFE pressed banks to work with other banks to provide or extend cooperative loans that would solve firms' liquidity problems.

In the wake of the crisis, which hit Korea in late 1997, MOFE, in consultation with the international financial institutions (IFIs), undertook two important administrative steps. In the first, colloquially styled the "Big Deals," it appears the government quietly pressed many of the largest *chaebol* (large, often family-owned conglomerates) to enter into a series of mergers, presumably to reduce competition and to shore up weak firms. This would also forestall huge bankruptcies that would limit losses to greatly weakened banks that were carrying huge non-performing loan portfolios.

Table 11.1 Sites of lawmaking on corporate insolvency reforms, 1992–2007

	Legislature	*Government ministries*	*Courts*
1992			1992 Supreme Court Guideline on Corporate Reorganization Proceeding
1996			1996 Revised Supreme Court Guideline on Corporate Reorganization Proceeding
1997		Anti-Budoo agreement (18 April 1997) Big Deals (1997–98)	
1998	Amendments to Corporate Reorganization Act (CRA), Composition Act (CA), Bankruptcy Act (BA)	Workout Accord (28 June 1998)	
1999	CRA amendments		Established Insolvency Division (March 1999)
2000	CA/BA amendments (Part of 1999 packet carried over into new year)		
2001	CRA amendments (pre-pack) Corporate Promotion Restructuring Act	Creditor Banks Agreement	
2002			
2003	Comprehensive draft submitted to National Assembly		
2004	Revised bill sent again	Workout Agreement for Small and Medium Enterprises	
2005	Comprehensive Act		
2006	Corporate Restructuring		Supreme Court Regulation
2007	Promotion Act		on DRBA

Source: Terence Halliday and Soogeun Oh, 'A Recursive Theory of National Lawmaking: Site-Switching in Korean Corporate Insolvency Reforms, 1992–2007', Working Paper, American Bar Foundation and Ewha Woman's University.

Note: DRBA, Debtor Rehabilitation and Bankruptcy Act.

In the second, MOFE and the IFIs agreed on a set of measures that would compel 210 domestic financial institutions to adopt practices under a framework of "Workout Accords." Banks were to target more than 100 weakened firms and develop workout plans with financial institutions that would be formalized in Memorandums of Understanding. MOFE styled this as Korea's equivalent to the much admired London Approach for financial restructurings that was pioneered by Britain's Bank of England. The Accords were premised partly on a desire to keep cases away from the courts.

In 1998, the government took a further step by pushing through a statutory amendment to increase the efficiency of corporate reorganizations. Based on a formula developed before the crisis at the Korea Development Institute, this measure sought to compel judges to decide whether or not companies were eligible for reorganization based on a bright-line "economic criterion test" that much reduced judges' discretion. As this coincided with the IFIs' interests in increasing the transparency of judicial decision-making, and compelled judges to take the hard decision of liquidating companies, it was done with IFI approval. Another statutory amendment followed in 1999 that was intended to expedite court proceedings. Rather than permit months for judges to decide whether insolvency cases should be accepted by the courts, the amendment compelled judges to make a decision on commencement of a case within one month, a decision that had a striking effect on reducing the time from filing to commencement.

From 2001 to 2004, the government introduced several measures to facilitate out-of-court workouts. The 2001 Corporate Reorganization Act Amendment set out provisions that would encourage domestic banks to undertake private workouts between creditors and debtors that would be taken to courts for their binding stamp of authority. A 2001 Corporate Restructuring Promotion Act sought to formalize and elaborate on the earlier Workout Accord. As its focus was on very large firms, it was followed in 2004 by a Workout Agreement for Small and Medium Businesses that was administered by the Financial Supervisory Service (FSS). Somewhat unexpectedly, the Corporate Restructuring Promotion Act was re-enacted in 2007 for another five years. The collective effect of all these Acts was a continuing push by skeptical economic technocrats in MOFE to keep cases away from the courts. The grounds, it seemed, were twofold. On the one hand, MOFE wanted to maintain its power over the destiny of major corporations. On the other hand, the economists doubted that a court-based process could efficiently and effectively preside over corporate reorganizations. The 2007 re-enactment of the Corporate Restructuring Promotion Act seemed to express this continuing reservation about court capacity.

The Debtor Rehabilitation and Bankruptcy Act, 2005

At the height of the crisis, the IFIs obtained a commitment from the government of Korea that it would consolidate its three insolvency laws into one comprehensive statute.[11] While the commitment was never formalized into a condition of IFI loans, the IFIs continued to press the issue once the dust settled after the most urgent reforms in 1998 and 1999. In 1999, the Ministry of Justice initiated a project to assist the reform of Korea's insolvency laws. Consulting law firms in Korea, Singapore, and the US entered discussions in 2000 to advise on a comprehensive reform of insolvency law under the auspices of the World Bank Technical Assistance Loan Program (TALP) project.[12] Around twenty aspects of corporate reorganization were put on the agenda. The final report, submitted in 2000, became the basis for the enactment of a new insolvency law.

Even though the government launched a deliberative process for consideration of the reforms, controversies continued over the legitimacy of new legislation. Most lawyers, especially judges, expressed strong criticism of such a comprehensive revision of laws in the wake of so many amendments to insolvency law since the crisis. But some industry sectors saw it as an opportunity to make the law more responsive to debtors. Creditor institutions did not resist change, probably because they did not want to offend the MOFE, which was leading the legislative initiative. It is not surprising that the parties to the reforms quarreled over the pace of deliberation. For lawyers, who were reluctant reformers, everything moved too quickly; for the government, and the MOFE in particular, the drafting dragged unnecessarily.

The deliberation committee had its first meeting in May 2001. Less than a year later, in March 2002, it issued a statement of principles for the consolidated insolvency law, which contained both the structure of the new act and conclusions on major issues. Drafting of the bill began in March 2002 and was completed by October 2002. The drafting committee needed more time to polish more than 600 articles, but the government pushed hard to enact a law during the term of the current President as one of his principal legislative achievements. After public hearings and review by the Ministry of Legislation, the bill was sent to the National Assembly on 21 February 2003, four days before the new president was inaugurated on 25 February 2003.

Except for some congressmen interested in personal bankruptcy proceedings, the National Assembly was not eager to deliberate over the bill. As the National Assembly was scheduled to be dissolved on 29 May 2004, the bill would automatically be discarded if not enacted. Given the growing severity of consumer bankruptcies, the governing political party decided to extract that part of the bill and enact the Individual Debtor Rehabilitation Act on 2 March 2004.

The new government, established in 2003, was nevertheless keen to enact the consolidated insolvency bill. After amendments to some troublesome provisions, a revised insolvency bill was sent to the National Assembly on 11 November 2004. When the Judiciary Committee asked for related government agencies to comment on the draft bill, the Supreme Court alone sent proposals for amendment on some ninety-seven issues. Talks between the Ministry of Justice, the Judiciary Committee, and the Supreme Court finally succeeded in agreement on a single revised bill. After its hearings, the Judiciary Committee amended several controversial provisions by deleting arbitration procedures in individual rehabilitation proceedings,[13] shortening the maximum period of repayment in individual rehabilitation proceedings,[14] and conferring on a foreign insolvency representative the authority to file a petition for the insolvency proceeding only after recognition.[15] The law was enacted in March 2005 and came into effect on 1 April 2006.

Configurations of change

To disentangle the global from the local in commercial lawmaking requires a methodology that systematically varies the origins and outcomes of law reform. We selected four areas of insolvency law that illustrate alternative trajectories of change: (1) instances where global pressure brought local acceptance (expediency of proceedings and judicial transparency); (2) cases where global norms were greeted by local rejection (automatic stay, specialized court); (3) examples of global norms that were initially resisted but eventually accepted (debtor-in-possession); and (4) an instance where legal innovations were developed domestically in response to international contexts (payment and settlement system).

1 Global pressure, local convergence

Global pressures can be exerted upon national policymakers in very different ways.[16] We contrast two forms of leverage. In the first, international financial institutions (IMF, World Bank) took advantage of the financial emergency that confronted Korea during the 1998 crisis to exercise economic coercion. Among other demands, they directed this coercion toward an increase in efficiency and expediency in corporate reorganization proceedings. In the second, an international governance organization, the United Nations Commission on International Trade Law (UNCITRAL) relied upon modeling and persuasion. Through a deliberative process that involved representatives of the world's nations and leading organizations of experts, UNCITRAL developed a Model Law on Cross-Border Insolvencies, which it urged member nations to adopt.

a Expediency in judicial proceedings

Concerns about delay in Korean corporate reorganizations extended back to the 1980s. Under Korean law, debtors and creditors could apply to the court for commencement of a reorganization proceeding, but it would take the court six to ten months or longer to make a substantive determination if indeed a company was eligible for the court protection. As in most jurisdictions, such delay created uncertainty in markets, undermined confidence in companies and their management, and provided a wide opening through which fraud and other efforts to minimize loss by creditors could effectively nullify the very object of reorganization itself. However, critics of the process and even judges had few ideas about how to solve the problem, partly because they assumed that such delays were due to the inevitable inefficiency of judicial procedure and partly because they were not serious about addressing the problem.

The crisis changed the attitudes of both sides completely. Rising numbers of failing companies in insolvency proceedings and delays in processing them drew public criticism of the judiciary and the government. This placed the inefficiency of insolvency proceedings firmly on the national agenda. In 1998, through amendments to the Corporate Reorganization Act, the Ministry of Justice sought to speed up reorganization proceedings by putting a time limit on certain procedures. They required that a provisional preservative order had to be issued within fourteen days from the date of application, the receiver was obliged to submit a reorganization plan within four months of the final date of the filing of claims, and the reorganization plan needed to obtain approval within one year of the date of commencement.

Nevertheless, these revisions were insufficient to bring an immediate end to delays in reorganization proceedings. Parties-in-interest did not see much change in the speed of proceedings. They wanted to know why corporate reorganization proceedings did not commence as soon as possible. To them, the lag between application and a court commencement order was too significant. IFIs too pressed for further revisions. Saving companies, insisted the IFIs, required rapid decisions and quick action.[17]

In response, the government of Korea pushed through reforms in 1999 that required that commencement of proceedings be decided within one month of the date of application. As such a short period of time did not permit the court to undertake substantive tests as to whether a debtor firm was eligible for the reorganization, the court's scope of examination for the commencement of a reorganization proceeding was limited to procedural formalities such as the proper use of forms and the payment of fees. As a result of the 1999 amendments, most cases were commenced less than one month from the application. It was a big change. The forceful entry of the IMF and World Bank on to the local stage produced a shift in the understanding of insolvency rules.

b Cross-border cases

In the case of cross-border insolvencies, the expression of global norms took quite a different form. Whereas the IFIs took an ad hoc approach to Korean reforms, seeking to apply their experiences from other national emergencies to Korea's particular case, UNCITRAL developed a set of explicit procedures, which it formalized and urged upon all countries. UNCITRAL confronted not a national emergency but a generic problem increasingly common with multinational corporations. Whereas a corporate insolvency can be handled in a relatively orderly and coherent manner in a single jurisdiction where all creditors are subject to the same court authority, a corporate failure of a multinational involves the coordination of creditors and their competing claims over multiple jurisdictions. Courts may compete for jurisdiction. Courts are also inclined to favor creditors resident within their jurisdictions over creditors outside their jurisdiction. As a result, not only is value frequently lost to creditors in a liquidation, but the prospect of a multijurisdictional rehabilitation becomes all the more challenging, if not impossible. UNCITRAL sought to solve this problem by developing a model law that laid out the procedures for cross-border corporate insolvency.[18]

Like other countries, Korea, too, had struggled with cross-border cases. Yet few options existed for their solution. While, in general, Korean reformers looked to US bankruptcy law and practice, because the US had most experience in rehabilitative insolvency laws, Article 304 of the US Bankruptcy Code, which dealt with multijurisdictional bankruptcies, was not a great help. As a broadly drafted section of the legislation, it relied on judicial development for specification and development. But for Korean reformers, this presented a formidable challenge. To confidently digest and analyze a large body of judge-made law from a variety of US courts placed an undue burden on lawmakers.

UNCITRAL's Model Law provided precisely the clear statutory provisions needed by Korean reformers. It was persuasive because it was in code law form. It had previously been adopted and tested in other countries, such as Mexico and Japan, and therefore provided some evidentiary base for its effectiveness. Moreover, it quickly became clear that other major regional and global economies, including Australia and the US, were planning to adopt it. As a result, in its comprehensive reform of bankruptcy statutes, Korea also adopted, with small modifications, the Model Law. It did so principally upon its merits and the functional necessity for such a cross-jurisdictional regulatory order. But it undoubtedly did not hurt that the primary sources of international norms in insolvency—UNCITRAL, IMF, World Bank, and the US—also concurred.

2 Global norms, local rejection

a The automatic stay

Corporate insolvency laws conventionally distinguish between the time of filing of an insolvency case and the commencement or acceptance of the case by a court. In most countries, as in Korea before the crisis, long delays between application and commencement can allow a great deal of activity that can hinder reorganizations or distract management from turning the company around. In a few countries, most notably the US, a provision called the automatic stay immediately forecloses all actions by creditors against the debtor at the moment of filing.

An automatic stay means that creditors are prohibited from exercising their claims from the time when a debtor applies for bankruptcy. If automatic stay exists, the insolvency proceeding commences immediately upon the debtor's application without any further court decision. Adopted initially in the 1978 Bankruptcy Code of the United States, most other countries have not followed suit. Rather, an insolvency proceeding commences when the court makes a decision to grant an insolvency application. At the point of the court's commencement decision, creditors are "stayed" or stopped from enforcing their claims. Most countries actively consider whether to adopt the automatic stay when they revise their insolvency law because it will change the balance of power between a debtor and their creditors. It is a powerful weapon to a debtor, as it can stop an attack by creditors simply by filing an application.

In international lawmaking, the automatic stay has been controversial. While it favors debtors and forestalls many preferential transactions that might occur between application and commencement, it also reduces judicial discretion on this issue to a formality and hampers creditors who may be scrambling to protect their assets. Moreover, in some countries, including Korea, the automatic stay can conflict with other provisions in civil procedure law. For that reason, UNCITRAL's Legislative Guide on Insolvency Law, adopted by the UN in 2004, encourages use of the automatic stay to facilitate reorganization, but it does not make it mandatory for national lawmakers.

Before the crisis, the automatic stay was not given any consideration by Korean reformers, although they were aware of its significance for US bankruptcy law. In part, it was not taken seriously because there seemed to be no urgency to do so, but in part, it was also resisted because the sudden blockage of all claims by creditors upon the debtor's application for insolvency proceedings could not be imagined in commercial practice. The law reformers from the World Bank and IMF, however, urged the Korean government to adopt the automatic stay in order to accelerate proceedings. This injunction, halting actions by creditors the moment the petition for commencement was filed, would replace the dual procedure of petitioning and subsequently obtaining a commencement order with a more immediate procedure to open reorganization proceedings. Financial creditors were opposed to this idea, vigorously asserting that the automatic stay would only become an exit for debtors seeking to violate the Control of Illegal Checks Act.[19] Emotionally, the idea of being restricted from exercising their rights upon the debtor's application for insolvency was difficult to accept for creditors. Judges also thought it impractical. Moreover, studies on potential side-effects of the automatic stay were non-existent and it had few proponents in Korea. Even if the IFI recommendations were to be followed, reformers in Korea had too little understanding of how it worked in practice to risk incorporating it in the law. For all these reasons, Korean reformers resisted pressures to adopt it.

Nonetheless, over the next several years, changing domestic circumstances also changed opinions about the value of an automatic stay for Korea. We have seen that reforms that took effect in 2000 reduced the gap between application and commencement to one month. Courts gave provisional protection orders within two to three days of application and strictly applied the one-month rule thereafter. As the gap between filing and commencement was already reduced to two to three days after 2000, creditors gradually realized that the automatic stay was not such a hardship and their emotional resistance to it eroded away. Resistance by creditors was further reduced by the passage of the Debtor Rehabilitation and Bankruptcy Act (DRBA) in 2005 as they observed the functioning in practice of a two- to three-day gap. As reformers have also come to understand the functioning of the automatic stay more fully, and to appreciate its potential efficiencies in reorganizations, the climate for reform has changed, so much so that, if there were to be a round of amendments to the insolvency law, it appears likely that changed domestic orientations would support the inclusion of the automatic stay in Korea's insolvency regime. However, to solve the problem would still require a resolution of criminal problems linked to check clearing.

b A specialized insolvency court

Some countries, including the US and Thailand, have specialized insolvency courts, which have exclusive jurisdiction over insolvency cases. They are recommended by IFIs because specialized insolvency courts can provide the expertise necessary for handling insolvency cases that ordinary courts do not have. The specialized insolvency court became an important issue in Korea because the creation of a new court would be costly and influence overall judicial structure.

When the IFIs arrived in Seoul at the height of the crisis, they made a quick judgment that Korea's insolvency system lacked the capacity to handle large numbers of consequential corporate reorganizations because its judges were inadequately trained and specialized. The IFIs' solution? To insist that the government of Korea establish a specialized insolvency court along the lines of the US Bankruptcy Court system.[20]

This proposal met fierce domestic opposition from all sides of the legal complex. In Korea, judges were characteristically rotated among courts every two to three years. Even specialized chambers, such as the Administrative Court and the Patent Court, kept judges only for the length of their usual rotation. To separate a specialized court from the normal court system would require a major restructuring of the judiciary and a shift from a model of the broadly experienced generalist judge to a specialist judge.[21] Moreover, the Supreme Court doubted that a specialized insolvency court would have enough cases to justify specialization over the longer term. The total number of cases under all three insolvency laws in 1997 was less than 500; by 1998, at the height of the crisis, this climbed toward 1,300; and by 1999 was back to less than 1,000 cases. Moreover, the government budget office believed that the cost of creating specialized courts would be prohibitive.

Instead of adopting a separate insolvency court, the Supreme Court chose instead to establish insolvency divisions that would exclusively handle insolvency cases. Leading judges were assigned to the insolvency division of the Seoul District Court to hear insolvency cases. They worked vigorously to establish a model that influenced other divisions nationwide. The insolvency division is now viewed as reliable and equipped with appropriate levels of knowledge and skill. Ironically enough, however, the recent rise in the number of insolvency cases has opened up new and more favorable inclinations from the court and the government toward the possibility of the establishment of a specialized insolvency court.

3 Global norms, local contestation, eventual acceptance: receivers and debtors-in-possession

In insolvency proceedings, the world's legal systems divide over which parties should be in control of a company once it enters reorganization. The overwhelming majority of countries remove authority from the company's management and vest it in an official who may be a private professional (variously labeled a receiver, an insolvency practitioner, a lawyer, an accountant) or a government official. Usually, these insolvency representatives are supervised by courts and creditors' committees. In a minority of countries, most notably the US, the managers that took the company into insolvency can continue to manage it. This is justified on several grounds. One is that it removes a disincentive for managers to file for bankruptcy. Who is likely to file if he or she knows they will be immediately replaced or superseded? Another is that the current managers know the company best and are thus well placed to turn it around with the protections of insolvency law.

This issue was hotly debated after the crisis. Until 1992, in practice, the incumbent management was apt to be appointed as the receiver by the court in corporate reorganization proceedings. But an avalanche of problems resulted from such practice. The inherent conflict between interested parties resulted in fraudulent activities of the management and, furthermore, the corporate restructuring process became inadequate and dysfunctional. Facing such problems, in 1996, the Supreme Court enacted a guideline (Supreme Court Guideline on Corporate Reorganization Proceeding) containing restrictions on the participation of the management of the firm prior to insolvency. Management was replaced in insolvency reorganizations.

While the IFIs did not press strongly for debtor-in-possession in the months following the crisis, the issue was put firmly on the domestic agenda by a distinguished Korean corporate lawyer, Y.S. Park, who was integrally involved in drafting teams for the several post-crisis law reforms. As a result of his involvement in the 1999 World Bank-funded TALP project, its preliminary report proposed that current management should be appointed as the receiver. The proposal generated fierce exchanges among parties to the reforms. Some lawyers strongly supported the idea because it would provide debtors with an incentive to file early for insolvency protection. As debtor-in-possession also puts the initiative for filing in the hands of debtors, and gives managers continuing power, industry groups added their support.

Judges, in contrast, were hostile to the idea. In 2000, for instance, the Central District Court of Seoul alone was handling more than 200 reorganization cases. The court could not imagine its ability to effectively monitor managers who were not selected by the court. And without effective monitoring, courts laid themselves open to the unwelcome accusation that receiver-managers were engaged in fraud or other loose practices that would rebound in criticism directed at the judiciary. Maximizing value mattered less to judges than protecting themselves from harsh public censure. In a workshop discussing the preliminary report of the project, the court representative made sure that the criticisms of the chief judge of the Insolvency Division of the Seoul District Court were delivered clearly. Giving the former management responsibility for the insolvent company, he said, was unthinkable, illicit, and absurd.

Opponents from creditor financial institutions obtained support from MOFE, which shared the views of the court. Keeping managers in control of their companies would facilitate cheating and create a moral hazard in favor of managers, a fear that dominated an alternative criterion that might be of greater concern to financial interests, namely the maximization of a firm's value which could be achieved by debtor-in-possession.

The argument continued even during the process of drafting the new, comprehensive bill. It was brought to a tentative conclusion in 2002 when the drafters prepared two separate options in the drafted bills: one stated that the incumbent management could act as the receiver; the other permitted an independent third party to act as the receiver. It was a policy choice by the government as to which would prevail. The difference between the options was not substantive, considering that both options left a possibility for either the incumbent management or a third party to become the receiver in exceptional circumstances.

However, as time passed, the courts' opposition became less vigorous. Courts gained confidence in their ability to control receivers. The management process became more transparent and the danger of cheating diminished. Courts also placed increasing emphasis on maximizing the value of the underlying business, an objective better served by permitting managers to act as their own receivers. By 2003, the courts had moved to a position somewhere between flat rejection and reluctant acceptance.

Two other developments changed the attitudes of the courts and the government. Courts became more and more concerned about the gradual decrease in the number of cases that were being filed, and they therefore became more amenable to incentives that would encourage early application. This recognition led the government to accept that incumbent management could act as receivers. Abolition of the composition procedure in which the incumbent management maintained its office gave more weight to the opinion that stressed the need for statutory grounds on cases in which the court is allowed to not appoint the receiver at all, i.e., small and medium enterprise insolvency cases. In 2003, the government inserted such a clause in the bill. The new law, Debtor Rehabilitation and Bankruptcy Act (DRBA), mandates the court to appoint the current management as the receiver in principle, but also stipulates cases in which the court is allowed not to appoint a receiver at all.[22]

In 2006, the courts went even further. The appearance of competition worked as a factor that changed the court's attitude toward the receiver. In 1998, the Korean government had established the so-called workout program that opened the door to non-judicial proceedings for ailing large firms. This diversion of cases from the courts compelled judges to consider how they might combat their loss of major cases to private workouts. In February 2006, just before DRBA came into effect, the Insolvency Division of the Seoul District Court invited insolvency lawyers from eight major law firms to a meeting at which they were told that the court would allow incumbent management to hold its office in rehabilitation cases.

This inspired the court to induce firms to use judicial proceedings by laying down a Supreme Court Rule in 2006 that expanded the range of cases in which the court is allowed not to appoint a receiver at all, including for listed companies.[23] As a result, even a big listed firm could go through the rehabilitation proceeding without a receiver under the DRBA.

In sum, in order to maintain a competitive advantage in a "market" for alternative ways of reorganizing companies, the Supreme Court took steps to encourage managers to file with courts without the fear that they would be removed from day-to-day control of their companies. This move, however, would not have been possible without a maturing of the insolvency bench itself as well as the broadening and deepening of the pool of lawyers with expertise in reorganizations. All these shifts also ultimately depended upon the progressive adoption of the overriding goal of maximizing the value of assets in insolvency for the benefit of creditors and debtors alike. The final result is that the US model has been progressively adopted in practice. The court appoints incumbent management as the receiver in most cases and appoints no receiver at all in about 20–30 percent of insolvency cases.

4 Global context, domestic innovation

Closeout netting is the mechanism that terminates all existing contracts among debtors and their creditors, calculates what is to be paid, pays the settled amounts, and closes out the legal relationship among the parties. It is used in financial transactions, usually among financial institutions. It was first adopted to deal with derivatives but is now widely used in various types of financial contracts. As financial transactions have sharply increased globally, international financial investors have sought a secure structure that can protect their contracts from insolvency rules. Closeout netting is the solution they found.

The International Swap Dealers' Association (ISDA) showed great interest in whether closeout netting was legally permissible in the process of insolvency in Korea. A decision handed by a district court[24] assumed that the closeout netting clause was valid, but practicing lawyers hesitated to advise whether closeout netting provisions in derivatives transactions were ensured.

In February 2003, attention was drawn to a Supreme Court decision that ruled that the act of enforcing the right of pledge after the commencement of reorganization proceedings was subject to the right of avoidance. In other words, a court could reverse the enforcement of the security.[25] The decision triggered intricate discussions over the applicability of insolvency law, especially in relation to the payment and settlement system for financial transactions.

After the decision, the ISDA directly approached the Ministry of Finance and Economy and the Ministry of Justice, and asked them to exclude closeout netting from the application of insolvency laws. The government agreed. It understood that, if the enforceability of closeout netting was left without any statutory grounds, Korea might face disadvantages in conducting international financial transactions in the future. Many academic experts also agreed. As a result, in 2003, a clause stipulating this exception was included in the 2003 Insolvency Bill and later enacted in a different form in 2005.

During the process of revising the Insolvency Bill in 2004,[26] the government faced additional requests related to the scope of exclusion from the application of insolvency laws. *Dambo*[27] call transactions were one of the first issues that the government confronted. A concept contrived in the development of the Korean financial market, a *dambo* call transaction refers to call transactions between financial institutions with security attached. Unlike traditional call transactions, which do not need security of any kind, demanding security for call transactions involving financial institutions with low credit became a common practice in Korea. Futures brokers who conducted these transactions insisted on an exception that included *dambo* call transactions, assisted later on by the Korea Securities Depository.[28] Experts acknowledged the need to ensure the finality of payment of *dambo* call transactions in spite of the distinction from derivative financial transactions, considering that they were conducted through the clearance and settlement system instituted by the Korea Securities Depository.

A second demand came from the Bank of Korea regarding the currency payment and settlement system. The Bank of Korea asked the government to legislate an exception regarding the currency payment and settlement system. The issue needed to be dealt with because the CLS bank (Continuous Linked Settlement Bank International), which the Bank of Korea at the time was seeking to join, required a substantive enactment that excluded the foreign exchange payment and settlement system from domestic insolvency laws. This decision was difficult to reach, and discussions were extended to the admissibility of the demand, as studies were unavailable on the necessity of the finality of payment in relation to the currency payment and settlement system.

A third demand was submitted by the Korea Securities Exchange regarding the clearance and settlement system in the securities market. After the experience of witnessing security brokers who become insolvent in 1998, experts understood the necessity of guaranteeing the finality of payment in case security brokers went bankrupt. The government and National Assembly, in contrast, found the idea hard to follow.

The legal scholar responsible for the revision project recognized that two tasks needed to be achieved in order to solve the problem.[29] The primary task, in light of the common objective to ensure finality of payment, was to create a single provision embodying the three kinds of transactions—the currency payment and settlement system of the Bank of Korea, the clearance and settlement system of securities and transaction of the securities market, and qualified financial transactions including derivative financial transactions. A secondary task was to hold workshops and seminars to promote understanding of unfamiliar concepts and legal theories and furthermore to gain the consent of the government, the court, the National Assembly, and lawyers. Article 120 of the DRBA, which ensures the finality of payment, is the final result of such efforts. Article 120 is the first enactment worldwide that has worked out the problem of the finality of payment in a single provision.[30]

Analysis

With these case studies in hand, we return to the reforms with an analytic eye and explore some of their theoretical elements.

Manifestations of the global

While it is clear that Korean insolvency reforms had a domestic trajectory, they all unfolded in a global context. That context, however, must be carefully disentangled because the constraints of its influence vary considerably depending on the nature of threads that linked the global to the local. We discern several threads.

First, Korean insolvency statutes enacted in the 1960s drew heavily on Japanese statutes. While Japan's insolvency statutes drew on other civil law countries, notably Germany and Austria, its corporate reorganization law derives from US bankruptcy law. That legal derivation, coupled with Korea's close economic, security, and educational links with the US since the Korean War, make it unsurprising that, as Korea's economy developed, a younger generation of Korean insolvency scholars looked to US bankruptcy law and practice for inspiration. This they did before any foreign constraints or without particular demands from IFIs or IOs.

Second, Korea itself has been an economically upwardly mobile country for decades. Its upward mobility, however, is not simply a matter of rising gross national product (GNP) or gross domestic product (GDP). While Korea rightly celebrated its admission into the Organisation for Economic Co-operation and Development (OECD), a club of rich nations, in the mid-1990s, Koreans calibrate their achievements in education, science, technology, and other areas by their international standing. The chair of a panel at a recent conference hosted by the prestigious Korea Development Institute proudly observed that all the Korean economists on the panel had doctorates from the University of Chicago's Economics Department, a comment with the unstated corollary that it is the most prominent department in the world, at least by the metric of current faculty who are Nobel Laureates. This vignette signifies a wider phenomenon—Korean institutions frequently orient their reforms to standards and practices to magnetic centers of global prestige. As an official from an influential IFI observed about the insolvency reforms, it was much more effective to persuade Korean lawmakers that their law fell below global standards than to try and exert crude financial pressures for change. As a result, Korean officials and Korean scholars orient themselves to global status indicators. In the insolvency field, these include the US, which is a normative leader in the international shift toward a rehabilitative ideal in insolvency regimes, and arguably the most prominent single global actor in the global norm-making of multilateral international organizations, such as the World Bank and, in the area of trade law, UNCITRAL.

Third, much of the foreign influence on Korean insolvency laws occurs diffusely through academic and professional epistemic communities. A small number of Korean academics and officials are closely integrated into international networks of insolvency specialists.[31] Leading law professors studied in the US, Japan, and Europe. Prominent Korean scholars participate in international professional associations, such as a recent International Bar Association world conference in Singapore. Korean specialists, judges, and law professors were integral to the global norm-making enterprises of the World Bank and UNCITRAL in the field of insolvency law. Korean academics and practitioners participate in the OECD's Forums on Asian Insolvency Law, which bring together scholars and practitioners across Asia and the world to Seoul and other Asian capitals.[32] Korean commercial lawyers come back from advanced degree courses overseas and a year or two of foreign practice with exposure to various insolvency regimes. The numbers of participating lawyers, scholars, and academics in the area of insolvency are quite small, but they are strategically placed within Korean reform circles to act as intermediaries between global and local reformist impulses.

Fourth, there is a quasi-functional element to the Korean law reforms that are adaptive to a wider embedding economic environment. The closeout netting impact on the insolvency legislation demonstrates that, as the Korean financial system became progressively more tightly integrated into global clearing systems, Korea had to find a mechanism that would conform to the global norms that regulate the clearing of financial transactions. Korea's solution was innovative. The functional problem that the legal innovation solved, however, was dictated by a global financial imperative.

It is in these contexts that the fifth and most dramatic form of foreign interventions must be situated. At the height of the financial crisis, the IMF and World Bank legal teams made explicit demands upon Korea to create a more effective insolvency system. Several of these were written into letters of intent from the government of Korea to the IMF. Others, such as the commitment to integrate three insolvency laws into one, were made subject to certain understandings. Beyond the formal conditions, for the most part, IFIs relied upon persuasion because their officials believed that the Korean government would respond in good faith and this will to reform would be reflected in a capacity to effect change.

We may therefore understand the influence of non-domestic forces on Korea as a combination of two sets of circumstances. The first were economic, legal, and academic conditions that created a general conduciveness toward legal changes that would simultaneously solve domestic problems and conform more closely to the global norms best exemplified by the US. The second were the precipitating events of the financial crisis, which certainly hastened and broadened the scope of reforms that had previously been envisaged by Korean lawmakers. It is no accident that the bulk of reforms occurred after the crisis, nor that the central tendency of reforms moved toward the US model and the global norms over which it had a disproportionate influence. As late as 2003, the IMF released an Article IV appraisal of Korea's economy that chided Korean lawmakers for not making further progress on consolidation of their laws, implicitly comparing them with US law before its three bankruptcy acts were unified in a single bankruptcy code.

Domestic politics

Let us now change the angle of orientation and appraise the Korean reforms from their domestic perspective. Here, too, however, we must broaden the context because insolvency politics have now been studied in numbers of countries and it is instructive to discover whether Korea conforms to patterns observed elsewhere.

In principle, all parties to commerce should have an interest in insolvency law: managers and owners; producers and consumers; creditors and debtors; trade creditors/suppliers and financial creditors; the state and private actors; and professionals. There are private interests in insolvency just as there are also public interests. But bargaining over the rules of the insolvency game is not merely a macrocosm of private interest negotiation. The "meta bargaining" over the rules that govern everyday bargaining has its own logic.[33] In most countries, the spectrum of actors involved in meta bargaining is a subset of those involved in everyday liquidations and reorganizations. Three differences are immediately obvious. First, there are problems of collective action in political mobilization, which characteristically work against trade creditors and small businesses. Second, the low probability of insolvency for any given business, coupled with a general aversion by business people to discussing corporate failure, produces a worldwide phenomenon that generally results in the absence of owners and managers from lawmaking in this field. Third, while civil society groups and non-governmental organizations (NGOs) sometimes mobilize for individual bankruptcies, they are seldom involved in corporate lawmaking. Finally, in most countries and circumstances, insolvency politics are remote from public interest. They are seen to be technical and difficult subjects where specialists are best equipped to make decisions. This technical quality of insolvency reforms therefore generally produces a bias away from broader participation and offers professions, in particular, disproportionate influence. The question then arises as to what biases are introduced by the technical politics of an area of law that in fact has significant distributional implications.

To assay systematically the degree of bias in public participation in Korea's insolvency reforms, we have identified all the domestic and international actors who mobilized on any of the five issue areas discussed above (see Table 11.2), from which we draw several general conclusions.

First, several groups of actors are constant across all issue areas. In every case, the MOFE, the Ministry of Justice, and the judiciary are actively involved in a variety of capacities—initiating reforms, taking responsibility for drafting of legislation, liaising with IFIs, negotiating with each other, managing the scope and direction of public participation. In every case, the legal complex[34] is also actively involved. The Korean case reinforces findings elsewhere that insolvency reforms are mediated, and sometimes dominated, by professionals—lawyers, judges, legal academics—who stand at the crossroads of public participation and government responsibility. Governments rely on these experts to filter foreign experiences, norms, and pressures and to adapt general policy concerns (e.g., the expediency of insolvency proceedings) to national circumstances. As insolvency law is thought to be technical and complex, this potentially privileges the technical authority of the legal complex.

Second, there are actors who are issue specific. Some are surprising. For instance, the legislature—the National Assembly—was not engaged on every issue, in part because some issues, such as a specialized insolvency court or the automatic stay, were debated and handled inside the legal complex, through exchanges among private lawyers, academics, and judges. Through its rule-making and advisory powers, the courts can operate independently of executive and legislative agencies. While the legislature always consulted with the courts, the obverse did not occur. It may also be surprising to observe that after the crisis IFIs were not universally involved in every issue area although their broad policy preferences are reflected in the general orientations of Korea's reforms. In part, direct IFI intervention was restrained for two reasons. On the one hand, as the years unfolded beyond the crisis, and Korea's economy rapidly regained its equilibrium, IFI leverage decreased until it amounted only to persuasion. On the other hand, IFI officials generally believed Korean policymakers to be responsive to international norms and thus did not require the degree of pressure IFI officials were inclined to exert in less responsive countries.

We observe also that two other forms of international influence are issue specific rather than generic, although in different ways. The TALP consultation funded by

Table 11.2 Actors in Korean insolvency reforms, 1992–2007

Actors	Management control in insolvency	Specialized insolvency court	Expediency and transparency	Automatic stay	Payment and settlement system
Supreme Court	Y	Y	Y	Y	Y
MOFE	Y	Y	Y	Y	Y
Ministry of Justice	Y	Y	Y	Y	Y
National Assembly / Judiciary Committee	Y		Y		Y
Korea Development Institute		Y	Y		
Lawyers: insolvency specialists	Y	Y	Y	Y	Y
Law firms					
Korea Bar Association			Y	Y	
Drafting team	Y	Y	Y	Y	Y
Insolvency law study group	Y	Y	Y	Y	Y
Law professionals	Y	Y	Y	Y	Y
Foreign lawyers in Korean practice	Y	Y	Y		
Central Bank/Bank of Korea					Y
Korea Securities Exchange					Y
Korea Bankers Association	Y		Y	Y	
Korea Federation of Industry	Y		Y	Y	
SME organization				Y	
IFIs		Y	Y	Y	Y
UNCITRAL	Y			Y	Y
ISDA					Y
Foreign private consultations (TALP)	Y	Y		Y	

Note: SME, small and medium-sized enterprise; IFI, international financial institution; UNCITRAL, United Nations Commission on International Trade Law; ISDA, International Swap Dealers' Association.
Y, engaged in lawmaking on an issue.

the World Bank was bounded temporally, beginning in 1999 and informing revisions of statutory law through 2003. It therefore had nothing to say to the expediency and transparency reforms of 1998 and 1999, nor to the later emerging issues of financial closeout and netting. UNCITRAL's Legislative Guide had a more diffuse impact. While the Guide itself was not adopted by the UN General Assembly until late 2004, the chief drafter of Korea's comprehensive insolvency legislation, Professor Soogeun Oh, was also Korea's official delegate to UNCITRAL. He participated in all UNCITRAL discussions and was thereby thoroughly informed about currents of expert and national opinion on every principal area of substantive and procedural insolvency law. Moreover, the Ministry of Justice and Judiciary Committee of the National Assembly asked him to compare the prospective Korean legislation in relation to UNCITRAL's Legislative Guide. It can be said that no feature of Korea's insolvency law is inconsistent with either explicit recommendations or permitted variations in the UNCITRAL Legislative Guide.

Third, Table 11.2 also reveals what is common to insolvency politics in other advanced economies. The banking industry and big business are given places at the table. Their representatives were on the formal drafting committee of the comprehensive reforms. They are less privy to technical reforms being discussed inside the legal complex and potentially formalized by the courts. In contrast, trade creditors and small business have no direct representation and, at best, have their interests treated either through lawyers speaking on their behalf or by legislators who are sensitive to the concerns of these particular constituencies.

In Korea, a revision committee for a certain law reform is usually formed by the Ministry of Justice. The Ministry of Justice selects experts, usually academics, and representatives from interested groups. To minimize the possibility of resistance at later stages, the Ministry tends to call upon the groups most likely to be outspoken. In the reform of insolvency law in South Korea, trade associations, labor unions, or civil society agents did not play a meaningful role. The Korea Federation of Industry (an association of large firms) and Korean Bank Association were each asked to send a representative on behalf of debtors and creditors respectively. Although some interested groups, including an organization for small and medium-sized industry, showed interest in participation in the Committee, they were not invited because of limitations on the size of the committee. Later, an organization for small and medium-sized industry made a written policy suggestion, which was reviewed by the committee. Only a few interested groups submitted any suggestions. The principal problem was that the people from invited interest groups were not experts in the field. Even though they were invited to the Committee, it was not certain whether they argued successfully for their interests. Further, to gain consensus and support among interest groups, the first draft of the bill was publicly announced and the call for the comments was made.

Among these actors, we can observe several fault lines that cut across the political landscape. The first arises out of professional epistemologies.[35] As augurs of the financial crisis loomed, and in its subsequent ripples, economists and lawyers differed sharply over the diagnosis of the problems and the prescriptions that would remedy them. Economists believed that law, lawyers, and judges stood in the way of efficient processing of cases and certain liquidation of companies that had no hope of rehabilitation. For instance, in response to a perceived failure of judges to take the hard decision to liquidate companies, economists at the Korean Development Institute designed an "economic criterion test" that would mandate liquidation, thereby reducing judicial discretion. At MOFE's behest, this was enacted in the initial wave of 1998 amendments. More generally, economists at MOFE thought of law as an instrumental lever that might recalibrate markets somewhat analogously to interest rates adjusted by central banks.

Lawyers, in contrast, disagreed both with the diagnosis that the failures of Korea's bankruptcy system should be laid at the door of lawyers and judges, and with the prescription that frequent statutory amendments could quickly produce a new and more satisfactory legal "equilibrium." For the legal complex, many problems arose from the failure of the banking sector to function responsibly, to make loans on financial rather than non-economic criteria, to monitor loans, and to resist governmental interference. The law does not function as a lever that can be pulled to obtain a quick and certain result. Every amendment introduces uncertainties and indeterminacy.

This divide in disciplinary analysis substantially corresponded with a second fault line that put MOFE at odds with the Ministry of Justice. Korea's astonishing path to economic development had been substantially guided by the sophisticated technocrats in MOFE and its predecessor agencies. When major companies got into trouble, government agencies had long been accustomed to solving their problems administratively. Sometimes, banks were compelled by the government to lend more or change the terms of their loans. At other times, takeovers by stronger companies were forced upon weaker companies. In contrast to MOFE, the Ministry of Justice was a weak cousin in the government. Its purview was narrow and its powers limited. MOFE officials looked upon their Justice counterparts from a historically conditioned position of superiority. In part, this derived from considerable skepticism among economist technocrats that law had the capacity to regulate markets without their guiding hand. This tension revealed itself repeatedly in competition between the two ministries over which would take the leadership in responsibility for insolvency reforms—and which would therefore shape the content of the law itself.

The IFIs did not have a direct channel to the Ministry of Justice. As the Ministry of Justice had nothing to ask the IFIs to do for it, the IFIs were strangers to the Ministry of Justice. It did not take IFIs as working partners, nor was it clever enough to use IFIs as free mercenaries. For the most part, IFIs seemed to be influenced by the information provided by MOFE, to which they were closer in any event.

A fault line also existed between MOFE and the courts. In Korea's remarkable rise from a third- to a first-world economy, the courts had played a constrained role. Up to and beyond the crisis, MOFE officials doubted that courts had the expertise or the probity to manage restructurings of large numbers of enterprises, especially those that were industry leaders. From their vantage point, MOFE officials observed judges who were slow, sometimes corrupt, often incompetent, and too often inefficient. From the opposite viewpoint, judges saw officials who had little real idea of what law could do, and who wanted little competition for regulation of the economy.

In this triad of intragovernmental competition, the Ministry of Justice and the courts had their own rivalries. In Korea's fierce competition for entry into the legal professions, on average, the highest ranking lawyers went into the judiciary, and the next rank was recruited to the public prosecutor's office. But actual power in the legal system resided not with judges but with prosecutors. Moreover, prosecutors exercised a measure of public leadership because many social problems brought prosecutors to the fore, not least corruption among politicians. Yet, while prosecutors complained about judges, the latter frequently criticized the former for the ways in which they handled cases.

The crisis compelled judges to look at themselves in a new light. Before the crisis, judges lived in an isolated and bounded world. They did not exercise public leadership, and there were few opportunities for them to be concerned or blamed about major social interests. Blame might be leveled at a single decision, but judges did not attract the attention of the public nor its threats.

The crisis changed this blinkered orientation. Courts came to see that they were handling cases that had an influence on the entire country. But as they stepped out on to the public stage, they were also more exposed to public critique, for instance on how efficiently they handled corporate restructuring. They began to comprehend an institutional interest in the national matrix of power, to view themselves as potential contenders in the national power elite. At the same time, the private market for senior retired judges was also constricting as the private profession expanded. Their career interests therefore aligned more fully with institutional development. As private career opportunities shut down, public institutional interests opened up. Now, judges began to show an interest in enlarging the regulatory pie and their control over it, just as they were also happy to see the domain of private legal services expand. In sociological terms, they envisaged expanding their "jurisdictional rights" over more extensive and more consequential terrain in the economic landscape.

Something of a fault line also existed between MOFE and the bankers on the one side, and lawyers and judges on the other. Korea's financial industry had been closely controlled by the government, so much so that foreign consultants questioned whether a viable private banking system had fully matured before the crisis.[36] After the crisis, as the government moved swiftly to stabilize the banking system, government regulators effectively became major stockholders in many banks, thereby effectively retaining a strong role in their governance. At the very time, therefore, that IFIs were preaching privatization, the government hand remained quietly in place behind many leading financial institutions. MOFE and the private financial sector preferred to find fault in the insolvency system in others, not themselves. Across the fault line, many private lawyers and legal academics resented finger-pointing that laid insolvency woes at the door of the legal system when it seemed obvious to them that bankers bore more than their share of responsibility. As we have seen, on several issues, financial creditors aligned themselves against lawyers and judges, not to mention debtors.

Conclusion

From 1992 until the present, the Korean insolvency system went through multiple cycles of reforms. In the years following the crisis, these came rapidly, and for a time, annually. These cycles may be understood as recursive, alternation of activity between enactment and implementation, between law-on-the-books and law-in-action.[37] These cycles should be characterized as neither domestic nor global. To varying degrees, they involve an admixture of both. The Korean reforms reflect three patterns of lawmaking activities: (1) cycles of substantially domestic lawmaking in a global context; (2) iterations of global norm-making that have national consequences; and (3) the mutual engagement of global norm-making and domestic reforms.

Recursive lawmaking is driven forward by several mechanisms, each of which is apparent in Korean insolvency reforms. Lawmaking, by its very nature, is *indeterminate*, opening up uncertainty of meanings and outcomes, producing inconsistencies within and between areas of law, and often revealing gaps that can be exploited in practice. Much of the struggle over a reduction in judicial discretion through an economic criterion test was intended by economists to reduce indeterminacy, but its results were perverse and required further rounds of lawmaking to forestall the unintended consequences.

Cycles of reform are often driven forward by *mismatch* between actors in practice and those in lawmaking. While we have not been able to expand upon this here, a notable case in point occurred when MOFE, over the objections of lawyers, sought to create a pre-packaged form of corporate workout[38] that courts would conform to without full judicial proceedings. As lawyers were heard but not heeded in this reform, they effectively nullified it by refusing to use it in practice on the grounds that it was impractical.

Contradictions also get internalized in law reforms when conflicting parties to reforms are unable to produce a real political settlement. Instead, the law builds in inherently contradictory tendencies that make it unstable in practice. We observe an example in the relationship between the IFIs and the courts in Korea. On the one hand, the IFIs were ideologically committed to the devolution of state regulatory powers to markets with the correlative emergence of courts as primary arenas for market restructuring. Yet IFI relationships in Korea were much stronger with MOFE than with the Ministry of Justice. They were therefore torn between listening to MOFE's insistence that courts were not yet ready to handle heavy responsibilities for market regulation and their own instincts that lawyers and courts, properly developed, were a better site for economic dispute settlement and corporate rehabilitation.

Finally, lawmaking invariably involves *diagnostic disputes*. In Korea, these tended to be systematic epistemologies borne by competing professions. It is noticeable that economistic diagnoses vied for ascendancy in the late 1990s but, after they were discredited by unsuccessful reforms, the government increasingly relied on the legal complex for its diagnosis of weaknesses in the system and for the prescriptions that would remedy them. Some strains of diagnostic tension also existed between IFIs and domestic reformers, the former relying on evaluations that pointed to solutions that adhered to global norms, whereas the latter produced solutions they believed appropriate for the particularity of Korea's own situation.

The settling of reform cycles in Korea and elsewhere depends on the resolution of these four mechanisms. Until indeterminacy is narrowed, contradictions are resolved in political agreements, actor mismatch is acknowledged as an impediment to implementation, and diagnostic struggles are revealed for their prescriptive consequences, cycles of reform are likely to recur with all the instability and uncertainty that they produce in law and markets. The more fully lawmaking is embedded in global contexts, the more difficult this may be to manage in domestic lawmaking, especially in a financial crisis where international actors may be at their strongest.

If domestic law reforms cannot be explained without understanding the dynamics of recursivity, neither can the insolvency reforms in Korea be understood without situating them in a wider struggle.

Korea's insolvency reforms were not only about insolvency. They are about the restructuring of the Korean state *vis-à-vis* the market.[39] We have alluded to the dominant role of the finance ministries and agencies in leading Korea's state development model of economic growth.[40] By the mid-1990s, however, both Korean and foreign analysts concurred that this model might have run its course.[41] The crisis gave IFIs fuel to preach the gospel of privatization, just as it also demonstrated to lawyers, judges, and courts that they might emerge from under the shadow of the powerful executive agencies that had steered the economy.

The insolvency reforms were yet another arena in which the restructuring of the state worked itself out, ironically enough, in this case, over the restructuring of corporations that had been enabled by the state. For the courts to shoulder responsibility for major corporate reorganizations, it required that MOFE pull back from its activist meddling in corporate affairs. That MOFE was reluctant to do so can be seen in several respects. From 1998 to the present, MOFE sought to construct ad hoc agreements, out-of-court arrangements, and even an out-of-court procedure based on a statute (the Corporate Restructuring Promotion Act), all of which were intended either to relieve pressure on the courts or to keep economic power away from the courts, depending on where one's sympathies lay.

The drama of commercial law reforms in Asian countries must therefore be seen for the magnitude of its stakes. In the insolvency domain, and other areas of commercial law, the stakes are not only to do with law and markets. They reach to the structure and functions of the state itself, the extent to which it will steer or drive the market, the degree to which executive agencies will yield power to courts, and the manner in which governance will devolve elsewhere in society.[42] In Korea, all the major parties to insolvency reforms recognized that these were the stakes behind the legal change. At once, they brought into the same arena of conflict competing professions, differing epistemologies of institutional regulation, changing career trajectories and opportunities, shifts in jurisdiction over areas of work and, most importantly, shifts in power to manage not only companies but economies.

It is also appropriate to ask how representative bankruptcy law was of commercial law reform more generally in Korea. Was its relation to the global typical or atypical of other areas of economic law, most particularly the Commercial Code? In fact, bankruptcy law was exceptional in its exposure to global influences. More than any other area of commercial law, it came under simultaneous domestic and foreign pressure. Almost at the same time as the bankruptcy reforms, the Commercial Code was amended many times.[43] The series of reforms in the Commercial Code, however, were initiated by local scholars in 1995 without any pressure from IFIs. Even after the crisis in the late 1990s, the demand from IFIs focused only on the rights of shareholders and the liability of directors, which were thoroughly discussed in academic circles long before the crisis. Hence, the interaction of foreign pressure and domestic pushback are distinctive to bankruptcy law.

We conclude with an observation or two about the metaphor that informs this book. "Pushing against" globalization has the merit that it questions the implicit premise of hyper-globalizers that legal change emanates predominantly from the global center. Yet this metaphor itself is premised on a dynamic of action versus reaction—that one party (a global actor) is pushing for something, while another party (a domestic lawmaker) is pushing back. Insofar as that dynamic resists the easy slide to inexorability that stalks some theories of globalization,[44] this is a useful corrective.

Nonetheless, we should remain alert to other dynamics. For instance, Dezalay and Garth,[45] among others, have shown that national law reforms often involve domestic actors who seek global allies in order to compensate for their political weakness at home. "Palace wars" get internationalized. We might therefore expect that Korean judges would welcome the ideology espoused by IFIs that devolves greater powers to courts and judges,[46] just as Indonesian reformers welcomed the IMF's bold effort to create a viable, competent, powerful, and independent commercial court. Rather than "pushing back," domestic reformers "pull" global actors into the local fray.

Or we might consider another metaphor altogether. Globalization of law could be seen as a general raising of temperature around an issue. Countries experience a common heating up of attention to insolvency, often for reasons that are common to them all. Their engagement with the issue may be informed through epistemic communities that span frontiers and bridge divides between advanced and developing economies. Their own bankers and corporations alert local lawmakers to problems they must solve as they encounter similar problems inside their countries to those manifest elsewhere, or they must have ways to deal with commercial relationships that cross borders. Sometimes, countries manage to insulate parts of their legal system from this overall rise in temperature. As often as not, however, a common movement takes place so imperceptibly that its currents can scarcely be discerned. Flows of ideas, networks of scholars, international organizations of professionals, and transnational links of legislators and judges might be captured by images that "pushing" and "pulling" might not fully connote.

Notes

1 Daniel Berkowitz, Katharina Pistor, and Jean-Francois Richard, 'Economic Development, Legality, and the Transplant Effect', *European Economic Review* 47, 2003, pp. 165–95.

2 Wolfgang Streeck and Kathleen Thelen, 'Introduction: Institutional Change in Advanced Political Economies', in Wolfgang Streeck and Kathleen Thelen, eds, *Beyond Continuity: Institutional Change in Advanced Political Economies*, New York: Cambridge University Press, 2005; Kathleen Thelen, 'Historical Institutionalism in Comparative Politics', *Annual Review of Political Science* 2, 1999, pp. 369–404; David Woodruff, 'Rules for Followers: Institutional Theory and the New Politics of Economic Backwardness in Russia', *Politics and Society* 28, 2000, pp. 437–82.

3 "Global norms" may be understood in contrasting ways. On the one side, they can be viewed as claims by international organizations (e.g., IMF, World Bank, UNCITRAL) to have developed and promulgated norms that are intended to be global in their impact. On the other hand, they could be seen as empirical descriptions of behavior around the world, i.e., that all nation-states or prominent nation-states behave according to these norms. This chapter adopts the former usage. By "global norms," we refer to any hard or soft laws that one or another influential actor on the global stage claims to be prescriptive for national and cross-national behavior.

4 Thomas L. Friedman, *The Lexus and the Olive Tree: Understanding Globalization*, New York: Anchor Books, 2000; David Held, Anthony McGraw, David Goldblatt, and Jonathan Perraton, *Global Transformations: Politics, Economics and Culture*, Stanford: Stanford University Press, 1999.

5 Terence C. Halliday and Bruce G. Carruthers, *Law's Global Markets: The Recursivity of Law in the Creation of Global Norms and East Asian Insolvency Regimes*, Palo Alto: Stanford University Press, 2009, forthcoming; Bruce G. Carruthers and Terence C. Halliday, 'Negotiating Globalization: Global Templates and the Construction of Insolvency Regimes in East Asia', *Law & Social Inquiry* 31, 2006, pp. 521–84.

6 Terence C. Halliday and Pavel Osinsky, 'Globalization of Law', *Annual Review of Sociology* 32, 2006, pp. 447–70.

7 Halliday and Carruthers, *supra*, forthcoming.

8 Held et al., *supra*, 1999.

9 For detailed analyses of Korean insolvency reforms from their inception, see Soogeun Oh, *An Institutional Perspective on Financial Reform in Korea*, Seoul: Korea Development Bank Report, 1999; Soogeun Oh, 'Bankruptcy Division and Commissioner', in *Insolvency Reform in Asia: An Assessment of the Recent Developments and the Role of the Judiciary*, Bali, Indonesia, 2001; Soogeun Oh, 'Drafting of New Insolvency Law of Korea', in *FAIR Conference*, Bangkok, Thailand, 2002a; Soogeun Oh, 'Government Intervention in Corporate Exit Mechanisms: The Corporate Restructuring Promotion Act of Korea', in *Hong Kong University Faculty of Law*, Hong Kong, 2002b; Soogeun Oh, 'Drafting of New Insolvency Law of Korea', in *World Bank Forum on Insolvency Risk Management*, Washington, DC, 2003a; Soogeun Oh, 'Insolvency Law Reform of Korea: A Continuing Learning Process', in *Forum on Insolvency Risk Management*, Washington, DC, 2003b; Soogeun Oh, 'Setting Insolvency Rules: A Course of Understanding and Persuasion', in *OECD FAIR III*, Seoul, Korea, 2003c; Soogeun Oh, 'Changes in Insolvency Practice, Restructuring of Ailing Firms and Risk Management after the Economic Crisis: The Korea Case', in *International Workshop on Reform of Corporate Governance: Corporate Rehabilitations in East Asia and its Lesson for China*, Beijing, China, 2005; Y.S. Oh and Keun Byung Lee, 'Korean Insolvency Laws Protect Foreign Investors', *International Financial Law Review* 17, 1998, pp. 30–33.

10 Soogeun Oh, 'Bankruptcy Division and Commissioner', in *Insolvency Reform in Asia: An Assessment of the Recent Developments and the Role of the Judiciary*, Bali, Indonesia, 2001.

11 Interviews 2040, 2305.

12 Orrick Herrington & Sutcliffe (US law firm), Shin & Kim (Korean law firm), and Bingham & Dana (Singapore law firm).

13 MOFE wanted to establish mandatory arbitration procedure in individual rehabilitation proceedings as it had a stake in individual workout programs among creditor financial institutions. The Court resisted MOFE's scheme, but failed to stop it. An academic persuaded congressmen to delete those provisions.

14 The maximum period of repayment in individual rehabilitation was eight years in the bill because the maximum period in individual workouts run by creditor financial institutions was also eight years. MOFE wanted to make them the same as each other because the short repayment period in the individual rehabilitation procedure might deprive individual workouts of competitiveness.

15 There was a tension between lawyers with cosmopolitan perspectives and those with rather conservative ones. The former wanted to have similar provisions to those in the UNCITRAL Model Law on cross-border insolvency law. The latter refused to accept the Model Law on its face and wanted to create more balance between cross-border cases and domestic cases.

16 John Braithwaite and Peter Drahos, *Global Business Regulation*, Cambridge: Cambridge University Press, 2000.

17 Immediately after the 1997–98 financial crisis, international financial institutions and the Korean government reached the following agreements:
IMF: "[Bankruptcy related law] will be reviewed and draft legislation will be prepared with the objective of streamlining bankruptcy procedure."
World Bank: (Objective) "Introduce market-based bankruptcy procedures and facilitate efficient liquidation of insolvent corporations,
World Bank: (Policy Measure 1) Submit to National Assembly insolvency laws (bankruptcy, composition, and corporate reorganization) to resolve jurisdictional conflicts, build administrative capacity, expedite procedures, enhance creditor participation in the reorganization process, and establish economic criteria for initiation of the reorganization process. (Monitoring Indicators 1) Appropriate amendment of laws.
World Bank: (Policy Measure 2) Review laws on bankruptcy, composition, and reorganization, with a view to harmonization and enhancing efficiency. (Monitoring Indicators 2) Preparation of study by end-1998 under TOR agreed with Bank, thereafter enactment of appropriate legislation."

18 United Nations Commission on International Trade Law (UNCITRAL), *UNCITRAL Model Law on Cross-Border Insolvency with Guide to Enactment*, New York: United Nations, 1999.

19 This Act penalizes the issuer of an unpaid check. If the issuer of a check got a commencement order, and the payment was prohibited by the order of the court, then the issuer would not be punished even though the issuer had no funds to pay the check.

20 Bruce G. Carruthers and Terence C. Halliday, *Rescuing Business: The Making of Corporate Bankruptcy Law in England and the United States*, Oxford: Oxford University Press, 1998.

21 It should be noted that this issue has been the subject of recurrent debate in many national insolvency regimes. On Britain and the US, cf. Bruce G. Carruthers and Terence C. Halliday, *Rescuing Business: The Making of Corporate Bankruptcy Law in England and the United States*, Oxford: Oxford University Press, 1998. On China, Indonesia, and Korea, cf. Terence C. Halliday, and Bruce Carruthers, 'Institutional Lessons from Insolvency Reforms in East Asia', in *Forum on Asian Insolvency Law Reform (FAIR), Insolvency and Risk Management in Asia*, Delhi, India: World Bank and Asian Development Bank, 2004b; Terence C. Halliday and Bruce G. Carruthers, *Law's Global Markets: The Recursivity of Law in the Creation of Global Norms and East Asian Insolvency Regimes*, Palo Alto: Stanford University Press, 2009, forthcoming.

22 Article 74 (Appointment of Receiver).
The court shall appoint as the receiver the person appropriate for performing the duty of the receiver, hearing the opinions of the Administrative Committee and the Council of Creditors.

Except for any of the following cases, the court shall appoint as the receiver the individual debtor, or a representative for the debtor who is not an individual:

1. If financial distress of the debtor is ascribed to property misappropriation, concealment, or mismanagement with serious liability by the following person

    A. An individual debtor;
    B. A director of the non-individual debtor; or
    C. A manager of the debtor.

2. If the Council of Creditors makes a request on reasonable reasons, and;
3. If it is necessary for rehabilitation of the debtor.

Notwithstanding Paragraph 1, in cases where the debtor is an individual, small and medium-sized enterprise or other person set in the Supreme Court Regulations, the court is allowed not to appoint the receiver. However, in cases where a matter of each subparagraph of Paragraph 2 is recognized during the rehabilitation proceeding, the receiver may be appointed.

In case of not appointing the receiver, the debtor (its representative in case of a non-individual debtor) shall be deemed as the receiver pursuant to this part.

In case of appointing the receiver, the court shall interrogate the debtor or its representative unless it is an urgent situation.

A legal person may become the receiver. In such case, the legal person shall nominate, out of its directors, a person to perform the duties of the receiver and make reports to the court.

23 Supreme Court Rule Article 51 (Debtor for whom a receiver may not be appointed) "other person set in the Supreme Court Regulations" of Article 74, Para. 3 refers to one of the following persons.

1. A non-profit organization or *habmyunghoesa, habjahoesa.*
2. A debtor who belongs to a listed company set in Article 2, Para. 13 of the Securities Exchange Act or a KOSDAQ listed company set in Para. 15 of the same article at the time of the commencement of the rehabilitation proceeding.
3. A debtor who has applied for the rehabilitation proceeding due to a temporary liquidity problem and is not under severe financial trouble at the commencement of the rehabilitation proceeding.
4. A debtor who is deemed to have the possibility of early rehabilitation through the rehabilitation proceeding based on technical skills, marketing ability, and market shares of a certain level acquired by the debtor at the time of commencement.
5. A debtor who has reached an agreement between major creditors and secured rehabilitation creditors at the time of the commencement of the proceeding on the main contents of the rehabilitation plan.
6. A debtor who at the time of commencement has acquired a plan for rehabilitation through the investment of a third party or former shareholders.
7. A debtor for whom the court deems that the absence of a receiver is necessary or helpful for the rehabilitation of the debtor.

24 Seoul District Court decision of 23 November 2001, case number 99GAHAP52591.
25 Supreme Court decision of 28 February 2003, case number 2000DA50275.
26 An earlier version of the bill had been introduced to the National Assembly in 2003. It lapsed on the dissolution of the National Assembly for a new election.
27 *Dambo* is a Korean term literally meaning security.
28 The public agency responsible for depositing securities.
29 The primary draftsman was Professor Soogeun Oh, Ewha Woman's University, Korea.
30 Article 120 (Special Provisions for Payment and Settlement System)

In the case where a rehabilitation procedure is commenced in respect to a participant in the payment and settlement system, which is designated for the finality of payment and settlement by the Governor of the Bank of Korea in consultation with the Minister of Finance and Economy (hereinafter "payment and settlement system" in this paragraph), transfer order or payment including payment-related performance, netting, deduction, provision or disposition or reimbursement of security like deposit money, and other payments are subject to what the manager of the payment and settlement system has stipulated, in spite of provisions of this Act, and are not subject to rescission, termination, revocation, and avoidance. Details regarding the designation of payment and settlement system shall be stipulated by the Presidential Decree.

In the case where the rehabilitation procedure is commenced in respect to a participant in the clearance and settlement system, operated by the entity who performs the business of clearance and settlement in the transaction of securities and financial derivatives, pursuant to the Securities Exchange Act, Forward Transaction Act, and other statutes, or others stipulated by the Presidential Decree, assumption of obligation, netting, deduction, provision or disposition, or reimbursement of security like deposit money, and other clearance and payment are subject to what the manager of the clearance and settlement system has stipulated in spite of provisions of this Act, and are not subject to rescission, termination, revocation, and avoidance.

In the case where the rehabilitation procedure is commenced in respect to a party dealing with any transaction of following subparagraphs (hereinafter "qualified financial transaction" in this paragraph), based on a contract that stipulates the basic matters about the specific financial transactions (hereinafter "master contract" in this paragraph), conclusion and netting of qualified financial transaction are subject to what parties agree in a basic contract in spite of provisions of this Act, and are not subject to rescission, termination, revocation, and avoidance, and the transaction of Subparagraph 4 is not subject to injunction order and comprehensive prohibition order. However, it shall not apply in cases where a debtor made a qualified financial transaction in conspiracy with a counterparty to do harm to rehabilitation creditors or secured rehabilitation creditors.

1. Derivative financial transaction stipulated by the Presidential Decree including forward, option and swap whose objects are the price of currency, securities, investment share, general goods, credit risk, energy, weather, fare, broadcasting frequency, environment or others, or interest rates, or numerical index or other indicator based on them.
2. Transaction of kinds, repo transaction of securities, borrowing and lending of securities, and transaction of *dambo call*.
3. Mixed transaction of Subparagraphs 1 and 2.

Provision, disposition and reimbursement of security accompanied to the transaction of Paragraphs 1–3.

31 Carruthers and Halliday, *supra*, 2006.
32 OECD (ed.), *Maximizing Value of Non-Performing Assets*, Paris: OECD, 2004; OECD (ed.), *Lawmaking and Institution-Building in Asian Insolvency Reforms: Between Global Norms and National Circumstances*, Paris: OECD, 2006.
33 Carruthers and Halliday, *supra*, 1998.
34 By "legal complex," we refer to all legally trained occupations that are actively engaged in some form of legal work on an everyday basis. Although the concept was originally coined to treat the politics of lawyers, judges, and others in mobilization for political liberalism (Terence C. Halliday, Lucien Karpik, and Malcolm M. Feeley, eds, *Fighting for Political Freedom: Comparative Studies of the Legal Complex for Political Change*, Oxford: Hart Publishing, 2007), its logic can be extended to the politics of commercial lawmaking and implementation. It has the promise of problematizing

much in the politics of professions that is taken for granted in conventional research on commercial law reforms.

35 Terence C. Halliday and Bruce Carruthers, 'Epistemological Conflicts and Institutional Impediments: The Rocky Road to Corporate Bankruptcy Reforms in Korea', in Thomas Ginsburg, ed., *Korean Law Reform*, London: Routledge Press, 2004a.

36 Booz-Allen and Hamilton, 'Revitalizing the Korean Economy towards the 21st Century', Seoul, Korea, 1997.

37 Terence C. Halliday and Bruce G. Carruthers, 'The Recursivity of Law: Global Normmaking and National Lawmaking in the Globalization of Bankruptcy Regimes', *American Journal of Sociology* 111, 2007b, pp. 1135–1202; Terence C. Halliday and Soogeun Oh, 'A Recursive Theory of National Lawmaking: Site-Switching in Korean Corporate Insolvency Reforms, 1992–2007', American Bar Foundation Working Paper, Chicago: American Bar Foundation, 2006.

38 This was loosely based on a practice in some other countries, most notably the London Approach in Britain, and "pre-packs" in US bankruptcy practice.

39 Soogeun Oh, 'Expansion of the "Rule of Law" in the Market: The Korean Experience after the Economic Crisis in late 1990s', in *Government Policies and Corporate Strategies*, Beijing, China: Korea Development Institute/Development Research Corporation, 2007.

40 Alice Amsden, *Asia's Next Giant: South Korea and Late Industrialization*, Oxford: Oxford University Press, 1989; David Chamberlin Cole and Yung Chul Park, *Financial Development in Korea, 1945–1978*, Cambridge, MA: Council on East Asian Studies, Harvard University, 1983; Karl J. Fields, *Enterprise and the State in Korea and Taiwan*, Ithaca: Cornell University Press, 1995.

41 Booz-Allen and Hamilton, *supra*, 1997.

42 Terence C. Halliday, 'Architects of the State: International Organizations and the Reconstruction of States in the Global South', Joint Socio-Legal Conference, Berlin, 2007.

43 For example, stock splits (§329–2), suggestions of agendas by a shareholder (§363–2), cumulative voting (§382–2), liability of a shadow director (§401–2), interim distribution of dividend (§462–63) in 1998; stock options (§340–42), committees of boards of directors (§393–2), audit committee (§415–2) in 1999; amortization of stock by the resolution of shareholders' general meeting (§343–2), comprehensive stock exchange (§360–62), comprehensive stock transfer (§360–15) in 2001.

44 cf. Freidman, *supra*, 2000.

45 Yves Dezalay and Bryant G. Garth, *The Internationalization of Palace Wars: Lawyers, Economists, and the Contest to Transform Latin American States*, Chicago: University of Chicago Press, 2002.

46 In fact, Korean judges actually perceived that IFIs were aligned with MOFE and its interests in maintaining substantial control over court restructuring. It is ironic that this failure to recognize IFIs' general ideology of development would be to their institutional benefit.

Bibliography

Amsden, Alice, *Asia's Next Giant: South Korea and Late Industrialization*, Oxford: Oxford University Press, 1989.

Berkowitz, Daniel, Pistor, Katharina, and Richard, Jean-Francois, 'Economic Development, Legality, and the Transplant Effect', *European Economic Review* 47, 2003, pp. 165–95.

Booz-Allen and Hamilton, 'Revitalizing the Korean Economy towards the 21st Century', Seoul, Korea, 1997.

Braithwaite, John and Drahos, Peter, *Global Business Regulation*, Cambridge: Cambridge University Press, 2000.

Carruthers, Bruce G. and Halliday, Terence C., *Rescuing Business: The Making of Corporate Bankruptcy Law in England and the United States*, Oxford: Oxford University Press, 1998.

——'Negotiating Globalization: Global Templates and the Construction of Insolvency Regimes in East Asia', *Law & Social Inquiry* 31, 2006, pp. 521–84.

Cole, David Chamberlin and Park, Yung Chul, *Financial Development in Korea, 1945–1978*, Cambridge, MA: Council on East Asian Studies Harvard University, 1983, distributed by Harvard University Press.

Dezalay, Yves and Garth, Bryant G., *The Internationalization of Palace Wars: Lawyers, Economists, and the Contest to Transform Latin American States*, Chicago: University of Chicago Press, 2002.

Fields, Karl J., *Enterprise and the State in Korea and Taiwan*, Ithaca: Cornell University Press, 1995.

Friedman, Thomas L., *The Lexus and the Olive Tree: Understanding Globalization*, New York: Anchor Books, 2000.

Halliday, Terence C., 'Architects of the State: International Organizations and the Reconstruction of States in the Global South', in *Joint Socio-Legal Conference*, Berlin, 2007.

Halliday, Terence C. and Carruthers, Bruce, 'Epistemological Conflicts and Institutional Impediments: The Rocky Road to Corporate Bankruptcy Reforms In Korea', in Thomas Ginsburg, ed., *Korean Law Reform*, Routledge Press, 2004a.

——'Institutional Lessons from Insolvency Reforms in East Asia', in *Forum on Asian Insolvency Law Reform (FAIR), Insolvency and Risk Management in Asia*, Delhi, India: World Bank and Asian Development Bank, 2004b.

——'The Recursivity of Law: Global Normmaking and National Lawmaking in the Globalization of Bankruptcy Regimes', *American Journal of Sociology* 111, 2007, pp. 1135–1202.

——*Law's Global Markets: The Recursivity of Law in the Creation of Global Norms and East Asian Insolvency Regimes,* Palo Alto: Stanford University Press, 2009.

Halliday, Terence C. and Oh, Soogeun, 'A Recursive Theory of National Lawmaking: Site-Switching in Korean Corporate Insolvency Reforms, 1992–2007', in *American Bar Foundation Working Paper*, Chicago: American Bar Foundation, 2006.

Halliday, Terence C. and Osinsky, Pavel, 'Globalization of Law', *Annual Review of Sociology* 32, 2006, pp. 447–70.

Halliday, Terence C., Karpik, Lucien, and Feeley, Malcolm M., eds, *Fighting for Political Freedom: Comparative Studies of the Legal Complex for Political Change*, Oxford: Hart Publishing, 2007.

Held, David, McGraw, Anthony, Goldblatt, David, and Perraton, Jonathan, *Global Transformations: Politics, Economics and Culture*, Stanford: Stanford University Press, 1999.

OECD (ed.), *Maximising Value of Non-Performing Assets*, Paris: OECD, 2004.

——(ed.), *Lawmaking and Institution-Building in Asian Insolvency Reforms: Between Global Norms and National Circumstances*, Paris: OECD, 2006.

Oh, Soogeun, *An Institutional Perspective on Financial Reform in Korea*, Seoul: Korea Development Bank Report, 1999.

——'Bankruptcy Division and Commissioner', in *Insolvency Reform in Asia: An Assessment of the Recent Developments and the Role of the Judiciary*, Bali, Indonesia, 2001.

—— 'Drafting of New Insolvency Law of Korea', in *FAIR Conference*, Bangkok, Thailand, 2002a.

—— 'Government Intervention in Corporate Exit Mechanisms: The Corporate Restructuring Promotion Act of Korea', in *Hong Kong University Faculty of Law*, Hong Kong, 2002b.

—— 'Drafting of New Insolvency Law of Korea', in *World Bank Forum on Insolvency Risk Management*, Washington, DC, 2003a.

—— 'Insolvency Law Reform of Korea: A Continuing Learning Process', in *Forum on Insolvency Risk Management*, Washington, DC, 2003b.

—— 'Setting Insolvency Rules: A Course of Understanding and Persuasion', in *OECD FAIR III*, Seoul, Korea, 2003c.

—— 'Changes in Insolvency Practice, Restructuring of Ailing Firms and Risk Management after the Economic Crisis: The Korea Case', in *International Workshop on Reform of Corporate Governance: Corporate Rehabilitations in East Asia and its Lesson for China*, Beijing, China, 2005.

—— 'Expansion of the "Rule of Law" in the Market: The Korean Experience after the Economic Crisis in late 1990s', in *Government Policies and Corporate Strategies*, Beijing, China: Korea Development Institute/Development Research Corporation, 2007.

Oh, Y.S. and Lee, Keun Byung, 'Korean Insolvency Laws Protect Foreign Investors', *International Financial Law Review* 17, 1998, pp. 30–33.

Streeck, Wolfgang and Thelen, Kathleen, 'Introduction: Institutional Change in Advanced Political Economies', in Wolfgang Streeck and Kathleen Thelen, eds, *Beyond Continuity: Institutional Change in Advanced Political Economies*, New York: Cambridge University Press, 2005.

Thelen, Kathleen, 'Historical Institutionalism in Comparative Politics', *Annual Review of Political Science* 2, 1999, pp. 369–404.

United Nations Commission on International Trade Law (UNCITRAL), *UNCITRAL Model Law on Cross-Border Insolvency with Guide to Enactment*, New York: United Nations, 1999.

Woodruff, David, 'Rules for Followers: Institutional Theory and the New Politics of Economic Backwardness in Russia', *Politics and Society* 28, 2000, pp. 437–82.

12 The people's prosperity?

Indonesian constitutional interpretation, economic reform, and globalization

Simon Butt and Tim Lindsey[1]

On 21 May 1998, Soeharto, President of Indonesia for thirty-two years, stepped aside (*lengser*) amidst economic and monetary crisis (*krismon*) and social and political unrest. The economic calamity—a flow-on from the collapse of the Thai baht in July 1997 that caused many foreign investors to re-evaluate their portfolios in Indonesia[2]—unraveled much of the economic development achieved during Soeharto's time in power, with Indonesia losing 13.5 percent of its gross domestic product (GDP) in 1997 alone, and its currency plummeting from Rp2,000 per US dollar to almost Rp20,000 by February 1998.

Crippled by the economic collapse, Soeharto's government sought foreign financial assistance primarily from the International Monetary Fund (IMF). As a condition for the injection of more than US$10 billion from the IMF,[3] the Indonesian government was required to commit to "far-reaching" reforms, the content of which was effectively dictated by the IMF, leading a group of other multilateral financial institutions.[4]

These so-called "conditionalities" required Indonesia to change aspects of its institutional and economic structures. In order to satisfy the IMF that it was responding to these concerns, the Indonesian government periodically issued letters of intent, explaining its progress towards economic and legal reforms. A reading of these letters (which were largely drafted under IMF auspices) indicates the extent to which the IMF was concerned that Indonesia move quickly towards privatization of many state-owned enterprises. This was because of their inefficiency, their exploitation "for the benefit of individuals and special interest groups" and, given their size in the economy, the "major drag" they were seen as imposing on Indonesia's overall economic performance.[5]

The Indonesian government's main response to IMF pressure was to commit to the privatization of a range of key state enterprises.[6] For some enterprises, however, restructuring and increase in efficiency, rather than privatization, was the preferred reform. One focus was the electricity sector, run primarily by the State Electricity Company (Perusahaan Listrik Negara or PLN). The Indonesian government pledged to "improve its performance"—particularly to "restore commercial viability, improve efficiency, and attract private investment."[7] In one letter of intent, the government pledged to enact a new Electricity Law, largely to establish a legal and regulatory framework for competition in the electricity market.[8]

Meeting these conditions has, however, never been straightforward. This chapter will show, for example, that compliance has been hampered—although not entirely thwarted—by some very significant legal and institutional reforms, most particularly those relating to Indonesia's recent radical democratic constitutional amendments.

Soeharto's resignation ushered in the so-called "Era of Reformasi" and, within a year, Indonesia had begun amending its previously "sacred" (*sakti*) Constitution of 1945. This process was repeated three more times annually, until on 10 August 2002, the Majelis Permusyawaratan Rakyat (MPR) or People's Consultative Assembly (Indonesia's highest representative assembly) completed the last of four major constitutional amendments.

These constitutional reforms have been discussed in detail elsewhere,[9] so we will not rehearse them here. However, two aspects of the constitutional reform process have affected the government's ability to "liberalize" the Indonesian economy. These are, first, the establishment of Indonesia's new Constitutional Court and, second, the retention of Article 33 of the Constitution, which provides for significant government intervention in the economy and has, from 1997, been a rallying point for opposition to the policies pushed by multilateral lenders and donors, as mentioned above.

This chapter focuses upon the Constitutional Court's interpretation of Article 33. We begin by setting out Article 33 and aspects of the 2001 MPR debates, which resulted in the retention of the provision without amendment. We then turn briefly to Indonesia's new Constitutional Court and its jurisdiction. The power of superior courts to review statutes is commonly referred to throughout the world as "judicial review,"[10] and the Constitutional Court has exercised its new powers of review with regularity and enthusiasm—the first Court to have done so in Indonesia since at least the late 1950s.[11] Key aspects of government reform to the electricity and water sectors through the 2002 Electricity Law and the 2004 Water Resources Law are briefly outlined. We then discuss the Court's treatment of Article 33, particularly its decisions reviewing these two statutes.

We show that, through its interpretation of Article 33, the Constitutional Court has attempted to thwart government efforts in providing greater scope for the private sector to participate in the exploitation of the branches of production and natural resources referred to in Article 33. Many aspects of its decisions—particularly in the *Electricity Law Case* of 2002—reflect or adopt arguments raised by MPR members who favored the retention of Article 33 during the 2001 constitutional amendment debates. If these government attempts reflect a desire to incorporate global trends by adopting features of a more liberal, free market economy, then it can probably be said that, consciously or unconsciously, the Court—along with some politicians, economic and legal commentators, and community groups—is "pushing back" against globalization or, at any rate, against the perceived global hegemony of free market economics.

These cases thus reflect the fact that attempts to transplant aspects of the liberal economic and legal systems into some developing countries have often proved problematic. We show, however, that the Indonesian government has found ways of circumventing the decisions, thereby countering judicial resistance and neutralizing the pushback, to some extent at least.

These cases also illustrate multidimensional tensions and conflicts. On a domestic political level, they bring out debates over the role of the state in the economy that have been controversial since well before Indonesia's independence in 1945. On a legal–institutional level, the cases underscore the tensions that exist in all political systems between the judiciary, on the one hand, and the executive and legislative arms of government on the other. These are tensions that are particularly significant in countries in which judiciaries have been granted new or enhanced powers of judicial review, and in countries still emerging from authoritarian rule. Because both these categories apply to Indonesia, the tensions will likely continue into the immediate future as Indonesia uses constitutional litigation to explore the complexities of implementing its new *Trias Politika* ("political triad" or separation of powers) arrangements.

The authors of this chapter, both lawyers, have deliberately tried to avoid engaging in debate about economic policy, such as the desirability or otherwise of privatization. We have also refrained from speculating upon the possible social, economic, or other consequences of the Constitutional Court (*Mahkamah Konstitusi* or MK) decisions. These are both important questions but are beyond the scope of this chapter.

Article 33: the people's economy

Article 33 of the Constitution reads:

1. The economy shall be structured as a common endeavor based upon the family principle.
2. Branches of production which are important to the state, and which affect the public's necessities of life, are to be controlled by the state.
3. The earth and water and the natural resources contained within them are to be controlled by the state and used for the greatest possible prosperity of the people.

Article 33 was originally inspired by a broad mix of Leftist, nationalist, and anti-colonial ideals that were influential at the time the Constitution was first drafted in 1945.[12] It did, however, survive the shift of the Indonesian state from the left under Soekarno to the right under Soeharto. And, as mentioned, Article 33 also lived through the major overhaul of the Constitution that took place after Soeharto's fall. In 2001, the MPR retained the "People's Economy" as the constitutional basis for Indonesia's economy; Paragraphs (1)–(3) of Article 33 escaped the deliberations untouched.[13] However, the retention of Article 33 did not proceed without significant debate, opposition, and fervor in the MPR.

Among MPR members, and the senior government officials, "experts," and commentators called in for the debates, three views prevailed on the meaning of Article 33.[14] The first group might be described as neoliberal, although its members would almost certainly not describe themselves as such.[15] This group, made up largely of non-parliamentarian experts and commentators, tended to support the types of economic liberalization policies pushed by the IMF. Some argued that Indonesia's 1997 economic collapse was, in part, the result of excessive government control over economic resources under Article 33.[16] Others argued that free market capitalism had become "mainstream" in the world economy, leaving Indonesia no choice but to adopt it in order to participate more substantially in global trade.[17] Others pointed to Indonesia's World Trade Organization (WTO) membership and the IMF conditionalities, which required Indonesia to—"like it or not" (*mau tidak mau*)—"open itself up and liberalize," and to become competitive in global markets.[18] These ideas were manifested in proposals to amend Article 33 to limit state intervention, such as by dropping Article 33(2) altogether,[19] which would presumably have allowed branches of production to be sold off to, or managed by, the private sector.

A second group pushed for a middle ground between liberalism and socialism—a social market system (*ekonomi pasar sosial*).[20] According to Susanti,[21] most members proposing this model sought an essentially socialist economy but with enough free market to enable participation in global markets. Most proponents of this view, however, failed to describe its features in any detail. For example, one Golkar member who appeared to support this system stated:

> … it is ok to go to the left, ok to go to the right, but not ok to go too far either way … [22]

Most MPR members, however, took a third view, favoring state protectionism and, hence, the retention of Article 33.[23] Proponents detested the free market as unjust, "very evil" (*sangatlah jahat*), or otherwise being unable to guarantee prosperity for ordinary Indonesians.[24] As one commentator stated during the debates:

> If someone says that competition is good, I say that competition is good if we win. If competition is the way that we are re-colonized, then competition is bad.[25]

An economic system with high levels of state involvement was preferable, they contended, largely because it was the system most likely to ensure the "prosperity of the people" (*kemakmuran rakyat*). This system was referred to variously by members as the family principle (*asas kekeluargaan*), collective endeavor based on the family principle (*usaha bersama berdasar atas kekeluargaan*), or the principle of the "people's economy" (*ekonomi keraykatan*), commonly translated as "Indonesian Socialism."[26]

What form should state intervention take? MPR members highlighted two main activities. First, the state should ensure that all Indonesians have the opportunity to participate in the economy and to share in its spoils,[27] including those arising out of the exploitation of natural resources,[28] with priority for cooperatives and small–medium enterprises over individual endeavors.[29]

Second, the state should protect the weak from domination by the economically strong, whether domestic or foreign.[30] According to one member, this did not require the absence of competition, but did require protection from excessive competition:

> In an *asas kekeluargaan* house, we have [several] children. We want all of them to advance; they must compete with each other to advance. But they cannot kill each other. The disabled and disadvantaged must be looked after. If the father allows the strong to win, the strong will eat more ... The weak will die because they cannot take back their food.[31]

Many of those in the third category justified their rejection of the free market system by emphasizing that the *asas kekeluargaan* system had been developed by Indonesia's "founding fathers" in 1945, including Indonesia's first Vice President, Mohammad Hatta. Members also appealed to Indonesia's national ideology— Pancasila—devised by Indonesia's first President, Soekarno.[32] The principles of Pancasila are contained in the Constitution's Preamble, and one of them is the principle of social justice.[33] Advocates also pointed to another part of the Preamble, which states that one of the purposes of independence was to create public welfare.[34] Presumably, these members thought that the free market could not appropriately guarantee this welfare.

Disappointment with the state's economic performance since Indonesia's independence was constantly raised during the debates, and prompted some members to question, rather rhetorically, whether *asas kekeluargaan* or *ekonomi keraykatan* were to blame. Most concluded that the misinterpretation of the principles, rather than the principles themselves, had caused these economic problems.[35]

The Constitutional Court

Constitutional amendments made in 2000 and 2001 required that Indonesia's first Constitutional Court (*Mahkamah Konstitusi* or MK) be established by 17 August 2003. Article 24C[36] of the amended Constitution provides for the jurisdiction of the new court, granting it the power to make first and final—and binding—decisions in the review of statutes (*undang-undang*) against the Constitution, to determine disputes concerning the authority of the state organs whose power is derived from the Constitution, to dissolve political parties, and to determine disputes on the results of a general election.[37] It also has the power to make decisions concerning the opinion of the People's Representative Council (*Dewan Perwakilan Rakyat* or DPR) regarding alleged violations of the Constitution by the President and/or Vice President—in other words, the power to have the final say in any impeachment proceedings.[38]

The MK has thus far reviewed the constitutionality of many statutes, that is has determined whether the legislation enacted by the DPR is consistent with the principles contained in the Constitution. The MK cannot, however, review other types of laws below the level of statute (*undang-undang*) such as government, ministerial and presidential regulations (*Peraturan*). These types of lesser laws fall firmly and exclusively within the review jurisdiction of the Mahkamah Agung (Supreme Court): Article 24A(1) of the Constitution. As will be seen below, this division of the review jurisdiction between the Constitutional and Supreme Courts is highly problematic, largely because the Supreme Court has not exercised its review jurisdiction regularly or vigorously and the issue of regulations rather than statutes has thus come to be seen by government as one way to avoid the MK's intervention in its legislative program.

The new MK has so far made important, if often controversial, contributions to the implementation of the amendments to the Constitution that brought it into being. It appears to be emerging as a professional and determined—even energetic—guardian of the new Constitution.[39] This has sometimes brought the new court into tension—and even, as this chapter will show, conflict—with the executive branch.

The MK's Article 33 decisions[40]

In its first three years of operation, the MK heard four cases in which applicants objected to government attempts to dilute its involvement in key economic sectors,[41] largely in an effort to encourage investment in infrastructure, arguing that this was contrary to Article 33 of the Constitution.

In the *Oil and Natural Gas (Migas) Law case*,[42] applicants sought a review of Law No. 22 of 2001 on oil and natural gas. In its decision, the MK made slight alterations to the law to bring it into line with the requirements of Article 33 of the Constitution.[43] In the *Forestry Law case*,[44] a group of many applicants[45] unsuccessfully disputed the constitutionality of Law No. 19 of 2004 on the Stipulation of Interim Law No. 1 of 2004 on Amendments to Law No. 41 of 1999 on forestry as a statute.[46] In the *Water Resources (SDA) Law case*,[47] almost 3,000 individuals and several non-governmental organizations (NGOs) requested the MK to review Law No. 7 of 2004 on water resources. A majority of the MK upheld the constitutionality of the Law, largely because the MK believed that the state retained control over the sector.[48] In the *Electricity Law case*,[49] three applicants requested the MK to review the constitutional validity of Law No. 20 of 2002 on electricity. The Court's decision will be discussed below.

These four Article 33 decisions raise questions that are now obviously of critical importance for economic policy in Indonesia. Many of these questions arise because the meanings of key terms used in Article 33 are not self-evident (not least because of the somewhat obscure and grandiloquent style in which the original document was drafted). They also arise because these terms have never been subject to definitive or binding legal interpretation, by reason of the absence until 2003 of any power of judicial review. Since then, however, both policymakers and the MK have been forced to confront a series of related and complex legal questions. What does "controlled by the state" mean? How much scope is there for private sector involvement in these sectors? Is the state's obligation with respect to important branches of production essentially the same as its obligation with respect to natural resources? How is an "important sector" to be defined? What is the meaning of "common endeavor"? What is "social justice"? Does Article 33 require the MK to assess government policy? In this chapter, we reveal the MK's answers to these questions through an examination of the reasoning relied on by MK judges.

Before doing so, however, it is important to note that decisions of the MK are, in general, more lengthy, discursive, and argumentative than decisions of other Indonesian courts. The case files reveal a multitude of arguments and issues too numerous for us to cover here. For reasons of space, we therefore focus our discussion on the *Electricity Law*—the first case ever heard by the MK—and, to a lesser extent, the *SDA case*. We refer only briefly to aspects of the *Migas* case.

Background to the electricity and water resources cases

As mentioned, the enactment of the Electricity Law appeared as an IMF conditionality term in a letter of intent sent by the Indonesian government to the IMF. Both the Electricity[50] and the SDA[51] Laws spawned significant controversy in the media and debate in the DPR, mainly because they sought to privatize elements of the sectors with which they respectively dealt.[52] They also sparked fears that prices would rise as a consequence of the relinquishment of state control.[53]

For example, turning to the *SDA case*, the SDA Law, which replaces Law No. 11 of 1974 on irrigation, allows the private sector to "play a role" in (*berperan*), and imposes a fee for, the provision and management of some types of water resources, such as drinking water and water for irrigation, the providers of which impose a fee themselves.[54] This is reflected in the Law's Introductory Considerations:

> ... in line with the spirit of democracy, decentralization and openness in the community, nation, and state, the community must be provided a role in the management of water resources (Part d).

This "community" role would, it appears, include private sector participation in the management of water resources. The applicants in the *SDA case* objected to several provisions of the SDA Law that allowed for this participation. One such provision was Article 45(3), which states:

> [t]he exploitation of water resources ... can be performed by individuals, legal entities, or in cooperation with legal entities.

The applicants noted that:

> [t]here is concern that [privatization] will lead to a relinquishment of state responsibility for fulfilling the people's right to water. In other words, the state's responsibility will be put on to individuals or private entities, both national and foreign ... This means that profits will become the main purpose of those entities, not the fulfillment of basic rights.[55]

The view that profits and rights are inherently at odds is often expressed in political discourse in Indonesia (although rarely reflected in formal policy). In this vein, Article 45(3), the applicants continued, contradicted "the soul and spirit" of the Constitution, as contained in its Preamble, which, as mentioned, sets out the state ideology, the Pancasila, and its call for "the realization of social justice for the Indonesian people."[56]

A further, widely stated objection to the SDA Law has been that the Law introduces a new "right to exploit" water resources (*hak guna usaha*). According to some commentators, this makes water a commodity when, in fact, it is a basic right that should be accessible to all.[57]

As for the Electricity Law, *Hukumonline*, Indonesia's leading legal information and commentary website, has described its effect as changing the sectoral policy from monopoly to competition.[58] Prior to the Law's enactment in 2002, the state electricity company (PLN, *Perusahaan Listrik Negara*) was, in essence, the sole distributor, transmitter, and seller of electricity.[59] The Law, however, provided much greater scope for private sector involvement in the sector. Using the vague and rhetorical style that is common in Indonesian legislative drafting, the Introductory Considerations of the Electricity Law state that:

> [e]lectricity must be provided efficiently through competition and transparency in a climate of healthy industry, through regulations that treat all business entities equally and provide a just and even benefit to consumers (Part b).
>
> In the framework of fulfilling national need for electricity and the creation of healthy competition, equal opportunity to participate in the electricity industry must be given to all business enterprises (Part c).

Consistent with this theme, the Law prohibited government monopolies in designated "competition areas," divided the "provision of electricity" into several activities, including generation, transmission, distribution, and sale, and allowed different entities to perform these activities.[60] Only in areas "not ready for competition" could the state retain its monopolies.

The applicants in the *Electricity Law case* used some of these criticisms of the Law as bases for constitutional argument before the MK. It is to these arguments that we now turn.

The Electricity Law case: *parties' arguments*

The applicants in the *Electricity Law case* contended that myriads of their constitutional rights had been damaged by the Electricity Law.[61] We will limit our discussion, however, to the arguments relating to Article 33.

The first applicant argued that the privatization of electricity—an important branch of production—contradicted Article 33 of the Constitution.[62] The second applicant argued that the Law's "unbundling" of the provision of electricity (that is dividing its provision into generation, transmission, distribution, sale, and the like, allowing different people or entities to perform these functions, and then allowing state companies to transmit and distribute electricity) undermined the state's control, as required under Article 33(2) of the Constitution. In this way, there would "no longer be protection for the majority of people who could not afford … electricity."[63] The third applicant argued that free competition would cause an electricity crisis in Indonesia, as was already occurring outside Java, criticized unbundling, and argued that leaving the market to determine prices was inconsistent with Article 33's emphasis on "the people's prosperity."[64]

In response, the government put forward several arguments. First, it emphasized that the Law was "desirable" because the government was having difficulties in meeting the demand for electricity by itself.[65] Private sector capital was, therefore, necessary to meet this demand. Second, the government contended that competition would help to make the provision of electricity more transparent and efficient, and it would assist in ensuring the "sufficient supply of electricity throughout Indonesia at an affordable price."[66]

Third, the government argued that it had decided to focus on regulating, rather than operating, the sector, because "Government's function is to Govern."[67] In this context, the government claimed that it would still "control" the sector: it would determine policy, regulate, and supervise the sector under the Law.[68] It could, therefore, ensure that those operating in the sector were providing equitable electricity distribution.

Fourth, the government acknowledged that "competition" in the electricity sector would not be successful through the whole of Indonesia. In anticipation of this, the government had allowed monopolies to remain in areas of Indonesia where competition would not ensure the adequate provision of electricity.[69] In these places, prices would be set only to recover costs.[70]

Fifth, the government noted that it would maintain complete control over some sectors of the electricity industry. The state would remain in control of distribution and transmission, and the private sector could be involved in only the sale and production of electricity.[71]

The Electricity Law case: *the Court's decision*

The Court's decision focused on the state's obligation to control important branches of production under Article 33(2) of the Constitution. It held that Articles 16, 17(3), and 68 of the Law, which sought to introduce competition and unbundling in the electricity sector, conflicted with Article 33(2) of the Constitution because they would, in fact, result in a relinquishing of control in the sense intended by that Article. It therefore declared them no longer legally binding.[72]

The Court, however, also found that competition and unbundling were at the "heart" of the Law. Quite extraordinarily, it therefore declared the entire statute invalid on the grounds that it was not in line with "the soul and spirit" of Article 33(2) of the Constitution, which, according to the Court, "forms the basis of the Indonesian economy."[73] The Court argued that it had no choice but to do this, because it believed that the invalidity of only a small part of the law would "cause chaos that would lead to legal uncertainty" in the Law's application.[74] The MK then reinstated the previous Electricity Law (Law No. 15 of 1985) on the logical basis that Article 70 of the 2002 Law—which declared the 1985 Law to be no longer in force—was, itself, no longer valid.

The most important aspect of the MK's decision was that merely regulating the electricity sector was insufficient to constitute control by the state as required by Article 33(2), although, of course, the term "regulate" is a broad one that can bear almost any form of interpretation. It is useful, however, to first dispose some of the Court's responses to some of the other arguments raised by the parties before returning to a more detailed discussion of this point.

The MK rejected most of the government's arguments in favor of privatization. First, the Court held that the increased transparency and reduced corruption that competition was presumed to bring was outweighed by the importance of the state fulfilling its (binding) obligations under Article 33.[75]

Second, the MK expressed doubts that privatization would necessarily improve capacity, quality, and price. The Court emphasized the testimony of an English expert,[76] who argued that restructuring of the electricity sector in Britain did not result in lower prices and greater efficiency. Instead, the Court said, many jobs were lost while investors enjoyed high returns. The expert also stated that Thailand, South Korea, Brazil, and Mexico had delayed or put off restructuring for these reasons.[77] The Court stated that the suggestion that the market would naturally provide available, evenly distributed, and affordable electricity was "far from realistic."[78]

In any event, the Court held that the government could improve the sector and attract private sector capital without privatization. According to the Court, PLN could seek financial assistance from, or work in partnership with, the domestic or foreign private sector. The Court also suggested that PLN delegate its functions to another state-owned enterprise or a regional state-owned enterprise with PLN as a holding company, although it did not explain what this might achieve.[79]

Third, the Court held that the state's obligation to ensure public prosperity would not necessarily be achieved by allowing competition, because the private sector would prioritize its own profits and would concentrate on established markets—primarily in Java, Madura, and Bali. The Court believed that cross-subsidies from these established markets would be required to support less competitive parts of Indonesia and that these subsidies could not be obtained from the private sector.[80] In this context, competition would "tend to undermine state enterprises and may not guarantee the supply of electricity to all parts of the community."[81]

It is worth noting here that many of the MK's arguments are similar to those made by the MPR members in 2001 in favor of the retention of Article 33, mentioned above. This issue is considered in the conclusion to this chapter.

Controlled by the state?

As indicated earlier, a crucial issue in all four Article 33 cases has been the Court's definition of the phrase "controlled by the state" contained in both Articles 33(2) and 33(3). Clearly, the Court saw Article 33 to be one of the Constitution's most fundamental provisions. In the *Electricity Law case*, for example, the Court even observed that state control over important areas of production "could be said to be the entire paradigm and legal ideal of the Constitution."[82]

In the *Electricity Law case*, the Court's discussion about the nature of obligations placed upon the government by this phrase was extensive, and was referred to in the *Migas* and *SDA Law* cases. The judges discussed whether "controlled by the state" in Article 33(2) required only that the government regulate important branches of production, or whether it imposed more onerous obligations upon the state, such as to own and operate the means of sale, supply, and distribution—even if this required prohibiting the private sector from operating in those areas. Further, was the state required to take control over sectors the private sector was already running, if those sectors became important enough to fall within Article 33(2)?[83]

The Court referred to expert testimony provided during hearings by Professor Dr. Harun Alrasid, a highly-regarded Indonesian constitutional law expert, who interpreted "controlled by the state" to mean "owned" by the state.[84] The Court also referred to the written submission of the State Enterprises Minister, who interpreted "controlled by the state" to mean "regulated, facilitated, and operated by the state," but "dynamically moving towards the state only regulating and facilitating."[85]

The Court took the view, however, that Article 33 required more than ownership over important branches of production in the civil law (*hukum perdata*) sense. Because state control exists within the Constitution's framework of "public law, political democracy, and economic democracy" (which it did not define), the Court stressed that the Indonesian people have ultimate power, and thus hold collective ownership over, those branches of production.[86] The Court argued that the civil concept of ownership was therefore insufficient because it did not, in itself, necessarily provide for the welfare of the people or social justice, as is required in the Constitution's Preamble.

> Viewing the Constitution as a system as intended, "controlled by the state" in Article 33 has a higher or broader meaning than civil law ownership. The concept of state control is a public law concept related to the principle of peoples' sovereignty adhered to in the Constitution, in both politics (political democracy) and economics (economic democracy). Within this concept of peoples' sovereignty, it is the people who are recognized as the source, owners, and also the holders of the highest authority in the state, in accordance with the doctrine "from the people, by the people, and for the people." This concept of highest authority encompasses public collective ownership by the people.
>
> If "controlled by the state" means only ownership in the civil sense, then the control will be insufficient to achieve the "greatest prosperity of the people," rendering the mandates to "advance public wellbeing" and "to create social justice for all Indonesian people" in the Elucidation to the Constitution impossible to achieve. Nevertheless ... civil ownership must be recognized as a logical consequence of state control, which also encompasses

collective public ownership by the people over the sources of those [natural] assets.[87]

Further, the Court refused to accept that "controlled by the state" could be interpreted merely as the government's right to regulate. According to the Court, the government would have inherent power to regulate, even if the phrase "controlled by the state" was not contained in Article 33.[88] "Controlled by the state," therefore, must have a broader meaning. The Court argued that, in light of the people's sovereignty over all natural resources and public ownership of those natural resources, the people, through the Constitution, had "provided a mandate to the state to make policy, organize, regulate, manage, and supervise to achieve maximum welfare for the people."[89]

The government exercises the state's administrative function by issuing and revoking permits (*vergunning*), licenses (*licentie*) and concessions (*consessie*). The DPR, using legislative power, and the government, through government regulation, exercises the regulatory function of the state (*regelendaad*). The management (*beheersdaad*) function is exercised through share ownership mechanisms and/or through direct involvement in the management of State-Owned Legal Entities, which, through the state, that is, the government, uses its control over those natural assets so that they are used for the greatest prosperity of the people. Similarly, the state, that is the government, exercises the state's monitoring function (*toezechthoudensdaad*) to ensure that the state's control over the sources of assets is truly exercised for the greatest prosperity of the people.[90]

Scope for private sector involvement?

The Court interpreted Article 33(2) to require state control over important existing branches of production—even if this requires prohibiting the private sector from operating in those areas or leads to the state taking over from the private sector areas that have become important.[91] Significantly, however, it did not prohibit all private sector involvement in the electricity industry. Rather, the Court held that the government could allow private sector involvement, provided that it did not extinguish its own control.[92] The Court also stated that the civil ownership included in the concept of control did not require 100 percent government ownership. Rather, the MK required only that the government own sufficient shares in the enterprise to enable the government to control decision- and policymaking.[93]

The Court also stated that the government could, from time to time, reassess the importance of these branches of production. If the government thought that a particular industry—such as electricity—was no longer of sufficient importance to the people, then policy, organization, regulation, management, and supervision could be left to the market.[94]

To support this stance, the Court engaged in historical interpretation, in which it reflected on the Elucidation to the Constitution as it stood before it was deleted during the amendment process. To do so was, of course, an act that severely strained the limits of the MK's authority, given that the whole purpose of deleting the Elucidation was precisely to prevent it being used to interpret the Constitution. Be that as it may, the MK emphasized that there should be economic democracy for the welfare of all and that the government should remain in control of important areas of production because, if production were to fall "into the hands of someone powerful, the community could be afflicted," a claim the court did not explain further.[95] The MK also referred to the interpretation of Article 33 proposed by "founding father" and Indonesia's first Vice President, Mohammad Hatta.[96] According to Hatta, the Indonesian government should control essential areas of production but, if it cannot meet demand, then it should seek foreign loans and, as a last resort, allow foreigners to invest in production.[97]

It is critical to note here that the Court has left it to the state to decide whether particular branches of production are important and therefore subject to state control. For example, in the *Electricity Law case*, the Court accepted that electricity was sufficiently important because the importance of electricity was emphasized in the Law itself.[98] This is significant, because it could potentially give latitude to a government to legislatively—and thus, in all likelihood, definitively—re-categorize a branch of production as no longer important, thus removing all legislation on that branch of production from the jurisdiction of the MK (at least so far as Article 33 is concerned).

Ignoring the difference between Articles 33(2) and 33(3)?

It appears that the Court ignored subtle but important differences between the text of Articles 33(2) and 33(3) in the *Electricity* and *SDA Law* cases, thus creating significant potential problems for rational regulation of energy and resources in the future.

Clearly, Articles 33(2) and 33(3) require state control over branches of production and natural resources, respectively, but they impose different obligations upon the state. Under Article 33(3), the government is required to use its control over natural resources "for the greatest public welfare." On its face, however, Article 33(2) does not require that important branches of production be managed to further public welfare. It merely requires that the state control them, leaving the purpose of doing so unstated.

It should be assumed that the differences between these two provisions were deliberate. It is, of course, possible that the drafters of the Constitution did intend the state to use both natural resources and branches of production to further public welfare, but simply neglected to convey this in the Constitution by mistake, or through a drafting error. Against this, however, it would seem obvious that, if the drafters had, in fact, intended no distinction between natural resources and branches of production, then they could quite easily have referred to both in one provision requiring the same level of state control to be maintained in the interests of public welfare. In any case, the provision has survived successive rounds of constitutional reforms in its original form, suggesting that its wording has received legislative reconsideration and has thus been implicitly reconfirmed.

Accordingly, the Court's failure to differentiate between these two provisions raises several questions. Has the Court simply overlooked the difference between them? Or has it presumed that the purpose of control of the supply of life's necessities (such as electricity) is no different from that of control of natural resources (such as oil and gas), and that, therefore, the Constitution's distinction between them is meaningless? This might be a logical stance, but the Court did not expressly justify or even adopt it.

Also, it is quite possible that the drafters envisaged that the level of state control required by Article 33(2) was different from that required by Article 33(3), given that the drafters appeared to attach more significance to natural resources than to branches of production. So, for example, was a stronger level of state control over natural resources required to ensure that they were used for the public benefit but, for important branches of production, was a lower level of state control (such as regulating and strictly monitoring the compliance of the private sector operators) justifiable, because the state was not required to exercise them for the greatest people's welfare? The Court did not discuss this issue at all.

Other evidence exists to suggest that the Court simply misunderstood the differences between these two provisions. Oil and natural gas are clearly natural resources and, therefore, it appears that Article 33(3)—not Article 33(2)—is relevant to them. In the *Migas Law case*, however, the Court appeared to distract itself with a discussion over whether oil and natural gas was an important branch of production. This was, quite clearly, irrelevant: Article 33 is explicit and unambiguous that all natural resources—whether they are important or affect the public's necessities of life, or not—must be controlled by the state. The following statement appears to indicate the Court's misunderstanding of this distinction.

> [I]f the Indonesian Government and DPR consider oil and natural gas—natural assets contained in the Indonesian earth within the meaning of Article 33(3) of the Constitution—to no longer be important to the state and/or to control the public's necessities of life, then it can hand over the regulation, administration, management, and supervision [of it] to the market. However, if the government and the DPR consider [it] to still be important for the state and/or to control the public's necessities of life, then the state, that is, the government, must control [it] by regulating, administering, managing, and supervising it so that it is truly used for the greatest prosperity of the people.[99]

This confusion goes to the heart of the Article 33 controversies and leaves policy-makers and legislators with little guidance for future attempts at regulation. The confusion may be compounded by the fact that all parties in the case appeared to make the same mistake, or shared the same interpretation, despite this contradicting the express words of the Constitution. According to the Court, the applicant, the government, the DPR, and experts all agreed that oil and natural gas was a branch of production important to the state, which controls the public's necessities of life.[100] This issue will probably remain unresolved unless the MK chooses to address it in a future case, leaving open the possibility that what seems to be an error may become doctrine through the passing of time.

The MK and government policy

In some of the cases it has decided thus far, the Court has gone to great lengths to emphasize that it lacks jurisdiction to assess government policy. The leading case on this issue is the Corruption Eradication Commission (*Komisi Pemberabtasan Korupsi* or *KPK*) *Law case*.[101] In it, the MK majority made the following statement.

> When performing material review, the MK must differentiate between [different types of] legislation … If the Constitution's provisions and spirit [require] a statute to contain *detail to achieve a particular aim*, but the statute takes a different or contrary direction, then the statute will go against the Constitution's provision and spirit. The MK then has jurisdiction to declare that statute to conflict with the Constitution and to declare that the statute has no binding legal force (emphasis in original).[102]

The Court went on to explain, however, that, if the Constitution establishes an end to be achieved by legislation, but not the means to achieve it, then the Court should not evaluate the means the legislature chooses to achieve that end, nor the effectiveness of those means.

> … [I]f the Constitution has underlined that the statute must contain the *means* to achieve a purpose, that is, it chooses an instrumental policy, lawmakers (the DPR and the President) can choose between a number of alternatives. Whichever alternative the lawmakers choose will be valid, provided that it remains within the *corridor* stipulated by the Constitution. The MK does not have jurisdiction to review the instrumental policy chosen by lawmakers.
> … In a democratic country in which the people are represented through elections, it is presumed that the people's will is represented by the people's representative institutions. Upon this premise, one can syllogistically … conclude that the people's aspirations are represented by elected people's representative institutions.
> Instrumental policy also relates to the *effectiveness* of a statute; that is, the extent to which the *means* chosen by lawmakers has successfully achieved the purposes mandated by the Constitution. The MK's jurisdiction does not extend to evaluating a statute's effectiveness. This does not mean that a statute's effectiveness cannot be reviewed [at all]. It can be reviewed at any time by lawmakers through *legislative review* (emphasis in original).[103]

The Court did not discuss the boundaries of its judicial review jurisdiction in the Article 33 cases. Nevertheless, it is arguable that Article 33(2) establishes an obligation on the government to enact laws that further people's welfare and, hence, a constitutional right that citizens and legal entities can seek to enforce. It is arguable, then, that, contrary to the MK's apparent concern to refrain from entering the domain of public policy, its own decisions have identified a constitutional obligation upon it to ensure that legislative policy in cases involving state control over natural resources furthers the people's welfare.

Indeed, some of the Court's arguments in the *Electricity Law case* set out above were, in essence, a critique of privatization. That is, the Court argued that privatization cannot guarantee the prosperity of the people, as required by Article 33(2). Determining whether government control is exercised to further people's welfare appears to verge on, or might, in fact, actually constitute, the MK intruding into the constitutional corridor within which the DPR can legitimately exercise discretion when legislating.

It is foreseeable that other policy choices might be subject to judicial review in future cases. For example, the Court might have cause to consider what constitutes an "important branch of production"—a concept not defined at all in the Constitution. In future legislation, the DPR might classify a branch of production as not being important purely in an attempt to privatize it without breaching Article 33. The MK may, therefore, need to establish objective criteria with which to identify important branches of production to prevent the apparently intended effect of Article 33(2) from being thwarted.

The extent to which the Court will continue to, or will increasingly, enter the policy debate is unclear, and should be clarified by the Court as it hears more Article 33 cases. Many questions remain, such as how the Court will assess whether public prosperity is in fact being achieved. For instance, how will the court view legislation that imposes a short-term financial burden but anticipated long-term economic benefits? Would the electricity price rises of 2005, if established by statute,[104] be reviewable by the Court on the basis that they could reduce the people's welfare? If so, would the Court have upheld the application because of the economic hardship the price rises caused for the poor, even if they freed up budgetary resources for the provision of other services? Or would the Court have rejected it on the basis that fuel subsidies were crippling the Indonesian economy and hence general welfare levels?

In the authors' view, the MK might now be well served by delineating more precisely the issues that it thinks it is competent to assess and those that should be left to the legislature. Like many other superior courts around the world that conduct judicial review, the MK faces the practical, political, and perennial question of the precise extent to which unelected judges, nine in this case, should be able to overrule the opinions of the majority of a democratically elected legislature, here comprising 550 members. Of course, the MK's constitutional mandate is to do precisely that—review (in certain circumstances) the constitutionality of statutes produced by the legislature—but that does not free the court from the political implications that inevitably arise from the exercise of that mandate. This is particularly true if the court remains unclear about the precise rationale for its decisions on key questions of national economic policy.

As mentioned at the outset, the effect of the MK's decision in the *Electricity Law case* has been to create potentially significant impediments to government's capacity to implement economic policies pushed by the IMF and other donors.

The implications of this decision for donors were, at time of writing, unclear, but they have probably been placated by the government's aggressive and, in our view, subversive regulatory response to the MK's decisions on privatization, which we now describe.

Statutory resurrection by government regulation and a pre-emptive strike?

In January 2005, around two months after the MK handed down its decision in the *Electricity Law case*, the government issued a regulation, the full title of which was "Government Regulation No. 3 of 2005, Amending Government Regulation No. 10 of 1989 on the Provision and Exploitation of Electricity." Part (a) of the Regulation's Considerations reveals its intent:

> ... in the framework of increasing the availability of electricity for the public interest, the roles of cooperatives, State Owned Enterprises, Regional State Owned Enterprises, the *private sector*, community groups, and *individuals* must be increased (our emphasis).

The government regulation was not framed as a formal and direct replacement of the Electricity Law struck down by the MK,[105] but it certainly appears to attempt to mitigate, even nullify, much of the effect of the MK decision. It has even been described as being "not much different"[106] from the Electricity Law the MK invalidated, and Hotma Timpul, a Jakarta lawyer, has said it was just a re-enactment of the Electricity Law "in new clothes."[107] Indeed, even a senior government official, J. Purnowo, the Electricity Management Administration Director, has admitted that the regulation was passed to provide certainty for private sector investors in the aftermath of the MK's decision.[108] More specifically, he hoped that the regulation would enable PLN to invite the private sector to compete for tenders.[109]

The main objections appear to center around Articles 6 and 11 of the regulation. Article 6 states that, provided that it does not damage the interests of the state, a permit can be provided to a cooperative or "another enterprise" to provide electricity in the public interest or in its own interest. Articles 6(2) and 6(3) provide that such "other enterprises" can include the private sector and individuals. Article 11 states that permit holders can buy and sell electricity. These provisions appear to directly contravene the MK's decision in the *Electricity Law case*, because they allow the state to evade its obligations under Article 33 by relinquishing its control over the provision of electricity to the private sector. It appears, therefore, that the government has successfully circumvented the decision.

The irony is that the MK can do nothing to remedy the apparent unconstitutionality of the electricity regulation because, as mentioned earlier, it cannot review lower level laws, such as government regulations. It can review only statutes (*undang-undang*), which regulations, as lower level laws, are (in principle at least) usually issued to implement. Only the Supreme Court (*Mahkamah Agung* or MA) has jurisdiction to review the consistency of lower level laws with statutes or the constitution, but this is a jurisdiction the MA has traditionally been extremely reluctant to exercise, with the result that such regulations are almost never struck down judicially.[110] It is therefore likely that the regulation will remain in force and applicable, a result that threatens to make a farce of the whole judicial review process.

The drinking water regulation

Similarly, after the MK had begun hearing the *SDA Law case*, but before its decision was handed down, Government Regulation No. 16 of 2005 on the Development of a Drinking Water Availability System was issued.[111] This regulation appears to achieve part of what the SDA Law aims to do—allow for private sector involvement in the provision of drinking water.

Article 37 of the regulation states that the government is responsible for ensuring that people have drinking water to fulfill their basic needs (Article 37(1)). State-owned enterprises or regional state-owned enterprises are to be formed to provide drinking water (Article 37(2)). If state-owned enterprises are, however, unable to increase the quantity and quality of drinking water, then it can involve others—including the private sector in the provision of the service (Article 37(3)).

Article 64(1) permits private entities to develop drinking water services in regions in which state-owned enterprises have not yet reached. Article 64(3) states that private sector involvement is to be conducted in accordance with the principles of healthy competition through a tender process. The tender process can encompass all, or some, of the stages in the development of drinking water (Article 64(4)). Some argue that the Article, if implemented, would absolve the state of its constitutional obligations[112] and, certainly, the provisions would appear to allow state-owned enterprises to simply withdraw from any activities they might be conducting in the area of drinking water, or to fail to expand their operations in order to allow the private sector to become involved.

The MK, however, did not, of course, invalidate the provisions of the SDA Law in its decision, and it is arguable whether the activities permitted under the regulation were permitted under the SDA Law in any event. Yet, given its timing, we speculate that the issuance of this regulation was an attempt at a pre-emptive strike by the government against the worst-case scenario decision that the MK might have handed down, building on the apparent success of the same strategy in the Electricity case. In other words, the government may have been concerned that, if the MK invalidated the statute, its opportunity to privatize aspects of the water resources sector would be lost, with serious implications for both policy and relations with major multilaterals and donors, and that this motivated it to create "regulatory insurance" to render the decision nugatory.

Conclusion: teething problems?

The MK Article 33/privatization cases show that the hoary Article 33 "people's economy" debate between state and market and between global economic orthodoxy and local political discourses is quite clearly still alive in post-Soeharto

Indonesia and, indeed, has even been revived by the MK. The debate continues now to have potentially enormous implications for both politics and the economy and, in particular, for the continuing process of transfer of state assets into the hands of private business, which forms so important a part of economic reform orthodoxy in post-Soeharto Indonesia and was a central feature of the post-1998 reform agenda sponsored by the IMF, the World Bank, and other donors.

The independence of the Court and the sincerity with which it approaches its constitutional tasks have been impressive so far.[113] But if the Court is too ambitious and its decisions are too far-reaching and unpalatable to the government, it runs the risk of being ignored by the government or having its decisions rendered meaningless—or even of having its powers curtailed through future legislation or constitutional amendment.

Further, the more directly the MK enters debates over legislative policy, the more likely it is to face stiff resistance—and even, as in the Electricity case, subversion—from government. Resistance or non-compliance has, in fact, already resulted, even though the MK has, in the decisions discussed in this chapter, appeared to give effect to the views of many MPR members on the continuing need for state intervention in the Indonesian economy. This resistance from DPR members and the government is somewhat incongruous, given that the majority of the MPR members who approved the retention of Article 33 and the establishment of the Constitutional Court were also members of the DPR which enacted the Electricity and Water Resources Laws. In reality, then, the Court has been forced to mediate the inconsistencies caused by the differing political and economic imperatives of the DPR and the MPR, which were, to a large extent, a result of the imposition of the IMF's conditionalities.

Resistance is all the more likely if, as we have shown, aspects of some of the Court's decisions and their implications are unclear or inconsistent, making compliance difficult. The same is true if the Court runs head on into major planks of economic policy, such as privatization, particularly when it does not seem to fully understand the complex economic issues involved or, at any rate, to be unable to unambiguously articulate a consistent and economically sophisticated rationale for its understanding. The Court had not, at the time of writing, had an opportunity to revisit its decisions in these cases. Although it did receive an application for review of the Migas Law again in 2007, the Court held that the applicants lack the standing required to bring the case and hence did not proceed to the merits of the case.[114]

It is not only the Court, however, that is having teething problems. The legislature and executive also appear to have trouble coming to terms with limitations being placed on them by being made answerable for legislation—for the first time in modern Indonesian history—to a bench comprising nine former academics and judges, from whom no appeal lies. The long "judicial winter" of the New Order, during which judicial review of statutes was expressly prohibited by law,[115] has left the democratic governments that follow with no experience of dealing with a judicial mechanism common in one form or another in most other democracies today. The government's responses to the *Electricity Law* and *SDA Law cases* appear to indicate that, in some matters, the government will simply not follow the MK's decisions, no matter what. This means that the MK will face political battles that it may lose. While that may, perhaps, not bode well for Indonesia's fledgling judicial review system, it is not unusual for effective courts of constitutional review to find themselves at odds with the legislature or executive.

The Article 33 cases have forced debate on the very basis of national economic policy and its relationship with global economic orthodoxy into the courts and thus into the public arena. That debate has now become entwined with continuing controversy regarding the relationship between the three main branches of government. The issues raised are therefore now not likely to be quickly or easily resolved by any of the institutions involved, but that is, again, not necessarily a bad thing. It is part of the reality of post-Soeharto reform as a process that will take decades, not years, to resolve, and which is evolving through political and institutional competition as the nature of the new Indonesian state is constantly contested, refined, tested, and revised. And that is, surely, hardly surprising for a young but vibrant democracy emerging from three decades of stifling and authoritarian rule.

Notes

1 This chapter draws in part on material in an earlier paper on these decisions that was published in Simon Butt and Tim Lindsey, 'Indonesia's Constitutional Court: Privatisation and Democratisation', *Bulletin of Indonesian Economic Studies*, Vol. 44, No. 2, 2008, pp. 239–262.

2 R. McLeod, 'Dealing with the Bank System Failure: Indonesia 1997–2003', *Bulletin of Indonesian Economic Studies* 40 (1), 2004, pp. 95–116, at p. 95.

3 See the IMF's website: http://www.imf.org.

4 T. Lindsey, 'The IMF and Insolvency Law Reform in Indonesia', *Bulletin of Indonesian Economic Studies* 34 (3), 1998, pp. 119–24, at p. 119.

5 *Letter of Intent*, 13 December 2001, point 29. Available from http://www.imf.org.

6 *Letter of Intent*, 7 September 2000, point 62; see also *Letter of Intent*, 20 January 2000, point 70. Available from http://www.imf.org.

7 *Letter of Intent*, 20 January 2000, point 77. Available from http://www.imf.org.

8 *Supplementary Memorandum of Economic and Financial Policies*, 16 March 1999, point 20. Available from http://www.imf.org.

9 For details of these amendments and the text of the Constitution before and after the amendments, see Tim Lindsey, 'Indonesian Constitutional Reform: Muddling Towards Democracy', *Singapore Journal of International & Comparative Law* 6 (1), 2002, pp. 244–301, on which this and the following paragraph draw.

10 Simon Butt, *Judicial Review in Indonesia: Between Civil Law and Accountability? A Study of Constitutional Court Decisions 2003–2005*, PhD thesis, Faculty of Law, Melbourne University, 2007. It should be noted that, confusingly, the term "judicial review" is often used in Indonesia as an English translation of *Peninjauan Kembali*, the final stage of appeal in the Supreme Court. *Peninjauan Kembali* or "PK" literally means "Reconsideration" and refers to a review on the papers of a cassation decision of the Supreme Court by a different panel of judges within the same court. The PK is the final level of "appeal" in the Supreme Court.

11 Asshiddiqie Jimly, 'Setahun Mahkamah Konstitusi: Refleksi Gagasan Dan Penyelenggaraan, Serta Setangkup Harapan' [One year of the Constitutional Court: Reflections on the Idea and its Implementation, and a Handful of [0][0]Hope]', in Refly Harun, Zainal A.M. Husein and Bisariyadi, eds, *Menjaga Denyut Konstitusi; Refleksi Satu*

290 Simon Butt and Tim Lindsey

Tahun Mahkamah Konstitusi [Guarding the Pulse of the Constitution: Reflections on One Year of the Constitutional Court], Jakarta: Konstitusi Press, 2004. See also Petra Stockmann, *The New Indonesian Constitutional Court: A Study into its Beginnings and First Years of Work*, Hanns Seidel Foundation, Jakarta, 2007.

12 See Phillipa Venning, *Determination of Economic, Social and Cultural Rights by the Indonesian Constitutional Court* (unpublished); Bivitri Susanti, *Neo-liberalism and Its Resistance in Indonesia's Constitution Reform 1999–2002*, Dissertation submitted for the Degree of Master of Law, University of Warwick, 2002, p. 4; Vedi R. Hadiz, 'The Failure of State Ideology in Indonesia: the Rise and Demise of *Pancasila*', in Beng Huat Chua, 2004, *Communitarian Politics in Asia*, London and New York: Routledge, p. 152; Mohamad Mova Al'Afghani, 'Constitutional Court's Review and the Future of Water Law in Indonesia', *Law Environment and Development Journal* 2, 2006, pp. 1 and 5; 'Ekonomi Indonesia di Masa Datang [Indonesia Economy in Future]', Pidato Wakil Presiden RI (Speech of the Vice President of RI], 3 February 1946 (copy on file with authors); and, generally, Sri-Edi Swasono et al., eds, *Mohammad Hatta: Demokrasi Kita, Bebas Aktif, Ekonomi Masa Depan* [Mohammad Hatta: Our Democracy, Non-aligned, Economy of the Future], Jakarta: UI-Press, 1992, pp. 5–8.

13 There was, however, some minor tinkering. The MPR added Articles 33(4) and 33(5):

4. The national economy is to be run on the basis of economic democracy, and the principles of togetherness, efficiency which is just, sustainability, environmentalism, and independence, maintaining a balance between advancement and national economic unity.
5. Further provisions to implement [Article 33] will be provided in legislation.

Further, the Elucidation to the Constitution—which included the Elucidation to Article 33 within it—was deleted. The Elucidation is the formal explanatory memorandum that accompanies most Indonesian regulations and is often read as if it were part of the regulation itself. The Elucidation to the 1945 Constitution has, however, always been controversial, as when the Constitution officially came into force on August 18, 1945, the Elucidation was not included. It was later promulgated in the *Government Gazette* in 1946. The full text of the Elucidation to Article 33 read as follows:

Article 33 embraces economic democracy under which production is carried out by all, and for all, under the leadership or supervision of members of the community. The main priority is the prosperity of the community, not the prosperity of individuals.

This is because the economy is structured as a collective endeavor based on the family principle. A business entity along these lines is a cooperative.

The economy is based on economic democracy, prosperity for all people!

Therefore, branches of production which are important for the state and which affect the lives of most people must be controlled by the state. If not, control of production might fall into the hands of individuals in power, who might exploit the people. Only businesses which are not important for the lives of many people may be left in private hands.

The land and water and natural resources in the earth are the fundamentals of community prosperity. For this reason, they must be controlled by the state and used for the greatest prosperity of the people.

See also Susanti's translation of the Elucidation to Article 33: B. Susanti, *Neo-liberalism and its Resistance in Indonesia's Constitutional Reform 1999–2002*, Dissertation submitted for the Degree of Master of Law, University of Warwick, 2002, p. 30.

14 These debates are available at http://www.mpr.go.id.

15 B. Susanti, *Neo-liberalism and its Resistance in Indonesia's Constitutional Reform 1999–2002*, Dissertation submitted for the Degree of Master of Law, University of Warwick, 2002, Ch. 4.

16 B. Susanti, *supra*, 2002, p. 11.

17 Drs. Achmad Hafidz Zawawi (F-PG), *Risalah Rapat Komisi A Ke-3 L St MPR*, 6 August 2002, p. 39.

18 Dr. Prasetiono (ISEI), *Risalah Rapat Ke-17 PAH I*, 21 February 2000, p. 14.

19 B. Susanti, *supra*, 2002, p. 66.

20 Dr. Sri Adiningsih (Tim Ahli), *Rapat Pleno Ke-13 PAH I*, 24 April 2001, p. 28; Drs. Achmad Hafidz Zawawi (F-PG), *Risalah Rapat Komisi A Ke-3 L S MPR*, 6 August 2002, p. 39.

21 B. Susanti, *supra*, 2002, pp. 69–70.

22 Ir. Ahmad Hafiz Zawawi, MSc (F-PG), *Risalah PAH I Rapat Ke-20*, 27 March 2002, pp. 31–32.

23 B. Susanti, *supra*, 2002, p. 9.

24 Erfan Maryono (LPTP), *Risalah PAH I Rapat Ke-8*, 28 February 2002, pp. 29–30.

25 Adi Sasono (CIDES), *Risalah PAH I Rapat Ke-8*, 28 February 2002, pp. 22–23.

26 B. Susanti, *supra*, 2002, p. 10.

27 H. Ali Marwan Hanan, S.H. (Menkopukm), *Risalah PAH I Rapat Ke-5*, 25 February 2002, p. 22; M. Hatta Mustafa, S.H. (F-UD), *Risalah PAH I Rapat Ke-20*, 27 March 2002, p. 9.

28 A.H. Hafild, 1999, *Membumikan Mandat Pasal 33 UUD 45* [Grounding the Mandate of Art 33 of the 1945 Constitution], Wahana Lingkungan Hidup Indonesia. Available from http://www.pacific.net.id/~dede_s/Membumikan.htm.

29 Drs. Ali Masykur Musa (F-KB), *Risalah Rapat Komisi A Ke-3 L St MPR*, 6 August 2002, p. 41; Drs. Hj. Chairunnisa (F-PG), *Risalah Rapat Komisi B Ke-2 St MPR*, 4 August 2002, p. 9.

30 Mayjen. Tni Affandi, S.IP (F-TNI/Polri), *Risalah PAH I Rapat Ke-20*, 27 March 2002, p. 23.

31 Ir. A.M. Luthfi (F-Reformasi), *Risalah PAH I Rapat Ke-20*, 27 March 2002, p. 35.

32 Drs. Sutjipno Mayjen. Pol. (Purn) (F-PDIP), *Risalah PAH I Rapat Ke-20*, 27 March 2002, p. 44; Harjono, S.H., MCL. (F-PDIP), *Risalah PAH I Rapat Ke-20*, 27 March 2002, p. 56.

33 The full text of the Preamble is as follows (the *Pancasila* state ideology is italicized): Whereas freedom is the inalienable right of all nations, colonialism must be abolished in this world as it is not in conformity with humanity and justice; And the moment of rejoicing has arrived in the struggle of the Indonesian freedom movement to guide the people safely and well to the threshold of the independence of the state of Indonesia which shall be free, united, sovereign, just, and prosperous; By the grace of God Almighty and impelled by the noble desire to live a free national life, the people of Indonesia hereby declare their independence. Subsequent thereto, to form a government of the state of Indonesia which shall protect all the people of Indonesia and their entire native land, and in order to improve the public welfare, to advance the intellectual life of the people and to contribute to the establishment of a world order based on freedom, abiding peace and social justice, the national independence of Indonesia shall be formulated into a constitution of the sovereign Republic of Indonesia which is based on the *belief in the One and Only God, just and civilized humanity, the unity of Indonesia, democracy guided by the inner wisdom of deliberations amongst representatives, and the realization of social justice for all of the people of Indonesia.*

34 H. Ali Marwan Hanan, S.H. (Menkopukm), *Risalah PAH I Rapat Ke-5*, 25 February 2002, p. 19.

35 Dr. Sri Adiningsih (Tim Ahli), *Rapat Pleno Ke-13 PAH I*, 24 April 2001, p. 28; Hobbes Sinaga, SH, MH (F-PDIP), *Risalah PAH I Rapat Ke-20*, 27 March 2002, p. 10; Ir. Ahmad Hafiz Zawawi, MSc (F-PG), *Risalah PAH I Rapat Ke-20*, 27 March 2002, p. 31). One expert, for example, mused that the family principle (*asas kekeluargaan*) had been misinterpreted as "the one-family principle" (*asas keluarga*)—that is the Soeharto family (Dr. Sri Adiningsih (Tim Ahli), *Rapat Pleno Ke-13 PAH I*, 24 April 2001, p. 28; see also Ir. A.M. Luthfi (F-Reformasi), *Risalah PAH I Rapat Ke-20*, 27 March 2002, p. 34.

36 Unless otherwise stated, all references to "Articles" are references to Articles of the 1945 Constitution of the Republic of Indonesia as amended.

37 Article 24C(1); Article 10(1) of the MK Law.

38 Article 24C(2); Article 10(2) of the MK Law.

39 See, for example, A. Irmanputra Sidin, 'Saat Harimau Itu Diompongkan Hakim: Pasal Eks PKI' [When Judges Remove the Teeth from the Tiger: the ex-PKI Provisions], *Kompas* 26 February 2004. Available from http://www.kompas.com. See also Benny K. Harman and Hendardi, eds, *Konstitutionalisme, Peran DPR, dan Judicial Review* [Constitutionalism, the Role of the DPR and Judicial Review]; Jaringan Informasi Masyarakat (JARIM) dan Yayasan Lembaga Bantuan Huku, Indonesia (YLBHI), 1999; Refly Harun, 'Bikin Lembaga Zonder KKN' [Creating an Institution without Corruption, Collusion and Nepotism], in Refly Harun, Zainal A.M. Husein and Bisariyadi, eds, *Menjaga Denyut Konstitutsi; Refleksi Satu Tahun Mahkamah Konstitusi* [Guarding the Pulse of the Constitution: Reflections on One Year of the Constitutional Court], Jakarta, 2004, pp. 309–27.

40 The MK publishes its decisions on its website (http://www.mahkamahkonstitusi.go.id) and also in hard copy. We refer to the soft-copy versions, as found on the website, in this chapter. All translations are our own, unless otherwise indicated.

41 Ross H. McLeod, 'Second and Third Thoughts on Privatisation in Indonesia', *Agenda* 9 (2), 2002, pp. 151–64.

42 MK Decision No. 002/2003.

43 'MK "Koreksi" Sebagian Materi Undang-Undang Migas' [MK "corrects" parts of the Migas Law], *Hukumonline* 21 December 2004.

44 MK Decision No. 003/2005.

45 The application was brought by eleven environmental or human rights NGOs, eighty-one Indonesian citizens who lived in locations where mining companies were operating in protected forests, and other environmental activists.

46 'Mahkamah Konstitusi Tolak Batalkan UU Kehutanan' [Constitutional Court refuses to invalidate Forestry Law], *Hukumonline* 7 July 2005.

47 MK Decision No. 058-059-060-063/2004 and 008/2005.

48 See, for example, 'Mahkamah Konstitusi Ogah Membatalkan UU Sumber Daya Air' [Constitutional Court Reluctant to Invalidate Water Resources Law], *Hukumonline* 19 August 2005. Two MK judges dissented, however: 'Mukhti dan Maruarar, Dua Hakim yang Ajukan Dissenting Opinion UU SDA' [Mukhti and Maruarar, Two Judges who issued Dissenting Opinions on the SDA Law], *Hukumonline* 17 August 2005.

49 MK Decision No. 001-021-022/PUU-I/2003.

50 See, for example, 'Ketua DPR Minta Pemerintah Aktif Sosialisasikan UU Ketenagalistrikan' [DPR Head Requests Government actively to socialise the Electricity Law], *Hukumonline* 27 September 2002.

51 'Dihujani Minderheidsnota, DPR Setujui RUU Sumber Daya Air' [Flooded with Objections, the DPR approves the Water Resources Bill], *Hukumonline* 20 February 2004; 'Pasca Disetujuinya RUU SDA, Petani se-Bandung Somasi Komisi IV' [After the Enactment of the Water Resources Bill, Bandung Farmers petition Commission IV], *Hukumonline* 20 February 2004; 'Undang-Undang Sumber Daya Air Terus Menuai Gugatan' [Water Resources Law continues to spurn Legal Action], *Hukumonline* 4 August 2004; 'Mengapa Judicial Review UU Sumberdaya Air?' [Why seek

Judicial Review of the Water Resources Law?], *Walhi website* 28, July 2004. Available from http://www.walhi.or.id/kampanye/air/privatisasi/040728_judrevuuair_li/.

52 See, for example, 'Akibat Privatisasi, Layanan Publik Jadi Barang Dagangan' [Privatisation turns Public Service into a Commodity], *Hukumonline* 15February 2003.

53 'Ini Dia, Kelemahan RUU SDA Versi LSM' [This is it: the Weakness of the NGO Version of the SDA Bill], *Hukumonline* 18 March 2004; 'Kampayne Menolak Privatisasi Dan Komersialisasi Sumberdaya Air' [Campaign to Reject Privatisation and Commercialisation of Water Resources], *Walhi website* 14 April 2005.

54 See, for example, Articles 7, 8, and 80 of the SDA Law. See 'Mengapa Judicial Review UU Sumberdaya Air?' [Why seek Judicial Review of the Water Resources Law?], *Walhi website* 28 July 2004. Available from http://www.walhi.or.id/kampa-nye/air/privatisasi/040728_judrevuuair_li/; 'Kampayne Menolak Privatisasi Dan Komersialisasi Sumberdaya Air' [Campaign to Reject Privatisation and Commer-cialisation of Water Resources], *Walhi website* 14 April 2005; Fabby VCM Tumiwa, 'Reformasi SUMBER DAYA AIR DI INDONESIA' [Reform of Water Resources in Indonesia], *Kompas* 15 August 2003; 'Privatisasi Air Melanggar Prinsip Air Seba-gai Hak Asasi Rakyat' [Privatisation of Water breaches Principle of Water as a Basic Human Right of the People], *Walhi website* 21 September 2003. Available from http://www.walhi.or.id/kampanye/air/privatisasi/030921_privairhak_sp/.

55 *SDA Law case*, p. 41.

56 *SDA Law case*, p. 41.

57 'Globalisme Dan Privatisasi Air di Indonesia' [Globalisation and the Privatisation of Water in Indonesia], *Sekitar Kita* [About us], no date, copy on file with author; Fabby VCM Tumiwa, 'Reformasi Sumber Daya Air Di Indonesia' [Reform of Water Resources in Indonesia], *Kompas* 15 August 2003; 'Ini Dia, Kelemahan RUU SDA Versi LSM' [This is it: the Weakness of the NGO Version of the SDA Bill], *Hukumon-line* 18 March 2004; 'Mendukung Mahkamah Konstitusi Menjaga UU 1945: Air Tidak untuk Diprivatisasi' [Supporting the Constitutional Court to Guard the 1945 Constitu-tion: Water is not for Privatisation], *Walhi website* 10 May 2004. Available from http://www.walhi.or.id/kampanye/air/privatisasi/050510_privair_sp/. Some commentators have gone so far as to suggest that this new right was introduced by the World Bank: 'RUU SDA Dinilai Diskriminatif dan Mengedepankan Ego Sektoral' [SDA Law Con-sidered to be Discriminatory and to promote Sectoral Egos], *Hukumonline* 19 Sep-tember 2003. As one legislator said during the DPR debates over the SDA Law, "Even the Dutch recognized water as a resource owned by the people": 'Pengesahan UU Air Diwarnai Walk Out' [Approval of Water Law coloured by Walk Out]. Available from http://estananto.blogspot.com/2004/02/uu-sumber-daya-air.html.

58 See, for example, 'Akibat Privatisasi, Layanan Publik Jadi Barang Dagangan' [Privatisation turns Public Service into a Commodity], *Hukumonline* 15 February 2003.

59 While private power companies existed in Indonesia prior to 2002, most had exclu-sive power purchase agreements with state-owned PLN. See, for example, Witold J. Henisz and Bennet A. Zelner, *The Political Economy of Private Electricity Pro-vision in Southeast Asia*, Working Paper of the Reginald H. Jones Center, Wharton School, University of Pennsylvania, 2001; David Hall and Emanuele Lobina, 'Pri-vate and Public Interests in Water and Energy', *Natural Resources Forum* 28, 2004, pp. 268–77.

60 See Articles 8(2), 16, and 17 of the Electricity Law.

61 The first applicant alleged that its rights under Articles 1(3), 28C(2), 28D(1), 28H(1), 33(2), and 33(3) of the Constitution had been damaged; the second applicant alleged a breach of Articles 27(2), 28D(2), 28H(1), 28H(3), 33(3), and 54(3); and the third applicant claimed its Article 28A, 28C(1), and 28H(1) rights had been breached.

62 *Electricity Law case*, pp. 342–43.

63 *Electricity Law case*, p. 343.

64 *Electricity Law case*, pp. 343–44.

65 Indeed, a government expert argued that PLN was incapable of meeting demand for electricity, despite electricity "being second only to food in importance to human life." *Electricity Law case*, pp. 339–40.

66 *Electricity Law case*, pp. 337, 340.

67 *Electricity Law case*, p. 338.

68 *Electricity Law case*, pp. 337, 340.

69 *Electricity Law case*, p. 338.

70 *Electricity Law case*, p. 338.

71 *Electricity Law case*, p. 338.

72 *Electricity Law case*, pp. 349–50.

73 *Electricity Law case*, pp. 349–50.

74 *Electricity Law case*, pp. 349–50. The Court did not, however, go so far as to invalidate contracts or licenses signed or issued under the Law, allowing them to continue until they expired.

75 *Electricity Law case*, pp. 348–49.

76 David Hall, Director of Public Services, International Research Unit, University of Greenwich, London, UK.

77 *Electricity Law case*, p. 342.

78 *Electricity Law case*, p. 331.

79 *Electricity Law case*, p. 348.

80 *Electricity Law case*, p. 347.

81 *Electricity Law case*, p. 347.

82 *Electricity Law case*, p. 330.

83 *Electricity Law case*, pp. 329–30. The MK stated (at p. 330) that any such takeovers must be carried out in accordance with just laws.

84 *Electricity Law case*, p. 332.

85 *Electricity Law case*, p. 332.

86 *Electricity Law case*, p. 333.

87 *Electricity Law case*, pp. 332–33.

88 *Electricity Law case*, p. 333.

89 *Electricity Law case*, p. 334.

90 *Electricity law case*, p. 334. *Migas Law case*, pp. 208–9.

91 *Electricity Law case*, pp. 329–30.

92 *Electricity Law case*, p. 336.

93 *Electricity Law case*, pp. 334–36, 346. Similar comments were made in the *Migas Law case* at pp. 210–11.

94 *Electricity Law case*, p. 335.

95 *Electricity Law case*, p. 331.

96 *Electricity Law case*, p. 332.

97 *Electricity Law case*, pp. 331–32, citing Mohammad Hatta, *Kumpulan Pidato II* [Collected Speeches II], compiled by I. Wangsa Widjaja and Mutia F. Swasono, Jakarta: PT Toko Gunung Agung, 2002, p. 231.

98 *Electricity Law case*, p. 345.

99 *Migas Law case*, pp. 209–10.

100 *Migas Law case*, p. 221.

101 MK Decision No. 006/2003, reviewing Law No. 30 of 2002 on the Corruption Eradication Commission (the *KPK Law case*).

102 pp. 94–95, 6/2003.

103 p. 95, 6/2003.

104 In fact, the electricity rises were introduced via Presidential Regulation No. 55 of 2005: 'Kenaikan BBM Diajukan Judicial Review' [Judicial Review sought of BBM Increase], *Hukumonline* 14 October 2005.

105 Although the MK's invalidation of the Electricity Law is mentioned in passing in the Elucidation to the Regulation.

106 Personal communication with Fultoni, Secretary of KRHN (Konsorsium Reformasi Hukum Nasional (National Legal Reform Consortium), 8 May 2005. See also 'PP Listrik Swasta Diajukan Uji Materiil', *Hukumonline* 17 July 2005.

107 'PP Listrik Swasta Diajukan Uji Materiil' [Review sought of Government Regulation on Private Sector Electricity], *Hukumonline* 17 July 2005.

108 'Pemerintah Segera Keluarkan PP Kemitraan Swasta Sektor Ketenagalistrikan' [Government immediately to issue Government Regulation on Private-Sector Partnerships in the Electricity Sector], *Hukumonline* 14 January 2005.

109 'Pemerintah Segera Keluarkan PP Kemitraan Swasta Sektor Ketenagalistrikan' [Government immediately to issue Government Regulation on Private-Sector Partnerships in the Electricity Sector], *Hukumonline* 14 January 2005.

110 In fact, an application has been lodged with the MA to review Government Regulation No. 3 of 2004, but had not been decided at the time of writing: 'PP Listrik Swasta Diajukan Uji Materiil' [Review sought of Government Regulation on Private Sector Electricity], *Hukumonline* 17 July 2005. See also A.W. Bedner, *Administrative Courts in Indonesia: A Socio-Legal Study*, London, The Hague: Kluwer Law International, 2003.

111 'Pemerintah harus ubah PP Air Minum yang Mendorong Privatisasi' [Government must change the Drinking Water Government Regulation which promotes Privatisation], *Walhi website* 20 October 2005. Available from http://www.walhi.or.id/kampanye/air/privatisasi/051020_pp-air-minum_1th-sby-jk_li/; 'PP Air Minum Muluskan Privatisasi' [Drinking Water Regulation Allows for Privatisation], *Walhi website* 15 July 2005. Available from http://www.walhi.or.id/kampanye/air/privatisasi/050715_pp_air_minum/.

112 'PP Air Minum Muluskan Privatisasi' [Drinking Water Regulation Allows for Privatisation], *Walhi website* 15 July 2005. Available from http://www.walhi.or.id/kampanye/air/privatisasi/050715_pp_air_minum/.

113 See Susi Dwi Harijanti and Tim Lindsey, 'Indonesia: General Elections Test Constitutional Amendments and New Constitutional Court', *International Journal of Constitutional Law* 4 (1), 2006, pp. 138–50.

114 MK Decision No. 20 of 2007. The applicants were members of the DPR who had voted against the Migas Law in parliament. The Court held, quite rightly, that, although DPR members have a right to vote, they cannot be considered to have had their constitutional rights or interests adversely affected by the passage of a statute to which they objected.

115 Prohibitions on judicial review were then contained in MPRS Decree No. III/MPR/1978 concerning the Position and Working Relationship between the Highest State Institution and Superior State Institutions, Article 11; Law on Judicial Power of 1970 (Law No. 14 of 1970), Article 26(1); Supreme Court Law of 1985 (Law No. 2 of 1985), Article 31(3). On the history of the Supreme Court during the New Order, see Sebastiaan Pompe[0][0], *The Indonesian Supreme Court: A Study of Institutional Collapse*, Ithaca, NY: Southeast Asia Program, Cornell University, 2005.

13 Law reform and corporate governance in Malaysia

Aishah Bidin

Introduction

Many countries in Asia have been seeking to overhaul their existing laws with a view to bringing them closely into line with international standards of practice. As the pace of legal harmonization and globalization is increasing in many Asian countries, Malaysia is no exception. This chapter will argue that Malaysia has undergone massive review in the commercial legal framework to ensure that it is in accordance with international practice of corporate governance standards, which have been developed by multinational bodies such as the World Bank and the Organisation for Economic Co-operation and Development (OECD). The major stimulus to reform corporate law in Malaysia was not primarily the harmonization of its law with other states but the increasing awareness that the current legal framework was found to be inadequate, lacking in clarity and detail, and based on an unsystematic approach.

Nevertheless, some of the imported models are not wholly compatible with the Malaysian corporate environment. This chapter will argue that the direct importation of foreign models may not be wholly appropriate for many of Malaysia's corporate governance problems. This has sometimes resulted in state intervention in formulating rules to preserve the rights and needs of specific groups in society or is reflected as pushing or resistance against the waves of globalization. Subsequently, state intervention also resulted in extensive powers given to the regulators on matters concerning penalties, enforcement, and power of review.

The Malaysian experience has illustrated that the British colonial legacy has left the Malay states with a British legal template, which forms the current present legal framework. However, the government has responded in a variety of ways, in particular in response to the need to preserve local interest, coupled with pressures by special groups in society. Within the corporate governance structure, the shareholding structure in Malaysia has also given rise to a specific agency problem, the powers of controlling shareholders, which was inadequately addressed by a corporate regime that focuses on the duties of directors.

There are other issues that affect the efficacy of corporate governance regulation in Malaysia, thus forming some limits and constraints to globalization. These include among others culture and value systems, the role of Islamic law/*Syariah* in legal development and society in Malaysia, the quality of legal institutions, issues relating to access to justice and judicial reform, and the influence of the state in businesses such as the rise of the Malaysian government link companies (GLC). The problems arising from these cannot be resolved either by reforming the law or by adopting foreign legal templates. In dealing with the pressure of global change, Malaysia is a clear example of a situation where globalization is an important element of legal, social, and economic advancement. Nevertheless, during the importation process, there will be occurrences of "pushing off" and severing some aspects of the global change in certain circumstances as a direct response to attempted assimilation with the local corporate structure.

Malaysian legal history

From the perspective of legal history, British colonization of Malaya left behind a lasting legacy of laws and legal system. English judges in the Straits Settlement and the Malay states made decisions pertaining to the local customs of the indigenous race and migrant races in those states. However, in matters pertaining to trade, commerce, and property, the position is different. This is due to a dearth of cases of local customs or established customary law about such matters, which could have formed the basis of the eventual development of local commercial domestic laws. Even customary laws that did exist were regarded as not sophisticated or developed enough and not on a par with English commercial law. Thus, in commercial matters or mercantile law, there was a wholesale importation of English law. It began through the work of English-trained judiciary but was subsequently formalized through the Civil Law Act 1937, which was applied to the Unfederated Malay States by the Civil Law Ordinance 1951. Today, the application of English law throughout Malaysia is accomplished under the Civil Law Act 1956. It can be seen that, even where the Civil Law Act has expressly excluded the application of English law in certain fields, Malaysian judges still refer to England to fill the lacunae in the local legislation. Where local legislation has not been based upon or borrowed from the UK, the peculiar habit of continuing to apply English law can perhaps only be explained on the basis of the strong influence that a "mother country" would continue to have over its former colony.

Impact of the financial crisis

As the East Asia financial crisis progressed, many listed companies in Malaysia faced increasing difficulties as the plunge in share prices increased investor risk aversion and tight credit conditions severely affected financing at a time when liquidity was most urgently needed. To help alleviate these pressures, the Malaysian government introduced a series of measures over the period 1997–2000 to ease the conditions for capital restructuring by distressed companies and to facilitate the necessary injection of capital to deal with the worst effects of the crisis. This included a review of the previous restriction on corporate restructuring and capital raising introduced by the government in December 1997. The overarching need to preserve stability and socio-political harmony amid the highly uncertain market conditions was an important consideration that brought about a turnaround in the government approach to crisis management. In view of the worsening economic climate, the then Prime Minister said frankly that, "We had no alternative but to pursue our own course of action to protect our economy."[1]

On 7 January 1998, the National Action Economic Council (NEAC) was established to act as a consultative body to the cabinet to deal with the economic crisis. On 23 July 1998, the NEAC released the National Economic Recovery Plan (NERP), which provided a framework for action to counter the negative effects of the currency crisis.[2] The months following the establishment of the NEAC saw a shift in a number of initial policies. A series of interest rate cuts were introduced in quick succession to improve liquidity conditions. Fiscal expenditures were increased with an expansionary Federal Budget tabled in October 1998 to pick up the slack on private demand. Previous proposals of government expenditure cuts were dropped and several stalled large infrastructure projects were revived. A fiscal stimulus package of RM7 million was announced, together with the establishment of an infrastructure development fund to help minimize delays in infrastructure projects.[3]

The government also put in place a dedicated institutional framework to ensure more effective and expedient restructuring of the financial and corporate sectors. A national asset management company, *Pengurusan Danaharta Nasional Berhad*, was established in 1998 with the task of acquiring and managing non-performing loans (NPL) in the banking system, which in July 1998 had risen to 10 percent of total loans, compared with the single digit figures recorded during the preceding five years. *Danamodal Nasional Berhad* (*Danamodal*), a recapitalization company for the banking sector, was also established in July 1998 as a special agency to ensure that banking sector recapitalization was commercially driven and the investment decisions were made according to market-based principles. In the same month, the Corporate Debt Restructuring Committee (CDRC) was set up to facilitate the restructuring of corporate debts through out-of-court settlements between debtors and creditors. This was soon followed by a number of high-profile corporate restructuring initiatives including those involving the DRB-HICOM (a large automotive manufacturing group), the Technology Resources Industries (TRI) Group, Malaysian Airlines, Naluri, and Renong.

The absence of International Monetary Fund (IMF) involvement in Malaysia allowed the reform process to unfold in a manner that fully reflected domestic political priorities and constraints. The IMF was never a serious problem for Malaysia as Malaysian external borrowing was relatively low compared with the IMF-assisted countries. More importantly, the major concern—would-be IMF conditionalities—would involve the eventual dismantling of Malaysia's ethnically based distributive policy as well as the removal of restrictions on foreign equity ownership in key economic sectors that are deemed to be of national interest. The Malaysian experience with the financial crisis also illustrates the tension between the global market that theoretically stresses market mechanisms and allocative agencies, namely capital on one hand and national markets on the other. Although the Malaysian economy has been described as a fairly open economy, there is, however, a more regulated sector in which the state controls the allocation of resources as well as the creation and distribution of economy.[4]

Malaysian corporate legal framework

The Malaysian corporate framework has undergone a massive legal change since the middle of the 1990s as a result of the financial crisis in Asia. This includes the introduction of asset management legislation in 1998, two new codes, namely on takeovers, mergers, and corporate governance, an ongoing major review of the Companies Act 1965 and insolvency laws (Table 13.1), the amendments to the Securities Commission Act 1993, new legislation on financial reporting in 1997 and money laundering in 2001, and the introduction of a new Capital and Market Services Act in 2007. In addition, the corporate changes also included setting up a new regulatory body, namely the Companies Commission in 2001, and the demutualization of the Malaysian Stock Exchange in 2004.[5]

Table 13.1 Legal changes in Malaysian corporate law, 1996–2007

Year	Legislation/statute/code/guideline	Regulatory body
1996	Amendment of the Securities Commission Act 1993—new disclosure-based regime introduced in Malaysia	Securities Commission
1997	Financial Reporting Act 1997	
1998	Pengurusan Danaharta Nasional Berhad Act 1998 Code on Takeover and Merger	
1999	Report on Corporate Governance	High Level Finance Committee on Corporate Governance
2000	Code of Corporate Governance	
2001	Companies Commission Act 2001 Money Laundering Act 2001 Capital Market Master Plan	Establishment of Companies Commission
2002		
2003		Establishment of the Corporate Law Reform Committee (CLRC)
2004	Demutualization Act New Listing Requirements for Public Companies	Demutualization of Malaysian Stock Exchange
2005	Repeal of the Pengurusan Danaharta Nasional Bhd Act 1998	
2006		
2007	Amendment of the Companies Act 1965 Amendment of the Securities Commission Act 1993 Capital Market Services Act Repeal of the Securities Industry Act 1983 Repeal of the Futures Industry Act 1993	

In terms of corporate regulation, Malaysia was generally regarded as having one of the best legal regimes in Asia, rivaling her closest neighbor Singapore and also Hong Kong.[6] Even to critical observers, Malaysia was seen to be committed to improving her corporate legal environment. As far back as 1994, the requirements for independent directors and independent audit committees had been put in place.[7] A new disclosure-based regulatory regime was introduced in 1996. The establishment of a Financial Reporting Foundation to oversee corporate reporting standards was established a year later.

Despite having all these rules and legal structures, Malaysia was not spared from the financial crisis that swept the region, beginning in 1997.[8] In fact, the crisis exposed some inherent problems in the Malaysian corporate governance regime, in particular relating to the protection of minority shareholders. The government took the initiative to address this by establishing the High Level Finance Committee on Corporate Governance in 1998 with a mandate to enhance the standards of corporate governance in Malaysia. The committee came up with the Report on Corporate Governance in early 1999, in which it proposed a draft code on corporate governance, together with some proposals for further reforms to improve governance. Since the publication of the Report, new governance measures have been taken, among them the publication of the Code of Corporate Governance in 2000, the requirement for beneficial owners of securities to declare their status,[9] quarterly reporting of financial information,[10] the requirement to include a director's report in the annual reports to shareholders, as well as income statements, balance sheets, cash flow statements, and details of equity changes,[11] and new laws imposing stringent disclosure standards for prospectuses and heavy sanctions for false or misleading statements or material omission.[12] All directors of listed companies are now required to attend an accreditation program to ensure competency, and a limitation has been imposed on the number of their directorships so that they might give better attention to their responsibilities.[13]

Pressures from non-governmental organizations (NGOs) also called for the setting up of a shareholder watchdog group in the form of a Minority Shareholder Watchdog Group, which was established by some large institutional investors. It was led by a public institution, the Employees Provident Fund (EPF), to establish the foundation for the growth of shareholder activism. These new governance initiatives were further enhanced with the publication of the Capital Market Master Plan by the Securities Commission in 2001.[14] The Companies Commission established a Corporate Law Reform Committee in 2003, which at the time of writing has published twelve Consultative Documents.[15] The following section will give an overview of the current corporate legal and regulatory framework in Malaysia.[16]

The main statute regulating companies in Malaysia is the Malaysian Companies Act 1965. The Companies Act deals with registration of companies, membership and internal management, debt capital, financial reporting and audit requirements, and administration of companies in financial difficulties. It also includes some provisions affecting takeovers and the regulation of securities. The Malaysian Companies Act was enacted in 1965. Prior to 1965, English law applied. As in other former British colonies, Malaysia inherited a British common law system and borrowed the British Companies Act. The first local company law statute was the Straits

Settlements Companies Ordinance 1889,[17] later replaced by successive Companies Ordinances of 1915, 1923, and 1940.[18] More importantly, these statutes reflected company law as it then existed in England. Following the formation of Malaysia in 1963, the Companies Act 1965 was enacted to replace the 1946 Ordinance. It was based on the British Companies Act of 1929, but in some respects was closer to the Australian Uniform Companies Act 1961, a modernized version of the 1929 Act. As a result of these transplantations, the doctrines of separate legal personality and limited liability as applied in Britain were made part of the law of the land.[19] This and the landmark decision by the House of Lords in *Salomon v. Salomon & Co. Ltd*[20] had formed the basis of the company's existence in Malaysia, as it has in Britain.

Although the Companies Act 1965 is the main statutory source of company law, it is not the only statute governing companies in Malaysia.

In addition to the Companies Act, company law rules can be found in:

- case law or common law (or precedent);
- the Companies Regulations 1966;
- the Securities Commission Act 1993 (SCA);
- SC exemptions, modifications, and guidelines;
- the accounting standards;
- the Bursa Securities Listing Requirements and Bursa Securities Rules;
- Securities Industry Act 1983 (repealed 2007);
- Futures Industry Act 1993 (repealed 2007);
- Code on Takeovers and Mergers 1998;
- Code on Corporate Governance 2000;
- Offshore Companies Act 1990;
- Demutualisation Act 2004;
- Pengurusan Danaharta Nasional Berhad Act 1998 (repealed 2004);
- Capital and Market Services Act 2007.

The most recent Capital Market and Services (CMSA) Act, which came into force in September 2007, has the following objectives, namely:

- enhance fund-raising activities;
- strengthen investor protection;
- promote Malaysia as a global Islamic financial hub;
- encourage the usage of technology in capital markets;
- promote self-regulation.

Impact of globalization and legal harmonization

While legal reforms and global change have resulted in an improvement in corporate governance, this chapter argues that there are also some constraints and limitations to globalization. As globalization of national economies progressed, the issue of the incompatibility of different regulatory and business system trading states became a matter of increasing concern. Differences in regulatory schemes about technical standards, taxation, environmental protection measures, labor standards, and other fields placed barriers in the path of enterprises when they sought to do business across borders. Such disparities could also take the form of the need to preserve national interest for the rights of special groups, namely the *Bumiputras*. In the Malaysian context, *Bumiputera* or "sons of soil" are regarded as natives that are indigenous to Malaysia. Among the groups recognized as Bumiputera are the Malays and the natives of Sabah and Sarawak. A Malay is defined under the Malaysian Federal Constitution as a person who professes the religion of Islam, habitually speaks the Malay language, conforms to Malay custom and:

a.   was born before Independence Day in the Federation (of Malaya) or in Singapore or has parents one of whom was born in the Federation or in Singapore or is on that day domiciled in the Federation or in Singapore; or
b.   is the issue of such a person.

The Federal Constitution also defines a native in the context of the recognition of their special position in Sabah and Sarawak. In Sarawak, a native means a person who is a citizen and either belongs to one of the races specified in Clause 7[21] as being indigenous to the state or is of mixed blood deriving exclusively from those races.[22] In relation to Sabah, a native is a person who is a citizen, is the child or grandchild of a person of a race indigenous to Sabah, and was born either in Sabah or to a father domiciled in Sabah at the time of birth.[23]

Other factors include differences in business customs and ownership structure, the rise of GLC (government link corporations), special protection for corporations, the role of *Syariah* in legal development in Malaysia, and the lack of access to justice and judicial reform. These issues will be discussed in the following section.

Preserving national interest and formulating national policy

In Malaysia, the authorities have always played a prominent role in ensuring that certain needs of society are being preserved and that the national policy will prevail.[24] A clear example of this is the establishment of Permodalan Nasional Berhad (PNB). Conceived as a pivotal instrument of the government's new economic policy to promote share ownership in the corporate sector among the Bumiputeras, PNB (Bhd) also played a role in developing opportunities for suitable Bumiputra professionals to participate in the creation and management of wealth. Prior to its establishment, efforts to increase Bumiputera ownership in the corporate sector were insufficient as shares allocated to individuals were seldom retained. Through PNB, substantial shares acquired in major Malaysian corporations from funds provided by Yayasan Pelaburan Bumiputera (Bumiputera Investment Fund Foundation) were transferred to a trust fund and sold to Bumiputeras in the form of smaller units. By employing this innovative investment model, PNB ensured that these shares were retained, resulting in the cultivation of widespread savings and the development of entrepreneurship and investment skills in Bumiputeras.[25] A direct impact of this social engineering was the creation of a bureaucratic corporate elite group among the Bumiputeras.[26]

An example of the extensive powers of the authorities can also be seen in the legislative process. A sample piece of legislation which has drawn critics, not only among the legal fraternity, is the asset management legislation passed in 1998. The Pengurusan Danaharta Nasional Berhad (*Danaharta*) was established in June 1998 to purchase non-performing loans (NPLs) from banking institutions and manage these NPLs to maximize their recovery value. *Danaharta*, like other asset management companies in the world, operates within the broad concept of rehabilitation, restructuring, and maximizing the recovery value of the assets. Once banking institutions have sold their NPLs to *Danaharta*, the latter would be able to impose conditions on borrowers, which may include, among other things, the reconstruction or rehabilitation of underlying assets and identification of cash flows. In 2000, Parliament passed the Pengurusan Danaharta Nasional Berhad (Amendment) Act 2000 to clarify existing provisions of the Act in order to remove any doubts about their intended effect and to overcome practical difficulties that arose after *Danaharta* began operations.

Danaharta is also empowered to appoint special administrators for viable companies that face temporary cash flow problems. The special administrators are vested with extensive powers,[27] which includes power to do all things (including the carrying out of works) as may be necessary for the management and realization of the assets and affairs of the affected person notwithstanding the memorandum and articles of association of the affected person or any other law. Most importantly, the act also provides that any decision of the corporation (*Danaharta*) through the appointment of a special administrator shall be final and binding and shall not be reviewed, quashed, appealed against, or set aside by any court of law.[28]

How does Danaharta *operate?*

Danaharta will buy the existing NPLs from the bank and manage the recovery of those debts that will be classified as viable or non-viable loans. Classification of viable loans would include the following criteria:

(1) rescheduling of loans repayments;
(2) debt/equity conversions;
(3) restructuring through the appointment of a special administrator or receiver and manager; or
(4) a scheme of arrangement under section 176 of the Companies Act.

For non-viable loans, asset management strategies will be applied. Under section 25 of the Pengurusan Danaharta Nasional Berhad Act 1998 (Danaharta Act), if there are loans of some value, a special administrator (SA) will be appointed by *Danaharta* to manage them before it undergoes the process of foreclosure. This in effect will give an opportunity to the debtor to have the loans treated as viable loans. In addition, *Danaharta* will only acquire NPLs of RM5 million and above. Section 44(3) of the *Danaharta* Act provides that *Danaharta* must first seek the approval of an oversight committee. Once approved, a SA will be appointed to take control of the management of the assets and affairs of the company concerned. The *Danaharta* Act also requires the appointed SA to prepare a workable proposal. The SA is an independent person who acts impartially in exercising all his or her powers. It resembles, to a certain extent, the position of judicial managers in Singapore. In this aspect, the SA is independent and is not answerable to the court. However, the *Danaharta* Act does not specifically state to whom the SA is accountable. However, the *Danaharta* Act requires the oversight committee, when approving the appointment of the SA, to determine whether he or she has discharged the requirements of being fully independent and whether he or she has acted fairly. On the other hand, in the UK, the Insolvency Act would require the SA to act fairly to both creditors and members of the company. *Danaharta* was specifically designed to be a finite life agency, established to carry out a specific mission. With the achievement of its mission by the end of 2005, *Danaharta* ended its operations on 31 December 2005. In the 2004 Annual Report, *Danaharta's* Chairman, Dato' Zainal A. Putih, pointed out that NPL resolution agencies such as *Danaharta* are not meant to be permanent institutions as their continued existence may present a moral hazard to the banking industry.

Criticism of Danaharta *and its implication for corporate governance*

Creditors do exercise a degree of control over companies and thus play a role in corporate governance, especially so in insolvent or near insolvent companies.[29] Their effectiveness will depend on the quality of monitoring and the enforceability of their rights in courts. Creditors do have rights that are generally enforceable in courts. One exception is where a court has granted a moratorium for a specified period to a company pursuant to a scheme of arrangement under section 176 of the Companies Act 1965. Under the scheme, safeguards are put in place to protect the rights of creditors. Another exception is provided by an Act of Parliament, Pengurusan Danaharta Nasional Berhad Act 1998. The Act not only affects the enforceability of debts, it also provides for the creation of a special company Pengurusan Danaharta Nasional Berhad (of *Danaharta*), which is given powers to circumvent governance rules provided by the memorandum and articles of association, the Companies Act, and Bursa Malaysia's Listing Requirements.

As mentioned above, *Danaharta* is a company incorporated under the Companies Act that has special powers conferred by the Act. Some of the provisions in the Act contain some of the most blatant contraventions of basic governance rules, yet it has escaped critical attention. *Danaharta's* main objectives are to remove NPLs from the balance sheet of financial institutions at fair market value and to maximize their recovery value.[30]

The Act confers on *Danaharta* two special powers, first, to buy assets through statutory vesting and, second, the ability to appoint SAs to manage the affairs of distressed companies. The SA's corporate powers are perhaps unrivaled by any other in the world, at least in the common law world. They include the power to exercise all the functions of the board and to remove or suspend from office any director regardless of memorandum and articles of association or any other law (this includes the Companies Act and all other corporate regulations).[31] As one High Court judge has noted, the SAs have much wider powers than the powers of a board of directors. No specific duty to act in the interests of any particular persons or group of persons was imposed on the SAs; thus, technically, the SA may act in the sole interests of *Danaharta* who appoints him or her to the detriment of shareholders and other creditors. More unusually, at least for a country professing to exercise democracy, these vast powers were effectively unchecked. Although there is the office of an oversight committee, it can hardly be described as independent as its members are appointed by the Executive.[32] Under the Danaharta Act, shareholders of the company that is put under administration will have their rights temporarily frozen and a moratorium is placed on the other creditors to recover their debts.[33] Unsecured creditors will find that they have no voice at all as they do not have a right to attend and vote at the creditors' meeting.[34]

Initially, shareholders, directors, or creditors of the company may challenge the actions and decisions by the SA based on the oppression remedy under section 181 of the Companies Act 1965, although no such action has ever been instituted. An action has been taken against *Danaharta* in 1998 seeking an injunction restraining the SA from acting. Challenges were made to the validity of the SA's appointment, the constitutionality of the Danaharta Act, and with an allegation of bad faith on the part of *Danaharta*.[35] Even though the action was dismissed by the High Court, the Parliament, to pre-empt further challenges, responded by amending the Danaharta Act by taking away the court's powers of oversight over the SA and *Danaharta*.[36] In addition, a new section 71 immunizes any act made in good faith by certain persons, including the SA, which may otherwise be a breach of the Act or any other law. The result is that the SA, once appointed, has unconstrained powers free from any possible challenges by shareholders, directors, creditors, or any other interested persons.

The provisions in the Danaharta Act that immunize them and the SA from legal challenges have been challenged in court for being unconstitutional. These have not been successful. It will be shown here that such failure is not because of any weakness in the case for the challengers; instead, it is the subservience of the judiciary that ultimately won the case for the authorities.

Ownership and shareholding structure

In addition, differences in shareholding structure, as well as economic, political, and cultural differences, mean that the nature of the problems and the solutions to them vary across markets. In Malaysia, a governance regime that has as its focus the shareholder–director agency conflict may not be wholly appropriate in a corporate environment where the excessive powers of controlling shareholders creates the biggest agency problem. The foundation of corporate governance regulation in Malaysia can be traced to the work of two US academics, Adolf Berle and Gardiner Means, in *The Modern Corporation and Private Property*.[37]

The assumption that underlies this "managerialism" theory was that shareholders as the providers of capital are the rightful owners of the company.[38] This therefore justifies the notion that the company should be managed primarily to further shareholders' economic interests. The concentration of powers in the hands of corporate managers, however, necessitates the control of such powers and the creation of incentive structures to align the interests of managers with those of shareholders.

Corporate governance regulation in Malaysia provides good evidence for this assertion. The law that has as its focus the agency problem of director–shareholder conflict was not designed for the concentrated nature of Malaysia's companies. In Malaysia, the high degree of concentration occurs not only in the concentration of control in specific companies, but also the concentration of control over the financial assets and productive capacity of the corporate economy. The concentration of control over these large companies is consolidated by the use of interlocking share ownership and interlocking directorates.[39] The state also plays a significantly different role in Malaysia. Not only is the state the majority or controlling shareholder in many of the largest listed companies (Table 13.2),[40] it also has direct influence on the management of many other companies.[41] To the extent that the state benefits as a direct and indirect beneficiary of these businesses, it cannot be considered as merely an impartial intermediary seeking to benefit the whole populace by implementing appropriate development strategies and ensuring free competition and fair play to all.[42]

Table 13.2 Market capitalization and share ownership in GLCs in Bursa Malaysia

Company	Market capitalization (RM million)	Total government shareholding (%)
1. Malayan Banking	44.708	63.5
2. Telekom Malaysia Bhd	34.871	63.8
3. Tenaga Nasional Bhd	32.968	73.7
4. Malaysian International Shipping Corporation	29.387	72.1
5. Sime Darby Bhd	14.244	57.3
6. Petronas Gas Bhd	14.148	89.5
7. PLUS Expressway Bhd	13.350	77.0
8. Commerce Asset Holdings Bhd	12.495	47.9
9. Golden Hope Plantation Bhd	5.460	78.8
10. Malaysian Airline System Bhd	4.838	80.8
11. Proton Holding Bhd.	4.586	68.8
12. Petronas Dagangan Bhd	3.954	78.0
13. Island and Peninsular	3.781	56.3
14. UMW Holdings Bhd	2.523	58.6
15. Kumpulan Guthrie Bhd	2.224	82.5
16. Affin Holding Bhd	2.112	54.3
17. Malaysian Airport Holding Bhd	1.639	77.3
18. Bintulu Port Holding Bhd	1.568	71.3
19. Pos Malaysia and Services Holdings Bhd	1.471	35.4
20. NCB Holdings Bhd	1.298	60.2

The transplantation effect is a primary reason why the regulation of directors' conduct is the focus of the governance regime in Malaysia. This is questionable because real control is exercised by the controlling shareholders, and not the directors. The Berle/Means theory of the separation of ownership and control and the kind of agency problems caused by such separation should, theoretically, be of limited relevance in Malaysia.

In countries with concentrated shareholding such as in Malaysia, the agency problems of the shareholder–director conflict is replaced by another agency problem, the controlling shareholder–minority shareholder conflict. Although it has never been conclusively proved that companies with concentrated ownership have a higher incidence of corporate misappropriation or other forms of abuses, it is generally thought that, where control rights are matched by cash flow rights, there will be incentive for the controlling shareholder to maximize the interests of shareholders generally, including minority shareholders. However, there is a persistent danger that controlling shareholders will transfer company resources out of the company to its controlling shareholders.[43]

The controlling shareholders are able to do this because of their influence over the board and domination in general meetings. Also, as shareholders, they are under no duty to act in the interests of the company or the other shareholders. Greater problems arise where there is a divergence between these two rights, i.e., where control rights are greater than cash flow rights, which is a widespread situation in East Asia. The divergence between control and cash flow rights creates an incentive for the controlling shareholders to expropriate minority shareholders and other stakeholders.

In relation to ownership and shareholding structures, some of the resistance was generated by the responses of certain groups in the country, namely active bodies such as the Minority Shareholder Watchdog Group (MSWG) and the Malaysian Institute of Corporate Governance (MICG). The arguments against these structures are, first, little attention was given to the concentrated nature of Malaysian companies. The Committee on Corporate Governance did acknowledge, albeit in passing, the "difficulties posed by ownership concentration," but did not make any worthwhile suggestion apart from recommending further studies and consultation.[44] Second, governance reform in Malaysia has so far focused on companies listed on Bursa Malaysia, while less attention has been given to general governance rules. In respect of listed companies, there have been many positive developments in governance rules applicable to these companies. These changes were attributable to the Code on Corporate Governance, which has resulted in some changes to Bursa Malaysia's Listing Requirements. Although the Code was described as voluntary, changes to the Bursa Malaysia rules means that listed companies must comply. It must be emphasized that the Code and Bursa Malaysia's rules apply only to listed companies. The Securities Commission has fully implemented the Disclosure Based Regulations regimes, which, together with Bursa Malaysia's improved disclosure requirements, should result in better corporate transparency. A shareholder watchdog group in the form of MSWG has been established by some large institutional investors, led by a public institution Employee Provident

Fund (EPF) to establish the foundation for the growth of shareholder activism. Thus, insofar as listed companies are concerned, these changes should result in better shareholder protection. A joint survey by Bursa Malaysia and PriceWaterhouseCoopers showed that this was indeed the case. This survey revealed the perception of a rise in Malaysia's corporate governance standards of listed companies.[45]

The rise of the Malaysian government link corporations (GLC)

Another form of vehicle in which the Malaysian government would be able to develop the next generation of Bumiputera Commercial and Industrial Community (BCIC) or preserving state control ownership is through the social engineering of GLCs.[46] As of December 2004, there were about forty GLCs, with a combined market value of approximately RM232 billion, accounting for 32 percent of the market capitalization of Bursa Malaysia. A GLC is defined as a company for which the government has the ability to appoint board members and senior management, and actively makes major decisions (e.g., contract awards, strategy, restructuring and financing, acquisitions, and divestments). There are three types of GLCs. In the first type, the government of Malaysia exercises controls directly through Khazanah, the National Pension Fund, and the Bank Negara Malaysia. The second type are companies controlled indirectly by other federal government-linked agencies, through the Permodalan Nasional Berhad, the Employees Provident Fund, and Tabong Haji. The third type consists of companies where control is exercised through state agencies.

GLCs are undergoing a series of reforms to promote a culture of high performance and to transform them into more efficient and globally competitive corporate vehicles.[47] The policy initiatives include the use of key performance indicators (KPIs), performance-linked compensation (PLC), and competitive contracts for the senior management of all GLCs. This policy signals greater emphasis on commercially driven strategies within the private sector, as well as on the government's gradual withdrawal from active micro-management of its private sector entities. In line with these initiatives, the government released thirteen guidelines to assist GLCs in their effort to implement KPIs and PLC. Initiatives to strengthen the process of nomination of directors and their independence, the protection of minority shareholders in listed GLCs and, more fundamentally, the organization of ownership function within the state would complement the ongoing reform process. Domestic institutional investors in the Malaysian capital market consist largely of GLCs, government-linked investment companies, mutual funds, pension funds, and investment companies. The most important institutional investors include Khazanah, Ministry of Finance Incorporated, the National Pension Fund, Permodalan Nasional Berhad, the Employees Provident Fund, Lembaga Tabong Haji, RHB Nominees (Tempatan) Sdn Bhd, Petroliam Nasional Berhad, Amanah Raya Nominees (Tempatan) Sdn Bhd, and Malaysian Venture Capital Management Berhad. GLCs are also said to play an important role in nation building.[48]

Access to justice and judicial reform

In many law reform projects, including Malaysian corporate governance reform, the emphasis is on substantive rules and regulations. However, law reforms, if not accompanied by measures to reform legal institutions, may be insufficient to create change. Legal institutions here mean the institutions that create, support, and enforce laws. It therefore covers a whole range of institutions—courts, legislative bodies, lawmaking and drafting agencies, enforcement agencies, law schools, and bar associations. A wide spectrum of issues are involved. In relation to the courts, issues include the appointment and training of judges, independence from external interference, court facilities (including a good library, research assistance, and an organized and networked system), case management rules, and court procedure.[49] There is not a lot of information and discussion on court-related issues in Malaysia, perhaps with the exception of issues relating to judicial independence. The judiciary crisis in 1988,[50] the irregularities in the trial of the former Deputy Prime Minister, Anwar Ibrahim,[51] and the Lingam tape affair have undermined the integrity of the judiciary and public administration. Relations between the judiciary and the Malaysian Bar have also been soured. Crucially, the strained relations affected the administration of justice.

There are several reasons for the relatively poor level of judicial independence in Malaysia. One is that judges seem to have had difficulty with their role as the protector of the Constitution, especially during the early phases of the Constitution. Rais Yatim attributed the deterioration in the protection of rights immediately after independence to the judicial inability to recognize constitutional supremacy.[52] Another factor is the value systems and political orientation of the judges themselves. Acceptance of social rank and loyalty to the ruler are established cultural traits.[53] Harold Crouch said that the judges are "essentially conservative custodians of a political system dominated by the Malay elite to which most judges belong," who "rarely showed interest in reinterpreting the law in ways that might restrict the prerogatives of the government and its bureaucracy," the reason being that they "shared the broad conservative outlook of the rest of the Malay elite."[54]

The acute shortage of judges and support staff, backlog of cases caused by a sharp rise in the number of new cases,[55] high levels of procedural formalism, and poor implementation of a comprehensive computerized system[56] have had a negative impact on efficiency. The lack of an extensive information system means that the task of compiling caseload statistics (counts of filed, pending, and disposed cases) for the purposes of identifying and solving problems and improving court performance becomes a much bigger task than it should be.[57] Some attention should also be paid to issues relating to access to justice. Rights are not very useful if not accompanied by means to enforce them. Access to courts is an important factor in determining the usefulness of a particular law. This is viewed as an important counterweight to the other key issue in judicial reform—improved court performance.[58]

As for law enforcement agencies such as the Securities Commission, the Attorney General's Chambers, the Companies Commission, and the Anti-corruption

Agency, the one common criticism often directed against them is their lack of independence and transparency. Legal enforcement is as important as the laws themselves and, furthermore, the high incidence and influence of the state in business makes independent law-enforcing agencies even more important.

Quite recently, the Domestic Trade and Consumer Affairs Minister and the Chief Executive Officer of the Companies Commission of Malaysia revealed that the failure to file annual returns was a common phenomenon, committed by 56 percent of registered companies in Malaysia. Other common offences include the failure to hold annual general meetings and failing to file annual accounts.[59] This gives a valuable insight into the efficacy of the commission's enforcement team. However, instead of promising to step up enforcement as one may reasonably expect, the Companies Commission recommended that all directors be required to attend a directors' training program, without detailing how such a massive project could be implemented and what the benefits of having such a training program might be.

It is not known whether resources for enforcement agencies and their enforcement powers are adequate. Most enforcement activities remain out of the public eye, as they are not publicized. Prosecutions are normally made at the subordinate courts, where the judgments remain unreported. It is imperative, therefore, that the enforcement agencies reveal the details of their work. The annual report of the commission's enforcement activities shows only data on the number of prosecutions carried out by them during the year. There is no mention about what these prosecutions are for, in which court, or their outcome. More significantly, the Report contains no critical account of the challenges faced by the commission in relation to their investigation and enforcement activities and how they have responded or intend to respond to these challenges. Further, the Anti-corruption Agency, the body responsible for the investigation and prosecution of corruption, is organizationally structured under the Prime Minister's Department.[60] Thus, the agency is not independent from the government. So too is the Attorney General's Chambers. Both these bodies have been criticized for lacking in transparency and exercising selected prosecutions.

Rights are not very useful if not accompanied by means to enforce them. Access to courts is an important factor in determining the usefulness of particular provisions. It is viewed as an important counterweight to the other key issue in judicial reform, improved court performance.[61] Leading thinkers in this area emphasize the issue of proper allocation of resources and not just merely efforts to reduce cost and delay. Anthony Jolowicz said that more effort should be made to understand and allocate priority areas in which to improve efficiency.[62] Adrian Zuckerman proposed that civil justice reforms employ the dual concepts of proportionality and fair allocation of resources, which depend on who benefits from litigation (public or private benefits), and that resources for the administration of justice be fairly distributed to all those who require access to justice, not only litigants.[63] Entitlement to legal aid should also reflect the allocation of resources. In contrast, it is very unlikely that any of the petitioners in Malaysia received any form of legal aid.[64]

Impact of *Syariah* (Islamic law) and its role in commercial legal development in Malaysia

In Malaysia, Islamic law, coupled with the customary law of the various races, represents the indigenous sources or basic foundation upon which the eventual growth of a legal system has been founded. It has been argued that, if not for the influence of colonization, which signified the introduction and application of English law into Malaysia, Islamic law would have developed to become the law of the land.[65] The eventual application of English law both through judicial process and through legislation in the Malay states effectively displaced Islamic law from its premier position. The role that *Syariah* now plays in the system is extremely limited. Under the Federal Constitution, *Syariah* is a matter over which the state legislature has jurisdiction but not the federal legislature.[66] The practice of *Syariah* differs among the various states due to the varied influences of custom; nevertheless, legal British transplantation had the effect of formalizing the manner in which *Syariah* was administered. *Syariah* was left to be administered by the respective states with the Sultans proclaimed as "Head" of the Islamic religion in each state, thus giving rise to the lack of uniformity of administration of *Syariah* in Malaysia, whereas there is uniform application of English law in the system.

As far as corporate governance is concerned, *Syariah* has played an important role in formulating the commercial system. One significant development was the adoption of the Islamic banking system in Malaysia. Islamic banking[67] in Malaysia is very well established and accepted by consumers both Muslim and non-Muslim since it was introduced in 1983 with the establishment of the first Islamic Bank, the Bank Islam Malaysia Berhad (BIMB). Although Islamic banking is now well entrenched in the financial system in Malaysia and more banks are licensed to operate Islamic banking, it is apparent that the Islamic banking system does not operate in its entirety on *Syariah* principles.[68]

Since the 1960s, investors seeking investment opportunities in line with Islamic principles had been doing so through the Pilgrims Funds Board.[69] While its *raison d'etre* was to facilitate pilgrimage activities for Malaysian Muslims, the board also provided an avenue for investors to channel their savings into investments considered permissible in Islam. In 1983, the Islamic Banking Act was passed, paving the way for the inception of Bank Islam Malaysia in 1983. This was followed by the enactment of the *Takaful* Act, which led to the first insurance company in Malaysia in 1984. The establishment of a Securities Commission (SC) in 1993 paved the way for a more focused approach to formulating a framework for the development of the Islamic capital market. The Islamic capital unit was set up by the SC as well, which was responsible for conceptualizing and proposing initiatives for the development of the Islamic capital market. The SC also initiated a series of dialogs among Islamic jurists, market practitioners, and regulators within an informal grouping, namely the Islamic Instrument Study Group (IISG).[70] With the approval of the Ministry of Finance, the SC Syariah Advisory Council (SAC) was formed in 1996 to replace the IISG. Currently, the SAC plays a significant role in advising the SC on matters pertaining to the development of a fully fledged

Islamic capital market and was given the mandate to promote the harmonization and convergence of capital market-related *Syariah* issues. In summary, *Syariah* played an important role in crafting legal development in Malaysia. The majority of people in the Malay population who profess the Islamic religion play a contributory factory in influencing the need to formulate a legal system that includes not only personal laws at state level but also an economic system that incorporates the good faith values of Islamic law. Clearly, Malaysia is a good example of how religion can play an important role in shaping public perception in society and forms an integral and influential part in the legal, social, and economic system.

Conclusion

Globalization is influencing legal systems in Asia as elsewhere in the world. Legal change and globalization are integral to the development of market-based societies. This has been recognized in many Asian legal systems where law reform and corporate governance have been major governmental priorities. The Asian economic crisis gave birth to a new international consensus about the need for increased and timely information to sustain developing markets. In the case of Malaysia, the law reforms have been largely led by the state with little evidence of concerted lobbying from business itself. The globalization process in corporate law in Malaysia has taken the form of adopting international standards developed by such multilateral bodies such as the World Bank, IMF, OECD, and also the United Nations Commission on International Trade Law (UNCITRAL). This can be seen from the massive corporate law review and reform undertaken since the financial crisis until today.

The social, political, and economic environment in Malaysia has resulted in great state influence on business, whether directly as corporate owners or indirectly through the influence politicians have on companies and business leaders. This has resulted in a situation of conflicts of interest. In certain cases, it is difficult for the regulators, appointed by the executive and answerable to the executive, to apply laws and regulations, which the executive-dominated parliament or the regulators themselves have created.

In a way, the Malaysian government has played a very pro-active role in implementing development-oriented policies and using law as an instrument of social change and control. Such events have also led to extensive discretionary powers given to the authorities under the name of transparency and accountability. Nevertheless, the combination of using law and legal reform as a tool of economic development and the complexity between law and economic efficiency has given rise to a more sensitive issue. Differences in shareholding structure as well as economic, political, and cultural differences mean that the nature of the problems and solutions will vary across markets, in particular, in a corporate framework where the excessive powers of controlling shareholders creates the biggest agency problems. In addition, cultures and value systems, the quality of legal institutions, issues related to access to courts, and the influence of politics in business have affected the development process.

Adopting legal transplantation based on a foreign model may result in an inappropriate corporate governance regime that has as its focus the shareholder–director conflict. It is therefore ill-suited for the local environment. The concentrated shareholding that is prevalent in Malaysian companies means that controlling shareholder–minority shareholder conflict poses more serious problems. The absence of dispersed shareholding and the dominance of family-based controlling shareholders in Malaysia have two major implications: (1) the agency problems that troubled the US and British models have limited relevance; and (2) there is no active market for corporate control which may serve to discipline corporate controllers. Although takeovers have become increasingly common in Malaysia, more often they have been the result of increasing competition brought about by globalization and are very rarely hostile. In addition, the controlling minority structure may exacerbate this problem by combining the agency problems associated with both dispersed and concentrated shareholding. Corporate governance problems in Malaysia cannot be overcome merely by copying corporate law development in other countries.

Legal global reform and transplanted laws will evolve as they interact with elements in the local environment. This evolution need not necessarily result in changes in the substantive law. Often, there will be differences in the way the law is used, administered, and enforced. The historical nature and the economic setting in the Malaysian corporate environment are a special case where the government has always played a dominant role in making any legal, social, and economic reform. This can be observed from the setting up of special vehicle mechanisms to protect special interests in society and transplanting authoritative power through legislation. Political and institutional transparency in corporate governance should not be underestimated. As global changes continue to affect Malaysia, developing new laws that are effective in these areas requires a good understanding of the socio-cultural environment in which these laws are to apply. This and other resistance and constraints discussed suggest that law reform in this region is still a long and winding road yet to be traveled.

Notes

1 Mahathir Mohamed, Federal Budget 1999 Speech, delivered at Dewan Rakyat on 23 October 1998.
2 National Economic Action Council, *National Economic Recovery Plan*, Kuala Lumpur: NEAC, 1998, p. 3.
3 Ministry of Finance, *Economic Report*, 1998/1999, Kuala Lumpur: Ministry of Finance, 1998.
4 See Helen Nesadurai, 'In Defence of National Economic Autonomy? Malaysia's Response to the Financial Crisis', *The Pacific Review* 13, 2000, pp. 73–113. See also T. J. Pempel, 'International Finance and Asian Regionalism', *The Pacific Review* 13, 2000, pp. 57–72; Garry Rodan, 'Do Markets need Transparency? The Pivotal Cases of Singapore and Malaysia', *New Political Economy* 7, 2002, pp. 23–47.
5 See Aishah Bidin, 'Insolvency and Corporate Rescues in Malaysia', *ICCLR* 15, 2004, p. 344.
6 Economic Analytical Unit, Department of Foreign Affairs and Trade Australia, *Changing Corporate Asia: What Business Needs to Know*, Vol. 2, Regional Economic Studies, Canberra: Department of Foreign Affairs and Trade, 2002.

7 Bursa Malaysia, Listing Requirements, paras 15.10, 15.10(1)(a), and 15.11.
8 The crisis started in Thailand and affected the currencies and stock markets of several Asian economies, including Malaysia. The combination of the currency devaluation, as well as depressed share and asset prices, resulted in a severe recession in the affected countries.
9 A 1998 amendment to the Securities Industry (Central Depository) Act 1991 now requires securities accounts to be opened in the name of beneficial owners or authorized nominees.
10 Bursa Malaysia, Listing Requirements, para. 9.22, amended in 1999.
11 Bursa Malaysia, Listing Requirements, para. 9.25.
12 Securities Commission Act, 1993 (Act 498) Pt IV, Div. 3.
13 Bursa Malaysia, Listing Requirements, paras 15.09 and 15.06.
14 Securities Commission Malaysia, Capital Market Master Plan Malaysia, 2001.
15 They are:

  * A Strategic Framework for the Corporate Law Reform Program, 2004;
  * Capital Maintenance Rules and Share Capital, Simplifying and Streamlining Provisions Applicable to Shares, 2005;
  * Engagement with Shareholders, 2006;
  * Company Liquidation—Reforms and Restatement of Law, 2006;
  * Clarifying and Reformulating the Directors' Role and Duties, 2006;
  * Memberships' Right and Remedies, January 2007;
  * Creating a conducive legal and regulatory framework in Malaysia, January 2007;
  * Capital maintenance rules and share capital: Simplifying and streamlining provisions applicable to the reduction of capital, share buyback and financial assistance, April 2007;
  * Review of provisions regulating substantial property transaction, disclosure obligations, and loans to directors, July 2007;
  * Reviewing the corporate insolvency regime; the proposed corporate rehabilitation framework; reviewing the company receivership process and company charges and registration process; improvements to the present registration system, August 2007;
  * Review of criminal, civil and administrative sanctions in the Companies Act 1965, December 2007;
  * Auditors' roles and responsibilities, December 2007.

16 See also Ian Ramsey, Aishah Bidin, Geof Stapeldon, Pamela Hanrahan et al., *Commercial Applications of Company Law in Malaysia*, 3rd edn, Singapore: CCH Asia Pte Ltd, Walter Kluwer, 2008, Chapter 13.
17 Prior to this, the Indian Companies Ordinance 1866 was applied in the Straits Settlements.
18 In 1956, a single Civil Law Ordinance was introduced in the Federation of Malaya, which replaced both the Straits Settlements Ordinance and the Federated Malay States Enactment. In 1972, the Civil Law Ordinance 1956 was revised and extended to Sabah and Sarawak by the provision of the Civil Law Act 1956 (Revised 1972). Section 3(1) of the Civil Law Ordinance provides that English common law, rules of equity, and statutes of general application may apply in Malaysia, subject to such qualifications as local circumstances render necessary.
19 Malaysian Companies Act 1965 sections 16(5), 18(3), and 214(1)(d). Section 16(5) of the Act provides that the company "shall be a body corporate ... capable forthwith of exercising all the function of an incorporated company."
20 13 [1897] AC 22.
21 Clause 7, among others, lists the races to be treated as native and indigenous to Sarawak, and these are the Bukitans, Bisayahs, Dusuns, Sea Dayaks, Land Dayaks, Kadayans, Kelabits, Kenyans, Penans, Tagals, and others.

22 Article 161A(6)(a) of the Malaysian Federal Constitution.
23 Ibid., Article 161A(6)(b).
24 According to the New Economic Policy (NEP), the government is committed to achieving the target of at least 30 percent Bumiputera equity share ownership in the economy. Although the NEP was first implemented in 1970, the goal of reaching corporate asset ownership distribution by the Bumiputeras has not been achieved. As of 2004, ownership of share capital among the Bumiputera in public companies is about 18.9 percent compared with 40.6 percent share ownership by the non-Bumiputera in Malaysia, with 32 percent in the hands of foreigners. Source: Economic Planning Unit, Prime Minister's Department, Putra Jaya.
25 In January 1981, the government launched a new scheme to transfer shares held by government agencies to the Bumiputera community using PNB as the intermediate vehicle. In April that year, PNB launched its flagship unit trust Skim Amanah Saham Nasional or the National Unit Trust Scheme. The launch was hugely successful with more than 170,000 individuals taking up units during the first week of its launch. Within two decades, it became the biggest single unit trust fund in the world. See KLSE, *Kuala Lumpur Stock Exchange: A Successful Symbiosis*, 1997. Also see PNB annual reports for 1978, 1979, 1980, and 1981.
26 See Helen Nesadurai, 'In Defence of National Economic Autonomy? Malaysia's Response to the Financial Crisis', *The Pacific Review* 13, 2000, pp. 73–113; H. Crouch, *Government and Society in Malaysia*, Sydney: Allen & Unwin, 1996; E.T. Gomes and K.S. Jomo, *Malaysia's Political Economy: Politics, Patronage and Profits*, Cambridge: Cambridge University Press, 1997.
27 Pengurusan Danaharta Nasional Berhad 1998, Second Schedule.
28 See section 25A, Pengurusan Danaharta Nasional Berhad Act 1998.
29 *Ring v. Sutton* (1979) 5 A.C.L.R 546. See also *Winkworth v. Edward Baron Development Co. Ltd* (1987) 1 ALL ER 114.
30 The Preamble to the Act provides the Act's objectives: (1) to assist financial institutions by removing impaired assets; (2) to assist the business sector by dealing with financially distressed enterprises; and (3) to promote the revitalization of the nation's economy.
31 Danaharta Act, sections 30, 33(2), and Second Schedule.
32 Danaharta Act, section 22.
33 Ibid., sections 41 and 46.
34 Ibid., section 45.
35 *Repco Holdings Sdn Bhd v. Pengurusan Danaharta Nasional Bhd* (No. 2) [2000] 5 MLJ 637.
36 Danaharta Act, section 72 was introduced by an amendment to the principal act in 2000. Section 72 reads:

Notwithstanding any law, an order of a court cannot be granted:

(a) which stays, restrains, or affects the powers of the Corporation, Oversight Committee, Special Administrator, or Independent Advisor under this Act;
(b) which stays, restrains, or affects any action taken, or proposed to be taken, by the Corporation, Oversight Committee, Special Administrator, or Independent Advisor under this Act;
(c) which compels the Corporation, Oversight Committee, Special Administrator, or Independent Advisor to do or perform any act, and any such order, if granted, shall be void and unenforceable and shall not be the subject of any process of execution whether for the purpose of compelling obedience of the order or otherwise.

37 A. Berle and G. Means, *The Modern Corporation and Private Property*, New York: Harcourt, Brace & World Inc., 1932; reissued New Brunswick/London: Transaction

Publishers, 1991. Writing in 1932, Berle and Means gave an insight into the division of powers in a modern company. The evolution of dispersed shareholding, they explained, was an incident of capital needs. Companies have grown so large that their capital requirements can only be met by a large and dispersed group of shareholders. Such ownership structure left a control gap, which was filled by corporate managers. Directors therefore have almost complete discretion in management. Berle and Means were concerned that management may not have the same objectives as directors and managers and they may not be accountable to shareholders. The core purpose of corporate governance regulation is thus to align the interests of directors and managers with that of the owners.

38 See A. Berle, 'Corporate Powers as Powers in Trust', *Harvard Law Review* 4 (1049), 1931 (arguing that the agency problem can be solved by regarding shareholders as beneficiaries, to whom the managers, as trustees, must serve). But see M. E. Dodd, 'For Whom Are Corporate Managers Trustees?', *Harvard Law Review* 45 (1145), 1932; A. Berle, 'For Whom Corporate Managers Are Trustees: A Note', *Harvard Law Review* 45 (1365), 1932.

39 M.H. Lim, *Ownership and Control of the One Hundred Largest Corporations in Malaysia*, Kuala Lumpur: Oxford University Press, 1981. See also The Economist Intelligence Unit, *Beyond the Bamboo Network: Successful Strategies for Change in Asia*, London, New York, Hong Kong, 2000, pp. 8–10.

40 Seven of the top ten listed companies in Malaysia are majority owned by the state through its investment arms. Most of these are privatized infrastructure companies in which the state maintains the majority shareholding (e.g., Tenaga Nasional Berhad (TMB), the national power company, and Telekom Malaysia Berhad (TMB), the national telecommunication company).

41 The Articles of Association of the privatized national utility company Tenaga Nasional Berhad (TMB), for example, has a provision for a "special share" held by a "special shareholder," a representative of the state. The special shareholder has the right to appoint a number of directors, including the Chairman of the Board and the Managing Director. The special shareholder also has extensive veto rights.

42 Privatization projects in Malaysia are examples of the politics–business nexus. See, for example, K.S. Jomo, 'Privatisation in Malaysia', in T. Clarke and C. Pitelis, eds, *The Political Economy of Privatisation*, London: Routledge, 1993, pp. 437–54; K.S. Jomo, 'Overview', in K.S. Jomo, ed., *Privatisation Malaysia: Rents, Rhetorics, Realities*, Boulder, CO: Westview Press, 1994. See also generally E.T. Gomez and K.S. Jomo, *Malaysia's Political Economy: Politics, Patronage and Profits*, Cambridge: Cambridge University Press, 1999.

43 Simon Johnson and Rafael La Porta, 2000, 'Tunneling', Unpublished Discussion Paper No. 1887, Harvard Institute of Economic Research, Cambridge, MA: Harvard University, used the term "tunneling" to refer to the transfer of resources out of a company to its controlling shareholder, whether illegally or otherwise.

44 Malaysian Committee on Corporate Governance, *supra*, note 22 at p. 46, para. 2.19.

45 The Kuala Lumpur Stock Exchange (KLSE) and PriceWaterhouseCoopers Malaysian Corporate Governance Survey, 2002.

46 See 'Clause 74, Building a Civilization to Elevate the Nation's Dignity', Speech by the Malaysian Prime Minister, The Honourable Dato Seri' Abdullah Ahmad Badawi, at the tabling of the motion on the Ninth Malaysia Plan, 2006–10, Dewan Rakyat, Kuala Lumpur, 31 March 2006.

47 In July 2005, the Putrajaya Committee on GLC High Performance (PGC) launched ten initiatives to drive and enhance the performance of GLC. One of the initiatives is the Silver Book, which is a set of principles and guidelines to be implemented by GLCs so they can proactively contribute to society while still creating value for their shareholders.

48 See Johan Jaafar, 'Memperkasa GLC, perkukuh amanah' [To Strengthen GLC is to Preserve Trust], Berita Minggu, Ahad, 9 July 2006. See also Aishah Bidin, 'GLC and its Role in creating Malay CEOs', Paper presented at the Malay Agenda Convention, November 2006, Kuala Lumpur.

49 See, generally, the World Bank's resource page for institution reforms at http://www1.worldbank.org/publicsector/legal/index.cfm.

50 For literature on the subject, see F.A. Trinidade, 'The Removal of the Malaysian Judges', *Law Quarterly Review* 106, 1990, pp. 51–86; H.P. Lee, 'A Fragile Bastion Under Siege – the 1988 Convulsion in the Malaysian Judiciary', *Melbourne University Law Review* 1990, pp. 386–417; A. Harding, 'The 1988 Constitutional Crisis in Malaysia', *International and Comparative Law Quarterly* 39, 1990, pp. 57–81; R.H. Hickling, 'The Malaysian Judiciary Under Crisis', *Public Law* 1990, pp. 20–27; M.S. Abas and K. Das, *May Day For Justice*, Kuala Lumpur: Magnus Books, 1989; Lawyers' Committee on Human Rights, Malaysia, *Assault on the Judiciary*, New York, 1990; T.A. Aziz, 'Malaysia Incorporated: Ethics on Trial', *Australian Journal of Public Administration* 58, 1999, p. 19.

51 Some aspects of Anwar's trial were covered by the International Commission of Jurists. Available from http://www.icj.org.

52 R. Yatim, *Freedom under Executive Powers in Malaysia—A Study of Executive Supremacy*, Kuala Lumpur: Endowment Publications, 1995. One reason for this was their training in England in which Parliament, and not the Constitution, is supreme. A Malaysian constitutional expert, Abdul Aziz Bari, openly criticized the judiciary who he said, when asked to resolve a conflict between the individual and public authorities, "invariably chose to abdicate themselves; citing lack of power and that the matter is beyond their purview." A.A. Bari, *Malaysian Constitution: A Critical Introduction*, Kuala Lumpur: The Other Press, 2003, p. 243.

53 See, for example, G.H. Hofstede, *Culture's Consequences: International Differences in Work Related Values*, 2nd edn, London: Thousand Oaks, 2001.

54 H. Crouch, *Government and Society in Malaysia*, NSW: Allen & Unwin, 1996, pp. 138–42.

55 Bar Council Press Statement, 'Shortages of Judges and Judicial Commissioners', 13 January 2003; and 'Clearing Backlog in the Courts', 24 December 2003.

56 Although an e-court project was first announced as far back as 1996, it has yet to be fully implemented.

57 For use of caseload statistics, see World Bank, 'Introduction: Using Caseload Statistics'. Available from http://www1.worldbank.org/publicsector/legal/CourtStatistics.pdf (accessed 12 January 2005).

58 World Bank, 'The Purpose of the Courts'. Available from http://web.worldbank.org/WBSITE/EXTERNAL/TOPICS/EXTLAWJUSTINST/0,contentMDK:20752673~menuPK:2035329~pagePK:210058~piPK:210062~theSitePK:1974062,00.html(accessed 8 December 2008).

59 The Star, 'Over Half of Private Firms' Directors Breach Rules', 13 July 2004.

60 The Agency is headed by a Director General, appointed by the Yang di-Pertuan Agong on advice from the Prime Minister. Officers of the Agency are members of the general public service: Anti-Corruption Act 1997, sections 3(2) and 4(3).

61 World Bank, 'The Purpose of the Courts', *supra*.

62 J.A. Jolowicz, 'General Ideas and the Reform of Civil Procedure', *Legal Studies* 3, 1983, pp. 295–314; *On Civil Procedure*, Cambridge: Cambridge University Press, 2000.

63 Adrian Zuckerman, 'Reforming Civil Justice System: Trends in Industrial Countries', The World Bank PREM, Note 46, 2000. Available from http://www1.worldbank.org/prem/PREMNotes/premnote46.pdf (accessed 13 January 2005). See also Steven Shavell, 'The Fundamental Divergence between the Private and Social Motive to Use the Legal System', *Journal of Legal Studies* 26, 1997, pp. 575–612; Adrian

Zuckerman, ed., *Civil Justice in Crisis: Comparative Perspectives of Civil Procedure*, Oxford: Oxford University Press, 1999.

64 To qualify for state legal aid, a person's disposable income must not exceed RM3,000 (approximately US$1,000) a year. In any case, legal aid is only given for a limited range of cases (shareholder suit is not one) unless the relevant minister gives special permission. Even when permission is given, there is the issue of competence of the legal aid solicitor.

65 R.J. Wilkinson, 'Paper on Malay Subjects', KL, 1971.

66 Federal Constitution, Article 74, Ninth Schedule. In this regard, matters over which the state legislatures have been permitted to make laws include personal and family matters, namely succession, betrothal, marriages, divorce, maintenance, adoption, guardianship, trusts, Islamic religious revenues, and matters in relation to Islamic mosques.

67 See Aishah Bidin, 'Islamic Banking in Malaysia: Reconciling Religious Law and the Common Law', *Journal of Banking Regulation* 1, 2000, p. 75. See also Aishah Bidin, 'The Impact of Islamic Law in the Banking System and Financial Market – A Malaysian Perspective', *Company Lawyer* 22, 2001, p. 154.

68 Specifically, Islamic banking litigation does not function on *Syariah* principles, but relies on civil law. In this regard, one would expect that disputes and disagreements between clients and the Islamic financial institutions resolved through the process of litigation must necessarily be guided by *Syariah*. Indeed, *Syariah* does not provide any single decree in which it gives all the rules and guidelines to be followed by the Islamic banks. The rules and guidelines, however, are abundantly described by the various sources of *Syariah*, namely *al-Quran*, *Hadith*, *Ijmak*, and *Qiyas*.

69 Also known as the Lembaga Urusan Tabung Haji and later renamed Lembaga Tabung Haji. This agency is responsible for the administration and financial planning of Muslims who intend to perform their pilgrimage to Mecca.

70 The IISG (Islamic Instrument Study Group) was primarily set up to foster greater cross-fertilization of ideas and understanding of Islamic issues by bringing together Islamic scholars in regulation and finance to provide input into development and policy issues. The tangible benefits of the work of the IISG provided strong justification for a more formal and permanent structure of consultations between the SC and Islamic capital market experts.

Index

Page numbers in *italics* refer to tables.